Tourism, Cult

_____

	DATE DUE	

To my dearest husband, Laci and my gorgeous son, Levi

Tourism, Culture and Regeneration

Edited by

Melanie K. Smith

Senior Lecturer in Cultural Tourism Management
University of Greenwich and Budapest
Business School Xellum Ltd
1055 Budapest
Szent István krt. II. III/30
Hungary

www.cabi.org

CABI is a trading name of CAB International

CABI Head Office	CABI North American Office
Nosworthy Way	875 Massachusetts Avenue
Wallingford	7th Floor
Oxfordshire OX10 8DE	Cambridge, MA 02139
UK	USA
Tel: +44 (0)1491 832111	Tel: +1 617 395 4056
Fax: +44 (0)1491 833508	Fax: +1 617 354 6875
E-mail: cabi@cabi.org	E-mail: cabi-nao@cabi.org
Website: www.cabi.org	

A catalogue record for this book is available from the British Library,
London, UK.

Library of Congress Cataloging-in-Publication Data

Tourism, culture, and regeneration/edited by Melanie K. Smith.
    p. cm.
  Includes bibliographical references and index.
  ISBN 1-84593-130-0 (alk. paper)
  1. Heritage tourism. 2. Cities and towns. 3. Tourism and city planning.
4. Urban renewal. I. Smith, Melanie K. II. Title.

  G156.5.H47T69 2006
  307.3'416--dc22

                                             2006002123

ISBN-10: 1 84593 130 0
ISBN-13: 978 1 84593 130 8

Typeset by AMA DataSet Ltd, Preston, UK.
Printed and bound in the UK by Cromwell Press, Trowbridge.

The paper used for the text pages of this book is FSC certified. The FSC (Forest Stewardship
Council) is an international network to promote responsible management of the world's forests.

Contents

Contributors

Editor

Melanie Smith is a senior lecturer in Cultural Tourism Management at the University of Greenwich in London, UK. She is also Chair of ATLAS (Association for Tourism and Leisure Education, http://www.atlas-euro.org). She has teaching and research interests in cultural tourism, regeneration and heritage management, and is author of *Issues in Cultural Tourism Studies* (Routledge, 2003), and co-editor of *Cultural Tourism in a Changing World* (Channel View, 2006) and *Tourism in the New Europe* (CABI, 2006). She is currently a visiting lecturer in Budapest, Hungary and can be contacted at the following address:

Melanie Smith, C/o Xellum Ltd, 1055 Budapest, Szent István krt. II III/30, Hungary, Tel: (0036) 204624443, E-mail: melaniesmith2004@hotmail.com

Authors

Rosita Aiesha is a research fellow currently completing research on the Engineering and Physical Sciences Research Council's Vivacity 2020 project on Urban Sustainability for the 24-hour City and is engaged in multidisciplinary research investigating the conditions for sustainability in mixed-use developments in urban environments. Rosita has a geography and planning background and has worked in planning in local government. Her research interests are in urban planning and policy processes, regeneration and gentrification processes.

Rosita Aiesha, Cities Institute, London Metropolitan University, Ladbroke House, 62–66 Highbury Grove, London, N5 2AD, UK, E-mail: r.aiesha@londonmet.ac.uk

Greg Andranovich is professor of political science and director of the master of science in public administration programme at California State University, Los Angeles. His research is in urban and regional politics and comparative public administration, where he most recently co-authored *Culture, Development, and Public Administration in Africa* (Kumarian Press, 2005).

Greg Andranovich, California State University, Los Angeles, Department of Political Science, 5151 State University Drive, Los Angeles, CA 90032-8226, USA, Tel: (323) 343-2235, Fax: (323) 343-6452, E-mail: gandran@earthlink.net

Patricia Avery is senior lecturer in cultural tourism at the University of Wales Institute Cardiff. She previously worked as a freelance journalist and art critic and has contributed to a wide range of conferences and publications engaging in the wide discourse exploring critical interpretations of the interplay between tourism, culture and regeneration. She has recently worked on interpretive strategies for several heritage sites in South Wales. Current research interests focus on the interface between culture, interpretation and social regeneration.

Patricia Avery, Welsh School of Hospitality, Tourism and Leisure Management, University of Wales Institute Cardiff, Colchester Avenue, Cardiff, CF23 9XR, UK, Tel: 029 20416316, E-mail: pavery@uwic.ac.uk

Brian Bath (BSc MTS MAHI – Interpretive Design Ltd) has worked at the Natural History Museum in South Kensington, London, as Head of Design and Interpretation for English Heritage, and as Interpretive Director for the Visual Connection. As an independent interpretive consultant, he has provided interpretive designs for art galleries, museums, heritage sites, theme parks and cities around the world. Brian has a particular interest in carrying capacity and was Chair of the Association of Heritage Interpretation from 1994 to 1997, is a member of the Tourism Society, the Visitor Studies Association and the Royal Society for Asian Affairs.

Brian Bath, 36 Carlisle Road, Hove, BN3 4FS, UK, Tel: 01273 724432

Anna Maria Bounds is a PhD candidate in urban and public policy at Milano, the New School for Management and Urban Policy. Her research interests include urban tourism, cultural policy and local governance. Her dissertation is titled 'The role of network management in cultural district initiatives: a case study of Philadelphia's Avenue of the Arts'.

Anna Maria Bounds, 300 Mercer Street Apt. #15E, New York, NY 10003, USA

Myrna M. Breitbart received her PhD in geography from Clark University and teaches urban studies at Hampshire College in Amherst, Massachusetts. Her interests focus on participatory planning, community development, conflicts over urban public space and the new cultural economy. She is committed to community-based learning and collaborates with many community partners in Holyoke, Massachusetts.

Myrna Breitbart, Hampshire College, Amherst, Massachusetts, USA

Matthew Burbank is an associate professor in the department of political science at the University of Utah. His research focuses on citizen participation in politics and urban politics. Professor Burbank teaches courses in American politics, political behaviour and research methods.

Matthew J. Burbank, University of Utah, Department of Political Science, 260 S Central Campus DR, Salt Lake City, UT 84112-9152, USA, Tel: (801) 581-6313, Fax: (801) 585-6492, E-mail: burbank@csbs.utah.edu

Professor **Graeme Evans** is Director of the Cities Institute at London Metropolitan University (www.citiesinstitute.org), which undertakes interdisciplinary research on city society and the urban environment. Contact: cities@londonmet.ac.uk

Graeme Evans, Cities Institute, London Metropolitan University, Ladbroke House, 62–66 Highbury Grove, London, N5 2AD, UK, E-mail: g.evans@londonmet.ac.uk

Paula Goncalves [AA Diploma, MA (Heritage management), MPhil (Urban renewal), DPhil (Oxon)] has worked at the Recife Urbanisation Company and Pernambuco State Government in Brazil and recently for the Planning Strategy Team of Brighton and Hove City Council in England. She has participated in a number of government plans and projects targeting historic areas in Recife and carried out various pieces of research that addressed the tensions inherent in heritage conservation and urban regeneration initiatives. She coordinated the local Monumenta Programme unit during the final phase of the Interpretative Plan for Bairro do Recife.

Paula Goncalves, 36 Carlisle Road, Hove, BN3 4FS, UK, Tel: 01273 724432

Daina Cheyenne Harvey is a lecturer and PhD candidate at Rutgers University. His primary research interests involve the intersection of culture, space and memory. He is currently engaged in ethnographic research that focuses on how tourist practices and the commemoration of space affects the collective memory of slavery.

Daina Cheyenne Harvey, Sociology Department, Rutgers University, 54 Joyce Kilmer Avenue, Piscataway, New Jersey, USA, Tel: 08854-8045

Charles Heying is associate professor of urban studies and planning at Portland State University. His scholarly interests include civic engagement, civic elites and the politics of urban life. Professor Heying's primary research focus has been on the political and economic impacts of mega-events such as the Olympics.

Charles Heying, Portland State University, Nohad Toulan School of Urban Studies and Planning, 506 S. W. Mill Street, Portland, OR 97207-0751, USA, Tel: (503) 725-8416, Fax: (503) 725-8770, E-mail: heyingc@pdx.edu

Andrew L. Jones is a senior lecturer at Swansea Business School-Swansea Institute-University of Wales and is a co-director of CELTaS (Centre for Leisure and Tourism Research @ Swansea). He has professional experience in planning at international, regional and local levels and has been an active member of the Royal Town Planning Institute (RTPI). Andrew has been an active practitioner, researcher and teacher in planning, conservation, regeneration and tourism planning since 1981. In his present post he is the Director for both postgraduate and undergraduate tourism programmes with subject specialisms in: town and country planning; cultural regeneration; and tourism development and environmental policy. He completed his PhD on investigating the relationship and tensions between regeneration, the environment and sustainable tourism.

Tel: 01792 481000/481212, E-mail: andrew.jones@sihe.ac.uk

Robert Maitland is Director of the Centre for Tourism at the University of Westminster. His research focuses on urban and cultural tourism in major cities, tourism policy and regeneration. As well as writing on these themes, he has advised a number of UK government departments and the National Audit Office.

Robert Maitland, Director, The Centre for Tourism, University of Westminster, 35 Marylebone Road, London, NW1 5LS, UK, Tel: 020 7911 5000 ext 3114, Fax: 020 7911 5171, http://www.wmin.ac.uk/tourism

Meiko Murayama is a senior lecturer in cultural industries at the University of Greenwich, London. Before arriving at Greenwich she worked as Associate Professor in tourism studies at Nihon University, Japan. She gained her PhD at the University of Surrey, UK, focusing on urban regeneration and tourism development and is the author of *Understanding Urban Tourism: the Regeneration and Development of Amenity in Birmingham, UK* (Bunshido Publications, 2004).

Meiko Murayama, Senior Lecturer in Cultural Industries, Business School, University of Greenwich, London, SE10 9LS, UK, Tel: 020 83319114

Gavin Parker is a senior lecturer and chartered planner based in the Department of Real Estate and Planning, University of Reading, UK. Dr Parker has wide ranging research interests, including the governance of leisure and tourism. He is also interested in Japanese policy and planning.

Gavin Parker, Senior Lecturer in Town and Country Planning, Department of Real Estate and Planning, The University of Reading, Reading, RG6 6AW, UK, Tel: 0118 378 6460, E-mail: g.parker@reading.ac.uk

Greg Richards is a partner in the Barcelona office of Tourism Research and Marketing. His main research interest is the relationship between culture and tourism, and he has edited a number of volumes on this topic, including *Cultural Tourism in Europe* (CAB International, 1996), *Cultural Attractions and European Tourism* (CAB International, 2001) and *Tourism and Gastronomy* (Routledge, 2002).

Greg Richards, Tourism Research and Marketing (Barcelona), Gran de Gracia 183 (4-1), 08012 Barcelona, Spain, Tel: (0034) 93 217 4826

Stephen Shaw is Director of TRaC Research Centre at the Cities Institute, London Metropolitan University. He has published a wide range of books and articles. His current topics include tourism and the built heritage of immigrant communities, social benefits of heritage environments, urban landscapes and cultural diversity in 'world cities'.

Stephen Shaw, Director TRaC Research Centre, London Metropolitan University, Stapleton House, 277/281 Holloway Road, London, N7 8HN, UK, E-mail: s.shaw@londonmet.ac.uk

Andrew Smith is a senior lecturer in tourism at the University of Westminster. He has written extensively about tourism, cities and regeneration, particularly on the image effects associated with flagship projects. Recently, Andrew has been involved in the evaluation of the Legacy Programme associated with the 2002 Commonwealth Games.

Andrew Smith, School of Architecture and Built Environment, University of Westminster, 35 Marylebone Road, London, NW1 5LS, E-mail: A.Smith24@westminster.ac.uk

Costas Spirou is Professor of social science at National-Louis University and Research Associate at the Center for Cultural Understanding and Change of the Field Museum in Chicago. His recent publications include the book *It's Hardly Sportin': Stadiums, Neighborhoods and the New Chicago* (Northern Illinois University Press, 2003) and articles in *Urban Affairs Review and the International Journal of Urban and Regional Research*.

Costas Spirou, National-Louis University, Department of Social and Behavioral Sciences, 122 S. Michigan Ave, Chicago, IL 60603, USA

Cathy Stanton received her PhD from Tufts University in Boston, Massachusetts. Her dissertation, 'The Lowell experiment: public history in a postindustrial city' is forthcoming as a book from the University of Massachusetts Press. She is currently an adjunct faculty member at Tufts and at Vermont College of Union Institute and University.

Cathy Stanton, Tufts University, Medford, Massachusetts, USA

Julie Wilson is Marie Curie Fellow in the Department of Geography, Autonomous University of Barcelona and a research fellow at the University of the West of England, Bristol, UK. She specializes in the field of tourism geographies, with interests in the production of urban space for tourism and cultural objectives, tourism place imagery and youth/independent travel.

E-mail: Julie.Wilson@uab.es

Preface

_____

The decision to edit this volume was prompted by a number of factors. A fascination with the increasingly prominent phenomenon of cultural regeneration seemed like a logical progression from earlier work undertaken in the field of cultural tourism (e.g. Smith, M.K. (2003) *Issues in Cultural Tourism Studies*. Routledge, London.). One small chapter in that publication hardly seemed to do justice to the diversity of projects that have been developing on a global scale in recent years. The government agenda in the UK and a large number of other countries worldwide has been focused on the potential of regeneration to transform cities. Whilst it is certainly not a panacea, it is exciting to watch relatively unknown and under-visited cities being transformed into well-known centres for culture, leisure and tourism. I knew that once I started choosing to holiday in former industrial rather than traditional historic cities, my interest in regeneration had gone way beyond academic!

Cultural regeneration is a diverse and exciting subject for academic research, as well as being a challenging field for practitioners. My own PhD work has been testimony to that. It is multidisciplinary and requires holistic or joined-up thinking. No one field can claim to 'own' this subject as it arguably sits equally comfortably in urban studies, planning, architecture, cultural geography or sociology. One can also draw upon cultural studies, anthropology, economics, environmental studies, leisure and tourism, heritage studies (and more) to shed further light on the complexity of the phenomenon. The fact that the subject is in its relative infancy means that many of the issues are still open to debate, but the sharing of good practice through interesting and innovative case studies can help to disseminate knowledge.

This volume therefore aims to contribute further to the latest discussions about cultural regeneration (theoretical and academic, as well as practitioner dilemmas), in addition to providing examples of contemporary practice. It was thought that a single-authored text could not do justice to the range of contexts, case studies and perspectives that could be encompassed in an edited volume. I am therefore grateful to the diverse range of authors for their valuable contributions to this project.

Melanie K. Smith
University of Greenwich
London, UK
2005

Acknowledgements

I am grateful to a number of people for their direct or indirect support for this project. First, I want to thank Laci for his love and patience, especially when I suffer from the terminal illness of academics everywhere – the inability to say 'no'!

Secondly, thank you to my two PhD supervisors, Noel Campbell and Grant Ledgerwood from the University of Greenwich, and my external advisor, Graeme Evans from London Metropolitan University, for their constant interest in and feedback on my work.

I would like to express my appreciation to my senior managers at the University of Greenwich, Les Johnson and Pat Baynes, for their ongoing support with research, and for granting me a sabbatical, which has allowed me to finish this project (amongst others!).

And as always, a big thank you to my wonderful family and friends for making the world a fun place to be and for giving me the enthusiasm and energy I need to bring such projects to fruition.

Introduction

Melanie K. Smith

The phenomenon of urban regeneration has become increasingly prominent on government agendas in recent years, particularly in those countries that have suffered a significant level of economic or industrial decline. Whilst there has been some confusion about definitional parameters, attempts have been made to clarify the concept and its remit, for example, the UK Government's consultation document entitled *Culture at the Heart of Regeneration* (DCMS, 2004). Here it is argued that 'culture' (howsoever defined) is pivotal to the success of regeneration strategies. Without a consideration of culture and (it is also argued) communities, it is not possible to achieve sustainable and integrated regeneration. This volume explores the extent to which this perspective is a valid one, emphasizing also the significant role played by tourism. This does not in any way subvert the importance of economics or business investment to the regeneration process, which are clearly baselines for any form of urban redevelopment. However, they have sometimes been viewed as uneasy bedfellows for cultural and community development, a perspective that needs to be redressed.

The Department for Culture, Media and Sport (DCMS) (2004) described regeneration as 'the positive transformation of a place – whether residential, commercial or open space – that has previously displayed symptoms of physical, social and/or economic decline'. This definition makes the point that the concept of regeneration can only be applied to areas that are being *re*-developed after industrial decline, and does not really apply to those that are in the first throes of industrial development. Thus the term has generally been used in the context of developed Western countries (e.g. Europe, the USA, Canada, Australasia). Similar case studies abound, documenting the apparent 'success' of waterfront or dockland developments or landmark buildings, icons or 'mega-events' that have been used as catalysts for regeneration. Increasingly, the remit of regeneration appears to have been broadened, focusing also on the role that festivals and smaller community arts projects can play in regeneration. Indeed, in cities like New York, regeneration appeared to be driven initially by clusters of artists and creative communities.

In his much-lauded book *The Rise of the Creative Class*, Richard Florida (2002) demonstrates how the creative classes have contributed enormously to urban transformation and (re)development in the USA. His research shows that those cities that have the highest level of economic growth and innovation are those that score highest on what he calls the 'Bohemian Index' (the relative concentration of artists, writers, musicians and other artistic professionals), as well as the 'Gay Index' (the relative concentration of gays). He suggests that such people are open-minded, diverse and are therefore conducive to creativity. For a long time now too, economists have found it difficult to deny the strength of the 'pink pound'! The links between culture, creativity and new technology are also paramount in encouraging economic growth, and therefore many cities that claim to have successful cultural regeneration have based their strategies on the so-called 'creative industries' (e.g. media, design, music, film, advertising).

The main message that comes out of Florida's work is that cities need to have a 'people climate' as well as a 'business climate'. This means addressing issues of inequality, intolerance, safety, as well as creating a vibrant atmosphere and an experiential economy. It also means 'community-building' and engaging in civic action, perhaps dealing with some of the more intangible issues relating to a sense of place, identity or integration. It is worth noting that many artists and creative projects have done far more for social inclusion than politics or business development could ever do. This aspect of regeneration is therefore a major focus of this volume.

In addition to the interesting and exciting projects taking place in the USA (many of which are referred to in detail in this volume), many of the most innovative approaches can also be seen in the oft-cited examples of European cities such as Barcelona, Bilbao, Glasgow, Liverpool, Rotterdam, Lisbon. What many of these cities have done is to build incrementally on a series of initiatives, usually starting with one major catalyst or 'flagship' project (e.g. the Olympic Games, European Cultural Capital status, a major museum, gallery or conference centre that puts it on the map). An interesting recent example of this is Liverpool, which will be European Cultural Capital in 2008. The day after the decision was announced, house prices had risen by around 25%! Investors were also waiting in the wings, ready to seize their opportunity. However, the main reason that this city was chosen over the other candidates was that it had led a bidding campaign that had involved numerous community groups, fostering local pride in the city. Similarly, Olympic bidding cities now have to demonstrate that there is local support for the event. Care must be taken that large iconic structures or 'flagship' projects connect with local people. For example, it

should reflect some aspects of their history, heritage, traditions, or contemporary cultures if it is to be accepted and visited.

A further problem that has been identified in the process of regeneration is the standardization of architectural and attractions development. Short (1989) refers to these as 'international blandscapes'. Florida (2002) also notes the proliferation of 'generica' – that is, heavily packaged commercial venues like chain restaurants and nightclubs. He notes that creative people tend to prefer more authentic, indigenous or organic venues. Questions should also be raised about how far tourists will want to visit a venue that reflects little or nothing of local culture or heritage. For example, why go to the waterfront development in Cape Town when it looks so similar to that of Cardiff or Vancouver? Do people travel to visit a shopping mall full of global brands that could just as well be in their own high street? Judging by the success of growing destinations like Dubai, it is possible that they do! However, this development of what Augé (1995) describes as 'non-places' arguably needs to be limited and offset by complementary developments that have their own individual identity, or reflect that of the location and its communities. Mixed-use or multifunctional developments may help to solve some of these dilemmas.

It is not just new attractions that have been criticized for their standardizing and homogenizing effect, however. Walsh (1992) suggests that many regeneration schemes create what he describes as a 'heritagisation' of space – that is, the original significance of history and place is overwritten by developments that reflect little of what was originally there, or what is important to local communities. Heritage is already an interpretation of history, which is already an interpretation of the past, therefore it can represent a third-hand representation of a place and its people. This can also be problematic in cases where heritage interpretation is 'hijacked' by politicians, who may use it as a tool for oppression, exclusion or manipulation.

Regeneration clearly does not happen overnight. It is an incremental process, and many former industrial, perhaps less aesthetically pleasing cities have had to accept that tourism may be a relatively late addition to their strategy. The phasing of regeneration is crucial, and often enforced, not least because public sector or business investment is hard to come by. Businesses are unlikely to invest in cities that do not already show signs of economic growth or potential, just as tourists will only visit those cities that have significant attractions and ideally an infrastructure to match. Firstly, the local economy must be diversified and strengthened, especially where there has been industrial decline. Jobs may be created in the service sector or creative industries, as advocated by Florida (2002). But this may require government incentives for start-up companies or training to encourage entrepreneurship in the first place. If regeneration is to be led by artists to boost the 'Bohemian Index', there may be a need for rent subsidies or affordable housing schemes (e.g. the UK Government's pledge to provide 20% affordable housing in all new residential developments). A common by-product of even the most successful regeneration schemes is that local people become displaced from their place of residence due to gentrification (e.g. rent increases and rising costs). The whole character of town centres (especially historic towns) can be completely eroded if rent increases are not curtailed. For example, small, independent shops and businesses can be priced out and replaced by ubiquitous global chains (e.g. McDonald's and Starbucks).

If tourism is to be encouraged, there may be a requirement for new infrastructural developments, such as transport and accommodation, especially if landmark buildings or 'mega-events' are not located centrally. Opportunities to increase length of stay and expenditure may be needed. Cities such as Bilbao struggled in the initial stages of regeneration and tourism development, despite the apparent 'success' of the Guggenheim Museum, as there was little else for tourists to see or do once they had visited this one attraction. Smaller, supporting attractions may be needed, even if these are only related to shopping (a major motivating factor for most tourists!), as well as a flourishing evening economy. However, animation is difficult to create in remote locations, especially if they are not frequented by local people either. Incentives may be needed like more frequent public transport connections, guaranteed taxi services, or closer links between hotels and attractions.

Once product development, diversification, or enhancement has taken place, then a city can work on its branding and image, positioning itself in relation to its competitors. This is, of course, much easier to do if a city has a unique selling point (e.g. a Guggenheim Museum). It is less easy to do if a city has implemented a range of copy-cat schemes based on other cities' successes. Indeed, research has shown that many such venues fail because they do not consider the links with their own local heritage and communities (e.g. Cardiff tried to develop a modern art museum similar to London's Tate Modern, but there was little local interest; and Sheffield's National Centre for Popular Music proved to be unpopular, unlike similar music-based initiatives in Liverpool and Manchester). Similarly, serial monotony (e.g. standardized developments that could be anywhere) do not constitute original attractions. Although ephemeral events like festivals and events are tourist magnets, they are of temporary duration and may not have such a long lasting impact as permanent attractions or iconic buildings. Having said that, Olympic and European Cultural Capital bids are required to include a detailed strategy for legacy and reuse. Barcelona is an example of a city that has managed this legacy admirably, constantly building new attractions in the former Olympic site. These days, with growing competition and changing consumer tastes, tourist destinations cannot afford to rest on their laurels. They must be constantly creative and innovative in their approach to attractions development and (re)branding. Some authors have suggested that there need to be more creative approaches to regeneration and tourism development. For example, Richards and Wilson (2006) advocate increasing the development of experiential creative spaces, creative spectacles and creative tourism.

Many academics and practitioners have been referring to the concept of 'cultural planning' in the context of regeneration for over 10 years now (e.g. Mercer, 1991; Bianchini, 1999, 2000; Evans, 2001; Ghilardi, 2001). This approach incorporates many of the issues and principles mentioned so far. That is, that culture should be central to the regeneration process, rather than a mere 'add-on' or appendage. This is clearly reflected in the DCMS (2004) document where the Secretary of State for Culture, Tessa Jowell, states that: 'Most people now accept that you cannot breathe new life into cities, towns and communities without culture.' Culture should be defined in the broadest sense as heritage, arts and creative industries, as well as incorporating peoples' everyday lifestyles into the equation (e.g. leisure, shopping, eating, drinking). Bianchini (2000) emphasizes the need to approach cultural regeneration in an integrated and socially inclusive way through joined-up policy. He also stresses the need to plan in creative ways, taking account of cultural diversity. Ghilardi (2001) highlights diversity and difference as key resources in cultural planning in terms of social inclusion (and often unique selling points for those cities that want to encourage tourism).

Recent analyses and evaluation of the true role of culture in regeneration (e.g. Evans and Shaw, 2004; Evans, 2005) have clearly moved the debates forward in terms of research, planning and management. Evans (2005) distinguishes between examples of locations where cultural activity is fully integrated into strategic planning and development, cases where culture is a catalyst for regeneration, and examples where it is more of an 'add-on'. Impacts therefore vary considerably from significant to marginal. Proving that culture really *does* matter is often problematic because of its elusive and intangible nature. Nevertheless, what is increasingly required by governments is evidence-based research on the role of culture in regeneration, an excellent starting point for which is given by Evans and Shaw (2004). This subject is also given some coverage in this volume. This is mainly presented in the form of case studies, where examples of good practice are offered.

It should be stated that regeneration strategies have often been overly ambitious in the past, trying to be all things to all people, or alternatively, over-promising and under-delivering. Some of the most 'successful' schemes have been limited to physical transformation and economic and business development (e.g. the Docklands development in the 1980s in London). Cultural attractions and tourism are only recent additions to the process, and the original local communities were largely excluded. This is not perhaps an ideal scenario, and it is arguably better to be aspirational and progressive in one's thinking. However, regeneration projects

need to be realistic and incremental, implemented in stages as and when investment becomes available, or where creative leadership becomes a driving force. A summary of responses to the DCMS's (2004) consultation document demonstrated that there is still a long way to go in terms of achieving the perfect model for cultural regeneration. There is a need for a better base of evidence for research and the development of toolkits of best practice. A combination of government support and regulation, and private sector innovation and investment is essential. Too much emphasis is still placed on buildings rather than more intangible, but equally important aspects of regeneration (e.g. social and community issues). A tourism imperative may not be the best starting point for a regeneration strategy, but it may follow naturally if a creative and innovative approach is taken. Overall, it is clear that regeneration is the new 'buzzword' in the transformation of urban environments. However, taking it from strategy to reality is the real challenge.

The authors in this volume therefore take up this challenge. The focus of the publication is on the destinations and sites that are being created for tourists, as well as for local people within a regeneration context. The volume's originality lies in its focus on tourism's relationship to regeneration and cultural developments, a subject that has so far only been given a cursory glance in other literature. The tourist gaze (Urry, 1990, 2002) is constantly being redirected towards new cultural attractions, venues and events; however, questions about standardization and 'authenticity' should be raised. What are the impacts of such developments on a local sense of place, heritage and identity? How far are the arts and artistic quality/integrity compromised by being used as a tool for regeneration? Can global/local debates be resolved within the context of regeneration, and if so, how?

These issues and others will provide the framework for the volume, and will be exemplified using a number of international case studies in North and South America, as well as in Europe and the UK. Authors will address a wide range of issues, including many of the contradictions and complexities inherent within this multidisciplinary field. Regeneration has featured regularly on the agenda of many governments in recent years, but the extent to which this phe-nomenon and its implications are truly under-stood is open to debate. It will be argued that there needs to be a shift away from the tokenism of 'buzzwords' towards a more practical and realistic approach to planning and strategic development.

The theoretical framework for the volume will be derived from a number of different fields including sociology, cultural geography and urban planning. The authors involved in the project have a wide range of experience within cultural tourism, regeneration and planning. Many of them are or have been practitioners within these areas of activity, as well as academ-ics and researchers. They therefore have a keen awareness of both theoretical and practical concerns.

In Chapter 1 Melanie Smith provides a framework for the rest of the volume, outlining some of the issues and problems inherent in implementing regeneration projects. She high-lights the increasingly important role that culture and tourism are playing in the process, focusing in particular on global and local tensions, standardization versus place-making, preser-vation of heritage compared to the promotion of contemporary cultures, and local community involvement. The chapter ends with a brief overview and discussion of a cultural planning approach, arguably the way forward for an integrated, democratic and creative future for regeneration.

In Chapter 2 Greg Richards and Julie Wilson examine the increasing importance of creative strategies for cities wishing to avoid the pitfalls of homogenization and serial monotony. Fol-lowing an analysis of four main types of regen-eration (e.g. using iconic structures, heritage mining, mega-events and thematization), they advocate models of creative development. Many of these are based on more experiential and interactive activities within the contexts of creative spectacles, creative spaces, and creative tourism. Using a range of examples, they demonstrate good practice and the positive effects of a more creative approach to regeneration.

In Chapter 3 Robert Maitland focuses on the regeneration of new or less familiar areas of cities, and their development for tourism pur-poses. Although many tourists seek a familiar

'bubble', others are keen to experience some-thing more 'real' or authentic. Often, the areas that such tourists seek tend to grow organically, rather than being specifically planned for. Indeed, it could be argued that too much plan-ning can stifle creativity, spontaneity and authenticity. Robert examines how the quality of places, their distinctiveness and sometimes even their 'ordinariness' can create tourist satis-faction. He also explores the role that tourists themselves can play in the process of discovery and re-invention.

In Chapter 4 Graeme Evans and Rosita Aiesha introduce the theme of mixed-use devel-opments in city fringe areas, especially those with culturally diverse or ethnic populations. Visitors and locals share common space, and usage is complex and varied. The sustainability of such projects is questioned, given that prob-lems of gentrification and congestion often abound. Mixed temporal use of space can result in significant social problems, particularly at night. The authors examine the policy and plan-ning implications for the management of such regeneration zones using a case study of Clerkenwell in North London (UK).

In Chapter 5 Stephen Shaw looks at the development of ethnoscapes (those areas of cities with a high concentration of ethnic minori-ties). He analyses the way in which multicultur-alism has become an increasingly attractive selling point for city tourism. Ethnic and cultural difference is frequently seen as being 'exotic', colourful and animated. He focuses in particular on examples from Canada, examining the role of Canadian provincial and city governments in supporting the redevelopment of ethnic minor-ity residential areas. He advocates more cre-ative and less formulaic approaches to both regeneration and tourism promotion in such culturally diverse contexts.

Chapter 6 by Daina Cheyenne Harvey focuses on the theme of black heritage sites in New Jersey (USA), examining some of the diffi-culties of interpreting and commemorating spaces of dissonant heritage. The re-imagining of such spaces for regeneration or tourism pur-poses can be problematic, especially where the past has been sanitized, distorted or only par-tially represented (e.g. the history of slavery). The emotional nature of such heritage for both residents and visitors alike requires careful planning and management, and is thus as much a political as a social issue. Daina makes the important point that whilst many sites can work as spaces for tourism, they can ultimately fail as instruments of cultural regeneration if they exclude or alienate the very minorities that they are supposed to serve.

In Chapter 7 Meiko Murayama and Gavin Parker use the example of Tokyo to illustrate many of the complexities that exist within large-scale, mixed-use development projects. They highlight tensions between the development of tourism facilities and provision for local residents, indicating the need for more integrated approaches to planning. A model is proposed wherein a balance between living, working and playing is suggested in accordance with principles of sustainability and the enhancement of quality of life.

Chapter 8 focuses on the role of major sporting events in regeneration. Andrew Smith questions the extent to which such events can truly boost tourism development, image enhancement and social inclusion. He looks at solutions for integrating sporting events into wider regeneration schemes, as well as ensuring a long-term legacy after the events. Using case studies of Manchester and London in the UK, he examines these issues and others in context, taking a refreshingly critical view of sports-led regeneration.

Following on from the theme of Chapter 8, Charles Heying, Matthew Burbank and Greg Andranovich focus specifically on the role of the Olympic Games in the regeneration of US cities in Chapter 9. Using a case study of Atlanta, they illustrate how multiple consumption-based strategies such as sports, public space, education, arts, heritage, and infrastructure development can be used to develop a comprehensive regeneration package. They also question the political, economic and social implications of the event. In addition, they consider the potential implications of the New York 2012 Olympic bid, demonstrating the complexity of the contemporary bidding process for mega-events.

Myrna Breitbart and Cathy Stanton in Chapter 10 discuss the role of the cultural industries in the regeneration of former industrial cities, focusing in particular on Lowell, Massachusetts in New England (USA). They examine the problems of addressing industrial decay, economic decline and negative images through the arts and culture. The widespread adoption of a cultural planning approach focusing on the cultural and creative industries is gently questioned. Contrary to good intentions, such approaches can lead to standardization and inadvertent marginalization of the 'local' if care is not taken to maximize community participation for the complete duration of projects. They also suggest that the dynamism of the arts and contemporary culture(s) can sometimes be more engaging than heritage-based initiatives.

Chapter 11 by Costas Spirou introduces an in-depth case study of Chicago (USA), a city that has engaged in regeneration following the decline of its manufacturing industry. Under the creative and dynamic leadership of the city's Mayor, many large-scale urban redevelopment projects have been constructed with tourism in mind. The outcomes have clearly been successful in this respect. However, less attention has been paid to the city's poverty stricken, unemployed and illiterate populations, despite political rhetoric. As in many similar examples, this imbalance needs to be redressed if urban restructuring is to be truly balanced.

In Chapter 12, Anna Maria Bounds looks at the example of the Avenue of the Arts in Philadelphia (USA), which was created to boost tourism development and the local economy. It is an example of a project that has been largely successful due to charismatic leadership, dynamic fund-raising campaigns and coordinated public and private partnerships. Despite the failure of some projects within the wider scheme, the case study demonstrates the power and potential success of aspirational and ambitious cultural regeneration projects.

Chapter 13 by Andrew Jones takes a balanced view of waterfront developments in the context of regeneration, examining both the problems and the potential benefits of such schemes. This critique enables the author to take the debates further, discussing models of good practice that are comprehensive and integrated. He contrasts the more commercially orientated examples of waterfront developments in the USA with the more publicly spirited approaches in Continental Europe and elsewhere, advocating a combination of the two, in which culture plays an increasingly important role.

Following on from the theme of the previous chapter, Patricia Avery in Chapter 14 examines the changing role of dockland cities and urban regeneration strategies, focusing in particular on case studies of Liverpool and Cardiff (UK). She includes within this a discussion of the European Cultural Capital initiative, a title won by Liverpool for 2008, and for which Cardiff was also bidding. Liverpool and Cardiff can be largely seen as 'success stories' in terms of cultural regeneration, as both cities have managed to engage in extensive redevelopment and image transformation. Liverpool's winning of the European Cultural Capital bid was mainly based on its consideration of local community issues (both social and economic), though there are still concerns about gentrification and commercialization. The bidding process for Cardiff also provided a catalyst to develop further cultural and community-based initiatives. Despite the inclusion of such positive examples, Patricia is also critical of many aspects of the cultural regeneration process in the context of dockland cities, highlighting the need for further research.

The final chapter, Chapter 15, by Brian Bath and Paula Goncalves discusses the use of interpretative planning in the context of Recife, Brazil. The case study looks at the interface between tourism, culture and regeneration, and emphasis is placed on the need to protect heritage and respect local cultures. Community consultation and involvement is seen as a prerequisite for successful regeneration planning.

References

Augé, M. (1995) *Non-Places: Introduction to an Anthropology of Supermodernity.* Verso, London.

Bianchini, F. (1999) Cultural planning for urban sustainability. In: Nystrom, L. (ed.) *City and Culture: Cultural Processes and Urban Sustainability*. The Swedish Urban Environment Council, Kalmar, Sweden, pp. 34–51.

Bianchini, F. (2000) From 'cultural policy' to 'cultural planning'. *Artsbusiness* 27 March, 5–6.

DCMS (2004) *Culture at the Heart of Regeneration*. Department of Culture, Media and Sport (DCMS), London.

Evans, G. (2001) *Cultural Planning: an Urban Renaissance?* Routledge, London.

Evans, G. (2005) Measure for measure: evaluating the evidence of culture's contribution to regeneration. *Urban Studies* 42(5/6), 959–984.

Evans, G. and Shaw, P. (2004) *The Contribution of Culture to Regeneration in the UK: a Review of Evidence.* A Report to the Department of Culture Media and Sport (DCMS). DCMS, London.

Florida, R. (2002) *The Rise of the Creative Class.* Basic Books, New York.

Ghilardi, L. (2001) *Cultural Planning and Cultural Diversity.* Noema Research and Planning Ltd, London.

Mercer, C. (1991) What is cultural planning? Community Arts Network National Conference. Sydney, Australia, 10 October.

Richards, R. and Wilson, J. (2006) Developing creativity in tourist experiences: a solution to the serial reproduction of culture? *Tourism Management* 27(6) (in press).

Short, R. (1989) *The Humane City: As If People Matter.* Blackwell, Oxford.

Urry, J. (1990) *The Tourist Gaze: Leisure and Travel in Contemporary Societies.* Sage, London.

Urry, J. (2002) *The Tourist Gaze: Leisure and Travel in Contemporary Societies,* 2nd edn. Sage, London.

Walsh, K. (1992) *The Representation of the Past: Museums and Heritage in the Post-modern World.* Routledge, London.

1 Towards a Cultural Planning Approach to Regeneration

Melanie K. Smith

Cities are cultural entities. The texture of social and economic life in them is defined by their cultural energy or lack of it, and cities all over the world – Glasgow, Barcelona, Seattle – have demonstrated that by changing the way their cultural life is perceived you can change everything about them.

(Jones, 2000)

Introduction

The aim of this chapter is to provide a framework for the volume as a whole, discussing some of the key issues in regeneration and examining the role of culture and tourism in the process. The concept of regeneration has become something of a 'buzzword' in the field of urban studies and planning in recent years. Its meaning is usually associated with the redevelopment of cities or areas of cities that have declined industrially, physically and economically. Numerous publications have been devoted to the process of urban regeneration documenting housing, welfare, environmental and economic policies, but surprisingly few have focused specifically on the role of culture within regeneration. It is perhaps true to say that the term regeneration was traditionally associated predominantly with an economic imperative, which may or may not have included cultural development. This volume therefore redresses this imbalance.

The term regeneration is not so much contentious as vague. It is often viewed as being synonymous with 'revitalization' (bringing new life to) or 'renaissance' (being reborn). It necessarily implies an initial de-generation. Bianchini (1993: 211) describes urban regeneration as 'a composite concept, encompassing economic, environmental, social, cultural, symbolic and political dimensions'. It is a process that aims to revitalize areas of cities that have declined using a range of tools (e.g. property, business, retail or arts development) to enhance the area physically, economically, socially or culturally. Urban regeneration strategies were largely developed initially in response to the post-war decline of cities, and the rising inequality, poverty, crime and unemployment that blighted inner cities, in particular. The deindustrialization process and subsequent global economic restructuring in the late 1970s and 1980s also acted as a catalyst for the development of urban regeneration strategies for many cities in the USA and Western Europe.

Many policy and strategy documents for regeneration would still suggest that regeneration is synonymous with economic development. The process often tends to be measured in economic terms, such as employment creation, multiplier effects or visitor expenditure. However, as concern for the supposed beneficiaries (i.e. the people living within target areas) of regeneration strategies has increased, the term appears to be more closely linked to the concept of 'community development'. Regeneration agencies are starting to consider the socio-economic or even socio-cultural impacts of regeneration, and although standardized measures for evaluation and monitoring have not yet fully emerged, there has clearly been a shift in priorities (at least in political rhetoric!).

The urban regeneration process is a complex one, and the motivations for embarking on large-scale regeneration projects are varied. They may form part of the government's agenda for the economic or cultural redevelopment of former industrial cities that have fallen into decline; the enhancement of external image may be viewed as a means of attracting inward investment and tourism; or projects may be a way of initiating wider environmental improvements and infrastructure developments. A key factor in all of these motivations is that initial funding will hopefully have a cumulative effect, acting as a catalyst for further inward investment and the development of other initiatives. There has been increasing interest in the role that culture can play in the urban regeneration process. Zukin (1995) describes how many cities in America and Europe started using culture as an instrument in the entrepreneurial strategies of local governments and business alliances from the 1970s onwards.

The Role of Culture in Urban Regeneration

In the context of urban regeneration, culture can refer to anything from architecture, heritage buildings and attractions, to the visual and performing arts, festivals and events, to entertainment and leisure complexes, as well as culture as the way of life of people. In many cases, culture is used as a tool to enhance or aestheticize declining areas of cities. Old buildings may be reused (e.g. power stations, factories and railway stations can be converted into museums and galleries); new spaces of consumption may be constructed on decontaminated wasteland (e.g. shopping malls, Olympic villages, Expo sites); industrial areas may be cleaned up and redeveloped (e.g. waterfronts). In some cases, close links are maintained with the history and heritage of place and local communities. In others, developments seem to be divorced from any sense of locality.

Culture and commerce have clearly become intertwined in the postmodern world of global consumption. Culture has become a commodity to be packaged and sold much like any other. Many regeneration projects therefore have a strong economic and business imperative, despite their apparent 'cultural' focus. Evans (2001: 226) argues that this is not a phenomenon that is any more prevalent in Western cities; in fact, the reverse might be true:

> The juxtaposition of commerce with culture, alongside or even in place of public culture ('realm') in the form of cultural venues, facilities and monuments appears more intense in New World cities undergoing modernisation than in the old cities.

Thus cities like Hong Kong, Singapore, Kuala Lumpur and others compete to construct 'monumental edifices' in the form of international hotels, shopping malls, entertainment complexes and such like. This has engendered debates about the problems of homogenization, serial monotony and placelessness (e.g. Relph, 1976; Short, 1989; Augé, 1995; Smith, 2005; Richards and Wilson, 2006). Some cities appear to be constructing similar 'global' landscapes, which could arguably be anywhere. They have little connection to a local sense of heritage or place. Many theorists are in agreement that 'place' must have a human dimension (e.g. Entrikin, 1991; Rotenberg and McDonogh, 1993; Lippard, 1997) therefore the role of communities in the development of cultural regeneration is pivotal if local or indigenous character and uniqueness are to be maintained. More recent theories are also focusing on the role of 'creativity' as well as culture in the regeneration of cities (e.g. Florida, 2002; Richards and Wilson, 2006). Florida (2002) also notes the close connections between place, community and a strong, creative economy.

Evans (2005) differentiates between approaches to regeneration, demonstrating examples of 'cultural regeneration', where cultural activities are integrated into a wider strategy; 'culture-led' regeneration, where culture provides a catalyst for further developments; and 'culture *and* regeneration', where cultural activities are less integrated and therefore play a more marginal role, often as a mere 'add-on'. This volume focuses on examples of all of these, but the majority of regeneration projects appear to be increasingly aspiring towards 'cultural regeneration', where cultural provision and its planning and management are fully integrated into wider urban strategies.

The following sections introduce some of the examples of culture-led regeneration that will be discussed further by the authors in this volume, highlighting in particular some of the inherent complexities and contradictions that frequently need to be addressed.

Cultural and Ethnic Quarters

Many cities create integrated 'cultural districts' or 'cultural quarters' as part of regeneration strategies. Wynne (1992: 19) describes a 'cultural quarter' as being 'that geographical area which contains the highest concentration of cultural and entertainment facilities in a city or town'. In many cases, these will be mixed-use development areas, which aim to provide attractions and facilities for locals and tourists alike. This may include entertainment facilities, retail outlets, eating and drinking establishments, as well as cultural venues or attractions (e.g. museums, galleries or theatres). Increasingly, its meaning can also include clusters of creative industries (e.g. media, design, technology) and creative individuals and groups. It is important in any cultural regeneration project that cultural and creative developments are integrated into mixed-use districts designated also for office space, residential, hotel, catering, retail and recreational use, rather than constructing isolated arts centres or cultural landmarks which fail to generate further economic and social benefits for the local communities.

Some cultural quarters develop more 'organically', for example, so-called 'ethnic quarters' or 'ethnoscapes' like 'China Towns', 'Arab Quarters' or 'Little Italies'. Such areas often become so popular with residents and visitors alike, that they regularly feature in tourist brochures as cultural attractions, with gastronomy, shopping and festivals topping the list of activities. However, there have been fears that such developments are leading to an appropriation or invasion of social space. For example, in London, many Asian women increasingly fear going out unaccompanied in Brick Lane as there are now so many (white) men frequenting curry houses there. Residents of Notting Hill are facing displacement from their homes as gentrification of the area increases and the Carnival becomes more of a 'white' spectacle.

Similar criticisms of appropriation have been directed at the development of gay quarters in cities. It is interesting to note that many gay areas of cities are becoming more gentrified, no doubt to capitalize on the strength of the 'pink pound'. This is certainly true of London's Compton Street (Soho) or Manchester's 'Gay Village' in the UK. Florida (2002) emphasizes the strong links between a high 'Gay Index' and clusters of creative and technological activities. The Gay Pride event or Mardi Gras is increasingly being used as a means of asserting gay identity, but also of attracting visitors. Manchester and Brighton Gay Pride events are becoming almost as popular as London's, and cities like Birmingham, Leicester and Sheffield in the UK are following suit. However, this event has recently been criticized for becoming depoliticized, mainly due to the growing number of heterosexual revellers 'crashing' the party. There are also concerns amongst the homosexual community about the 'de-gaying' of certain spaces as heterosexuals are becoming more frequent visitors to such areas and venues.

The 2005 riots in Paris and elsewhere in France also perhaps reflected some of the social and racial inequalities omnipresent in quarters where the concentration of ethnic minorities is high. This demonstrates only too clearly that regeneration sometimes needs to focus on economic and community issues, rather than being sidetracked into cultural and tourism development.

The Arts, Festivals and Community Development

In Britain, the USA and most other Western countries, there has been an emergence of 'arts-led' urban regeneration strategies in recent decades. It was hoped that such strategies would serve to reconstruct cities' external image, making them attractive to potential investors and visitors, as well as triggering a process of physical and environmental revitalization. Inspiration was drawn from the American experience of the 1970s in cities like Pittsburgh, Boston and Baltimore. Mayors in these cities were keen to relaunch the image of downtown areas, develop cultural districts and mixed-use areas, and to boost the local economy through art-related activities (Bianchini, 1993).

Jacobs (1961: 386) emphasized the importance of a thriving cultural life for American cities: 'We need art, in the arrangement of cities as well as in other realms of life, to help explain life to us, to show us meanings, to illuminate the relationship between the life that each of us embodies and the life outside us.' She later added that 'lively, diverse, intense cities contain the seeds of their own regeneration' (Jacobs, 1961: 462). Arts activities can make a positive contribution to community life, attracting people to an area, creating a lively ambience and improving safety on the streets. As noted by Fisher and Owen (1991), the arts are just as essential for a city's identity as any other civic services. Sharp et al. (2005) suggest that public art can contribute to local distinctiveness, attract investment, boost cultural tourism, enhance land values, create employment, increase use of urban space and reduce vandalism. However, the arts typically suffer from problems of under-funding and under-valorization. Governments frequently take a rather tokenistic approach to the arts, exploiting their economic and social potential, but without adequate reinvestment and support. More research and evaluation is therefore needed to prove the true worth of the arts to the process of regeneration (unfortunately, often a time-consuming, difficult and expensive process).

Clearly, large, cosmopolitan cities have become more culturally diverse over the past few decades. The consequence has been a proliferation of exciting and colourful festivals, events and spectacles, many of which have global appeal. As stated by Sandercock (1998: 213): 'Our deepest feelings about city and community are expressed on special occasions such as carnivals and festivals.' Tourism has helped to raise the profile of ethnic festivals, and tourists are clearly motivated by an interest in the cultural origins of festivals. Quinn (2005) outlines

the benefits of festivals in the context of regeneration. These include contributing to the democratization of culture, celebrating diversity, animating and empowering communities, and improving quality of life. However, she notes the need for better research and more holistic management if festivals are to succeed in providing such benefits.

The 'Heritagisation' of Urban Space

Many theorists have been somewhat cynical about the way in which heritage has been used as a tool for regeneration. Sudjic (1992: 166) states that 'When there is nothing else left to sustain their economies, cities start to rediscover their own history, or at least the history that they would like to have had. They use it as a catalyst for their attempts at regeneration.' Soja (2000: 246) suggests that this is linked to a sense of urban nostalgia 'a longing for what is called the "historical city", a once more clearly definable urbanism that is believed to have been civilized, urbane, and richly creative'. This may be true, but it is difficult for many cities (especially former industrial cities) to sell themselves otherwise, given that the urban landscape has often been blighted by heavy industry. The alternative is perhaps to develop a series of new, global attractions, only then to be accused of creating 'blandscapes' (Short, 1989) or 'placeless' environments. However, there is perhaps a need to take into consideration local connections and meanings. Walsh (1992) complains of a phenomenon which he calls 'heritagisation', whereby the past is transformed by a process of 'ahistoric aestheticization' creating fantasy spaces, which are home to no one and have few local associations or affiliations. Similarly, Hughes (1998) suggests that care must be taken not to 'overwrite' the original significance of heritage spaces when developing tourism, and Middleton (1987) comments on the problems of towns becoming too sanitized in insidious attempts to clean up and prettify. Regeneration initiatives arguably need not only to conserve as much local heritage as possible, but to encourage the representation of hidden or alternative histories, especially those of local or diasporic communities. The reuse of heritage buildings (e.g. former factories, railway stations) for modern purposes is a common regeneration strategy, but this can be problematic as the original workers may feel no affiliation with the new structure (and not all ex-factory workers can or want to be retrained as curators or retail managers!).

'Grand Projects' and 'Flagships'

Some cities use cultural flagship projects or events as catalysts for the environmental, social, economic and cultural regeneration of an area. This may include the development of new cultural attractions, such as museums, galleries or theatres, or cultural events, such as festivals and exhibitions.

Cities clamour to host the next Olympic Games, the Expo, or the European Cultural Capital initiative. However, the legacy of 'mega-events' and their contribution to urban regeneration is a subject that has concerned a number of researchers. Sandercock (1998) suggests that many governments have fast-tracked mega-projects, often short-circuiting established planning processes and isolating such developments from public scrutiny and democratic politics. Sudjic (1999) states that cities and governments are unfortunately not very good at hosting mega-events. The legacy is often one of high levels of debt, redundant buildings and a community that has been displaced or bypassed. However, they are high profile events that generate international publicity, therefore the host city often considers the prestige to outweigh other considerations.

Sudjic (1992: 201) is fairly scathing about the standardization of such large events, stating that 'The Expo is Disneyland's alter ego, an insight into the gaudy mixture of the mundane and the fantastical that lies close to the surface under the banality of the modern city.' Such developments could technically take place in almost any city in the world, and their attempts at engaging local people rather than tourists or visitors are often tokenistic. But in some ways, perhaps they are simply 'external' rather than 'internal' events, aiming to put cities on the tourist map or the international stage. And tourists generally find them rather fun! However, once the event is over the question of legacy

needs to be considered if 'white elephant' status is to be avoided. Olympic bids, for example, now have to include detailed plans for future legacy as part of the application criteria.

Jones (2000) suggests that a number of projects have failed for financial reasons, but also because they are largely inappropriate for the local community and cultural infrastructure. He cites the example of the Centre for Visual Art in Cardiff, which has not met with the same success as the flagship rugby stadium or Cardiff Bay Waterfront Development. He attributes this to a local lack of interest in modern art, suggesting that popular culture and sport generally tend to strike more of a chord with local audiences in Cardiff than high arts. Sheffield's National Centre for Popular Music perhaps failed because it does not have a particularly strong musical heritage in the way that Liverpool or Manchester does. Whereas Tate Modern has appealed to London audiences and international tourists alike, it should not be assumed that it is possible to reproduce such an effect elsewhere. The same is true of the Guggenheim Museum in Bilbao. Although many cities are now hankering after their very own Guggenheim, it is the uniqueness of the structure, its location and cultural context that partly shape its success.

However, the Guggenheim was developed specifically to attract international tourists and to raise the city's profile, rather than attracting local people or promoting their heritage. Sudjic (1999: 180) cynically suggests that this development was symptomatic of 'the neurotic difficulties of small nations attempting to be noticed on an international level'. He notes that an American architect was imported to design the building and a collection was franchised from the Guggenheim, and he highlights the tensions between 'metropolitan culture and a people's distinctive local sense of self and identity'.

But can and should such developments and attractions attempt to be all things to all people? They are essentially icons and tourist attractions, perhaps, but there are mechanisms that can be used to enhance local attendance and engagement. International art galleries such as Tate Modern in London have fairly extensive outreach and educational programmes, for example. Differential pricing or free passes for locals can encourage visitation. Residents may benefit indirectly from big events like Expos and Olympic Games if infrastructural improvements are made or new (affordable) housing is created. However, all of this needs to be taken into consideration at the planning and consultation stages.

Waterfront Development Schemes

Sieber (1993) describes how the revitalization of urban waterfronts is a seemingly ubiquitous process in North America, Europe and Australasia, and is one that inevitably seems to involve gentrification. Despite the intentions of developers and planners to create integrated mixed-used development, combining residential, recreational and cultural developments, the result is often a gentrified space largely occupied by strangers to the city (e.g. urban professionals, suburban communities and tourists). The failure to provide access for locals or, worse still, the displacement and exclusion of local communities is an issue that needs to be addressed by governments in their regulation of private sector development and planning.

Cooper (1993) suggests that geographers liken waterfronts to 'urban frontiers'. They have largely become isolated 'landscapes of consumption' awash with gentrified cultural and recreational activities, which often fail to reflect the diverse cultural traditions of local people. Cooper claims that this is true of Toronto. It is also starkly in evidence in Cape Town, where the commercialized, internationalized, 'could-be-anywhere' sense of space experienced at the waterfront stands in sharp contrast to the troubled heritage of the Black and Coloured Townships. Given the city's history of spatial and racial segregation, it is surprising to encounter a contemporary version of a similar process. Cooper suggests that whatever diversity exists at the waterfront, it is certainly not local heritage. Nevertheless, the waterfront is immensely popular with international tourists arguably *because* of its cosmopolitan environment and its rather safe and sanitized atmosphere!

Edwards (1996: 93) states that many waterfront developments have been criticized because of their 'poor design, lack of character and generally unimpressive environments'. Hoyle (2002) discusses different models of

waterfront regeneration, some of which create bland standardization, globalization and gentrification, and others which focus more on heritage renaissance, community development or contemporary culture. Such conflicts are not easily resolved within the context of urban (re)development. Similarly, the resolution of global/local tensions is a key dilemma as discussed earlier in the context of 'flagship' projects.

Tourism and the Globalization of Urban Space

Hughes (1998) describes how tourism is a spatially differentiating activity, which can lead to the homogenization of culture, but which can also help to 're-vision' or 're-imagine' space:

> Tourism [. . .] differentiates space in a ceaseless attempt to attract and keep its market share. In the face of growing global cultural homogenisation, local tourist agencies strive to assert their spatial distinctiveness and cultural particularities in a bid to market each place as an attractive tourist destination.
> (Hughes, 1998: 30)

Something similar could be said of the regeneration process. Various destinations are actively engaging in the reconfiguration of their identity in an attempt to reposition themselves or to put themselves on the tourist map. However, Walsh's (1992) fears about bland standardization and the 'heritagisation' of public space are not unfounded. It is evident that numerous town centres, particularly in Britain, are starting to rely on inward investment from global businesses, which render them at best homogenous, and at worst, soulless. The same is true of some rural areas, which are becoming more standardized and losing their character (see Campaign for the Protection of Rural England (CPRE), 2003). Although it is clear that former industrial cities often have little option but to court such investment, it can quite feasibly be channelled into the development of innovative new projects, initiatives and attractions, rather than bland retail developments. Tourism development is likely to be threatened if all places start to look the same (Ritzer, 2004).

Nevertheless, the tastes of the postmodern tourist or 'post-tourist' are clearly changing, and increasing numbers of tourists are drawn to the excitement of 'hyper-real' experiences, often within enclavic bubbles, such as shopping malls, theme parks or leisure complexes. This is part of the 'playfulness' of tourism (Rojek, 1993). The production of such spaces therefore appears to be a prominent characteristic of postmodern urban planning, and thus an inherent part of regeneration.

Planning for Cultural Regeneration and Tourism Development

Planning must take into consideration local structures of meaning and experience if it is to avoid the aforementioned problems of serial monotony, blandscapes, placelessness, etc. Philo (2000) suggests that we should emphasize the particular, the local and the specific over the general, the universal and the eternal. Destinations clearly need to be unique in order to place themselves on the tourist map, but they also need to offer certain levels of familiarity, comfort and security. Enclavic bubbles are often the favoured retreat of both the masses and the 'cosmopolitan elite' (Bauman, 2001), even if they appear to be characteristic of 'non-place' (Augé, 1995).

Planning for the regeneration of tourist destinations and spaces is a complex process. As demonstrated by failed 'flagship' projects, it is not simply enough to 'beam in' an attraction of supposed international significance and acclaim. It must have some local resonance and connections with a sense of place and identity; otherwise, dissent becomes inevitable. The same is true of World Heritage Sites, which promote themselves as panaceas for the regeneration of industrial or rural areas. Local people should be involved in their interpretation and representation as national or global icons. As stated by Evans (2001: 226):

> The focus on world and symbolic heritage sites in the cities of both developed and developing countries requires that a balance be struck between local and national imperatives – qualities of life, economic and physical access, minimising gentrification effects . . .

A postmodern approach to planning appears to favour more integrated approaches and mixed-use developments, which cater for numerous social and cultural needs simultaneously. There is also more emphasis on the entertainment function of cities and the creation of 'hyper-real' environments and themed spaces, which generally seem to appeal to the masses, especially the young. Jacobs and Appleyard in Gates and Stout (1996: 169) advocate less traditional approaches to urban planning and design:

> A city should have magical places where fantasy is possible, a counter to and an escape from the mundaneness of everyday work and living. Architects and planners take cities and themselves too seriously; the result too often is deadliness and boredom, no imagination, no humour, alienating places.

Despite earlier critiques of standardization and 'placelessness', it is interesting to note the increasing proliferation of unique and fantastical architectural features and public art across the urban landscape in recent years. Although local people may not immediately engage with new architectural features, familiarity and frequent usage help to break down barriers. Such unique selling points, however controversial, can also aid promotional campaigns for tourism.

Evans (2001) describes how place and culture are inextricably intertwined, with culture helping to shape local character and place differentiation. However, he suggests that geographers and urban planners have often failed to appreciate the significance of culture and arts practice and participation in urban planning. He therefore redresses this imbalance, advocating a cultural planning approach. He describes it as a means of integrating cultural resources into strategic urban development. If a sense of place is to be maintained or enhanced, a balance must be struck between the emphasis that is placed on heritage and the celebration of contemporary culture and the arts. Care must be taken not to 'overwrite' the significance of heritage with new developments, whilst adequately representing the diversity of both indigenous and non-indigenous local community cultures. If it is to have any resonance with local communities, urban planning needs to take into consideration peoples' lifestyles, cultural associations and identity. A more 'discursive' form of planning may help to ensure that the true meaning and significance of city space are not overlooked. Ploger (2001: 64) looks at planning as a 'discursive practice', which 'produces a sense of place, place-identity and common cultural schemes'.

Sandercock (1998: 183) strongly advocates that 'the cities and regions of the future must nurture difference and diversity through democratic cultural pluralism'. She describes how the foundations of postmodern planning praxis should be built on the acknowledgement of multiple publics. She describes how the 'voices from the borderlands' – i.e. those of the marginalized, displaced, oppressed or dominated – are increasingly being listened to. Cultural differences should not simply be tolerated, they must be valorized, which requires a new kind of 'multicultural literacy'. An important part of this is a familiarity with the multiple histories of urban communities, especially where these intersect with struggles over space and place claiming. This includes the histories of 'imagined communities' such as gays and lesbians, and women, as well as ethnic and diasporic communities. Sandercock (1998: 54) suggests that we have moved from 'planning history to planning's histories', thus challenging familiar notions of culture, difference and identity.

Box 1.1 offers a summary of the main principles of a cultural planning approach to urban regeneration, based on an in-depth analysis of both theory and practice in a range of contexts. Here, we are reminded of many of the complex issues discussed so far in this chapter.

Box 1.1 demonstrates that the role of creativity in the development of cities and tourist spaces is of increasing importance. Many destinations can no longer compete simply on the strength of their heritage attractions, especially where repeat visitation is desirable. Many cities (e.g. industrial or global) have relatively few heritage attractions to develop and promote, thus the emphasis on contemporary, experiential and creative tourism becomes of pivotal importance. Csikszentmihalyi (1996: 28) notes the potential of creativity: 'Creativity is any act, idea, or product that changes an existing domain, or that transforms an existing domain into a new one.' Creative cities arguably need creative governments and creative leadership (Florida, 2002). They also need creative communities,

Box 1.1. Key principles of cultural planning.

- Culture at the centre of and integral to planning
- Democratic and community-orientated (Mercer, 1991)
- 'Bottom-up' approach
- Pluralist, multi-stakeholder approach (Evans, 2005)
- Predominantly 'anthropological' in approach (Bianchini and Ghilardi, 1997)
- Local participation in the arts and cultural activities
- Emphasis on 'quality of life'
- Takes account of cultural diversity (Ghilardi, 2001)
- Negotiation of the local versus the national and the global (Evans, 2001; Richards, 2005)
- Recognition of multiple histories/heritages (Sandercock, 1998; Graham et al., 2000)
- Multiple representations
- Recognition of hybrid and multiple identities (Bhabha, 1994; Sarup, 1996)
- Fostering civic pride, a sense of local identity and ownership (DCMS, 1999)
- Awareness of intangible aspects of culture (Mercer, 1991)
- Animation of the cities through culture and creativity (Landry and Bianchini, 1995)
- High 'Creative' and 'Bohemian' Indices (Florida, 2002)
- Access to public spaces (physical and psychological)
- New, more 'tolerant' spaces for social interaction (Ghilardi, 2001)
- Spiritual and 'sacred' spaces (Sandercock, 1998)
- 'Aesthetics discourse' (Ploger, 2001)
- Space for fantasy (Sandercock, 1998)
- 'Place' and culture inextricably intertwined (Evans, 2001)
- Emphasis on place-identity and place marketing (Ploger, 2001)
- Retention of local 'authenticity' (Gibson, 2005)
- Creative approaches to development (Richards and Wilson, 2006)

who depend on that leadership for encouragement and support.

Many theorists and practitioners advocate an anthropological or community-based approach to cultural planning, and it is true that an area's people are often its most unique asset. A sense of place and animation is arguably created through and by the people resident in an area, coupled with the social and cultural programmes that are provided for and supported by them. Public spaces need animation, perhaps through the development of cultural festivals or the presence of public art. Increasingly, areas of high ethnic concentration and cultural diversity are becoming the most popular areas of cities (e.g. see Shaw *et al.*, 2004). Areas become attractive to creative practitioners because of their unique atmosphere or character (and of course, affordable rents and property). Florida's (2002) seminal work shows clearly that the most attractive and economically successful cities tend to be those with the highest concentration of creative and bohemian people, including gay residents.

Sandercock (1998) suggests that spaces for fantasy are essential to a city. Often fear of public dissent leads to conservative approaches to architectural development, but evidence suggests that the long-term benefits of iconic and unique structures far outweigh concerns for 'aesthetics' or social convention. In a competitive market, tourism destinations rely heavily on unique features as selling points. These need not erode a local sense of history or 'authenticity' – they can be complementary juxtapositions.

Rojek (1993) emphasizes the importance of 'playfulness' in tourism and leisure. Many tourists enjoy fantastical spaces with high levels of technological interaction (the enduring popularity of theme parks is testimony to that). New global destinations that might be described as 'hyper-real' (e.g. Dubai) are currently some of the most appealing, because of their innovative and creative approaches to architectural and attractions development, and their clear understanding of the 'experience economy' (Pine and Gilmore, 1999).

Conclusion

The common characteristic of both the tourism development and the regeneration process is that they seek to transform old spaces whilst recreating new ones. Tourism lifecycle models often imply that old destinations rarely die, they simply rejuvenate. Whilst it is seldom possible to rectify environmental damage and the destruction of natural resources, culture is arguably more resilient and can withstand changes of fortune. Cultures rarely disappear; they simply evolve. Ideally a balance should be maintained between the conservation of heritage, the promotion of the arts and festivals, and the development of new entertainment complexes. Notwithstanding the sweep of globalization, many destinations are exploring innovative and creative ways of expressing or representing regional or local cultures, all of which serve as unique reminders of their individualism and identity. A cultural planning framework that adopts a creative approach is arguably the most effective way forward. Sometimes all of this is easier said than done. As stated by Kunzmann (2004), planners are often restricted by legal, financial and political regulations, as well as social resistance. Nevertheless, it is arguably better to be aspirational in one's approach to regeneration, albeit keeping a realistic eye on what is actually achievable. The authors in this volume outline some examples of positive and innovative practice, which suggest that the future potential of cultural regeneration is truly inspirational.

References

Augé, M. (1995) *Non-Places: Introduction to an Anthropology of Supermodernity*. London, Verso.

Bauman, Z. (2001) *Community: Seeking Safety in an Insecure World*. Cambridge, Polity.

Bhabha, H. (1994) *The Location of Culture*. Routledge, London.

Bianchini, F. (1993) Culture, conflict and cities: issues and prospects for the 1990s. In: Bianchini, F. and Parkinson, M. (eds) *Cultural Policy and Urban Regeneration – The West European Experience*. Manchester University Press, Manchester, UK, pp. 199–213.

Bianchini, F. (1999) Cultural planning for urban sustainability. In: Nystrom, L. (ed.) *City and Culture: Cultural Processes and Urban Sustainability*. The Swedish Urban Environment Council, Kalmar, Sweden, pp. 34–51.

Bianchini, F. and Ghilardi, L. (1997) *Culture and Neighbourhoods: a Comparative Report*. Council of Europe, Strasbourg.

Campaign for the Protection of Rural England (CPRE) (2003) *Lie of the Land*. CPRE, London.

Cooper, M. (1993) Access to the waterfront: transformations of meaning on the Toronto Lakeshore. In: Rotenburg, R. and McDonogh, G. (eds) *The Cultural Meaning of Urban Space*. Bergin and Garvey, Westport, Connecticut, pp. 157–171.

Csikszentmihalyi, M. (1996) *Creativity Flow and the Psychology of Discovery and Invention*. HarperCollins, London.

Department for Culture, Media and Sport (DCMS) (1999) *Local Cultural Strategies: Draft Guidance for Local Authorities in England*. DCMS, London.

Edwards, J.A. (1996) Waterfronts, tourism and economic sustainability: the United Kingdom experience. In: Priestley, G.K., Edwards, J.A. and Coccossis, H. (eds) *Sustainable Tourism? European Experiences*. CAB International, Wallingford, UK, pp. 86–98.

Entrikin, J.N. (1991) *The Betweenness of Place: Towards a Geography of Modernity*. Macmillan, Basingstoke, UK.

Evans, G. (2001) *Cultural Planning: an Urban Renaissance?* Routledge, London.

Evans, G. (2005) Measure for measure: evaluating the evidence of culture's contribution to regeneration. *Urban Studies* 42(5/6), 959–984.

Fisher, M. and Owen, U. (eds) (1991) *Whose Cities?* Penguin, London.

Florida, R. (2002) *The Rise of the Creative Class*. Basic Books, New York.

Gates, R.J. and Stout, F. (eds) (1996) *City Reader*. Routledge, London.

Ghilardi, L. (2001) *Cultural Planning and Cultural Diversity*. Noema Research and Planning Ltd, London.

Gibson, L. (2005) *Cultural Planning and the Creative Tropical City*. Available at: http://www.cdu.edu.au/cdss0406/presentations/papers/Lisanne%20Gibson.pdf (accessed 24 September 2005).

Graham, B., Ashworth, G.J. and Tunbridge, J.E. (2000) *A Geography of Heritage: Power, Culture and Economy*. Arnold, London.

Hoyle, B. (2002) Waterfront revitalization in East African port cities. University of Greenwich Seminar, 27 November.

Hughes, G. (1998) Tourism and the semiological realization of space. In: Ringer, G. (ed.) *Destinations: Cultural Landscapes of Tourism*. Routledge, London, pp. 17–33.

Jacobs, J. (1961) *The Death and Life of Great American Cities*. Penguin, New York.

Jones, J. (2000) The regeneration game. *Guardian Unlimited*. Available at: http://society.guardian.co.uk/regeneration/story/0,7940,395020,00.html (accessed 14 March 2006).

Knox, P.L. (1993) Capital, material culture and socio-spatial differentiation. In: Knox, P.L. (ed.) *The Restless Urban Landscape*. Prentice Hall, Englewood Cliffs, New Jersey, pp. 1–34.

Kunzmann, K.R. (2004) Culture, creativity and spatial planning. *Town Planning Review* 75(4), 383–404.

Landry, C. and Bianchini, F. (1995) *The Creative City*. Demos Comedia, London.

Lippard, L.R. (1997) *The Lure of the Local: Senses of Place in a Multicentred Society*. The New Press, New York.

Mercer, C. (1991) What is cultural planning? Paper presented to the Community Arts Network National Conference, Sydney, Australia, 10 October.

Middleton, M. (1987) *Man Made the Town*. The Bodley Head, London.

Philo, C. (2000) Foucault's geography. In: Crang, M. and Thrift, N. (eds) *Thinking Space*. Routledge, London, pp. 205–238.

Pine, J.B. and Gilmore, J.H. (1999) *The Experience Economy*. Harvard Business School Press, Boston, Massachusetts.

Ploger, J. (2001) Millennium urbanism – discursive planning. *European Urban and Regional Studies* 8(1), 63–72.

Quinn, B. (2005) Arts festivals and the city. *Urban Studies* 42(5/6), 927–943.

Relph, E. (1976) *Place and Placelessness*. Pion, London.

Richards, G. (ed.) (2005) *Cultural Tourism: Global and Local Perspectives*. ATLAS (Association for Tourism and Leisure Education), Arnhem.

Richards, R. and Wilson, J. (2006) Developing creativity in tourist experiences: a solution to the serial reproduction of culture? *Tourism Management* 27(6), (in press).

Ritzer, G. (2004) *The Globalization of Nothing*. Sage, London.

Rojek, C. (1993) *Ways of Escape: Modern Transformations in Leisure and Travel*. Macmillan Press, London.

Rojek, C. (1997) Indexing, dragging and the social construction of tourist sights. In: Rojek, C. and Urry, J. (eds) *Touring Cultures: Transformations of Travel and Theory*. Routledge, London, pp. 52–74.

Rotenburg, R. and McDonogh, G. (eds) (1993) *The Cultural Meaning of Urban Space*. Bergin and Garvey, Westport, Connecticut.

Sandercock, L. (1998) *Towards Cosmopolis*. John Wiley, Chichester, UK.

Sarup, M. (1996) *Identity, Culture and the Postmodern World*. Edinburgh University Press, Edinburgh.

Sharp, J., Pollock, V. and Paddison, R. (2005) Just art for a just city: public art and social inclusion in urban regeneration. *Urban Studies* 42(5/6), 1001–1023.

Shaw, S., Bagwell, S. and Karmowska, J. (2004) Ethnoscapes as spectacle: reimaging multicultural districts as new destinations for leisure and tourism consumption. *Urban Studies* 41(10), 1983–2000.

Short, R. (1989) *The Humane City: As If People Matter*. Blackwell, Oxford.

Sieber, R.T. (1993) Public access on the urban waterfront: a question of vision. In: Rotenburg, R. and McDonogh, G. (eds) *The Cultural Meaning of Urban Space*. Bergin and Garvey, Westport, Connecticut, pp. 173–193.

Smith, M.K. (2005) Space, place and placelessness in the culturally regenerated city. In: Richards, G. (ed.) *Cultural Tourism: Global and Local Perspectives*. ATLAS (Association for Tourism and Leisure Education), Arnhem.

Soja, E.W. (1996) *Thirdspace: Journeys to Los Angeles and Other Real-and-Imagined Places*. Blackwell, Oxford.

Soja, E.W. (2000) *Postmetropolis: Critical Studies of Cities and Regions*. Blackwell, Malden, Massachusetts.

Sudjic, D. (1992) *The 100 Mile City*. Flamingo, London.

Sudjic, D. (1999) Between the metropolitan and the provincial. In: Nystrom, L. (ed.) *City and Culture: Cultural Processes and Urban Sustainability*. The Swedish Urban Environment Council, Kalmar, Sweden, pp. 178–185.

Walsh, K. (1992) *The Representation of the Past: Museums and Heritage in the Post-modern World*. Routledge, London.

Wynne, D. (ed.) (1992) *The Culture Industry: the Arts in Urban Regeneration*. Avebury, Aldershot, UK.

Zukin, S. (1995) *The Cultures of Cities*. Blackwell, Oxford.

2   The Creative Turn in Regeneration: Creative Spaces, Spectacles and Tourism in Cities

Greg Richards and Julie Wilson

In recent years the term 'creativity' has been liberally applied to regeneration projects around the globe. Whereas a few years ago 'culture' was the key to urban regeneration, now 'creative districts', 'creative clusters' and the 'creative class' are in vogue. Every city seems to want to position itself at the leading edge of creative development, attracting creative producers, wooing creative consumers and consolidating a higher position in the rankings of 'creative cities'.

One of the keys to regeneration is attracting people to live in, work in and visit a city. Tourism has an important role in this process, because it allows people to see cities at first hand, to make a contribution to the local economy, and perhaps in the longer term to return to live or work in the city. The new creative development strategies therefore often incorporate tourism, stimulating the production of cultural icons and creative activities to persuade people to visit. Many new forms of tourism and tourist-related activity are therefore developing in response to this trend.

This chapter focuses on the increasingly important role of creativity in urban regeneration, looking at how and why cultural development is utilized by cities, and the growing challenge of serial monotony in cultural production. The analysis draws on work undertaken in the field of creative development in New Zealand, Spain, the Netherlands, the UK and Canada.

The Rise of Culture

The new centrality of culture in the urban development process has its roots in the 1970s, when the first major redevelopment projects began to use cultural facilities, such as museums, concert halls, theatres and cinemas, as a focus to generate visitation and to improve the image of run-down urban districts.

Zukin (1995: 268) identified this process within the general development of the symbolic economy. She argued that the contemporary emphasis on culture is:

> a concerted attempt to exploit the uniqueness of fixed capital – monuments, art collections, performance spaces, even shopping streets – accumulated over the past. In this sense, culture is the sum of a city's amenities that enable it to compete for investment and jobs, its 'comparative advantage'.

Similarly, Amin and Thrift (2002: 124) argue that cities are seeking to develop comparative advantage by re-engineering the experience of cities through a process of theming, as a result of which 'spaces compete with each other by promoting their performativity across a whole set of activities formerly set apart, such as shopping, dining, recreation and even education (in visits to increasingly "hands-on" museums)'. In this development of what Pine and Gilmore (1999) also term the 'experience economy', culture has come to be viewed as a crucial resource in the post-industrial economies of cities in creating animation and developing their 'socio-economic vibrancy'.

Cultural resources were also identified by George Ritzer (1999) as one of the 'means of consumption' underpinning the consumer society. Cultural and leisure facilities are transformed into 'cathedrals of consumption'. The cathedrals of consumption include fast food restaurants, department stores, shopping malls, casinos, theme parks and 'eatertainment'.

Culture is therefore increasingly being included in urban regeneration strategies as a means of stimulating physical redevelopment, adding animation to areas of the city and generating economic and cultural benefits. However, as Evans (2004) points out, culture may be included in regeneration strategies in different ways, ranging from 'culture-led regeneration', in which culture provides the engine for development, through 'cultural regeneration', where culture is an integral part of regional strategy, to 'culture and regeneration', which is the default model of non-integrated or incidental cultural development.

These different strategies adopted by cities to counter the challenge of economic and social restructuring through cultural development seem to have distinct goals and methodologies, but Richards and Wilson (2006) have argued that there is a high degree of equifinality in terms of development outcomes. They identify four main types of development stemming from such regeneration processes: iconic structures, heritage mining, mega-events, thematization.

Iconic structures

Cities are increasingly constructing iconic landmarks as a means of creating or changing an image and focusing cultural and economic activity. The development of the Bilbao Guggenheim Museum is a good example of this, but there are numerous others (e.g. the Tate Modern in London, The Angel of the North on Tyneside).

Heritage mining

When cities decline, they are usually forced to conserve the past because they do not have the resources to redevelop it. In these situations, cities are often left with a rich historical legacy, even when other economic resources may be missing. Cities such as Bruges, Venice, New Orleans and Kyoto have led the way in valorizing their past to stimulate current economic activity.

Mega-events

Many cities have tried to use major international events as a stimulus to development. In addition to sporting events, such as the Olympic Games, cultural events, such as World Expos, the European City of Culture or the United Nations Educational, Scientific and Cultural Organization (UNESCO) sponsored Universal Forum of Cultures, have become popular means of stimulating economic development and improving city image.

Thematization

Some cities have tried to distinguish themselves by developing a specific cultural theme. For example, cities such as London and New York compete for the title of 'world cities', with New York in particular positioning itself as the 'cultural capital of the world' (Zukin, 1995). Other less well-endowed cities have selected more humble alternatives, such as 'walled towns' (Den Bosch in the Netherlands) or the 'garlic capital of the world' (Gilroy, California). It therefore seems that for many cities being oneself is not enough, but you have to borrow recognition by becoming the *something of somewhere*: The Venice of the North (Stockholm, Bruges, St Petersburg, Amsterdam), the Athens of the North (Edinburgh) or the Edinburgh of the South (Dunedin, New Zealand).

Such strategies have been successful in a range of different settings, but the most spectacular results have arguably been achieved in what Bianchini and Parkinson (1993) term 'declining cities', where the need to replace lost manufacturing employment has driven a search for cultural development as a new source of jobs and income. Well-known examples of this type of redevelopment include Baltimore, which has used culture to attract visitors and regenerate its waterfront and Rotterdam, which has used cultural events including the European Cultural Capital to improve its image and cultural infrastructure (Richards and Wilson, 2004).

The new-found role for cultural facilities, particularly museums, as generators of economic value, has not been without problems. In addition to the moral objections from cultural actors about their changed role as generators of economic 'value' as well as cultural 'values', the new strategies of differentiation have themselves arguably run into problems of serial reproduction.

The Rise of Serial Reproduction

The problem with culture-led initiatives such as the Guggenheim in Bilbao is that 'nothing succeeds like success' (Richards and Wilson, 2006). Examples of urban regeneration that are perceived as being successful (or which are successfully sold as a success) are readily copied by other cities. Barcelona, with its mega-event redevelopment strategy centred on the 1992 Olympics, has been the inspiration for cities the world over who want to change their image and develop new cultural facilities. For example, Cork in Ireland has built itself a new 'Rambla' as a centrepiece of the European Cultural Capital event in 2005, designed by Catalan urban designer Beth Galí. Edinburgh is said to be considering a similar move for the Leith area of the city. In fact, Barcelona's administration has recently admitted to 'borrowing' many of its development ideas from American cities such as Baltimore and European cities such as Liverpool and Hamburg.

The circulation of similar development models based on a narrow range of elements (among which culture is prominent) leads to a problem of 'serial reproduction'. Borrowed ideas have the advantage of being 'proven', they can be readily communicated to the electorate (because examples are to hand) and this is seen as a relatively safe strategy (Richards and Wilson, 2006).

Serial reproduction is also paradoxically stimulated by the search for distinction. Cities hire signature architects to build distinctive buildings and create a new image, but these very same architects end up producing similar icons in different cities across the world. Rodgers, Calatrava, Foster and Gehry are now virtually household names in urban development circles. Cities want unique icons, but architects want to recycle their ideas and underline their own distinctive style. For example, Frank O. Gehry's Guggenheim in Bilbao is very similar to his Los Angeles concert hall, which was actually designed before the Bilbao museum but which had the misfortune to be finished later.

As a result of the proliferation of similar development models, new projects across the world are running into problems. There is a growth in competition, which stimulates a greater need for distinction, while at the same time the physical shape of developments and development strategies seem to be converging. As Evans (2004) notes, this is already leading some regions to reject the idea of cultural regeneration based on 'new landmark investments'.

The problems of serial reproduction seem to underwrite the idea that globalization is creating more 'placelessness' in cities, as similar environments are copied across the globe. However, as Richards (2007) has pointed out, the distinctiveness of places is dependent not just on the nature of the physical environment, but also on the people who inhabit them. Creative uses of 'standardized' spaces can make them into unique places.

The building styles of new developments may be homogeneous, but the way they are used can be very different. This was one of the concepts behind the creation of 'hard plazas' in the redevelopment of Barcelona in recent years. Unlike open spaces in many northern cities, the new plazas carved out of the fabric of Barcelona's Old City are devoid of greenery or landscaping. They provide a *tabula rasa* which different groups can use as they please. The plaza in front of the Museum of Contemporary Art (MACBA) has now become a favourite haunt for skateboarders from all parts of the world, keen to combine skating with iconic architecture. Next to this plaza is also a graffiti wall, which has a similar attraction for artists from many countries. These activities are combined with local community uses to provide a flexible space whose character is defined by creative use.

This may suggest that we should pay more attention to individual expressions of creativity in the development process, rather than emphasizing the structures in which these take place. This in turn indicates that we should pay more attention to cultural processes that can serve to foreground the role of creativity in the development process.

The Creative Turn

The need to identify new models of development to create greater differentiation and avoid problems of serial reproduction has arguably stimulated a shift away from the 'cultural industries' towards the 'creative industries'. This was one of the early strategies adopted by New Labour in the UK (Smith, 1998), and was also given a fresh impulse by Richard Florida's (2002) concept of the 'creative class'.

As O'Donnell (2004) remarks, 'Pop management theory has, since the early 1980s, raised "creativity" to the level of an entrepreneurial imperative.' There are a number of reasons why creativity has become particularly popular in urban development strategies. The creative industries are often viewed as new and dynamic, and therefore have a wider appeal than the (now) old-fashioned cultural industries. In addition:

- Culture is associated with 'high culture', which has a traditional, staid image.
- The cultural sector is not perceived as being very flexible or dynamic.
- The creative sector is broader than the cultural sector alone.
- The creative sector is directly linked to innovation.
- The creative industries include many more aspects of visual consumption (advertising, cinema, design, fashion, video games).
- Women often play a key role in the development of the creative industries.

As a result, the creative industries are being embraced by regions of the world where the traditional cultural industries had problems gaining a foothold. For example, Yusuf and Nabeshima (2005) describe the development of the creative industries in East Asia. In Hong Kong, for example, annual growth rates of the creative industries have an average of 22% over the past decade. The film industry in Hong Kong now employs 9000 people, and is being used as one of the spearheads for urban redevelopment.

One of the advantages of the creative industries in development terms is their tendency towards clustering and the high degree of linkage between creative enterprises. Creative producers also tend to cluster relatively close to the centre of cities, making this an attractive sector for the regeneration of run-down inner city areas. In fact, it is also argued that the most important locational factor for the creative industries is often the quality of urban facilities (particularly cultural facilities), which suggests that creative development strategies can have wider quality of life benefits as well.

Cities are therefore increasingly dependent on animation, liveliness and 'atmosphere' to attract and hold on to creative people. These strategies are also arguably a reaction to the anti-urban stance taken by the suppliers of authenticity (Prentice, 2001). Because urban areas are not seen as 'authentic' landscapes in physical terms, they are forced to opt for other experiential qualities, notably 'liveliness' or 'ambience'.

This idea is taken to its logical extreme in the work of Richard Florida (2002), who suggests that the success of cities now depends on their ability to attract and retain creative people, or the 'creative class'. The attractiveness of cities for the creative class, according to Florida, depends not just on physical factors, but the cultural climate of the city and the liveliness of its creative scene. On the basis of such ideas, in Austin, Texas: 'A city-council economic-development subcommittee . . . adopted the slogan "Keep Austin Weird" to emphasize its belief that support for offbeat culture is essential to the city's economic future' (Malanga, 2004). Such exogenous models are arguably problematic, because they rely on attracting external creativity. In fact there is also a circular logic in needing to develop a creative class in order to attract more people from the creative class. Florida's work has also attracted criticism for trying to turn creative people into a 'class', and in the USA, his relatively interventionist arguments have also come under fire.

The answer to this problem seems to lie in more endogenous models of creative development. By stimulating local creativity, the intellectual property developed through the creative process can be more easily rooted in a particular location.

Models of Creative Development

The typology of cultural development outcomes outlined above emphasizes the physical basis of many cultural development strategies, even where these are firmly based in the symbolic economy. With the creative turn, paradoxically, the materialization of cultural development seems to have increased, as the intangible nature of creativity forces cities to develop spatial expressions to make creativity visible. This process is evident in a number of discrete creative strategies that have been employed in cities.

The creative cluster or creative district is perhaps the most widespread strategy, providing as it does a physical focus for a wide range of creative activities and actors. In some cases, the city may opt to develop a creative lead industry such as fashion, film or festivals, which in turn leads to a physical development of spaces for performance and reproduction, as well as theming of the city to fit the industry. This is the case in Edinburgh (City of Festivals), Bristol, UK (City of Animation), Barcelona (City of Design) and many other cities.

The arguably more comprehensive *creative city* strategy presupposes that the city as a whole must be involved in the creative process. This often implies a combination of physical spaces (particularly creative clusters) and creative theming. Such strategies have been employed by cities such as Huddersfield (UK), Newcastle (UK), Brisbane (Australia) and a whole group of cities in Canada (Creative Cities Network).

The remodelling of districts or whole cities along creative lines is, however, a complex process. Creativity has many different dimensions and can be manifested in different forms, for example both as individual creativity and as collective creativity. Much attention has been focused on individual creativity because creativity is seen largely as an individualized talent. However, creative individuals need a 'creative environment' in which to function. This includes both groups of like-minded people who can help to spark ideas and provide support, but also a constant flow of new ideas and contacts. In Putnam's (2000) terms, therefore, creativity is dependent to a certain extent on both bonding capital (which holds communities together) and bridging social capital (which creates links between different communities).

Usually the collective dimension (and particularly bridging capital) is overlooked, and yet this would seem to be one of the most important aspects of creativity for cities. The key question for any city should be: What can a particular location add to the creativity of the individual? Particularly in the context of serial reproduction, it is the interplay of individual and collective creativity that holds the key to creating distinction, because creative individuals and groups creatively remake spaces and places. The creativity that is available to cities involves not just its permanent residents, but also its visitors, and the creative ways in which visitors and residents interact. Without bridging social capital, such interactions are less likely to produce positive impacts.

In view of these relationships, there would seem to be a number of key elements that are important in any creative development, recognizing the need to transform space, stimulate creative production and consumption and attracting the attention of investors and consumers.

Clustering

Creative enterprises need a network of colleagues and suppliers, and clustering is therefore seen as providing an impulse to both individual creativity and collective creativity. The spatial clustering of activities also makes it easier for the public sector to intervene in the development of the creative industries, as well as providing the critical mass necessary to stimulate visitation.

Consumers

Audiences are vital to the creative industries, and in many cases creative enterprises need to attract audiences or consumers to specific locations. This in turn reinforces the tendency towards clustering, as many enterprises will gravitate towards locations where there is a large potential audience. Large numbers of consumers also help to generate the ambience which is important to make spaces and districts attractive to live in.

Co-makership

In order to function well, creative clusters need to involve both producers and consumers in a process of co-makership of creative experiences. One of the differences between creative and cultural attractions in cities should be the level of involvement of audiences. Attractions that do not allow space for the consumer to create their own experiences or help to shape the experiences produced by creative enterprises, are arguably not exploiting the full potential of creative tourism (Richards, 2001).

Clarity

Clarity can be important to creative development in two senses. First, attracting audiences depends on a certain level of *visibility* within the urban fabric. If a 'creative district' is not well defined or well known, it will have problems attracting attention.

Secondly, even if a creative cluster or district manages to achieve a certain level of visibility within the city, it is important that the creative enterprises have a certain level of *permeability* for the consumer. Creative enterprises such as architects' practices, for example, do not lend themselves readily to public consumption, which vastly reduces their utility as attractive elements within the cluster. There is therefore a very important role for cultural programming in the mix of enterprises in each cluster (Hitters and Richards, 2002).

Confidence

Confidence is a vital issue in a number of ways. Confidence comprises not just having the faith to invest in creativity, but also involves the essential issue of trust. Banks *et al.* (2000) show how important trust is in making the creative industries tick. Creative clusters therefore need

to integrate both dimensions of social capital: bonding capital, which brings creative people together; and also bridging capital, which enables clusters to link more effectively to the outside world.

Confidence in one's ability to make such developments work is also an essential element in selling the idea of success. One of the important qualities of most successful urban strategies is the ability to convince stakeholders that development initiatives have been successful, even if the objective evidence may suggest otherwise. This is a strategy employed widely in the city of Barcelona in turning itself into an urban development model for many other cities (Richards, 2004a).

Materializing Creativity

Although the principles outlined above give some guidance on the key elements of creative regeneration strategies, at a basic level, the success of any creative development will lie in its ability to materialize the effects of creativity in the city. Too much attention has been paid in the past to intangible and symbolic aspects of development. The recent rematerialism focus in geography is one recent sign of the recognition that symbolic development has very real physical consequences that are embodied in real space and real time.

Given the increasingly important role of tourism in the urban economy, it is not surprising that the physical remodelling of cities (and particularly city centres) for creative purposes is strongly related to tourism and leisure. Richards and Wilson (2006) have identified a number of forms in which these aspects of creativity can be integrated into urban and tourism development. These are creative spectacles, creative spaces and creative tourism.

Creative spectacles

Many major arts festivals have effectively become what we might term creative spectacles. For example the 'World of Wearable Art' forms the basis of an annual awards show staged in New Zealand. Garment entries are received from all around the country and increasingly from all around the world. The 2003 show sold out, and over two weekends was estimated to have generated NZ$6.5 million for the Nelson region. In 2005 the event relocated to Wellington to accommodate larger audiences, and the new host city organized an 'Excessive Accessories Street Parade' to mark the event. The Cirque du Soleil is also an interesting example of a creative spectacle which has expanded from its original base in Canada to cover a number of permanent locations worldwide (including Las Vegas) as well as an extensive touring programme.

Creative spaces

Creative spaces are often empty of fixed ideas; blank slates; spaces that are multifunctional and that can be used to develop different narratives. Creative spaces can be designed to house a core of permanent residents, such as the formal creative clusters now being developed in cities such as Manchester, Toronto, Rotterdam and Barcelona. Clusters can help creative producers to tap a common audience among the creative classes, but there is a tendency for the relatively fixed nature of these spaces to depress creativity in the long term.

Creative tourism

The major difference between creative spectacles, creative spaces and creative tourism is that creative tourism depends far more on the active involvement of tourists. Creative tourism involves not just spectating, not just 'being there', but reflexive interaction on the part of tourists, who are usually thought of as 'non-producers' in traditional analyses.

The most developed creative tourism network can be found in the city of Nelson, New Zealand, where Creative Tourism New Zealand has been established as a network of creative businesses offering products to tourists (www.creativetourism.co.nz). The network provides a wide range of creative experiences, including bone carving, Maori language classes, native flora, weaving, felting, woodwork and New Zealand gastronomy.

These types of developments can be initiated in many different locations, but in most cases cities have been at the forefront of creative tourism development. The following section provides some more detailed cases of creative urban redevelopment strategies linked to tourism.

Examples of Creative Urban Development

Barcelona

Barcelona has arguably re-invented itself in the past two decades, changing its image from that of an industrial and commercial city into that of a cosmopolitan Mediterranean metropolis. At the centre of this transformation has been the much-vaunted 'Barcelona Model' (see, for example, Benach and Albet, 2005), which among other things has emphasized urban design and public–private partnership in redevelopment.

The city has also made much use of mega-events to redevelop specific areas of the city, most notably the World Fairs of 1888 and 1929, the Olympics in 1992 and the Universal Forum of Cultures in 2004. In developing these major creative spectacles, Barcelona has emphasized the upgrading of infrastructure and creation of public space. The physical legacy of the Forum, for example, includes the 'second largest public square in the world' (after Tianenmen Square).

These post-event spaces (now known collectively as 'Port Forum') have in turn provided arenas for more localized creative activities, including music performances, street theatre, outdoor cinema and human statues. Some of the new spaces are also linked to the emergence of creative clusters, such as in the Poble Nou district of the city, a former manufacturing district now being regenerated with creative industries. The 22@BCN project designed to revitalize the Poble Nou area is based on a combination of knowledge, design, IT, music and other 'creative' businesses, together with communication infrastructure and housing. It should be noted, however, that this scheme has run into considerable local opposition, who see this creative development strategy as backdoor gentrification, particularly in the speculation that is involved in new housing developments.

In spite of the designation of new cultural clusters and the provision of incentives, it seems that the creative sector still exhibits some degree of traditional industrial inertia. Most creative enterprises are still concentrated in areas of the city centre such as St Gervasi, the Eixample and Gràcia, which have stronger existing ties between firms and a more ready flow of consumers than newer clusters in the periphery (Interarts, 2005).

Barcelona has also discovered creative tourism, which is rapidly becoming an important adjunct to its largely heritage-based cultural tourism market. The new creative tourism products are usually tied to creative spaces or events. For example during the 2005 Year of Gastronomy, visitors to La Boqueria Market (which attracts over 2500 tourists a day) were offered a tour of the market during which participants bought fresh ingredients to be used in a cookery lesson, the product of which was taken as lunch, accompanied by a wine tasting. Tours around the creative businesses of the Ciutat Vella (old city) are also being offered by tour operators as an addition to the cultural tourism product.

All of these developments have helped to strengthen the image of Barcelona as a creative city, an image that is as strong among tourists as it is among planners (see Fig. 2.1).

Rotterdam

Rotterdam is a good example of Bianchini and Parkinson's (1993) 'declining' European cities. Economic restructuring in the 1960s and 1970s left the second largest city in the Netherlands with a severe decline in manufacturing employment and much of the city centre had to be rapidly redeveloped following the destruction of the Second World War (McCarthy, 1998). The result was arguably that Rotterdam became the only 'American' style city in the Netherlands, with high-rise buildings and offices, but lacking the cultural advantages of Amsterdam, its closest cultural and economic rival (Richards and Wilson, 2004).

In its long trajectory of post-war development, Rotterdam, much like Barcelona, has adopted an event-based strategy to tourism generation, but unlike Barcelona it does not have the physical advantages of climate or an attractive coastal environment. Cultural events

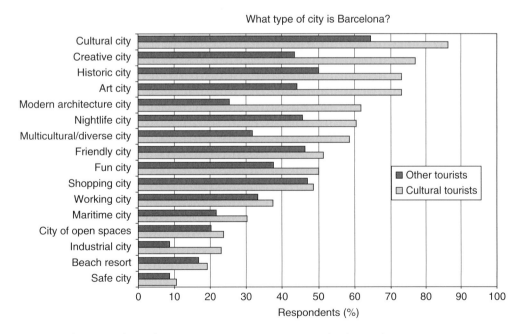

Fig. 2.1.   The image of Barcelona among visitors, 2004 (Source: Richards, 2004b).

have therefore arguably been even more important in generating tourism.

The city embarked on a policy of developing arts festivals and leisure events in the 1990s,
which was subsequently supported by the development of new creative spaces, including the
expansion of the Boijmans Museum, a new
National Architecture Museum and the Kunsthal
art gallery (McCarthy, 1998). Such developments
were marked by an entrepreneurial approach to
the arts and leisure, which included the establishment of a 'leisure industries' department of
the city government and the staging of privately
managed publicly funded events. This strategy
was arguably very successful in attracting visitors to the city, which saw a threefold increase in
event visitation between 1993 and 1998 and a
further 50% growth between 1998 and 2001
(OBR, 2003).

As part of this strategy, Rotterdam staged
the European Cultural Capital event in 2001. The
event had a very broad, ambitious programme,
which was supposed to appeal to a wide range of
target groups and to turn Rotterdam into a festival city. The Cultural Capital year included over
500 events, which attracted more than 2.3 million
visitors (Gemeente Rotterdam, 2003).

However, according to many in the cultural sector, the most successful events were not
necessarily those that attracted large numbers of
visitors. Instead, they emphasized small-scale,
creative activities such as Preaching in Another
Man's Parish, which involved ministers of different faiths preaching in each other's churches
(Richards and Wilson, 2004).

The development of small-scale facilities
for artists has also been a major weapon in
the cultural struggle between Rotterdam and
Amsterdam. Rotterdam has developed a number
of creative clusters that offer atelier and performance spaces for artists at relatively low rents.
Both cities have been developing policies of
providing 'nurseries' for the creative sector, but
in Amsterdam the process has been com-
plicated by high land prices and speculation.
Rotterdam has the advantage of a rich supply of
disused industrial spaces that have been turned
over to creative use. As a result, many artists
have relocated from Amsterdam to Rotterdam,
at least to work.

Rotterdam has also developed different
types of cultural clusters, ranging from highly

centralized, managed clusters such as the Van
Nelle Fabriek to the more diffuse cluster around
the Witte de Withstraat (WdW) (Hitters and
Richards, 2002). Arguably, the WdW has been
more successful, linking new creative enterprises
with existing cultural attractions along the 'cultural axis' of the city and adopting a bottom-up
model of development and management.

According to research by Hitters and
Richards (2002), the visitors to the WdW cluster
are highly educated, often with professional or
managerial positions, indicating that the area is
largely populated by representatives of the 'new
middle class' or 'new cultural intermediaries'.
They come for a combination of museum and
gallery visits and eating and drinking. They see
the area as 'diverse', 'lively' and 'attractive',
indicating that many visitors come for the
'atmosphere'. They see the WdW cluster as a
distinct area of the city, but only 51% of visitors
recognized a relationship between the different
elements of the cluster.

The WdW visitor research therefore tends
to confirm the image of the cluster as a geographically defined consumption-led cluster.
Creativity lays the basis for clustering of productive activities, which then attract consumption,
mainly in the form of bars and restaurants
rather than pure 'culture'.

In the case of the WdW cluster, therefore,
success seems to be based on production-led,
consumption-supported processes, which in many
ways mirror wider gentrification processes. It
can be argued that such models work in inner
city areas of large cities, where location tends to
ensure a large customer base.

Lewisham

Lewisham is an inner city municipality in London
with a population of over 240,000, with 22%
drawn from ethnic minorities. The area suffers
from a relatively high level of unemployment
and social problems. In response to such problems, in 2000 Lewisham set about developing
a creative redevelopment strategy, based on the
creative cities concept of Landry (2000). The
Creative Lewisham Agency was then set up to
oversee the development process.

The Projects being developed in Lewisham
include creative spaces, such as the new Laban

Centre at Creekside, Deptford, designed by 'World-renowned architects Hertzog and de Meuron', and a refurbishment of the Horniman Museum 'to create a new extension and several associated spaces'. Cockpit Arts opened their new premises on Deptford Creekside in December 2002 after extensive refurbishment to transform the building into studio facilities for developing design and craft businesses.

The Creative Lewisham website (http://www.creativelewishamagency.org.uk/) also includes a map of creative resources in the borough, and a grid which relates resources (spectacles) of different types (visual arts, music and dance) to specific types of spaces or locations (performance space, exhibition space, studios, shops and meeting spaces).

Creative Lewisham is also contributing to the borough-wide animations (festivals) strategic review, and is working with particular festivals and events to enhance their offerings and improve their marketing. The agency has appointed a Creative Enterprise Zone Manager, and is working to strengthen and protect the existing 'creative sector cluster' around Deptford and New Cross, as well as marketing it as a destination for cultural tourism.

These developments seem to be bearing fruit, with a commendation from the Royal Institute of British Architects (RIBA), which specifically praised 'the Creative Enterprise Zone and the opening of the Laban Centre by Herzog and de Meuron'. The Laban Centre for Contemporary Dance also won the RIBA Sterling Prize for Building of the Year in 2003.

Lewisham has therefore begun to attack its image as a declining area by stimulating creativity. The initiative combines creative spectacles, creative spaces and creative tourism, although the apparent need to concentrate on iconic architecture to draw attention to creativity is evidence of the problems of making creativity visible.

Toronto

The city of Toronto in Ontario, Canada, has a population of over 4.5 million, including 40% from 'visible ethnic minority groups'. In 1991, Toronto commenced a planning approach to cultural provision, with widespread consultation. The plan included the development of artists'

studios and housing in old factories, brokered by a social property development organization, Artscape (Evans, 2001).

The Toronto Artscape project echoes the symbolic economy logic of Zukin (1995), in its argument that 'creativity needs space'. Artscape is a non-profit organization that undertakes physical development for the arts and creative sector. It is active in 'property management, master planning, development of arts districts, creation and management of multi-tenant arts centres, engagement of stakeholders in creative cluster projects, and research on monitoring the impact of arts-driven revitalization projects' (Toronto Artscape, 2005). This implies a very holistic approach to the management of space for creative uses, which in turn can be used to shape those spaces.

The cluster concept is grounded in a focus on 'multi-tenant centres that serve artists, non-profit arts groups and local communities' that are developed by 'forging a common vision from diverse interests, building community partnerships, raising funds, as well as all of the technical aspects of capital project planning and construction'.

For example Artscape developed the Gooderham and Worts Distillery, a national heritage site with Victorian industrial architecture. Artscape took a cheap lease on two buildings on the site and let most of the 4000 m^2 within a year. Sixty new tenants moved into the Case Goods Warehouse and Cannery Building including artist and designer/maker retail studios, non-profit theatre, dance, music, and arts-in-education organizations and artist work studios.

Artscape also leases affordable space to professional artists in Toronto. Studios under Artscape management include artist work and live/work spaces, designer/maker retail studios, offices, production, performance and exhibition facilities for non-profit arts organizations, and complementary ancillary uses. One of the problems with providing relatively cheap space for creative entrepreneurs is the sticky problem of defining who is a 'professional artist'. Thanks to the conflation of the arts into the creative industries, beneficiaries may arguably include many who previously would not have been considered artistic and therefore worthy of 'subsidy'.

Artscape's Creative Clusters Development Programme is designed to create more like-minded organizations and to develop their capacity to establish and run multi-tenant arts centres in their community. The programme includes a workshop series on developing and managing creative clusters and a helpline to provide advice on project development.

Artscape organizes creative spectacles, such as the Queen West Art Crawl, which it describes as 'a weekend-long festival celebrating the arts'. This event, which had its third edition in September 2005, featured open ateliers, galleries, businesses, shops and restaurants. An outdoor art exhibition displayed the work of visual artists and artisans. The event has attracted a good flow of visitors to creative spaces in the city:

> The Queen West Art Crawl inspired a great sense of community. I had a minimum of 300 people through my gallery – someone visited who had never bought art before and walked out with two pieces!
> (Jamie Angell, Director, Angell Gallery – www.torontoartscape.on.ca)

As in many other developments of this type, the Toronto Artscape includes elements of creative spaces, creative spectacles and creative tourism. These are not necessarily mutually exclusive models of development, but facets of creative development that can usefully be combined.

The impacts of the Toronto project have been assessed by Jones et al. (2003), who indicated that the area around the Artscape developments had lower unemployment, higher educational attainment and better occupation structures than nearby control areas. Business surveys indicate that there are more cultural events taking place and that there have been improvements in a range of areas, including better cleanliness, less crime and higher safety. There were high levels of business turnover in the early years of development, but this seemed to settle down after 5 to 6 years.

These positive effects have to be set against some potentially negative ones, such as gentrification, which has stimulated land and property values to increase faster than average for the city. Rising property prices may be good for developers and home owners, but are not necessarily conducive to maintaining diversity and affordable living costs for existing residents. In addition, there has been criticism of tax increases,

which are seen as linked to public subsidy of projects such as Artscape (Kheiriddin, 2006) and fears that the new developments are promoting 'Disneyfication' (Hirschmann, 2003).

Conclusion

The examples of creative development indicate that creativity is not just becoming an important buzzword in urban regeneration, but is also beginning to be accompanied by real physical change. As Zukin (1995) suggests, the growth of culture tends to demand ever more space, but in the shift from culture to creativity, the spatial demands grow, as cultural institutions stimulate creative clusters and cities transform themselves into creative cities. This is not necessarily a progressive change, because as the examples cited above seem to indicate, different forms of creative strategy may be combined in one place at the same time.

Creative development is also being combined with more 'established' forms of cultural development, such as the creation of iconic structures and the development of heritage. In many cases some combination is necessary, because the creative industries are not always very visible, and they need to be linked to more legible forms of consumption in order to attract consumers and to convince planners and investors.

One significant change that is taking place is the shift towards more private sector participation in creative developments relative to their 'traditional' cultural counterparts. Because the creative industries are more readily viewed as 'commercial', there is a much greater expectation that creative enterprises will generate their own income and be less dependent on subsidy than other forms of culture. In fact, as Bayliss (2004) points out, cultural industries developments that have relied too heavily on public funding (such as Sheffield's Cultural Industries Quarter) may be perceived as failures because they cannot sustain themselves without public funds.

Whether or not this is strictly true, public–private partnership has emerged as an important model for the development of the creative industries, in an arena that has traditionally been the preserve of the public sector. As Hitters and Richards (2002) show in the case of the Westergasfabriek in Amsterdam, the cultural manager becomes creative programmer of commercially run space, trying to utilize the more lucrative activities to cross-subsidize new creative activities and community events.

The area in which all of these creative developments seem to converge is in their dependence on a steady flow of consumers. In this context, tourism becomes a central part of creative development, since it is an important mechanism for bringing new income into the city. The attraction of creative development is therefore not just the stimulation of endogenous creativity, but also the economic benefit to be gained from attracting the 'creative class' and their spending power.

We should be wary of seeing creativity as a panacea for urban regeneration. Although there are many examples of successful creative development, there are also many potential problems. One of the major challenges lies in maintaining the creativity of creative clusters. Paradoxically, as clusters become more successful, they attract new tenants who tend to squeeze out the original creative producers. This may lead to a formerly creative space increasingly becoming a consumption space (an effect seen in a number of existing clusters, such as the MuseumsQuartier in Vienna).

Local residents may also be forced out by the gentrification that almost inevitably follows successful creative redevelopment. The extent to which creative development strategies contribute to gentrification processes is still unclear, but the evidence of rising property prices around the creative clusters in Toronto and Vancouver (Jones *et al.*, 2003) suggests that there is a direct impact. Studies of the 'creative class' in cities such as New York (e.g. Beveridge, 2004) also suggest that the creative influx will tend to be more homogeneous than the inner-city populations it tends to replace. Importing creativity along the lines suggested by Florida (2002) may therefore leave the city with the problem of creating jobs and homes for the original residents. Those outside the creative class may also be excluded from the cultural fruits of creative development as well, as 'creativity' is not always designed to be accessible and inclusive.

The examples we have examined also raise the question of how far creativity is able to stimulate regeneration on its own. In many cases, the regeneration process seems to require a mix of physical icons and spaces that can make the creative process more visible and tangible. Without this, creative development strategies may seem extremely abstract to local residents, taxpayers and politicians. This suggests that cities may need to think in terms of combining creative spaces, creative spectacles and creative tourism to underpin successful regeneration.

References

Amin, A. and Thrift, N. (2002) *Cities: Reimagining the Urban*. Polity, Cambridge.

Banks, M., Lovatt, A., O'Connor, J. and Raffo, C. (2000) Risk and trust in the cultural industries. *Geoforum* 31, 453–464.

Bayliss, D. (2004) Creative planning in Ireland: the role of culture-led development in Irish planning. *European Planning Studies* 12, 497–515.

Benach, N. and Albet, A. (2005) Barcelona 1979–2004, entre modelo y el espectáculo. In: Minca, C. (ed.) *Lo spettacolo della città/The Spectacle of the City*. CEDAM, Padova.

Beveridge, A. (2004) New York's creative class. *Gotham Gazette*. Available at: www.gothamgazette.com (accessed 14 October 2004).

Bianchini, F. and Parkinson, M. (eds) (1993) *Cultural Policy and Urban Regeneration: the West European Experience*. Manchester University Press, Manchester, UK.

Evans, G. (2001) *Cultural Planning: an Urban Renaissance?* Routledge, London.

Evans, G. (2004) Measure for measure: evaluating the evidence of culture's contribution to regeneration. *Urban Studies* 42, 959–983.

Florida, R. (2002) *The Rise of the Creative Class: and How it is Transforming Work, Leisure, Community, and Everyday Life*. Basic Books, New York.

Gemeente Rotterdam (2003) *Evaluatie Rotterdam Culturele Hoofdstad 2001*. Bestuurdienst/Culturele zaken, Rotterdam.

Hirschmann, T. (2003) Strange brew: the distillery historic district opened to raves, but is it art zone or theme park? *Now* 22(39). Available at: http://www.nowtoronto.com/issues/2003-05-29/art_reviews.php (accessed 11 October 2004).

Hitters, E. and Richards, G. (2002) Cultural quarters to leisure zones: the role of partnership in developing the cultural industries. *Creativity and Innovation Management* 11, 234–247.

Interarts (2005) *Les industries creatives a Barcelona*. Fundació Interarts, Barcelona.

Jones, K., Lea, T., Jones, T. and Harvey, S. (2003) *Beyond Anecdotal Evidence: the Spillover Effects of Investments in Cultural Facilities*. CSCA, Toronto.

Kheiriddin, T. (2006) Toronto the bad: proposed 2006 city budget a disgrace. Available at: http://www.canadafreepress.com/2006/business010506.htm (accessed 5 January 2006).

Landry, C. (2000) *The Creative City: a Toolkit for Urban Innovators*. Earthscan, London.

Malanga, S. (2004) The curse of the creative class. *City Journal* Winter. Available at: http://www.city-journal.org/html/14_1_the_curse.html (accessed 15 October 2004).

McCarthy, J. (1998) Reconstruction, regeneration and re-imaging: the case of Rotterdam. *Cities* 15, 337–344.

OBR (OntwikkelingsBedrijf Rotterdam) (2003) *Economische Verkenning Rotterdam 2003*. Gemeente Rotterdam, Rotterdam.

O'Donnell, A. (2004) Just who works for the new creative class. *The Age* Monday 2 August, p. 11.

Pine, B.J. and Gilmore, J.H. (1999) *The Experience Economy*. Harvard University Press, Boston, Massachusetts.

Prentice, R. (2001) Experiential cultural tourism: museums and the marketing of the new romanticism of evoked authenticity. *Museum Management and Curatorship* 19, 5–26.

Putnam, R. (2000) *Bowling Alone: the Collapse and Revival of American Community*. Simon and Schuster, New York.

Richards, G. (ed.) (2001) *Cultural Attractions and European Tourism*. CAB International, Wallingford, UK.

Richards, G. (2004a) Globalising the local? Selling Barcelona to the world. 13th Nordic Symposium in Tourism and Hospitality Research, November. Aalborg, Denmark.

Richards, G. (2004b) *Symbolising Catalunya*. AGAUR Fellowship Report, Department of History and Geography, Roviria I Virgili University, Tarragona.

Richards, G. (2007) *Cultural Tourism: Global and Local Perspectives*. Haworth Press, Binghampton, New York.

Richards, G. and Wilson, J. (2004) The impact of cultural events on city image: Rotterdam cultural capital of Europe 2001. *Urban Studies* 41(10), 1931–1951.

Richards, G. and Wilson, J. (2006) Developing creativity in tourist experiences: a solution to the serial reproduction of culture? *Tourism Management* 27(6), (in press).

Ritzer, G. (1999) *Enchanting a Disenchanted World: Revolutionizing the Means of Consumption*. Pine Forge Press, Thousand Oaks, California.

Smith, C. (1998) *Creative Britain*. Faber and Faber, London.

Toronto Artscape (2005) Home page. Available at: www.torontoartscape.on.ca (accessed 15 July 2005).

Yusuf, S. and Nabeshima, K. (2005) Creative industries in East Asia. *Cities* [London] 22(2), 109–122.

Zukin, S. (1995) *The Culture of Cities*. Blackwell, Oxford.

3 Culture, City Users and the Creation of New Tourism Areas in Cities

Robert Maitland

Introduction

A few days after the bombings of 7 July 2005, the writer John Lanchester was prompted to muse about the area around London's Tavistock Square, and what it meant to him, and how his feelings about it would be affected (Lanchester, 2005). He reflected on the place and how, for him, its meaning came from a mixture of many things – personal memories, architecture and cultural associations – to which memories of the bombing would now be added. One of his favourite spots is a church; another is:

> a passageway . . . where there was a sandwich bar run by gloomy Italians with a plaque saying that WB Yeats had lived there. What the plaque didn't tell you was that that was also where Yeats lost his virginity, at the decidedly late-starterish age of 31. He and Olivia Shakespear had to go to Heal's specially to order a bed before finally consummating the relationship, and he found the experience – that of ordering the bed – deeply traumatic, since 'every inch added to the expense'.

Sense of place arises from many disparate elements – some associated with markers (MacCannell, 1976, 1989) such as an official blue plaque, others arising from the knowledge or personal associations the viewer brings to a particular spot. The mix of elements that combine to create a sense of place are part of the culture of a city. As Lanchester goes on to say,

everybody has their own version: history, personal memory and images from books, films and other media combine and overlap to create it. But 'everybody' includes not just residents but others who use the city, such as tourists. This discussion looks at how a sense of place and search for a distinctive experience can draw visitors beyond traditional tourist zones, and at how tourists can combine with residents and workers in the process of reconfiguring and regenerating a city.

Tourism, leisure and cultural activities are now seen as a natural and integral part of the way in which cities in developed economies make their living, and an obvious element in strategies for regeneration and economic development: 'what distinguishes the present era is that virtually every city sees a tourism possibility, and has taken steps to encourage it' (Hoffman et al., 2003:8). This represents a big change in attitudes and in ideas about the urban economy. Of course, towns and cities have always attracted visitors, and that has been particularly true of world cities such as London or New York. But until comparatively recently, these tourist activities were not seen as a significant part of city economies, nor as a particularly desirable form of employment or one that should be encouraged by public policy. Writing about London's tourism industry almost 30 years ago, Lipscomb and Weatheritt (1977: 17) drew attention to the industry's low pay and inconvenient working hours before conceding that it offered employment to 'poorer families and to workers whose employment prospects have suffered so much in London's population decline'.

The extensive acceptance of tourism as an element in cities' regeneration strategies has been accompanied by adoption of standardized approaches to development, based around the planned reconfiguration of parts of the city to deal with dereliction and add visitor attractions in new tourism zones or quarters. Far less attention has been paid to the way in which visitors and tourism pervade other parts of the city, link with the activities of residents and workers, and represent part of a wider process of change.

This chapter examines how tourism can develop outside tourism zones and how less familiar areas can cater for the demands of some segments of the visitor population. It draws on research in London and New York City to argue that subtle combinations of the qualities of place draw visitors to regenerating areas, and that these are qualities also enjoyed by residents and workers. In these cases, the role of tourism in regeneration is less planned, and can be seen as more organic and part of a response to changing lifestyle demands.

Converting Cities for Leisure and Tourism

Significant tourism development in former industrial cities or 'converted cities' (Judd and Fainstein, 1999), and in formerly industrial areas of polycentric cities like London, was an innovation that began in the late 1970s in the USA (for example, Baltimore, Maryland; Lowell, Massachusetts). It reflected the major economic change and spatial restructuring that has taken place in advanced capitalist economies over the last quarter century, changes which have had both material and symbolic effects on places (Harvey, 1989) and have seen cities transformed from centres of production to centres of consumption. Britain quickly took up the idea – partly as a result of active promotion by the national tourism organization (English Tourist Board (ETB), 1981) and partly because the severity of unemployment caused by the restructuring and recessions of the 1980s led to a vigorous search for new sources of jobs (Department of

Employment, 1985). During the 1980s tourism and leisure development became a recognized element of the inner city and regeneration agenda, and evaluative research pointed to its effectiveness (Beioley, Maitland and Vaughan, 1990). Tourism development has since become a familiar element of regeneration strategies in cities around the world, but, the process is rather poorly understood, particularly in terms of the development in new areas of large polycentric cities (Pearce, 1998).

Judd and Fainstein (1999) describe how many cities have sought to attract visitors by creating a planned tourist zone. This frequently seeks to attract visitors with a series of stereotypical attractions such as flagship museums and galleries, aquaria, Imax cinemas or casinos, combined with leisure shopping such as music stores, and internationally branded bars and restaurants. Judd (1999) sees these collections forming a 'mayor's trophy collection'. The new attractions are intended to provide economic activity and jobs directly, but also to mark and symbolize broader change and regeneration. In this approach, areas become 'tourist bubbles' (Judd, 1999: 36) or urban entertainment districts (Hannigan, 1998), based around attractions that are interchangeable between cities and not rooted in the locality and its culture. They attract investment and so contribute to the physical and economic regeneration of the immediate area, but they are solipsistic: separated from the ordinary fabric of the city physically and symbolically, even when they reuse rehabilitated historic buildings. In one sense, this separation promotes their tourist and leisure functions, since it demarcates them from other 'unregenerated' areas of the city that visitors might be expected to find unattractive or perceive as unsafe. This reconstruction of the city to create safe spaces can be seen as part of a process of regulating the converted city to make it more attractive to visitors (Hoffman et al., 2003). However, it creates a paradox. Development and attractions are standardized, yet visitors are thought to want an experience that is in some sense authentic, and related to the city and its culture (Fainstein and Gladstone, 1999). We return to this point in the next section.

Subsequently, the development of 'cultural quarters' (Montgomery, 2003, 2004) has sought to root tourism and leisure more firmly in the existing fabric and culture of the city. Cultural quarters like Dublin's Temple Bar in Ireland, or Hindley Street in Adelaide, Australia are planned developments, but the intention is to build on existing cultural activities and the history and built form of the district to create a new tourism cluster (Law, 2002). Again, reuse and rehabilitation of historic buildings is key to development, and deliberate attempts have been made to focus development around city culture and place characteristics and to favour a mix of local small- and medium-sized enterprises (Montgomery, 2003, 2004). Despite this, the dangers of serial reproduction persist as ideas are copied by other cities – there are similarities here with earlier waterfront developments (Jones, 1998; Law, 2002). Equally, the locally based activities that contribute distinctive place and culture-specific elements may be driven out by more profitable and ubiquitous businesses, such as branded bar chains (Chrisafis, 2004). This tendency towards serial reproduction and uniformity of activities and brands links to wider debates about 'placelessness' in the global economy – the sense that many localities have been homogenized into standardized spaces that could be anywhere (for example, Relph, 1976; Harvey, 1989; Entrikin, 1991; Kunstler, 1994; Lippard, 1997; Smith, 2003).

These approaches take a supply-side perspective to attracting visitors to cities. New attractions are provided and localities are reconfigured to draw in visitors – the assumption apparently being that 'if we build it, they will come' (Norris, 2003). Tourism development in cities is seen as a process of planned intervention to regulate and reconfigure cities with visitors in mind. But this fails to account for the growth of tourism in other places where public policy and investment have not been used to produce planned tourist development. In such areas it seems tourism can develop more organically, in cities perhaps in part through a process of 'exploration' by visitors. We look at examples of such development in London and New York City later, but first we need to remind ourselves of the complexity of visitors' demands and activities.

What Do Visitors Want?

Whilst considerable attention has been given to the increasing role of tourism in city development,

there has been comparatively little research into the characteristics, attitudes and wants of visitors or to the role they play in shaping new tourism areas. As mentioned above (Fainstein and Gladstone, 1999), tourists are often thought to value an 'authentic experience', but a substantial debate has developed about their motivation and the nature of the authenticity [for example MacCannell (1976, 1989)], the extraordinary (Urry, 1990) or liminal moments (Judd and Fainstein, 1999) they are assumed to value. Indeed some authors argue that authenticity is pluralistic (see Wang (1999) for a review). Urry suggested that whilst 'authentic elements' might be an important component of what tourists sought this is 'only because there is in some sense a contrast with everyday experience' (1990: 11). This suggests that it is difference rather than 'authenticity' that draws visitors to a place. Perhaps rather than framing what a city offers in terms of authentic or inauthentic, it may be more helpful to think of the distinctive and the over familiar. Actually seeing a sight may be an anti-climax if it is already so familiar because of perceptions formed before the visit – particularly since images and accounts are so often designed to show the sight in the best possible light (Rojek, 1997) – Big Ben on a sunny but uncrowded day, for example. Equally, if a destination simply offers another version of the 'mayor's trophy collection' in a rather different setting, it may prove a let-down for those who have seen similar collections of attractions before. A more satisfying visitor experience may be had from places that are not so familiar, for which there are fewer preconceived images or which offer a different mix. These may be no more 'authentic' but they may be experienced by visitors as more distinctive, and thus valued.

Distinctiveness may be more important to particular segments of the visitor market. Commentators such as Poon (1993) and Lash and Urry (1994) see a division between mass tourists and emerging 'post-tourists' or 'new tourists'. They see the latter as more experienced, independent and discriminating in what they seek from destinations – more authentic experiences, at the same knowing and being aware about the experience of being a tourist – 'self-conscious, cool, role distanced' (Urry, 1990: 101). Whereas mass tourists may be content with a planned tourist bubble or cultural quarter, more experienced visitors may want something else. We do not have to accept a simple division between 'mass' and 'new' tourists to see that some segments of the visitor market may want to move beyond tourist zones. Exploration by visitors has long been seen as an important element in tourism development [for example Butler (1980) and Plog (1973)] but the idea has tended to be applied to leisure visitors going to 'new' and 'exotic' destinations – for example, presenting Vietnam as the 'new Thailand'. But the desire for distinctiveness is complex, and needs to be set alongside other demands. More experienced visitors to large cities may want to move away from traditional tourist beats, and some may see tourism as the sense of experiencing 'ordinary everyday life' rather than an extraordinary attraction or event that constitutes a 'tourism experience' (Maitland, 2000). These may be seen as 'exotic' (Sassen and Roost, 1999) urban environments, and are likely to appeal especially where they can be easily accessed. But at the same time, visitors may want elements of predictability in their experience. The move away from 'mass tourism' in part means that tourists want to enjoy a more eclectic mix of experiences in their visit. The 'cosmopolitan consuming class' (Hoffman et al., 2003: 243) with more experience of travel and possibly more sophisticated tastes may want to experience the local. But for parts of their visit, for example in choosing their hotel, they may value the availability of 'commodified . . . standardized' but reassuringly familiar 'facilities . . . devised to meet [their] needs' (Fainstein et al., 2003:8). Returning visitors to London may welcome the growth of reliable branded budget hotels as an alternative to frequently low quality local independents. The enjoyment of distinctive places may in part be the opportunity to determine the mix of the novel and local with the international and familiar – providing choices unavailable in pre-planned tourism bubbles or urban entertainment destinations.

Pursuing the ideas of exploration and the everyday raises two further points. First, tourism to large polycentric cities need not be dominated by leisure visitors. In London for example, only 42% of overseas visitors say that the main purpose of their visit is a holiday, whereas a total of 47% are on business or visiting friends or relations (VFR) (VisitLondon, 2004). Business and

VFR tourists have access to colleagues, friends or family living and working in London, and that potentially gives them access to information not available to other visitors and may affect their behaviour and activities. Second, it is increasingly difficult to identify tourism as a 'discrete activity, contained tidily at specific locations and occurring at set periods' (Franklin and Crang, 2001:5), especially in large cities. There is increasing overlap between what tourists do, what day visitors do, and what residents and workers do on their evenings and days off. Tourism's contribution to regeneration may go beyond the reconfiguration of specific localities for tourism, and be part of a wider process of development and change in the city. New aesthetic demands by visitors may chime in with those of residents – for example the gentrification of former working-class areas and working-class housing, and the reaestheticization of former factories and warehouses (Zukin, 1995).

Investigating these ideas means gaining a better understanding of what type of visitor moves beyond traditional tourist beats and what draws them to new areas. However, evidence is hard to come by; there are generally no regularly collected, consistent and reliable data on tourism activity at the local level in major cities. To begin to fill this gap, surveys were organised by researchers from the University of Westminster (London, UK) in areas of London and New York City that are not traditional tourist locations. In this way the characteristics and perceptions of overseas visitors could start to be explored. The findings are reviewed briefly below, and used to inform a discussion of the role tourism can play in a broader process of regeneration.

The London surveys took place in Islington and in North Southwark, both areas that had not traditionally been a focus for tourism but which were known to be attracting more visitors. Islington is immediately to the north of the City of London, and well connected to familiar tourist areas of central London by public transport. It has no flagship attractions but a variety of cultural assets including the Sadler's Wells and Almeida theatres. There are independent and speciality shops, and a busy evening and night-time economy with small theatres, a cinema, pubs, bars, nightclubs and a variety of restaurants. The area has been subject to a long process of gentrification reflected in a complex mix of land-uses including both high value Victorian and Georgian terrace housing and mass housing estates dating from the 1960s and 1970s. There has been no attempt to reconfigure the area as primarily a tourism destination, but the local council supported tourism initiatives from the mid-1980s until 2001. However, there was never a comprehensive tourism plan for the area or structured tourism development, and the local tourism agency was closed in 2001. In common with other localities in London, data on tourism are severely limited and irregular. However, a study in 1998 made it clear that tourism had become important to the area – it was estimated that over four million visitors spent some £105 million, and that visitor numbers were growing (Carpenter, 1999).

A questionnaire survey was carried out amongst overseas tourists visiting Islington. The topics covered included visitor characteristics, how they had found out about the area, and what they thought of it. In many cases, questions were designed to be compatible with the Survey of Overseas Visitors to London (SOVL), a sample survey carried out annually by London's tourism organization (formerly London Tourist Board and Convention Bureau, now VisitLondon). This meant that it was possible to compare some of the characteristics of visitors to the area with characteristics of visitors to London as a whole. These findings have been reported more fully elsewhere (Maitland, 2003; Maitland and Newman, 2004). In summary, it turned out that visitors to Islington had characteristics that distinguished them from overseas visitors to London as a whole. They tended to be older, and to have had considerably more prior experience of London – over half of them had made three of more previous visits to the city. They were more likely to be visiting friends and relations than all London visitors, and more likely to make use of friendship networks along with guidebooks in deciding which areas to visit. Perhaps most interesting is their perception of the area, and what they liked about it. They were not drawn by particular individual attractions. Instead they liked the broader qualities of place – the physical environment created by architecture, building, streetscape and physical form, combined with socio-cultural attributes such as atmosphere, and

being in an area perceived as 'cosmopolitan' and 'not touristy'. Whilst shops, bars and restaurants were valued, it was as part of a broad landscape of consumption adding to the quality of place: *particular* shops or restaurants were not attractions.

A similar survey was carried out in the Bankside area of North Southwark (see Maitland (forthcoming) for more details). Bankside stretches along the south bank of the Thames from London Bridge westward to Blackfriars Bridge and beyond, and extends north into previously rundown areas of south London. It is much closer than Islington to traditional tourism hotspots. A new pedestrian bridge spans the river and creates a route to and from St Paul's cathedral, whilst a riverside walk linking Tower Bridge to Westminster Bridge runs through the area. There are new flagship attractions in the Tate Modern art gallery (adapted from a disused power station) and the recent re-creation of Shakespeare's Globe Theatre. There has been a substantial programme of urban regeneration, coordinated by two urban regeneration partnerships (Pool of London Partnership and Cross River Partnership). The area has seen substantial office development and the adaptive reuse of former warehouses and industrial buildings to create new residential apartments and lofts, bars and restaurants. Along with these developments, the creation of cultural clusters and coherent urban design, leisure and tourism have been significant in the planned regeneration of the area. It has been argued, however, that changes have been driven primarily by property speculation (Newman and Smith, 1999).

The presence of two flagship attractions in Bankside, along with its location and easy connections to established tourist areas might have been expected to mean that it would attract a range of visitors that was little different to overseas visitors to London as a whole. That proved not to be the case. There were notable differences in Bankside visitor characteristics, though not to the extent found in Islington. They tended to be rather older and more likely to be have been to London before (69% compared with 55% for all London visitors), although most (68%) were on their first visit to Bankside. Friendship networks and guidebooks were again most important in the decision to make the visit.

Despite the presence of major attractions, it seemed to be the qualities of place that proved most important in drawing visitors – the sense of history, the river, views, architecture and the overall atmosphere.

The London surveys suggest that we can see a somewhat different set of visitors exploring new tourism areas. In Bankside, close to established tourism hotspots, the difference is less pronounced than in Islington, which is not contiguous with established areas. But in both cases we can see that visitors are drawn by the qualities of place rather than specific attractions from the 'mayor's trophy collection', and this raises important concerns for tourism and regeneration which might be expected to apply to other areas too. A preliminary survey in New York City (NYC) allowed the researchers to investigate this possibility.

Surveys were undertaken, employing substantially the same questionnaire, at sites in western Queens and central Brooklyn, both acknowledged to be 'off-the-beaten-path' city attractions by NYC and Company (the official tourism office for New York City). The findings were consistent with the London surveys. Compared to visitors to NYC as a whole, survey respondents were more likely to be repeat visitors to the city, to be older, to have arranged their visit independently, to have obtained information from friends and relatives and guidebooks and to be visiting friends or relatives as the main purpose of their visit. As in London, they were not drawn primarily by individual attractions but by qualities of place and culture – 'architecture', 'people', 'food', 'culture', 'diversity' (Genoves et al., 2004).

Regeneration: Visitors, Residents and Workers

Underlying much of the discussion of tourism in cities is an implicit assumption that it makes sense to see visitors as separate from the host community – wanting different things from the city and thus behaving differently. But sustaining this separation is becoming more problematic as visitors and cities change rapidly. For many tourists, the stereotypes of mass tourism are becoming outdated. Our surveys showed

that at least some visitors have characteristics to be expected of 'new' or 'post-' tourists. At the same time, cities like London are being transformed. Demographic changes and increased population mobility (regionally, within the EU and globally) affect the make up of the host community, and are accompanied by changing patterns of consumption and lifestyle.

Much contemporary discussion about cities stresses the importance of quality of life, the rise of a more affluent urban class, the importance of individual consumers and differences of taste in consuming culture (Glaeser et al., 2000; Florida, 2002; Clark, 2003). These writers see the future economic success of cities as depending on their qualitative assets (for example, pleasing aesthetics, a high quality public realm, or low crime rates). Florida argues that in an era of city competition, winners will be those that can attract the 'creative class' of talented professionals in growing service industries. For him, the key element in attracting such talented workers is amenity – a combination of the intangible qualities of places and their cultures, and more tangible public goods, efficient transport, for example. In this view, amenity is required to attract the workers that make the city competitive – but of course amenity matters to visitors too. Amenity and the distinctive qualities of places help attract the discriminating urban tourists we have been discussing. 'Locational decisions that emphasise taste and quality of life, and the rise of leisure and concern about the arts' (Clark, 2003: 497–498) are becoming more important, and this means that the interests of residents and workers are brought closer to the concerns of visitors. Increasingly, these different groups of city users all behave in a 'touristic manner' (Franklin, 2003).

How does this affect our understanding of the creation of new tourism areas, and the role that visitors play? Gordon and Goodall (2000) identify many different elements that lie behind the creation of tourism places, ranging from general economic and social factors affecting demand – evolving tastes, holiday behaviour patterns and important characteristics of the tourism industry – to local factors such as the functioning of labour markets, property development processes, local politics and place images. They argue that these factors 'all come together' (p. 292) to define tourism places.

in 'real' places the experience is conditioned by a range of services independently provided within a physical, social and cultural environment shaped (in both intended and unintended ways) by past patterns of development, as well as by the presence of visitors arriving independently.

(Gordon and Goodall, 2000: 291)

This raises an important point. Creating a planned tourism district like a tourism bubble can be readily understood as systematic master planning and deliberate investment. In other areas, the development of tourism will result from a combination of very different factors – the image of places, past interactions, the physical environment and a range of economic and social forces, and visitors themselves. It is unlikely that we can explain this complex procedure by searching for simple causal processes. As Molotch et al. (2000) argue, the character of a place is the product of connections between 'unlike' elements and the analytical task is to understand the success of these connections rather than pointing to a single causal factor. From this point of view, we can see how new areas can emerge from the success of connections between unlike elements – local culture and associations, historic architecture, buildings that are reaestheticized as they are adapted for new uses, changes in the local housing market, improved urban design, together with consumption opportunities that include both local offers and familiar international brands. It might be difficult to see these areas as authentic, but they will be distinctive, since the combination of unlike elements will differ between places. They offer amenity that appeals to (some) residents, workers and visitors alike.

Visitors can be actively engaged in the creation or 'transformation' (Ashworth and Dietvorst, 1995) of areas like this, perhaps as regular visitors, who are familiar with and attached to the place. The kind of global forces shaping urban tourism identified by Fainstein et al. (2003) suggest we need new perspectives on the roles of visitors who 'belong' to the cities they visit as much as to their cities of primary residence, and of temporary migrants working or studying in the place. Tourism areas come together in part through the decisions and values of visitors, and visitors are one of the elements shaping new tourism areas. The idea of visitors

'belonging' suggests some affinity with residents. In some cases elements of belonging will be part of the motivation for the visit. Most business and VFR travellers have some pre-existing link to the city they are visiting and to residents or workers there. We might describe them as connected visitors. Other visitors may see themselves as having affinity with (some) residents. The *City Secrets Guide Book for London* (Adams, 2001: 7) introduces itself as a guide for 'discriminating strangers' by contributors 'who know the city best' – who are all resident writers, artists, historians and architects. Its recommendations include Islington, Bankside and the area around Tavistock Square, and it suggests unlike elements – architecture, galleries and museums, shops and restaurants – that its readers might enjoy. We could imagine the educated 'cosmopolitan consuming class' (Fainstein et al., 2003) comprises discriminating strangers, connected visitors and some residents and workers who value amenity and are drawn to and play a key role in regenerating areas of the city.

Conclusions

We can draw four points from this discussion. First, focusing on the supply side, and the planned reconfiguration of new areas for tourism is too limited a way of understanding the role of tourism in regenerating converted cities and areas of polycentric cities. We need to pay more attention to the demand side, and the role that visitors and their demands can play in creating and shaping places. Second, categorizing city users as 'visitors' on the one hand and 'the host community' on the other may not be helpful analytically. In some polycentric cities like London or New York there may be substantial overlap in the demands and tastes of visitors to some new tourism areas (such as those in our surveys) with a 'host' population characterized by high levels of mobility. It may be more helpful to think in terms of a 'cosmopolitan consuming class' comprising residents, workers and visitors alike who want to consume amenity and culture, and enjoy familiar landscapes of consumption.

Third, these visitors may be drawn away from more familiar tourist attractions (Maitland and Newman, 2004) to new 'cultural clusters'

(Mommaas, 2004) or new areas of gentrifica-tion that offer the restaurants and other ameni-ties demanded by young professionals. They will contribute to the process of gentrification and regeneration. Of course the creation of amenity and revalorized aesthetics may conflict with some tourists' search for 'authenticity'. In turn some residents may feel that the neigh-bourhood is no longer recognizable. For others enhanced amenities meet lifestyle demands. Close analysis of how place characteristics oper-ate and develop over time will be helpful to understanding how such issues of taste contri-bute to distinctive places. Over time the 'success of connections' (Molotch *et al.*, 2000) is dis-played in 'tradition', or, on the other hand, con-ditions may combine to make a radical shift of direction. But this perspective argues that any planned change of direction will need to take account of existing complementarities. 'Plop-ping in a new museum . . . [carries] the risk of artificiality' (Molotch *et al.*, 2000: 818) and may not draw visitors seeking the distinctive. It seems that localities do not need to be deliberately planned and reconfigured for tourism to attract visitors. But we need to know more about how the elements creating new tourism areas come together and where complementarity between tourists and others may be a creative force in regeneration. Further research is planned to explore in more detail the attitudes and demands of visitors, residents and workers, and their interactions.

Finally, there are obvious policy implica-tions to be drawn from the discussion. If new areas can attract visitors not through the planned development of a tourist bubble or a contrived

cultural quarter, then the role of local policy-makers in managing tourism is very different. If transformation of an area results from the deci-sions of individual visitors, linked to broader processes of change as residents and workers seek more amenity, then it may be difficult for policymakers to intervene in the process. In London, a key aim of policy is to disperse tour-ism across the city, particularly to poorer areas of East London, where it is seen to have potential to create jobs (London Development Agency, 2004). London's recent success in securing the 2012 Olympic Games may contri-bute to that ambition. But whilst the planned development of new sports facilities is a straight-forward (if expensive) means of attracting visi-tors to their immediate vicinity, at least in the short term, creation of new tourism areas in the wider locality is more complex. Ensuring the 'success of connections' between unlike ele-ments such as local culture, amenity, housing markets and consumption is beyond the control of local policymakers, certainly until our know-ledge of the process is substantially improved. There is no simple replicable model like that of the tourist bubble. Lanchester begins his descrip-tion of the area around Tavistock Square by saying that its appeal is that it is 'full of history, but at the same time scrappy-feeling and unplanned and random and all the better, all the more characteristic of London, for that' (Lanchester, 2005). Many city users would also enjoy the distinctiveness of the place, but find-ing ways to encourage the creation of such areas in desired locations provides a formidable challenge, and one unlikely to be achieved by conventional planning approaches.

References

Adams, T. (2001) *City Secrets Guide Book for London*. The Little Bookroom, London.
Ashworth, G.J. and Dietvorst, A.G. (1995) *Tourism and Spatial Transformations*. CAB International, Wallingford, UK.
Beioley, S., Maitland, R. and Vaughan, R. (1990) *Tourism and the Inner City*. Her Majesty's Stationery Office (HMSO), London.
Butler, R. (1980) The concept of a tourist area cycle of evolution, implications for management of resources. *Canadian Geographer* 24(1), 5–12.
Carpenter, H. (1999) *Islington: the Economic Impact of Visitors*. Discover Islington, London.
Chrisafis, A. (2004) Ibiza on the Liffey: but where are the Irish? *Guardian*, 8 November.
Clark, T.N. (2003) *The City as an Entertainment Machine*. Elsevier, San Diego, California.

Department of Employment (1985) *Pleasure, Leisure and Jobs: the Business of Tourism*. Her Majesty's Stationery Office (HMSO), London.

English Tourist Board (ETB) (1981) *Tourism and Urban Regeneration: Some Lessons from American Cities*. ETB, London.

Entrikin, J.N. (1991) *The Betweenness of Place: Towards a Geography of Modernity*. Macmillan, Basingstoke, UK.

Fainstein, S. and Gladstone, D. (1999) Evaluating urban tourism. In: Judd, D. and Fainstein, S.S. (eds) *The Tourist City*. Yale University Press, New Haven, Connecticut, pp. 21–34.

Fainstein, S., Hoffman, L.M. and Judd, D.R. (2003) Introduction. In: Hoffman, L.M., Fainstein, S.S. and Judd, D.R. (eds) *Cities and Visitors. Regulating People, Markets and City Space*. Blackwell, Oxford, pp. 239–253.

Florida, R. (2002) *The Rise of the Creative Class*. Basic Books, New York.

Franklin, A. (2003) *Tourism: an Introduction*. Sage, London.

Franklin, A. and Crang, M. (2001) The trouble with tourism and travel theory? *Tourist Studies* 1(1), 5–22.

Genoves, R., Hogan, M., Mallory, P., Murphy, M. and Roman, J. (2004) *The Real New York*. New York City University, New York.

Glaeser, E., Kolko, L. and Saiz, A. (2000) *Consumer City*. Harvard Institute of Economic Research, Cambridge, Massachusetts.

Gordon, I. and Goodall, B. (2000) Localities and tourism. *Tourism Geographies* 2(3), 290–311.

Hannigan, J. (1998) *Fantasy City: Pleasure and Profit in the Post-modern Metropolis*. Routledge, London.

Harvey, D. (1989) *The Condition of Postmodernity*. Blackwell, Oxford.

Hoffman, L.M., Fainstein, S.S. and Judd, D.R. (eds) (2003) *Cities and Visitors. Regulating People, Markets and City Space*. Blackwell, Oxford.

Jones, A. (1998). Issues in waterfront regeneration: more sobering thoughts – a UK perspective. *Planning Practice and Research* 13(4), 433.

Judd, D. (1999) Constructing the tourist bubble. In: Judd, D. and Fainstein, S.S. (eds) *The Tourist City*. Yale University Press, New Haven, Connecticut, pp. 35–53.

Judd, D. and Fainstein, S.S. (eds) (1999) *The Tourist City*. Yale University Press, New Haven, Connecticut.

Kunstler, J. (1994) *The Geography of Nowhere*. Touchstone, New York.

Lanchester, J. (2005) Story of a street. *Guardian*, 12 July.

Lash, S. and Urry, J. (1994) *Economies of Signs and Space*. Sage, London.

Law, C.M. (2002) *Urban Tourism: the Visitor Economy and the Growth of Large Cities*. Continuum Books Continuum International, London.

Lippard, L.R. (1997) *The Lure of the Local: Senses of Place in a Multicentred Society*. The New Press, New York.

Lipscomb, D. and Weatheritt, L. (1977) Some economic aspects of tourism in London. *Greater London Intelligence Journal* 42, 15–17.

London Development Agency (LDA) (2004) *East London Sub-Regional Tourism Development Strategy and Action Plan 2004–2006*. LDA, London.

MacCannell, D. (1976, 1989) *The Tourist: a New Theory of the Leisure Class*. Sulouker Books, New York.

Maitland, R. (2000) The development of new tourism areas in cities: why is ordinary interesting? Keynote paper given at Finnish University Network for Tourism Studies Opening Seminar 2000/01: *Managing Local and Regional Tourism in the Global Market*. Savonlinna, Finland, 18 September 2000.

Maitland, R. (2003) Cultural tourism and new tourism areas. Paper at Association for Tourism and Leisure Education (ATLAS) Cultural Tourism Meeting *Globalising the Local – Localising the Global*, Barcelona.

Maitland, R. (forthcoming) Cultural tourism and the development of new tourism areas in London. In: Richards, G. (ed.) *Cultural Tourism: Global and Local Perspectives*. Haworth Press, Binghamton, New York.

Maitland, R. and Newman, P. (2004) Developing metropolitan tourism on the fringe of central London. *International Journal of Tourism Research* 6, 339–348.

Molotch, H., Freudenburg, W. and Paulsen, K. (2000) History repeats itself, but how? City character, urban tradition, and the accomplishment of place. *American Sociological Review* 65, 791–823.

Mommaas, H. (2004) Cultural clusters and the post-industrial city: towards the remapping of urban cultural policy. *Urban Studies* 41(3), 507–532.

Montgomery, J. (2003) Cultural quarters as mechanisms for urban regeneration. Part 1. Conceptualising cultural quarters. *Planning Practice and Research* 18(4), 293–306.

Montgomery, J. (2004) Cultural quarters as mechanisms for urban regeneration. Part 2. A review of four cultural quarters in the UK, Ireland and Australia. *Planning Practice and Research* 19(1), 3–31.

Newman, P. and Smith, I. (1999) Cultural production, place and politics on the south bank of the Thames. *International Journal of Urban and Regional Research* 24(1), 9–24.

Norris, D.F. (2003) If we build it, they will come! Tourism based economic development in Baltimore. In: Judd, D.R. (ed.) *The Infrastructure of Play*. M E Sharpe, Armonk, New York, 125–167.

Pearce, D.G. (1998) Tourism development in Paris – public intervention. *Annals of Tourism Research* 25(2), 457.

Plog, S.C. (1973) Why destination areas rise and fall in popularity. *Cornell HRA Quarterly* November, 13–16.

Poon, A. (1993) *Tourism, Technology and Competitive Strategies*. CAB International, Wallingford, UK.

Relph, E. (1976) *Place and Placelessness*. Pion, London.

Rojek, C. (1997) Indexing, dragging and the social construction of tourist sights. In: Rojek, C. and Urry, J. (eds) *Touring Cultures: Transformations of Travel and Theory*. Routledge, London, pp. 52–74.

Sassen, S. and Roost, F. (1999) The city: strategic site for the global entertainment industry. In: Judd, D.R. and Judd, S.S.F. (eds) *The Tourist City*. Yale University Press, New Haven, Connecticut, pp. 143–154.

Smith, M. (2003) Space, place and placelessness in the culturally regenerated city. Paper at Association for Tourism and Leisure Education (ATLAS) Cultural Tourism Expert Meeting, Barcelona.

Urry, J. (1990) *The Tourist Gaze: Leisure and Travel in Contemporary Societies*. Sage, London.

VisitLondon (2004) *London Visitor Statistics 2003/04*. VisitLondon, London.

Wang, N. (1999) Rethinking authenticity in tourism experience. *Annals of Tourism Research* 26(2), 349–370.

Zukin, S. (1995) *Cultures of Cities*. Blackwell, Oxford.

4   VivaCity: Mixed-use and Urban Tourism

Rosita Aiesha and Graeme Evans

Introduction

This chapter will draw on contemporary research on the themes of sustainability and the mixed-use city. This is based on a national research programme, Sustainable Urban Environments, in which the authors are investigating the concept and practice of mixed-use development in inner urban areas of UK cities, with case studies in city centre and fringe areas of London, Manchester and Sheffield (VivaCity, 2005; see http://www.vivacity2020.org/). In London this includes the historic 'urban village' and cultural production quarter of Clerkenwell, which has transformed into a venue for evening economy, creative industries and heritage tourism activity.

Such ordinary areas of cities (Lefebvre, 1991; Robinson, 2005) differ from the heritage districts and upmarket office, residential, entertainment (Sassen and Roost, 1999) and retail areas in which urban tourism is most visible, in that they retain a residential population and mix of amenities, built environment and employment activity not dominated by tourism. They therefore combine a range of social, economic and cultural activity within which visitors, particularly evening, business and event-based, share time and space with everyday urban life. This mix also has implications for neighbourhood management, branding and marketing, and urban sustainability. 'Mixed-use' is a phenomenon, and now a ubiquitous response to

the Compact City (Jencks, 1999), Urban Village (Aldous, 1992; Urban Villages Forum (UVF), 1992) and New Urbanism (Marshall, 2004) movements, which look to higher urban density and the design of mixed-use buildings/blocks combining living, workspace, commercial and entertainment/leisure uses (Office of the Deputy Prime Minister (ODPM), 2005; Evans, 2005a). According to the English Planning Ministry, sustainable communities should be:

> well designed and built – including appropriate size, scale, density, design and layout, including mixed-use development, high quality mixed-use durable, flexible and adaptable buildings, with accessibility of jobs, key services and facilities by public transport, walking and cycling, and strong business community with links to the wider economy.
>
> (ODPM, 2005)

Diversity in terms of mixed-use and mixed communities (social, tenure) also extends to the temporal use of space – built and open, e.g. markets, parks/squares, festivals, public art/animation – through the evening economy and events.

The spatial impact of fringe area regeneration therefore offers the opportunity for visitor activity to spread geographically out from the city core, tourist hotspots and highly concentrated hotel districts, and to provide a more diverse, 'edge' experience for visitors – local, domestic and international tourists – whilst fulfilling the goals of physical and economic

© CAB International 2007. *Tourism, Culture and Regeneration* (ed. M.K. Smith)

regeneration for declining neighbourhoods and their residents. This widening of the visitor economy therefore seeks to capture the day-visit and entertainment market, which significantly exceeds traditional international and domestic tourist flows, and offers an economic and regenerative potential to areas otherwise limited to local economic activity, with little 'passing trade'.

This chapter will review these urban and cultural concepts in terms of policy and practice. The detailed critique of the city fringe district and local areas is based on surveys of residents, businesses, visitors to local events and intermediaries (town planners, regeneration partnerships, developers/agents, destination promoters, police), and utilizes GIS-based mapping of land-use linked to demographic and social survey data (VivaCity, 2005). Visual images of street scenes and the built environment complements local area mapping to describe the spatial relationships and the extent of diversity and flows which these mixed-use areas generate. This will include festival and event strategies, late-night activity ('club scene'), as well as cultural and heritage trails through this otherwise low-key historic workshop area.

Urban and City Tourism

Since the early 1990s, urban tourism and more specifically city tourism, has joined the canon of tourism studies, and latterly urban studies (Law, 1992; Page, 1995). Cultural tourism was fêted in Europe as one of the fastest growing sectors of the tourism market (CEC, 1996; Richards, 1996) and seen as a panacea for heritage conservation and development worldwide (ICOMOS, 1998). This was also adopted as part of the European Project, as regional development and other structural funds were concentrated in major cultural flagship schemes, reliant upon attracting a visitor market to downtown and revitalized areas of post-industrial city sites (Evans and Foord, 2000). This was fuelled by a growth in heritage attractions and venues, the improved marketing of existing traditional historic sites in Europe (six out of ten countries hosting the highest number of World Heritage Sites are in Western Europe, notably Italy,

France, Spain and the UK) and a widening world heritage list in 'long haul' as well as emerging destinations in Central and Eastern Europe. Urban heritage sites have also sought United Nations Educational, Scientific and Cultural Organization (UNESCO) inscription, as a universal 'brand' (Evans, 2002) with 'Maritime' Greenwich (south-east London) and Liverpool; Royal Botanic Gardens, Kew (south-west London), Saltaire (Bradford), joining Bath and Edinburgh, as city attractions which have extended the tourism map of the city. At the same time, supply-led factors such as low-cost airline 'city to city' routes and latent demand from Eastern Europe and the packaging of city-breaks, leisure shopping, cultural and entertainment tours, have together facilitated city regeneration designed around this growing visitor consumer group, which could not have been imagined in the former declining areas of Temple Bar, Dublin and Barcelona [El Raval, El Born and Poblenou (Evans, 2006)].

Larger cities (Law, 1993, 1996) which attract major tourism flows, combining business/convention, leisure, education and migration-based movement, have been less affected, or at least less reliant upon the city-break phenomenon. They do however need to maintain their market share and visitor numbers, through high repeat visits from more savvy tourists (Urry, 1995). At the same time they have faced the need to regenerate major tracts of former docklands/waterfront, and residual light industrial areas, including the city fringe areas which have become interstitial zones between the Central Business District (CBD) and inner suburban areas where employment and residential usage is most concentrated. They have therefore been potential sites for alternative economic, cultural and urban design experiments, in relatively close proximity to office workers, incumbent working class and new urban lifestyle dwellers. Whilst such fringe areas lack major visitor attractions and tourist hotel accommodation, they do contain urban heritage and contemporary consumption experiences which mainstream city venues lack, and with an all-year-round local and sub-regional visitor market. In this sense they are not so vulnerable to the vagaries of international tourism and transport markets, notably exchange rates, safety – e.g. crime and terrorism – and inter-city competition.

Writing over a decade ago, Ashworth called for:

> a coherent body of theories, concepts, techniques and methods of analysis which allow comparable studies to contribute towards some common goal of understanding of either the particular role of cities within tourism or the place of tourism within the form and function of cities.
>
> (Ashworth, 1992: 5)

Since then numerous texts on urban and city tourism, case studies of regeneration area types such as waterfronts, city centres, and the role of festivals and events in cultural tourism, have established this *genre* within the tourism literature and case study exemplars. What is less evident over this period is how far the city-tourism dialectic has accompanied and moved forward these analyses. In many respects these have treated urban tourism as just another destination and market type, with little or no conception of the complexity or even history of the city itself. Urban tourism is also messy – distinguishing the 'local', from the 'visitor', from the 'tourist', let alone isolating this activity from the ebb and flow of city life, is very difficult (Tyler *et al.*, 1998) and costly in resource terms, as compared with tourism resort analysis and sites which can be controlled and ring-fenced in terms of impacts. But resort tourism is also atypical, compared with domestic activity and consumption within which much urban tourism coexists. Attitudes of residents to tourism activity in, say, heritage zones of cities such as York (Bahaire and Elliott-White, 1999) and Quebec (Evans, 2002), provide some insight, but again these relate to designated and delineated heritage sites and buffer zones, not to mixed-use (as opposed to mono-use) and regular areas of the city.

What this study exposits therefore is a study of an 'urban village' area, of neighbourhoods, mixed communities and land-uses, within which the visitor economy is a function of endogenous economic and social activity, as well as being destination-based. This has also developed incrementally to include tourist stays (overnight) and itineraries, but in a predominately working environment. A key question is how far this diversity represents a sustainable approach to urban living and working, in contrast to the sterile heritage and touristic zones

familiar in many cities, and the seemingly inevitable gentrification effects which accompany city/fringe regeneration.

Tourism and Urban Development

Urban development tied to a range of social, economic and physical regeneration goals, varies according to the political regime, local conditions and how far 'degeneration' and market failure have reached in an (economic) cycle. This is of course reflected in social effects, such as poor housing and environment, worklessness, crime, under-capacity and spirals of deprivation, which collectively typify areas 'in need' of regeneration. In industrial and mining areas, multiple deprivation due to structural unemployment (wholesale closures) can present extremes. In major cities this is more likely to be area-based, influenced by poorer housing, lower paid employment and settlement by migrant and other groups with higher barriers to social and economic access and participation. This includes areas of deprivation in close proximity to better-off areas, as well as city fringe estates.

Regeneration intervention by the public sector varies, again in line with political ideology, in terms of a focus on inward investment and flows (for example London Docklands development in the 1980s under the Heseltine/Thatcher regime), or in a more bottom-up approach which seeks to improve the capacity of incumbent communities, through a variety of skills and training, physical improvement (housing, amenity, public realm) and 'neighbourhood renewal' – or 'gentrification from within'. In practice, property markets, inward and outward migration and hard-to-reach communities, conspire to undermine both of these approaches unless public intervention programmes are sufficiently long term, integrated across social, economic and physical effects, and mediate the extremes of private sector and dependency cultures.

Where tourism is most evident in the regeneration cycle and programmes, is in site-based projects which look to visitor activity to support new facilities such as cultural, sport/stadia and leisure attractions, linked to physical redevelopment, transport and flagship schemes. This formula is long established, if not rigorously analysed (Evans, 2005b) and is represented in the literature on US 'downtown revitalisation' (National Building Museum, 1998), arts and urban regeneration (in the UK/USA: Arts Council, 1986; BAAA, 1989; and in Europe: Bianchini and Parkinson, 1993), hallmark/ mega-events (Hall, 1992), French *Grands Projets* (Looseley, 1997; Pearce, 1998) and in the iconic projects which anchor place-making, competitive city and branding strategies (Evans, 2003). Most well known projects include *Guggenheim Bilbao*, the *Grand Travaux Culturel* in Paris (e.g. Pompidou, La Défense), the UK's Millennium projects (e.g. Tate Modern, Baltic Gateshead, Eden Centre) and entire city cultural strategies, notably Barcelona, and their emulators such as Montreal and Marseille. One element they share, apart from often-imported star architects, is a reliance on cultural tourism to justify public investment and city repositioning strategies.

Outside of these key downtown and water-front regeneration schemes, many local urban areas also look to the twin benefits of tourism and branding, to stimulate local economies and achieve a range of social, economic and environmental improvements, without the single flagship or more mono-cultural zoning associated with 'festival marketplace' and entertainment districts. These seek to build on a more diverse range of activities and consumption possibilities, including local heritage, contemporary crafts and galleries (including showcasing, fairs), events and festivals, speciality retailing, markets (covered and 'street'), food and evening entertainment, including late-night music and dance clubs. This diversity also seeks to attract a wider range of visitor in terms of age, taste and income group, and to benefit, in theory at least, local residents, workers and visitors alike.

Tourism Development Action Programme

In the late-1980s the English Tourist Board (ETB) promoted the idea of tourism development action programmes (TDAPs), in part to stimulate tourism in less developed visitor areas, and to assist in local area regeneration and thereby to fulfil the strategic goal of spreading tourism activity over a wider geographic area and beneficiary community and to relieve congestion and crowding out in over-developed areas. This policy was also reflected Europe-wide, nationally as well as regionally and at city level, with capital cities such as London exhibiting highly concentrated tourist and hotel provision (Evans and Shaw, 2001). Whilst major regional cities looked to US-style tourism and convention marketing as part of their boosterist approach – underpinned by major city centre redevelopment (e.g. Birmingham, Manchester) and major events (e.g. Glasgow, Montreal) – local area regeneration looked to more subtle interventions, in the absence of major attractions, venues and marketing budgets.

The first TDAP in London was located in the borough of Islington, an inner urban area to the north of the City of London. Its location outside the symbolic and administrative boundary of the medieval city walls afforded it freedoms from city controls and guilds: 'lawless, taxless places where actors, chancers and whores thrived', and where according to Porter, 'rich and poor lived in decent reciprocity' (Lynch, 2004: 105). For similar reasons, this habitus was sustained as radicalism and social activism thrived in the industrial and post-industrial periods. Residents included Karl Marx (celebrated in the Marx Memorial Library), and Berthold Lubetkin, whose experimental housing and health centres (e.g. Finsbury) were exemplars in social provision, prior to the post-war establishment of the National Health Service. A thriving crafts and print trade also flourished, including numerous publication presses, and this continues today in high concentrations of 'new media', architects and designer-makers occupying managed workspaces and studios (Evans, 2004).

In 1991 the TDAP was established, with Discover Islington (DI), an arm's length company (i.e. an autonomous but related company) but funded in cash and kind by the ETB and the local authority. This initiative effectively took over from the local council's economic development function, which had included a dedicated tourism development officer, a post that was then made redundant. This reflected a move from tourism as an economic development and planning issue, to tourism as an area branding opportunity (Long, 2000). The first action programme focused on destination marketing, raising the profile of the tourism economy and 'offer' (Discover Islington, 1992) and most effort during the TDAP was to establish the area's tourism presence, define its character and strength, as the basis for internal and external marketing and promotion. This included developing bed and breakfast provision, since the area lacked hotel provision at all scales; booking/information systems; and assessing the impact that tourism activity had on the local economy. Towards the end of the programme, and as it turned out, the DI organization's life, the focus shifted towards that of urban sustainability: 'a commitment to high yield, low impact tourism that also benefits local people' (Carpenter, 1999). Like many public tourism programmes (PACEC, 1990), the issue of dependency and subsidy arose, as the ETB funding expired, and more local funding was required. This coincided with a change in political control within the local council (from Labour to Liberal Democrat parties). This conspired to end the DI organization, as the new regime made substantial public spending cuts to 'non-essential' public services and looked to greater private sector/business-led enterprise. In some respects, however, the tourism policy had failed to engage or make the case for local benefits, in part a reflection of the highly skewed and gentrified nature of business organization, with few opportunities for lower skilled/entry level jobs in the sector, and also a failure to interpret and benefit from the regeneration regime which was emerging from a New Labour national government, around notions of social inclusion and a 'New Deal' for communities. This fell foul of the spatial inequalities which separated the touristic areas from poorer residential areas (in this case a north–south local divide), and also the market-led, mixed-use phenomenon which was taking place in the southern, Clerkenwell area of the borough.

Urban Heritage

The morphology of the Clerkenwell area reflects its medieval past and its host to migrant groups – from Hugenots, Jewish, Bangladeshi and recently Eastern European settlers. Today it is also inhabited by a younger ('child-free')

residential group living in converted 'lofts' and most recently, new, mixed-used premises built on infill or brownfield sites, mainly former light industrial/office and utility buildings. The area's high dwelling density is far less than during its industrial era heyday, when live-work, male and female craft and industrial workers cohabited with commuting workers – and tourists – drawn to the entertainment and 'freedoms' it offered. The reuse of industrial and institutional buildings (e.g. schools, libraries) is a feature of inner city regeneration and the more organic mixed-use areas, which has enabled an increasing inner city residential population, reversing decades of decline, as well as a day and night visitor economy, as in the past. This built environment also represents examples of architectural form and style, from Georgian and Victorian terraces, historic sites and buildings including its former role as a healthy spa area (Clerk's Well, Sadler's Well), small alleyways and underground rivers – an urban ecology spanning several hundred years.

The value attached to the architectural heritage was recognized in the designation of several Conservation Areas, protecting against development and change to façades (see Fig. 4.1). This also responded to the rapid redevelopment of such inner urban areas as modernization and new building technology (offices, tower blocks) cut swathes through many cities. The urban heritage and conservation movement came out of this era, but too late to save many architectural legacies, prior to the value now placed on such urban assets in both tourism and property investment terms.

Commercial and residential property markets and the restructuring of employment and workplace needs, have also shifted the profile of economic and social activity, with light industrial workspace converted into offices in this City overspill district during the late-1970s/1980s, then office/industrial premises to residential 'loft living' in the 1990s, a trend which has continued apace to date. With a high architect and designer fraternity in the area, design experiments in both conversion and new-build provide an exceptional mix of old and new styles in close proximity, coupled with historic trails, sites and a popular 'foodie' and club culture. Designer restaurants, bars and clubs serve weekday, evening and weekend users, interspersed

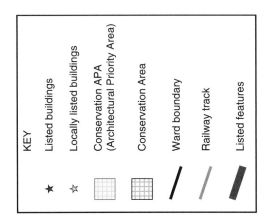

KEY

★   Listed buildings

☆   Locally listed buildings

    Conservation APA
    (Architectural Priority Area)

    Conservation Area

    Ward boundary

    Railway track

    Listed features

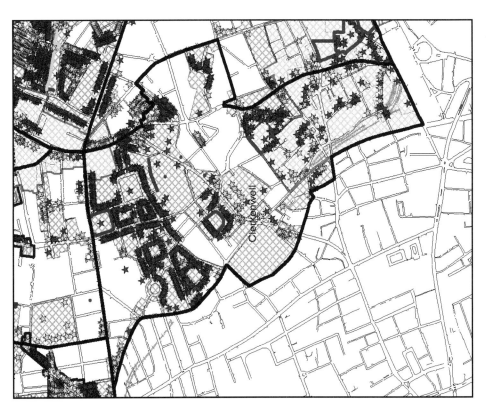

Fig. 4.1.   Map of the Conservation Areas and listed buildings in Clerkenwell (not drawn to scale) (Source: London Borough of Islington, 2004).

with established and incomer residential communities, the latter occupying more mixed-use areas, the former in residential estates on the fringe of the commercial neighbourhood.

Urban Festivals

As already noted, Clerkenwell does not offer the same sort of primary tourist attractions as those found in central and west London's *beaux quarters*, such as St Pauls, Tower Bridge or Madame Tussaud's, or the neoclassical architectural sites on tourist itineraries (Lasansky and Greenwood, 2004), which attract a large number of overseas and day visitors. This also points to a certain type of visitor being attracted to areas such as Clerkenwell, those perhaps wanting a more fringe or alternative experience of London. Major cities also receive a high proportion of return visitors, both business and leisure and for whom, like residents, the traditional sights and experiences are of little interest. They seek new areas to visit and a more contemporary experience, and hold greater knowledge of what is on offer and 'new'.

The facilities for such visitors tend to be specialized and do not require an overnight stay, although more recently two boutique-style chain hotels (Malmaison, Zetter's) have opened, supplementing the area's 'designer image' and dining circuit. Clerkenwell in this respect provides a set of 'secondary' but more authentic attractions for overseas tourists and a sizeable day visitor group. The visitor attractions tend to target very tailored messages to different groups about what is available in Clerkenwell, although its medieval, Victorian and crafts heritage is one that is commonly projected. Places like the Clerkenwell Visitors' Centre run a series of heritage trails, some promising an authentic experience of a bygone Clerkenwell based on real historic buildings, many of which are listed, such as the House of Detention, The London Spa, Clerkenwell Green, The Clerk's Well (from which Clerkenwell derives its name). However, some attractions promote varying degrees of 'authenticity' providing themed entertainment based on re-interpreting history and conjuring up a darker 'rough and ready' Dickensian image of Clerkenwell – such as the 'Murders,

Monasteries and Martyrs Tour' run by the Clerkenwell and Islington Guides Association.

Literary associations from books such as *Clerkenwell and Finsbury Past* (Thames, 1999), *London: the Biography* (Ackroyd, 2001) and the *Rough Guide to Britain* (Andrews *et al.*, 2004) devote time to Clerkenwell's rich history and Peter Ackroyd's *The Clerkenwell Tales* (2004) attempt to recreate a new 'popular' imagining of the past by mixing factual and fictional elements with literary musings about the place and context of its complex history. Alongside this, place-marketing literature such as the annual *Clerkenwell Guide* and *Time Out* guides provide information about where to eat, where to stay and what you can do in Clerkenwell. This type of marketing not only promotes the potential for tourism and leisure activities but also highlights the mixed uses and diversity of the area by also selling it as a place in which to live and work. This has helped raise both the positive image and the investor confidence in the residential and commercial property market in an area that has been attempting to recover from the impact of deindustrialization and urban population decline over the last 30 years.

Annual themed events such as the Clerkenwell Festival, Literary Festival, Exmouth Market Festival, Italian Festival, exhibitions such as 'Clerkenwell Dressed' – are mainly independent sector-led endeavours which attempt to celebrate and create a sense of place, all of which have had a cumulative effect of raising the profile of the area. These events originally celebrated the locality and its heritage, primarily by/for local residents, including a long-established migrant Italian community. However, more recently, contemporary events have highlighted the areas' design past and present, as host to one of the highest concentrations of creative industry firms in London (and therefore in the UK). This encompasses traditional designer-makers in jewellery, textiles, metalcrafts, printing and publishing, to new economy activity such as graphic design, digital media and a large number of architectural practices and ancillary services (interior design, furniture). The latter cluster builds on the architectural heritage itself, including architectural innovation in building conversions, new build and loft-style live-work developments. Two London-wide events have therefore developed which promote the area's creativity and design production base. The first 'Hidden Art: Open Studios', which is hosted by the Clerkenwell Green (Crafts) Association, makes designer workshops and products available to the public over a one to two week period each year. Hidden Art is part of an established East London initiative to promote artists working in the sub-region (Foord, 1999). Open Studios are linked by a map, website (www.hiddenart.com) and list of participating artists, as a marketing opportunity for both the producers and the area itself. Visitors get to enter the artists' and designers' workspaces, purchase their work and visit buildings otherwise not open to the public.

Most recently, the London Architecture Biennale was first staged in Clerkenwell in June 2004, as a first attempt to promote the area's architectural heritage and contemporary design practices. By taking the biennale format (Venice, Berlin etc.), exhibitions were curated, design firms opened their studios to the public, and talks and presentations from historians, architects and writers combined with street markets to produce a 10 day event. Over 25,000 visitors attended the opening exhibition over the first weekend (Fig. 4.2), during which the main road leading to Smithfield meat market was closed to

traffic, grassed over and cattle driven down it, in reference to this last produce market to still operate in the city. Over 90% of surveyed attendees rated the event as good or excellent and, as with most cultural venues and cultural tourism generally with a highly knowledgeable visitor (Richards, 1996), 46% of attendees were 'professional' (e.g. architects, designers/students), but 54% were 'non-professional', including local residents.

A *vox pop* survey of Biennale visitors using a number of open questions provided a snap shot of views about what people living, working or visiting Clerkenwell thought about the area. Significantly, the survey revealed that up to 70% of those attending were residents in the neighbourhood, and of those 52% stated they took part in some form of leisure or work-related activities within Clerkenwell.

The aspects they most liked about the area were the range of leisure and entertainment facilities on offer (Fig. 4.3). Residents not only specified particular facilities such as the pubs, bars, restaurants and clubs, but also features such as the built heritage and historical associations, accessibility, vitality and attractiveness of location. For some, including local residents, dislikes were expressed in terms of

Fig. 4.2.   Biennale visitors – launch and street celebration (© Evans, 2004, with permission).

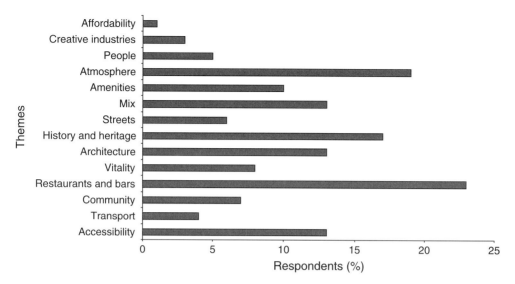

Fig. 4.3. What people living, working or visiting Clerkenwell liked about it.

the lack of green space and convenience shops, and environmental problems of litter, parking and noise were cited. The area's centrality, transport links and mix of activities are therefore both an advantage, as well as a disadvantage to some.

One of the key environmental and planning issues for urban tourism, indeed tourism in established residential areas generally, is the impact from visitor activity and the relationship between visitor activity and residents with regard to the local economy. Related factors include economic crowding out (price inflation, property/rents), conflicts of usage, pollution (noise, air, water, traffic congestion and litter) and symbolic effects on identity and community cohesion. Mixed-use areas in several respects already face some of these issues with the combination of social, economic and physical activities in close proximity, including mixed-use buildings and shared amenities. The addition of sustained visitor activity in daytime and evening periods extends this mix and obviously heightens these effects.

The results of a detailed household survey and a business survey reveal the impact of mixed-use on its different users and occupiers and the mixed messages concerning city centre living and quality of life, particularly in relation to the visitor economy (Evans, 2005a). The analysis suggests that respondents are trading

(positive or negative) factors against each other in their assessments of mixed-use/central city environments (i.e. dwelling type, land-use mix, location, provision of additional security and public transport networks). For those respondents who did express a positive preference for locating in mixed-use neighbourhoods, they did so principally for reasons of high levels of amenity. The profiles of the respondent households and key aspects of living in the area are shown in Table 4.1.

The surveys suggest that, generally, whilst some aspects of leisure, entertainment and local amenities are of importance to both residents and business occupiers, other aspects are of importance to only one of these interest groups. Both groups are significant users of the local shops and restaurants and are less likely to use local nightclubs. Business occupiers are more likely to be users of banking, financial services and pubs than local residents. By contrast, local residents are much more likely than the business occupiers to use health centres, local parks, playgrounds, libraries and museums (Table 4.2).

Around 40% of both residents and business occupiers identified the presence of mixed-use buildings and activities in the area as a positive factor for living in or locating to Clerkenwell. Most residents found the presence of mixed-use activities beneficial all of the time. The greatest

Table 4.1. Profile of respondents in a household survey of Clerkenwell.

Factor	Respondents	
Premises		
	33%	lived in accommodation with non-residential activity in building
	67%	lived in a flat/maisonette
	29%	lived in a house
Open space		
	75%	felt that private open space was important
	59%	were affected by antisocial behaviour in parks/public space
Tenure		
	52%	rented their accommodation
	45%	owned their accommodation
Age group		
	33%	under-35
	18%	35–45
	14%	46–55
	34%	56 +
Work		
	58%	working
	18%	retired
	12%	workplace in home
	19%	worked in neighbourhood
Transport		
	58%	did not have a car
	30%	felt that parking space was important
	77%	felt that parking for visitors was important
Transport to work		
	8%	car
	58%	walk/cycle
	22%	bus
	8%	tube/train
Noise		
	33%	lost sleep due to noise disturbance

Table 4.2. Activities and amenities ranked as important by residents and businesses.

Type of activity valued	Business occupiers (%)	Residents (%)
Shops (e.g. convenience, post office)	96	80
Bank or building society	81	13
Gym or leisure facility	16	25
Health practice (e.g. GP/dentist)	14	77
Restaurant/cafés	77	60
Park/playground	28	62
Library	18	49
Art gallery or museum	20	46
Pubs/bars	80	51
Nightclub	14	13

benefit to residents of mixed-use development is the presence of convenience shops and services (40%). The presence of more people in the streets, and the lively atmosphere contributed in part by 'good' non-residential activities, creates a highly diverse residential environment. However, these perceived benefits are given their lowest value during the night and early morning. At all times the lowest valued benefit was additional security; in fact no respondents felt mixed-use development provided additional security during the night.

We can see that the business activities found within mixed-use areas bring with them costs and benefits. The costs are often the result of the activities necessary to carry out a business but are not valued similarly by residents. Litter is identified at all times as the worst problem encountered by residents as a result of non-residential activities (Fig. 4.4). Other problems become pronounced at particular periods of the day. Antisocial behaviour hardly features during the day or early evening but is considered to be a problem in the late evening and at night. By contrast, in the early morning the key concerns of residents are from noise, deliveries

(loading and unloading) and litter. Unpleasant smells are only identified by a significant number of people as a problem late in the evening.

Whilst both residents and non-residents (business occupiers) find noise and litter of significant concern, residents generally tend to find fewer aspects of the mixed-use environment a problem than business occupiers. Business occupiers are more likely than residents to find difficulties with parking for visitors and customers and for loading and unloading of deliveries. Furthermore, residents are far less likely than business occupiers to report problems with antisocial behaviour or security.

The findings highlight that the pros and cons of mixed-use development are different for residents and business occupiers in several ways (although a significant proportion of business owners are also residents). However, for both groups the overall benefits outweigh the problems that such developments create. Importantly, the results also show that noise, poor litter collection and parking problems are the three main externalities cited by both residents and business occupiers. However, despite these negative factors, respondents seem to be

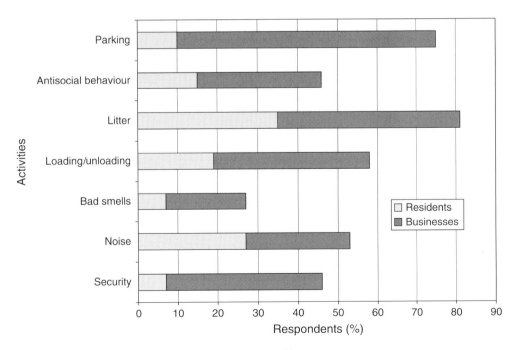

Fig. 4.4. Problems of mixed-use activities for residents and business occupiers.

trading these off against what they perceive as more positive attributes of the neighbourhood (i.e. a central location and access to a well connected bus service).

The residential quality-of-life factor most associated with mixed temporal use, relates to night-time activity, particularly dance and music clubs, and antisocial behaviour on the streets as well as from 'neighbours'. Data from noise complaints in the area confirm the prime source of nuisance. Of over 2200 complaints in the year 2003/04, 1100 were from 'music' of which 88% occurred during the night-time. The highest daytime noise complaints were from construction and machinery, as well as loud music. Six nightclubs with late-night music licences are located in the central area, including Fabrica, Dust and Turnmills – the first 24-hour licensed club in London. Late nights tend to run Thursday through Sunday with 20,000 clubbers attending over this period. The local police maintain a close relationship with club management, mainly over drug use and parking. They sweep local streets to deter parking in/near residential areas to prevent noise after closing and in fact few resident complaints relate to late-night club activity – many owners live locally and have a detailed knowledge of the area and the community. Noise pollution therefore emanates from smaller bars and restaurants located on the ground floor of residential blocks. Environmental issues, including antisocial behaviour and street crime (e.g. bike theft) represent the prime challenge for mixed-use involving visitor activity, whilst gentrification effects impact on the character and amenity for residents, and ultimately threaten the mix itself.

> There's Exmouth market. Twenty-five years ago it was a market, you had food stores and utility stores, somewhere to get your boots sorted or your clothes and there was a Woolworth's at the end of the road. There has been a change from traditionally working class things – you had a pie and mash shop down there. Now, you have wine bars and flash restaurants.
>
> (Resident, 2004)

Conclusion

The views and experience of those who live and work in a mixed-use (partial) 24-hour visitor economy reveal a great deal about the potentials for reconciling problems in the development of a more successful mixed-use environment – for all the differing demands of its users. This is of particular value as advantageous features can be identified and barriers to mixed-use activities reduced. It suggests for example what conditions may need to be considered in order to make city centres more viable places to live and work whilst at the same time managing the competing interests from other user groups such as that of leisure and entertainment attractions. This inevitably raises questions about the range of interactions that take place, and about the degrees of separation of land-uses within a mixed-use neighbourhood, all of which bear implications for future policy and practice.

Perceptions about the potential externalities are a function of the people associated with specific uses (customers of pubs or clubs are likely to be viewed more negatively than customers to an office) and reactions to the amenity value (users of a club are likely to be viewed more negatively than users of a shop). It seems certain types of uses are likely to result in externalities and 'user' aversion to them. This has significant implications for planners and policymakers as it emphasizes the importance of addressing the externalities through good design and management. What is clear is that planners have a key role in making mixed-use more acceptable to residents and particularly careful that in promoting certain practices which are considered sustainable, such as the Government's policy of encouraging higher density and car-free development, they do not create more problems in the process. This means that it should not be assumed that mixed-use is good whatever the uses. Of particular importance is the scale of area and mix of uses (land, social, economic, temporal) that provides the right (i.e. sustainable) balance.

Areas of mixed social, economic and temporal activity, hosting incumbent communities and new residents, as well as day and night visitors, offer a particular model of contemporary urban life which at its best can support these various uses – of space, amenities, work and leisure – whilst retaining a character which touristic zones have long lost. The compact city concept in one sense is enabled by the visitor economy by generating local trade and providing more innovative opportunities for production and consumption activities to collaborate in a managed way, where mainstream (urban) tourism has otherwise degenerated into a consumption 'experience'. Issues of carrying capacity, gentrification and environmental management arise here as in other visitor scenarios. However, it is the mix of uses that militates against any one activity or form of capital dominating to the exclusion of others. Maintaining this mix therefore requires a detailed understanding of what works, what doesn't, and how far local zoning and licensing still needs to apply in order to protect local amenity (including local shops, open space) and local quality of life.

An imbalance or neglect of an area's liveability risks the commodification all too familiar in tourism and other mono-cultural usage of urban sites (e.g. major retail and leisure developments). Local area planning and consultation approaches, as being developed under the VivaCity project (VivaCity, 2005) and GIS-based participatory (GIS-P) 'planning for real' systems, attempt to bring together what have been parallel spheres of social (residential, tenure, demographic), economic (employment, business, live-work) and physical (design quality, open space, transport, environmental qualities) interaction. This may in turn contribute to Ashworth's (1992) earlier call for 'understanding . . . the particular role of cities within tourism or the place of tourism within the form and function of cities'.

References

Ackroyd, P. (2001) *London: the Biography*. Vintage, London.

Ackroyd, P. (2004) *The Clerkenwell Tales*. Vintage, London.

Aldous, T. (1992) *Urban Villages: a Concept for Creating Mixed-Use Urban Developments on a Sustainable Scale*. Urban Villages Group, London.

Andrews, R., Brown, J., Humphreys, R., Lee, P. and Reid, D. (2004) *Rough Guide to Britain*. Rough Guides, London.

Arts Council (1986) *An Urban Renaissance: the Case for Increased Private and Public Sector Co-operation*. Arts Council of Great Britain, London.

Ashworth, G. (1992) Is there an urban tourism? *Tourism Recreation Research* 17(2), 3–8.

BAAA (1989) *Arts and the Changing City: an Agenda for Urban Regeneration*. British American Arts Association (BAAA), London.

Bahaire, T. and Elliott-White, M. (1999) Community participation in tourism planning and development in the historic city of York, England. *Current Issues in Tourism* 2(2/3), 243–276.

Bianchini, F. and Parkinson, M. (eds) (1993) *Cultural Policy and Urban Regeneration: the West European Experience*. Manchester University Press, Manchester, UK.

Carpenter, H. (1999) Measuring the economic impact of local tourism – making the most of local resources. *Tourism – the Journal of the Tourism Society* 102, 10–11.

CEC (1996) *Report on the Evaluation of the Community Action Plan to Assist Tourism 1993–95*. 92/421EC. Commission for the European Community (CEC), Brussels.

Discover Islington (1992) *A Tourism Strategy and Programme for Islington*. Discover Islington Tourism Action Development Programme, London.

Evans, G.L. (2002) Living in a world heritage city: stakeholders in the dialectic of the universal and the particular. *International Journal of Heritage Studies* 8(2), 117–135.

Evans, G.L. (2003) Hard branding the culture city – From Prado to Prada. *International Journal of Urban and Regional Research* 27(2), 417–440.

Evans, G.L. (2004) Cultural industry quarters – from pre-industrial to post-industrial production. In: Bell, D. and Jayne, M. (eds) *City of Quarters: Urban Villages in the Contemporary City*. Ashgate Press, Aldershot, UK, pp. 71–92.

Evans, G.L. (2005a) Mixed-use or mixed messages? *Planning in London* 54, 26–29.

Evans, G.L. (2005b) Measure for measure: evaluating the evidence of culture's contribution to regeneration. *Urban Studies* 42 (5/6), 959–984.

Evans, G.L. (2006) Branding the city – the death of city planning? In: Monclus, J. and Guardia, M. (eds) *Culture, Urbanism and Planning*. Ashgate Press, Aldershot, UK (in press).

Evans, G.L. and Foord, J. (2000) European funding of culture: promoting common culture or regional growth. *Cultural Trends* 36, 53–87.

Evans, G.L. and Shaw, S. (2001) Urban leisure and transport: regeneration effects. *Journal of Leisure Property* 1(4), 350–372.

Foord, J. (1999) Creative Hackney: reflections on hidden art. *Rising East. Journal of East London Studies* 3(2), 38–66.

Hall, C.M. (1992) *Hallmark Tourist Events: Impacts, Management, Planning.* Belhaven, London.

ICOMOS (1998) *International Cultural Tourism Charter. Managing Tourism at Places of Heritage Significance,* 8th Draft. International Council of Monuments and Sites (ICOMOS), Paris.

Jencks, M. (ed.) (1999) *The Compact City: a Sustainable Urban Form.* E & FN Spon, London.

Lasansky, D.M. and Greenwood, D.J. (eds) (2004) *Architecture and Tourism.* Berg, Oxford.

Law, C.M. (1992) Urban tourism and its contribution to economic regeneration. *Urban Studies* 29(314), 599–618.

Law, C.M. (1993) *Urban Tourism: Attracting Visitors to Large Cities.* Mansell, London.

Law, C.M. (ed.) (1996) *Tourism in Major Cities.* Routledge, London.

Lefebvre, H. (1991) *Critique of Everyday Life* (trans. Moore, J.). Verso, London.

London Borough of Islington (2004) Map of the Conservation Areas and listed buildings in Clerkenwell. London Borough of Islington, London.

Long, P. (2000) Tourism development regimes in the inner city fringe: the case of discover Islington, London. *Journal of Sustainable Tourism* 8(3), 190–206.

Looseley, D.L. (1997) *The Politics of Fun. Cultural Policy and Debate in Contemporary France.* Berg, Oxford.

Lynch, P. (2004) Urbanism: the death of Hoxton. *Icon,* London, June, 105.

Marshall, S. (ed.) (2004) New urbanism. *Built Environment* 29(3), 189–192.

National Building Museum (1998) *Building Culture Downtown: New Ways of Revitalizing the American City.* National Building Museum, Washington, DC.

ODPM (2005) *What is a Sustainable Community?* Office of the Deputy Prime Minister (ODPM), March, p. 3.

PACEC (1990) *An Evaluation of Garden Festivals.* Inner Cities Research Programme, Department of the Environment, PA Cambridge Economic Consultants (PACEC), London.

Page, S. (1995) *Urban Tourism.* Routledge, London.

Pearce, D. (1998) Tourism development in Paris: public intervention. *Annals of Tourism Research* 25(2), 457–476.

Richards, G. (ed.) (1996) *Cultural Tourism in Europe.* CAB International, Wallingford, UK.

Robinson, J. (2005) *Ordinary Cities: Between Modernity and Development.* Routledge, London.

Sassen, S. and Roost, F. (1999) The city: strategic site for the global entertainment industry. In: Judd, D.R. and Fainstein, S. (eds) *The Tourist City.* Yale University Press, New Haven, Connecticut, pp. 143–154.

Thames, R. (1999) *Clerkenwell and Finsbury Past.* Historical Publications, London.

Tyler, D., Guerrier, Y. and Roberton, M. (eds) (1998) *Managing Tourism in Cities: Policy, Process and Practice.* Wiley, Chichester, UK.

Urry, J. (1995) *Consuming Places.* Routledge, London.

UVF (1992) *Urban Villages: a Concept for Creating Mixed Use Urban Developments on a Sustainable Scale.* Urban Villages Forum (UVF), London.

VivaCity (2005) Home page. Available at: http://www.vivacity2020.org (accessed 21 November 2005).

5 Ethnoscapes as Cultural Attractions in Canadian 'World Cities'

Stephen J. Shaw

Introduction

In many North American and European cities that are gateways of immigration, ethnic 'quarters', 'enclaves' or 'neighbourhoods' are conspicuous features of the 21st century urban landscape. Particular streets and public spaces – usually on the fringe of the city centre – are gazed upon as the locus of 'exotic' commercial, religious and social practices. In some cases, the same streetscapes and thoroughfares have been home to successive waves of new migrants, the buildings adapted and reused. In recent times, some have been selected, developed and marketed with the support of city governments as new destinations for leisure and tourism consumption. Thus, they are being made accessible, safe and visually appealing to people who are generally more affluent than the local population. Places whose very names once signified the poverty of marginalized urban communities are now being promoted to appeal to visitors with sophisticated and cosmopolitan tastes.

Through such re-imaging strategies, expressions of multiculturalism in the built environment can be exploited as a picturesque backdrop, while 'ethnic' markets, festivals and other events are used to 'animate' the scene. Signifiers of ethnic and cultural difference inscribed into the urban landscape may thus assume a dual function. As 'texts' they communicate meaning between people of a minority group, but they are also 'read' by people of the dominant national culture, and in some cases international tourists. As with tourism development in less developed countries, the responses of local entrepreneurs to the varied demands of visitors may produce dissonant landscapes of multiple realities (Shaw and MacLeod, 2000; Shaw et al., 2004). Both theorists and practitioners are deeply divided over the appropriateness of developing and promoting such areas to attract high-spending visitors, and how the longer-term issues for the 'host' communities should be addressed.

This chapter considers these debates with particular reference to multicultural districts in the gateway cities of Canada, where immigration has for over two centuries been regulated by the governing elite of settlers originating from Britain and France (Québec). Districts where minority groups settled were defined and socially constructed as Chinatown, Greektown, Petite Italie, Quartier latin, and so on. The following section introduces the processes through which such places have been aestheticized and transformed into attractions in the North American and European metropolis, highlighting the significance of urban landscapes and ethnic cuisine. The mediating role of city governments is then explored with reference to leisure and tourism-led regeneration. A case study of Quartier chinois, Montréal provides the context for critical discussion of the drivers of change and initiatives that trade upon themes of diversity to add value to the place-product.

Host to Visitors from the Host Society

Immigrants adapt (as well as adapt *to*) their new urban environments in gateway cities. Where regulations allow, they may re-create the architecture of former homelands with a marked emphasis on correct design and execution, most notably in places of worship. Faithful maintenance of food preparation and customs associated with hospitality to family and friends may also constitute an important element of 'symbolic ethnicity': a nostalgic allegiance to cultural identity and the 'Old Country' (Gans, 1979). Conversely, through restaurants oriented to the tastes of customers from the dominant national culture, they may exploit familiar stereotypes. In his pioneering study of 'the roving palate' Zelinski (1985: 53–54) argues that ethnic restaurant cuisine has been an important factor in the transnationalization of North American urban culture. A welcome reprieve from workaday environments is provided, not only through the food itself, but also through exterior design, furniture, tablecloths, china, wall decorations, costumed staff and background entertainment: 'an effortless voyage into some distant enchantments'. In Valene Smith's (1989) terminology, ethnic minority restaurateurs may thus play host to visitors from the 'host society'.

Historical evidence suggests that the role of ethnic cuisine in the diffusion and acceptance of cultural diversity by mainstream North American society has been more contentious than Zelinski (1985) implies. In her longitudinal study of Chinatown in Vancouver 1875–1980, Anderson (1995) documents the social construction of the area by European settlers as a place of squalor and disease. From the city's foundation through to the Depression years, Chinese were treated as 'aliens' whose rights of citizenship were severely restricted. The area had an unsavoury reputation for its gambling and opium dens; the moral protection of European women prevented them from working as waitresses in Chinese cafés and restaurants. By the mid-1930s, however, as the economy picked up, restaurateurs in Vancouver's *Little Orient* were welcoming a rising trade from non-Chinese customers who viewed the area more positively. To encourage this trend, its merchants accentuated romantic images of Old Cathay through the building facades; their contribution to the city's Golden Jubilee celebrations in 1936 was an elaborate 'Chinese Village' (Anderson, 1995: 155–158). The official guidebook (Yip, 1936: 6) promised that the streets would be 'most artistically and becomingly decorated with . . . hundreds of Oriental splendours'. Major attractions included an ornate 24 m bamboo arch, a nine-tier pagoda and a Buddhist temple.

In the USA, the attitudes of White Anglo Saxon Protestant (WASP) society towards the inner city neighbourhoods of ethnic minorities also changed significantly over the course of the 20th century. As Lin (1998) observes, Chinatowns, Mexican barrios, Jewish and African–American '*ghettos*' – along with settlements of other minorities such as Southern Europeans – were features of an unstable 'zone-in-transition' (Burgess, 1925). Their very place names expressed the marginalization of their impoverished communities, for example in Los Angeles: *Sonora* 'Dogtown' and *Calle de los Negros* 'Nigger Alley' (Pearlstone, 1990: 72). In the 1950s and 1960s, as cities sought to modernize their downtown areas and improve motorway access, the bulldozing of low-rent non-WASP districts was prioritized. Nevertheless, as the Civil Rights and other urban social movements gathered strength and more broad-based support, such wholesale clearance was resisted (with varying success). By the 1976 Bicentennial, more inclusive attitudes prevailed, at least at Federal level, and 'ethnic heritage recovery' entered the political mainstream, with symbolic renovation of landmark buildings and the founding of museums that celebrated diversity. In New York, these included the Chinatown History Museum, the Eldridge Street Synagogue and Lower Eastside Tenement Museum; in Los Angeles, the *El Pueblo* Historical Monument and the Japanese American National Museum in Little Tokyo.

During the 1950s and 1960s, the UK government encouraged immigration from former colonies to satisfy industrial labour shortages. As Hall (1996: 79) observes, in the postcolonial city, memories of Empire are reactivated through the presence of transnational communities: a 'web of connections which have . . . never moved from "centre" to "periphery", but rather have criss-crossed the globe'. In Birmingham – former 'Workshop of the World' – interracial tensions have resurfaced periodically (cf. Rex and Moore, 1967). Nevertheless, as Henry *et al.* (2002) demonstrate, postcolonial, post-industrial Birmingham now capitalizes on the wealth of cultural industries associated with its ethnic diversity, for example British *Bhangra* music and the 'Birmingham Balti'. These are promoted as cultural assets that complement the city's flagship projects. In London's East End in the 1980s, wide media coverage was given to ugly scenes of conflict in Brick Lane, where race-hate groups attacked and intimidated the local Bangladeshi population. By 2000, however, the *Banglatown* brand was being used to promote the area's restaurants and events such as the Bengali New Year (Shaw *et al.*, 2004).

Immigration from former colonies has also transformed gateway cities in the Netherlands. Rotterdam City Council has endorsed 'City Safaris', an initiative which encourages visitors to make their way to deprived multicultural districts. Itineraries are arranged to addresses that include a centre for asylum-seekers, a *halal* butcher and several mosques. These self-guided tours are designed to challenge the visitors' preconceptions of the everyday lives of recent migrants (Biles, 2001). Although the object of their quest is in the European inner city, they may have much in common with 'ethnic tourists' who search for the 'exotic in as untouched, pristine, authentic form' as can be found (Van den Berghe, 1994 quoted in Hitchcock 1999: 17). In post-war German cities, minority neighbourhoods have developed as a consequence of particular labour requirements, rather than a colonial heritage. In West Berlin, after the Wall was erected on 1961, *Gastarbeiter* from Turkey migrated to the working class district of Kreuzberg, along with artists and young Germans avoiding military service. By the 1990s, the area had entered mainstream tourist guidebooks as the colourful bohemian quarter of the new Federal capital.

The examples given above suggest considerable variation on the underlying theme of the exoticized Other, according to the predilections and prejudices of the dominant national culture: a point emphasized by Said (1978) in his historical analysis of the Orient in the Western imagination. The fabrication of exotica to appeal to particular national cultures has expanded from art objects and the interior world restaurants into the street. At this very local level, minority entrepreneurs have played an important role in creating communities that 'sit astride political borders and that, in a very real sense, are "neither here nor there" but in both places simultaneously' (Portes, 1997: 3). They have transformed everyday features of the North American and European metropolis. In more recent times, city governments have actively supported this process and promoted such areas as 'ethnic cultural quarters' (Taylor, 2000; Chan, 2004). It is therefore important to consider the relationship between global cultural flows and the policies and changing practices of urban governance.

Cultural Flows, 'Ethnoscapes' and Urban Governance

Arjun Appadurai (1997: 32) – social anthropologist and influential commentator on globalization – discusses the 'complex, overlapping, disjunctive order' of the 'new cultural economy'. Like Hall (1996), he argues that global cultural flows can no longer be understood in terms of existing centre–periphery models. In exploring such disjunctures, he highlights the concept of *ethnoscapes*: the landscapes of those who 'constitute the shifting world in which we live: tourists, immigrants, refugees, exiles, guest workers, and other moving groups' (Appadurai, 1997: 33). In a later work, Apparurai (2001: 5) expands upon the interplay of mobility, stability and governance in a world 'characterised by floating populations, transnational politics within national borders, and mobile configurations of technology and expertise'. The rising 'world cities' of Canada, and their inner urban ethnoscapes, provide some pertinent illustrations of these concepts as they position themselves to attract footloose industries, creative knowledge clusters, highly educated residents and discerning visitors.

The city governments of Canada's three largest metropolitan centres – Toronto, Montréal and Vancouver – have been the main receptors of immigration. For the past half-century, successive civic leaders of all three have placed a very high priority, not only on competing successfully with other metropolitan centres in North America, but on attracting inward movement of capital, people and knowledge spanning all continents. Distinct phases are, however, apparent: stages that correspond fairly closely with Kotler *et al.*'s (1993) model chronicling the evolution of place-marketing in post-war North America. In the 1950s and 1960s, city governments preoccupied with crude civic boosterism lured industrialists and other inward investors. Such 'hard sell' place promotion emphasized the provision of hard infrastructure, fiscal incentives and the supply of sites for development for new plants that would provide employment and contribute to local tax revenues.

In the 1970s and 1980s, 'smoke-stack chasing' gave way to a multiplicity of goals, including an increasing concern with urban amenity. Informed by analysis of market positioning, cities began to adopt a more selective approach to encourage growth sectors that would generate jobs without adverse consequences for the urban environment. A third phase then emerged in the early 1990s, as they began to develop more sophisticated place-marketing strategies tailored to specific audiences such as entrepreneurs in knowledge-based industries, immigrants with managerial and professional skills, and high yield/low impact tourists. Their efforts began to focus on niche products that create value for target customers. In this context, a premium was placed on a distinctive and vibrant ambience for city-centre living, as well as a business-friendly and stable workforce, free from social and inter-ethnic tensions (Mason, 2003; Shaw, 2003).

In Canada, as in the USA (Judd and Fainstein, 1999), municipalities have striven to create an attractive built environment and a cohesive urban society against a background of falling Federal and Provincial transfer payments. According to Porter's (1995: 57) influential thesis, urban governance must capitalize on the inherent strategic advantages of inner city areas, rather than depend on government subsidy. For competitive markets for inward investment, desirable residents and visitors operate *within* as well as between cities. Public intervention should be minimized and municipalities should work in harmony with market forces to build upon the true competitive strengths of inner city firms, especially their proximity to downtowns, entertainment and tourist attractions.

Further key advantages are identified as low-cost labour and the entrepreneurial drive of ethnic minority businesses. Through their symbiotic relationship with the Central Business District, inner city ethnoscapes can thus be seen as crucibles for wealth-creation that will benefit the city as a whole.

Neo-liberalism and the Canadian Cosmopolis

Municipalities in Canada have adopted regeneration strategies that reflect this neo-liberal model. Intervention through the 'bureaucracy' of city governments is eschewed, while every encouragement is given to entrepreneur-led, 'self-help' initiatives at the local or neighbourhood level. With suitable place-marketing support, minority business enclaves can build on their existing social capital and business networks to rejuvenate themselves. The astute response of minority entrepreneurs to business opportunity will thus provide badly needed, if low-paid jobs, helping to reduce local unemployment, especially among low-skilled residents. Some pump-priming through targeted public intervention may be required to create the necessary confidence for private investors to upgrade the built environment. The visitor appeal of the main thoroughfares will thus be developed and enhanced. Measures will generally include the creation of safe and attractive pedestrian routes from the city centre and public transport, parking and loading for traders, improved street lighting as well as business advice, training and marketing support. The staging and promotion of events may also be used to draw visitors to the locality.

Enabling legislation enacted by Canadian Provincial governments has encouraged a 'self-help' approach that builds upon the structures and resources of local business associations. In his discussion of urban planning and multiculturalism, Quadeer (1994) commends the Business Improvement Area (BIA) scheme in the Province of Ontario for its success as a tool for revitalizing ethnic business enclaves. With the consent of the majority of commercial property owners, a compulsory supplementary BIA levy is collected by the municipality, but managed by a non-profit board of local businesses. The levy can be spent on hiring staff and activities that include place promotion, events, beautification, street furniture and other improvements to the spaces between buildings. Quadeer highlights the role of BIAs and other business-led initiatives in celebrating urban cultural identities. However, he notes that in Ottawa's 'Chinatown' identities were less straightforward as other (non-Chinese) groups reside in the locality. Planning guidelines therefore had to stress the 'multicultural identity of the area, instead of affirming it as the turf of any one group. Its design guidelines recognise cultural elements and allow for their architectural expression'.

In Toronto, where the BIA model was first developed, the appeal of the city's 'neighbourhoods' has been greatly enhanced through upgrading of the public realm, instigated and managed by commercial property owners. For example, in *Greektown on Danforth*, the streets are identified by Greek signage; public spaces are beautified by classical statues, other public art and stylized street furniture. Toronto's downtown 'Chinatown', once the city's Jewish Quarter, was narrowly saved from destruction in the early 1970s when an elevated expressway was proposed. The area has since been developed as a major attraction, through investment directed by a strong and well-established Chinese business association. The attractions of these areas on the fringe of downtown are described in a recent guidebook *Ethnic Toronto: a Complete Guide to the Many Faces and Cultures of Toronto* (Kasher, 1997). The would-be tourist is introduced to a place transformed in the past 30 years from 'one of the most narrow-minded and uncosmopolitan of the British colonial cities' (Kasher, 1997: ix–xi):

> Toronto has become an international microcosm of different cultures in its neighbourhoods. You can buy products from around the world in ethnic speciality shops, as well as find special foods, delight in unique and exotic entertainment, and just enjoy the ambience of being in a different world for a little while as you walk through neighbourhoods like Corso Italia or Little India.

Strategies for leisure and tourism-led urban 'makeovers' to regenerate multicultural neighbourhoods in the inner city have, however, attracted considerable scepticism, especially in the USA. With particular reference to initiatives in Baltimore and Detroit, Judd (1999: 53) highlights the development of 'Disneyfied Latin Quarters' where 'tourist bubbles are more likely to contribute to racial, ethnic and class tensions than to an impulse towards local community'. Urban tourism may lead to deepening alienation of those among local residents as it may lead to displacement of established low-rent residents and small businesses (Zukin, 1991, 1999). In their discussion of the regeneration strategies of post-industrial North American cities, Smith and Deksen (2003) concur that capital and culture have been interwoven in 'generalised gentrification' that excludes the urban poor and creates new cityscapes to accommodate the lifestyles of affluent consumers.

It can be argued, nevertheless, that in Canada, city governments have developed policies and practices that remain distinctive from their counterparts in the USA. In all three of the major gateway cities, urban social movements in the 1970s and 1980s led to the election of influential Councils that rejected the doctrine of 'growth at any cost'. Today, city governments across the political spectrum are acutely aware of the vulnerability of low-income and ethnic minority residents to the effects of redevelopment and rising real estate values in inner city areas. Issues relating to gentrification have been a major focus of debate in municipal politics, and some civic leaders have taken a strong position in support of zoning and other measures to protect communities from intrusion and displacement. The City of Vancouver – an important gateway between North America and the Pacific Rim – received a considerable boost in the mid-1990s from immigration and investment from South-east Asia, especially Hong Kong. This large-scale development of redundant industrial and waterfront land has been achieved within a discretionary though powerful regulatory framework and release of municipally-owned land that has produced important community gains, especially the provision of low-rent housing (Mason, 2003).

Montréal's Chinatown as Cultural Attraction

After a long period of highly centralized, 'growth machine politics' from the mid-1950s to the mid-1980s, Ville de Montréal has also adopted a distinctive approach to cultural integration, planning and regeneration (Shaw, 2003). The reformist policies of the Montréal Citizens' Movement-led Council (1986–94) represented a new departure for the city. There was a strong emphasis on reconciliation, not only across the Francophone and Anglophone *solitudes* of the city, but also inclusion and active participation of residents from other long-established communities, notably Greek, Italian, Jewish and Chinese Montréalers. Neighbourhoods around the downtown area were now home to many low-income households that included a rich diversity of cultural and ethnic identities, for example new migrants from Vietnam. Mayor Doré (Ville de Montréal 1992: iii) introduced a new City Plan, which was to be: 'both an instrument to be used to improve Montréalers' quality of life as well as a social contract uniting them in a common goal: the economic and cultural development of our city'.

Montréal's *Quartier chinois*, which developed in the late 19th century in the liminal zone between the Francophone and Anglophone sectors of the city was a notable illustration of the new approach. As in many other Chinatowns in North America (Ng, 1999; Guan, 2002; Yan, 2002), it had lost customers and merchants as new car-oriented Chinese shopping and entertainment malls were built away from the traditional downtown core. This decline was further exacerbated by the isolating effects of an urban motorway, development on adjacent land and the urban blight that followed. Within the district, vacant lots and derelict buildings were visible signs of low investment. Following lobbying from various organizations of Chinese residents, merchants and voluntary societies, a 'Chinatown Development Consultative Committee' was set up by Ville de Montréal in 1990. *Inter alia*, this established certain principles for development. Incorporated in the City Masterplan for *secteur Ville-Marie* (city centre), the key issues identified by the local Chinese community were to:

1. Define the boundaries of Chinatown;
2. Produce clear land use and design guidelines within this area;
3. Improve its public spaces, and action on related issues, especially parking, rubbish collection and street cleansing.

By the late 1990s, the beginnings of recovery were apparent. Developments in downtown

and the adjacent *Quartier international*, where prestigious headquarter offices have located, were creating significant opportunities for Chinatown merchants, especially in business and conference-related tourism. The city planners recognized, nevertheless, that without appropriate management of the area as an urban 'visitor destination', an upswing would also bring problems of traffic, parking and intrusion by visitors into the everyday life of the community, as well as pressure on residential accommodation through rising land values. In accordance with the guidelines of the Masterplan, the 'Chinatown Development Plan' was adopted to provide a framework for action:

> so that all efforts can be channelled in the same direction, and it is hoped, stimulate the growth of Chinatown and truly reflect the ever-growing importance of the Chinese community in Montréal and Québec society.
>
> (Ville de Montréal, 1998: 13)

The over-arching aim of the Chinatown Development Plan was to consolidate the commercial core of *Quartier chinois*. Where necessary, land use (zoning) controls would be used to protect the character of the neighbourhoods to the east and west from incompatible activities, and to prevent displacement. Improvements to existing residential buildings would also be encouraged, and it would be necessary to rationalize access, parking and delivery times.

Improvements carried out under the Action Plan have included extension and upgrading of the public realm: refurbishing the pedestrian mall and widening pavements; murals, street trees and landscaping; conservation of heritage buildings; and the creation of a new Sun Yat Sen Park for the local community. As in other cities, the entrances to the *Quartier chinois* are marked by impressive gateways, and these have been complemented by further 'traditional' and contemporary public art. The Plan stressed that as well as being an attraction for all tourists, the *Quartier chinois* would continue to serve as a venue for a broad range of trading, social and religious activities for the wider Chinese population, and a potent symbol of their identity, since:

> it provides a major point where Chinese in Québec can meet those from other areas in the north-eastern part of North America

(New York, Boston, Toronto), as well as other Quebécers. Chinatown is thus the heart of commercial and cultural exchanges within the community itself, and an eloquent statement of the dense, thriving urban culture that the Administration wishes to promote within downtown areas of Montréal.

(Ville de Montréal, 1998: 11)

Chinese businesses engaged in servicing the city's expanding visitor economy are thus regarded as prime movers in the regeneration of their locality. Nevertheless, Ville de Montréal rejects the notion that the interests of the area and of the city as a whole are best served by freeing landowners and traders from the 'burdens' of regulation and control by the municipality. Nor does it accept that improvements to streets and other public spaces should be financed, planned and managed by local business associations alone. Indeed, the pressures to redevelop sites associated with the expansion of the nearby city centre are seen as an important rationale for more stringent zoning, traffic and parking controls to ensure that Chinatown continues as a living mixed-use neighbourhood.

Conclusion

The cases discussed above do not suggest a single or simple type of place-consumption in ethnic quarters. First and foremost, established and often historic ethnoscapes – such as the downtown Chinatowns of Montréal, Vancouver and Toronto – continue to function as commercial, cultural and social hubs, not only for the 'neighbourhood', but also for visiting members of the minority group across the city-region, North America and overseas. Such areas may also appeal to members of the dominant national culture and international tourists. In any given city, such visitors will have diverse motivations and requirements. Some are attracted by colourful street markets, ethnic cuisine, festivals, world music and other performance art; some by the bars, clubs and late-night entertainment in quasi-exotic settings. Recent studies have highlighted the discerning tastes of 'cultural omnivores' for whom an appreciation of contemporary, fine ethnic cuisine is regarded as a marker of distinction (Warde, 1995). Some are curious to 'discover' the

heritage of immigrant communities. Some quest for knowledge and understanding of other contemporary cultures.

Inner city municipalities have generally inherited worn-out and badly maintained public infrastructure. This, together with low levels of private investment contributes to a general air of neglect that contrasts sharply with the bright lights of the nearby city centre. In most cases, the majority of the 'host' population remains poor, with high levels of underemployment. From a neo-liberal perspective, welfare dependency does not provide a sustainable solution to the entrenched problems of the inner city. In place of subsidy from governments and municipalities, it is argued that removal of bureaucratic obstacles will enable minority businesses to develop niches in heterogeneous, post-industrial markets. If such entrepreneurial talent can be unlocked, business confidence in the locality will increase, encouraging restoration and care of urban landscapes. Astute responses to market opportunities that include a demand for exotic goods and services will thus create a virtuous circle. If they are willing to adapt to the demands of the new, globalized urban economy, inner city residents will find employment that compensates for decline in older trades.

According to this paradigm, the role of city government is to capture local benefits from the global ebb and flow of capital, people and their cultures so that the urban centre becomes a node of lucrative trans-national networks. As demonstrated in the BIA initiatives in Ontario, 'self-help' initiatives at the micro-level led by local associations of minority businesses can greatly enhance municipal investment and promotion. A mutually beneficial relationship is nurtured between knowledge industries located in the city centre and a visitor economy rooted in adjacent multicultural districts. Important components of such regeneration strategies are physical accessibility and improvements to urban design to make the public realm of public spaces attractive and safe for casual strollers. If such transformations are successful, inner city ethnoscapes will no longer be regarded as 'revenue sinks' that drain local taxes and discourage inward investors. Instead, they are promoted as cultural attractions that 'celebrate diversity', and complement the cosmopolitan 'buzz' of the nearby city Central Business District.

As with the internal space of restaurants, exotic motifs of the streetscape are accentuated to create an enclave conducive to leisure and tourism consumption. Critics may argue that this packaging of 'a racialized construct tuned to multicultural consumerism' (Jacobs, 1996: 100) denies the very essence of identity and place. A simplified, 'monocultural' approach helps to create a strong unifying theme that is easy to communicate, but the imagery projected to visitors may misrepresent complex and shifting ethnic geographies, as demonstrated in the proposals for Ottawa's 'Chinatown'. There are also justifiable concerns that formulaic development may reinforce rather than challenge stereotypes. As with the proliferation of festival malls, they may come to resemble 'glocalized' versions of a universal brand, with little sense of place or time (Hannington, 1998; Neill, 2004; Bell and Jayne, 2004). Ironically, the sign posting of difference may produce an anodyne and relatively homogenous culture of consumption, disconnected from the social life of the local population.

The successful development of visitor economies and cultural industries in disadvantaged, multicultural districts pays tribute to the active role of minority entrepreneurs as active agents of regeneration. The process may help to develop social capital and foster pride in areas where low self-esteem has, for many years, been reinforced by the negative perceptions of outsiders. However, few can predict with any certainty how it will impact on the everyday lives of local residents and small businesses. The attention of visitors may become intrusive. An evening economy may bring problems of noise and antisocial behaviour. In some cases, as wealthy visitors enter a relatively poor neighbourhood, it is associated with rising street crime and disorder, drug dealing and prostitution. Without interventions to ensure the continued availability of affordable accommodation – especially zoning, rent controls and social housing provision – the rising property values associated with gentrification may drive out low-income residents.

If city governments are to mediate between the tides of global capitalism and the sustainable regeneration of urban neighbourhoods, a balanced and continuing dialogue with the diverse communities of people who live and work in inner city areas must inform their strategies. The interventionist approach demonstrated in Montréal's *Quartier chinois* underlines the wisdom and long-term benefits of including a wider range of local stakeholders in plan formulation and management. It suggests the need to strengthen rather than relax regulation; it highlights the desirability of benefits such as public space and facilities for local community use. This model of cultural tourism development acknowledges the profound uncertainties over the impact of an emerging visitor economy, and the importance of the participation and goodwill of residents and small businesses. Without such involvement and the development of mutual trust, an emerging visitor economy may promote discord and conflict rather than harmony and cooperation.

References

Anderson, K. (1995) *Vancouver's Chinatown: Racial Discourse in Canada, 1875–1980.* McGill-Queen's University Press, Montreal and Kingston.

Appadurai, A. (1997) *Modernity at Large: Cultural Dimensions of Globalisation.* University of Minnesota Press, Minneapolis, Minnesota.

Appadurai, A. (ed.) (2001) *Globalization.* Duke University Press, Durham, North Carolina.

Bell, D. and Jayne, M. (eds) (2004) *City of Quarters: Urban Villages in the Contemporary City.* Ashgate, Aldershot, UK.

Biles, A. (2001) A day-trip to the urban jungle. *Regeneration and Renewal* 17 August, 14–15.

Burgess, E. (1925) The growth of the city: an introduction to a research project. In: Park, R.E., Burgess, E. and McKenzie, R. (eds) *The City.* University of Chicago Press, Chicago, Illinois, pp. 47–62 [republished 1967].

Chan, W. (2004) Finding Chinatown: ethnocentrism and urban planning. In: Bell, D. and Jayne, M. (eds) *City of Quarters: Urban Villages in the Contemporary City.* Ashgate, Aldershot, UK, pp. 173–187.

Gans, H. (1979) Symbolic ethnicity: the future of ethnic groups and cultures in America. *Ethnic and Racial Studies* 2, 1–20.

Guan, J. (2002) Ethnic consciousness arises on facing spatial threats to the Philadelphia Chinatown. In: Erdentug, A. and Colombijn, F. (eds) *Urban Ethnic Encounters: the Spatial Consequences*. Routledge, London, pp. 126–141.

Hall, C. (1996) Histories, empires and the post-colonial monument. In: Chambers, I. and Curtis, L. (eds) *The Post-colonial Question*. Routledge, London, pp. 65–77.

Hannington, J. (1998) *Fantasy City: Pleasure and Profit in the Postmodern Metropolis*. Routledge, London.

Henry, N., McEwan, C. and Pollard, J.S. (2002) Globalisation from below: Birmingham – postcolonial workshop of the world? *Area* 34(2), 117–127.

Hitchcock, M. (1999) Tourism and ethnicity: situational perspectives. *International Journal of Tourism Research* 1, 17–32.

Jacobs, J.M. (1996) *Edge of Empire: Postcolonialism and the City*. Routledge, London.

Judd, D. (1999) Constructing the tourist bubble. In: Judd, D. and Fainstein, S. (eds) *The Tourist City*. Yale University Press, New Haven, Connecticut, pp. 35–53.

Judd, D. and Fainstein, S. (eds) (1999) *The Tourist City*. Yale University Press, New Haven, Connecticut.

Kasher, R. (1997) *Ethnic Toronto: a Complete Guide to the Many Faces and Cultures of Toronto*. Passport Books, Glencoe, Illinois.

Kotler, P., Haider, D. and Rein, I. (1993) *Marketing Places: Attracting Investment, Industry, and Tourism to Cities, States and Nations*. The Free Press, New York.

Lin, J. (1998) Globalization and the revalorizing of ethnic places in immigration gateway cities. *Urban Affairs Review* 34(2), 313–339.

Mason, M. (2003) Urban regeneration rationalities and quality of life: comparative notes from Toronto, Montreal and Vancouver. *British Journal of Canadian Studies* 16(2), 348–362.

Neill, W. (2004) *Urban Planning and Cultural Identity*. Routledge, London.

Ng, W.C. (1999) *The Chinese in Vancouver 1945–80: the Pursuit of Identity and Power*. UBC Press, Vancouver.

Pearlstone, Z. (1990) *Ethnic Los Angeles*. Hillcrest, Los Angeles, California.

Porter, M. (1995) The competitive advantage of the inner city. *Harvard Business Review* May–June, pp. 55–71.

Portes, A. (1997) Globalization from below: the rise of transnational communities. Transnational Communities Programme, WPTC-98-01, Oxford: University of Oxford and Princeton University. Available at: www.transcomm.ox.ac.uk (accessed 5 July 2005).

Quadeer, M. (1994) Urban planning and multiculturalism in Ontario, Canada. In: Thomas, H. and Krishnarayan, V. (eds) *Race Equality and Planning*. Avebury, Aldershot, UK, pp. 187–200.

Rex, J. and Moore, R. (1967) *Race, Community and Conflict: a Study of Sparkbrook*. Oxford University Press, Oxford.

Said, E. (1978) *Orientalism*. Routledge and Kegan Paul, London.

Shaw, S. (2003) The Canadian 'world city' and sustainable downtown revitalisation: messages from Montréal 1962–2002. *British Journal of Canadian Studies* 16(2), 363–375.

Shaw, S. and MacLeod, N. (2000) Creativity and conflict: cultural tourism in London's city fringe. *Tourism, Culture and Communication* 2(3), 165–175.

Shaw, S., Bagwell, S. and Karmowska, J. (2004) Ethnoscapes as spectacle: reimaging multicultural districts as new destinations for leisure and tourism consumption. *Urban Studies* 41(10), 1983–2000.

Smith, N. and Deksen, J. (2003) Urban regeneration: gentrification as global urban strategy. In: Douglas, S. (ed.) *Every Last Building on 100 West Hastings*. Arsenal Pulp Press, Vancouver.

Smith, V.L. (ed.) (1989) *Hosts and Guests: the Anthropology of Tourism*. University of Pennsylvania Press, Philadelphia, Pennsylvania.

Taylor, I. (2000) European ethnoscapes and urban redevelopment: the return of Little Italy in 21st century Manchester. *City* 4(1), 27–42.

Van den Burghe, P.L. (1994) *The Quest for the Other: Ethnic Tourism in San Cristobal, Mexico*. University of Washington Press, Seattle, Washington.

Ville de Montréal (1992) *City Plan: Master Plan of the Ville-Marie District*. Ville de Montréal Service de l'urbanisme, Montréal.

Ville de Montréal (1998) *Chinatown Development Plan*. Ville de Montréal Service de l'urbanisme, Montréal.

Warde, A. (1995) *Consumption, Food and Taste: Cultural Antinomies and Commodity Culture*. Sage, London.

Yan, A. (2002) *Revitalization Challenges for Vancouver's Chinatown*. Carnegie Community Action Project, Vancouver.

Yip, Q. (1936) *Vancouver's Chinatown, Vancouver Golden Jubilee*. Pacific Printers, Vancouver.

Zelinski, W. (1985) The roving palate: North America's ethnic restaurant cuisines. *Geoforum* 16(1), 51–71.

Zukin, S. (1991) *Landscapes of Power: from Detroit to Disney World*. University of California Press, Berkley, California.

Zukin, S. (1999) Urban lifestyles: diversity and standardisation in spaces of consumption. *Urban Studies* 35(5–6), 825–839.

6 (Re)Creating Culture through Tourism: Black Heritage Sites in New Jersey

Daina Cheyenne Harvey

Introduction

The tendency to use tourism as a means to regenerate the space of the city has been well documented (Judd and Fainstein, 1999; Thorns, 2002; Judd, 2003; Miles and Miles, 2004). Recently, problems that stem from attempts at urban regeneration, whether due to diverting monies away from the local infrastructure and towards a visitor class (Eiseniger, 2000, 2003; Perry, 2003), merging tourist development and cultural authenticity (McIntosh and Prentice, 1999; Apostolakis, 2003; Chhabra et al., 2003), or simply the commodification of heritage through tourism (Taylor, 2001; Apostolakis, 2003; Miles and Miles, 2004) have captured the attention of academics. Less examined, however, have been attempts to regenerate culture through tourism and the ensuing difficulties in re-presenting spaces of contested history or multiple histories as heritage (Smith, 2003).

Whereas academic work on tourism has struggled with the dichotomization of production and consumption (Ateljevic, 2000; Ateljevic and Doorne, 2003), work on regeneration has struggled with conceptualizing its main term. Indeed the two, tourism and regeneration, are often conflated. Regeneration has been conceptualized both as the (re)creation of niche villages within the city, whether based on urbanity, ethnicity or sexuality, to foster a sense of place for (potential) residents (Bell and Jayne, 2004) and

as the construction of flagship enterprises which come to define or symbolize a city for tourists (Law, 2002). Part of the coalescing of these terms is due to the prevalence of understanding regeneration from a planning or consumption perspective. Although it has been noted that attempts at regeneration can potentially exacerbate existing social inequalities (Parkinson et al., 1988), rarely has regeneration itself been problematized or even examined from the perspective of the marginalized communities that regeneration schemes are supposed to benefit. Still less examined have been attempts at regeneration where the basis of regeneration has been contested. Thus this chapter attempts to go beyond the dichotomization of these perspectives by examining the politicized acts of commemorating space and place in historically marginalized communities.

This chapter focuses on the problems of regenerating minority culture through tourism and the re-imagineering of place. In particular, I concentrate on the difficulties in interpreting and commemorating spaces of dissonant heritage and on a number of questions, including, how do we physically commemorate minority heritage spaces that are already commemorated by the dominant culture? Also, is it possible to regenerate the culture of marginalized groups through tourism or does tourism further complicate the relationship between heritage and history? Finally, can cultural regeneration occur if we fail to fully acknowledge the past and only commemorate selected aspects of heritage? I look at attempts in New Jersey, specifically Burlington County, to regenerate Black culture through commemoration and tourism.

Problems of Commemoration, Heritage and Identity

The nexus of commemoration, heritage and identity is complex. David Blight has recently argued that the American Civil War is commemorated as the enduring struggle against racial oppression and for racial equality (2001). In an equally persuasive effort, Barry Schwartz, arguing that 'commemoration often insinuates itself into and distorts history' (2004: 63), uses Blight's text to show how society has misremembered both Lincoln (Schwartz and Schuman, 2005) and the Gettysburg Address (Schwartz, 2004). For Schwartz the Gettysburg Address commemorates the American Civil War as a struggle for democracy and national unity and not as Blight and others have argued as a precursor to the civil rights movement. Schwartz maintains that as our need to commemorate events, texts, or places changes, so does our memory (commemoration). The Blight and Schwartz exchange is interesting in and of itself, but also because of its relationship to tourism and cultural regeneration.

Athinodoros Chronis has recently written on how the past is constructed to suit the needs of the present. In his ethnographic study on Gettysburg, Chronis notes that national culture is regenerated by the tourists themselves to fill the contemporary desires of patriotism and national unity offered by the Gettysburg storyscape (2005). At Gettysburg a national culture is regenerated by revisiting and recreating the storyscape. Although such an attempt is futile, as tourists encounter the storyscape with varied levels of historical knowledge and for multiple purposes, for Chronis, historic sites become a 'praxis of poesis through which cultural meaning is created' (2005: 402). Tourism thus becomes a tool by which to study cultural production and the transformations in the meaning(s) of culture.

Bruner (2004) similarly shows us how cultural meaning is (re)created to remake or re-imagine

a particular space and identity. His focus is on New Salem, the space that is promoted for tourists as the place that transformed Lincoln into the statesman that he is remembered for being. Bruner shows that not only was the space of New Salem consciously re-imagineered by the locals to promote an identity that would facilitate selling the town to tourists, but that this particular act of commemoration greatly changed the identity of Lincoln and the heritage of those living in New Salem (Bruner, 2004).

Taken together, Schwartz, Blight, Chronis, and Bruner, portray the dilemmas inherent to commemorating virtually the same object and how the act of commemoration can question how we remember the past. What is missing, however, is an analysis of the contested act of commemoration and how re-imagineering space for tourists produces contemporary dissonant claims to that space. In other words, in the case of Gettysburg and New Salem commemoration is seen as univocal and monological, while what is being commemorated may result in multiple interpretations of culture, none the less it is the same act of commemoration. Consequently, for the tourist, the act of commemoration and the cultural meaning of the space is not one of dissonance, but fluidity. While tourists may approach these spaces with a particular sense of identity and heritage, because the landscape/storyscape offers a single dominant commemoration the cultural meaning of the space is not contested.

Both Paul Shackel (2003) and Diane Barthel (1996) note the rush to commemorate space as important for historical identity. Immediately after the Civil War acts and agencies to commemorate the victory of the North and to regenerate the culture of the South were initiated throughout the USA. These efforts were instigated to claim the landscape (Shackel, 2003) and to avoid negotiations on the past (Lowenthal, 1998). However, as Shackel notes '[t]he meaning of sacred sites on the American landscape is continually being negotiated and reconstructed' (2003: 209).

The reason for the reconstruction and negotiation of not only the American landscape but also the national culture has been the attempt to incorporate the culture of groups that have traditionally been marginalized from the production of heritage spaces. Thus unlike Gettysburg and New Salem, many spaces of heritage that are promoted for tourist consumption offer dissonant cultural images and lead to interpretations that contradict the dominant group's hold on the cultural landscape. In his epilogue Paul Shackel describes a number of approaches to challenge the dominant group's hold on interpreting the cultural landscape that is built for tourist consumption (2003). While Shackel provides several strategies for marginal groups to re-present their heritage or history (where history is defined as examinations of selected aspects of the past and heritage is the contemporary use of history) (Graham et al., 2000 in Smith, 2003), what he fails to consider are sites where both the dominant and the marginalized groups fail to fully commemorate the past.

Representations of contested spaces for tourist consumption are usually dichotomized into existing commemorations and those that challenge the traditional representation of the space. Whether it is the attempt to differentiate Cornish and Anglican heritage in Cornwall that has resulted in the vandalism of tourist signs owned by the English (Hale, 2001), the exclusion of Palestinians in commemorating Israeli heritage sites (Bauman, 1995), the contestation between promoters of communist heritage sites in Central and Eastern Europe and those engaged in the construction of a post-communist identity (Light, 2000), or the symbolic deflection of African-Americans on southern plantations in the USA (Eichstedt and Small, 2002), commemoration of the landscape is usually seen as a struggle between groups with opposing ideologies. While some of this contestation has been worked out during the time of what Kammen (1991) calls the heritage phenomenon, we have not given adequate attention to instances where both groups eschew the past and attempt to commemorate a narrow version of a heritage space or where this carefully delimited celebration of the past has been used as a mechanism for cultural regeneration.

Black Culture and Regeneration in New Jersey

New Jersey is framed as a space of freedom and abolition. A recent article on New Jersey's involvement in the Underground Railroad, *Steal Away, Steal Away . . . a Guide to the Underground Railroad in New Jersey* (Wright, 2002),

inspired a 12 day commemorative march replicating paths connecting sites along the Underground Railroad. Concerning the march, then Secretary of State Regena Thomas said 'I would like New Jersey to be the home for a museum dedicated to the Underground Railroad' (Magyar and Martinez, 2002). This comment is noteworthy for two reasons. First, by using the indefinite article 'a', Thomas ignores that an Underground Railroad Museum already exists in Ohio. Second, by using the definite article 'the', as in 'the home', she implicitly suggests that New Jersey should specifically, naturally be the place for such a museum.

New Jersey has recently taken a number of steps to promote tourism. In addition to 'Celebrate New Jersey' the 2005 annual statewide festival (actually 2005 marks its first year), the niche segmentation of the tourist industry through the successful establishment of Eco-Tourism and New Jersey Lighthouse guided tours, the acknowledgement of The Red Bank Jazz and Blues Festival and the Cape May Food and Wine Festival as 'Top 100' events for 2005 by the American Bus Association (the trade association for the motorcoach industry), the New Jersey Commerce, Economic Growth and Tourism Commission has highlighted its African-American heritage for the last 5 years. The celebration and marketing of its African-American heritage through the *New Jersey's African American Visitors Guide* has, according to the Commission, been the most successful in promoting tourism (New Jersey Commerce, Economic Growth and Tourism Commission, 2005: 1). While the content of the booklet is virtually identical from year to year, each year the guide promotes less of New Jersey's general tourist attractions and more of New Jersey's Black tourist attractions; the 2005 theme is 'The African American Family Reunion' which borrows heavily from 'Reunions Master Plan for a Successful Family Reunion' (New Jersey Commerce, Economic Growth and Tourism Commission, 2005). The *Guide* encourages visitors to 'enjoy New Jersey's African American heritage' (New Jersey Commerce, Economic Growth and Tourism Commission, 2004) by visiting particular museums and sites where 'New Jersey's African American history comes alive' (New Jersey Commerce, Economic Growth and Tourism Commission, 2005). While the booklet does feature typical tourist attractions such as taking in a baseball game, shopping at malls and golfing, the booklet primarily focuses on Black cultural and heritage attractions in each of New Jersey's six tourism regions.

Visiting the Commission's and other historical societies' recommendations, Secretary of State Thomas's remarks are understandable. Most of the places marked for tourist consumption are spots on the Underground Railroad. Despite, as Giles Wright, New Jersey's primary authority on Black history, has suggested, that only 1% of all slaves escaped the South through the Underground Railroad (UGRR) and that most of the sites commemorated as UGRR stops in New Jersey are fictitious (1998), the number of commemorated UGRR stops increases each year. Many of the tourist attractions are Algeresque. The Peter Johnson House in Morristown is commemorated as one of the first homes built in the state by a freed slave. Likewise commemorated are the Peter Mott House and Museum in Lawnside (one of the first free Black farmers and businessmen and one of the few Black-run UGRR sites) and the Heath Farm in Middletown (one of the first free Black farms). These heritage spaces act as points of origin for the Black community. That is, these spaces mark the beginning of the storyscape, what comes before is ignored or denied.

The booklet and the efforts at promoting New Jersey's Black culture for tourists have also led to a regeneration of Black culture in New Jersey. Various historical societies and associations have focused on Black heritage in their collections and exhibits. In addition, several spaces important for Black heritage have been placed on the 'Endangered Historic Sites' by Preservation New Jersey and a number of other sites have been extensively developed. Other places in New Jersey have attempted to re-present themselves simultaneously to tourists and residents as heritage places for African-Americans. Most of these spaces, however, have been re-imagined as to sever the connection with slavery, which in light of New Jersey's past, is troubling.

The role that New Jersey played in the 'peculiar institution' has often been minimized; Watson (2002) notes that the proportion of the population enslaved in New Jersey has often been undercounted by over 100%. New Jersey more so than any other northern state, with the exception of New York, encouraged the importation of slaves (Lyght, 1978; Wright, 1988; Harris, 2004). Despite the assumption that slavery was abolished comparatively early in the state's colonial history, New Jersey was the last of the northern states to fully abolish slavery and actually entered the Civil War as a supplier of slaves to the South (Pingeon, 1991). Not only has the history of slavery been forgotten in New Jersey, what Melish (2000) calls the 'disowning of slavery', but the role New Jersey played in the abolitionist movement has been greatly exaggerated (Magyar, 2002).

Dunkerhook, in Paramus, for example, in oral tradition was an extensive slave community. Recently, however, Lutins (2002) has argued against oral tradition and local history. Using historical documents he cites Dunkerhook as home to one of the first free African-American communities in New Jersey. According to Lutins, the impoverished condition of the Black community in general and their low social status contributes to the belief that residents of Dunkerhook were enslaved. Lawnside likewise has recently transformed its history. Lawnside was initially used by enslaved African-Americans who rented the land to grow crops to supplement the food that their owners provided for them. Today Lawnside's founding is attributed to free Blacks and celebrated on the fourth Saturday in June as 'Heritage Day' (it was originally celebrated on 4 July but failed to attract supporters and later changed to 19 June but because the significance of the date was widely unknown it was changed again). Today both Dunkerhook and Lawnside are commemorated for tourists as places where African-Americans began their struggle for freedom and racial equality. While it is true that both communities served in that capacity, the history of slavery has been removed from the storyscape and as such regenerates an artificial past. Perhaps, though, the most troubling attempt in New Jersey at cultural regeneration through tourism can be found in Burlington County.

Burlington County

Burlington County was selected as a case study because the city of Burlington is presented as the 'abolitionist city', it is the site of the first Black presence and first all-Black community in

New Jersey (Wright, 1988) and is actively promoted for African-American tourists (Wright, 1998). Burlington also represents an interesting example for two other reasons. First, Burlington County differs from most areas that are undertaking expansive attempts at cultural regeneration because most of the sites presented for tourists are not materially commemorated or if commemorated are marked and preserved for reasons other than the sites' association with Black heritage. Second, Burlington County warrants examination as it engages in what Melish (2000) terms the disowning of slavery. That is, by only re-presenting sites of abolitionism for tourists, Burlington County avoids sites involving thanatourism (Dann, 1998; Dann and Season, 2001) or dissonant heritage (Tunbridge and Ashworth, 1996), thus complicating the already troubled relationship between heritage and history (Hewison, 1987; Barthel, 1996, 2001; Kirschenblatt-Gimblett, 1998).

Burlington's need to re-imagineer their city stems from their dependency on the industrial cities of Philadelphia, Camden and Trenton. Because of its presence in the agricultural industry (Burlington County to date has more acres devoted to agricultural production than any other county in the USA), Burlington's farmers were severely affected by the deindustrialization in Philadelphia. Burlington was the main supplier of agricultural goods, especially wheat and corn, for Philadelphia and as deindustrialization took hold of American cities in the 1950s, the market for agricultural goods coming from Burlington declined. Residents of Burlington County not engaged in agricultural production were also affected by deindustrialization as they either worked in Camden or Trenton. Both New Jersey cities experienced even greater affects from deindustrialization than Philadelphia; in New Jersey deindustrialization was compounded by the degree of white flight. While Philadelphia lost 26% of its population from 1950 to 2000, Camden and Trenton lost 36 and 34%, respectively, the majority of which were replaced by unskilled Black labourers (Cox, 2005). Despite attempts at redeveloping downtown Camden through urban renewal, the city became increasingly impoverished and overwhelmingly Black (Cowie and Heathcott, 2003). (According to the 2000 census, Camden's Black population was 53.3% compared to 13.6% for the state.)

Trenton has suffered a similar plight and likewise has tried to rebuild its image. In the early 20th century Trenton was one of the largest industrial centres in America. The large neon sign over the bridge into Trenton that read, 'Trenton Makes – The World Takes', is nationally known. Rebuilt in 2005, the city wondered aloud if the slogan still fitted Trenton. Similar to other deindustrialized cities Trenton has attempted a number of times to rebuild its urban space through urban renewal. In Burlington, however, the radical economic change of deindustrialization here served as the impetus, not for a search for new means of economic growth, as Harvey (1989) and others (Law, 2002; Miles and Miles, 2004) have claimed, but rather to regenerate culture.

Deindustrialization and white flight contributed to the urban sprawl that now characterizes most of New Jersey's landscape. Increasingly, Whites who fled Camden and Trenton for the suburbs found themselves encroaching on historic Black communities. One such historic fight in Burlington County involving the city of Mount Holly reached epic proportions. When Whites threatened to remove the historic Black community by redeveloping the area, especially through suburbanization, local prominent members of the Black community resisted (Kirp et al., 1997). Mount Holly was able to stave off the identity crisis facing neighbouring cities such as Trenton and Camden by regenerating its historic Black culture through tourism.

Ernest Lyght begins his book Path of Freedom: the Black Presence in New Jersey's Burlington County 1659–1900 by stating that 'As early as 1664 there was a Black presence on Burlington Island in the middle of the Delaware River' (1978: 1). The island was originally inhabited by slaves, who were sold to planters in Maryland, and was most likely the first site of a Black presence in New Jersey (Wright, 1988). While the African American Visitors Guide does cursorily mention Burlington Island, a tour guide developed in 1998 by the Burlington County Cultural and Heritage Department (Burlington County's More to Explore, 1998) proclaims its importance. Still the Island is not physically commemorated. In fact the on-line city reference guide for Burlington County describes the Island as once being a site of tribulations among the Lenape Indians and English, an amusement park, vast farmland which funded the first free public school system in the nation, and today serves as 'an uninhabited scenic landmark in the river' (Birchall, 2004). The failure to physically commemorate Burlington Island or to engage it in Burlington County's heritagescape is illustrative of other sites in Burlington County.

Timbuctoo, like Burlington Island, only exists as a space of Black heritage in cyberspace. There are no signs indicating a Black presence. All that survives of the first all-Black community in New Jersey, and the site of a number of legendary battles between alleged runaway slaves and Whites who attempted to sell both free Blacks and runaway slaves into slavery, is a non-commemorated graveyard of Grand Army of the Republic soldiers – all of whom were Black. The failure of the New Jersey Commerce, Economic Growth and Tourism Commission to recognize these spaces in Burlington County stems from their overemphasis on spaces of abolitionism and the avoidance of spaces that deal with slavery.

However, even the sites that the Commission recognizes in Burlington County, those on the UGRR, are not physically commemorated. The Burlington Pharmacy, which according to oral tradition served as an integral site on the UGRR and was a meeting place for abolitionist activities, is commemorated as New Jersey's oldest continuously operating pharmacy. The Dr George Haines House in Medford, also in oral tradition a stop on the UGRR, where recent excavations have confirmed the existence of underground tunnels and hiding spots, commemorates Haines as being the first physician in the area and instrumental in building the first bank. Neither site commemorates Black heritage.

Two other structures preserved for tourists in Burlington County are the Burlington Friends Meeting House and the William R. Allen School. The Meeting House was the site where the first abolitionist tract was read in the USA. While preserved, primarily for its historical association with the Quakers, it is not physically commemorated. The William R. Allen School in Burlington is the site of a once all-Black school and the school that figured prominently in the case that desegregated New Jersey's schools. While the School is preserved it is not open to tourists nor does it appear in the Commission's tourism booklet. Neither site is commemorated

for its Black heritage yet both appear in the 1998 Burlington County Cultural and Heritage Department tour guide.

A site that eludes both the Commission's tour guide and the Burlington tour guide is Peachfield Plantation. While the Burlington County Historical Society recommends Peachfield Plantation to visitors, it is currently closed to tourists. Until 2004, in its tours and promotional literature, Peachfield was promoted as a vital site for the abolitionist movement in New Jersey. The tour and the literature highlighted the role of the Quaker family that owned the plantation and their reluctance to use slave labour. Central to Peachfield's theme was Black Maria. Black Maria was the last domestic slave owned by the Burr family and her manumission was the cause for much abolitionist fervour in Burlington County. Tourists were allowed to view the manumission document and Henry Burr's will in which he recorded which possessions Maria could take with her when manumitted. Today, rather than highlight its past history with slavery and even abolitionism, the curators focus on Peachfield's colonial revival architecture and have completely removed references to Black Maria, slavery, or abolitionism from their promotional literature and private tours. While Peachfield is featured prominently in Burlington County's landscape it is not as prominent in its heritagescape.

Thus despite the 1998 tour guide of African-American Heritage Sites issued by the Burlington County Cultural and Heritage Department (Wright, 1998) there has been no effort at either promoting these spaces on the part of the State (Commission) nor has the original promulgation of the guide (it only exists on-line now) resulted in the commemoration of these spaces. Burlington County, the epicentre of Black life in New Jersey (Lyght, 1978), has been unable to regenerate its Black culture through tourism as it is unable to merge the spaces of thanatourism and dissonant heritage. While both New Jersey in general and Burlington County in particular are trying to promote Black cultural regeneration through tourism, disagreement over which sites should be incorporated into the heritagescape, the reluctance to commemorate Black heritage sites, and the failure to include sites of slavery while promoting sites of abolitionism prevent a full realization of the past.

A problem for Burlington County, one that Shackel (2003) addresses in general, is that most of the sites claimed by the Black community as important for their past have already been commemorated by the dominant group. Shackel's solution, and one that would readily work in the case of Burlington, is to offer multiple commemorations and interpretations. Thus sites can equally partake in commemorating Black, Quaker, English, or simply White heritage. A much more central problem for Black heritage sites in Burlington is the relationship between heritage and history and the failure to completely embrace the past.

The desire to tell tourists a positive story and thus not engage in a critical examination of the past plagues most heritage sites (Barthel, 2000; Smith, 2003). While the heritage sites in Burlington are free and thus avoid economic commodification, they have none the less been culturally commodified. Although the distinction between history and heritage often hinges on critical interpretation, that is whereas history can be critical, heritage is suppose to be edutainment (Urry, 1990), experiential and imaginative (Schouten, 1995), and selective (Lowenthal, 1998), the real distinction is that we have culturally commodified heritage. We cull and winnow the past to produce a commodity that as consumers we can feel good about consuming. Heritagescapes all too often allow the present to use the past for its own purposes. Thus we interpret the past and history to fit the needs of the present rather than merging past(s) and present(s) to critically examine how we socially construct heritage. While we can never fully approximate the past in the constructions of heritage sites or heritagescapes, we owe it to the past to be more inclusive. Heritage sites commemorated and interpreted for tourists cannot lead to cultural regeneration; it has even been demonstrated that tourists do not want critical examinations of heritage or as we might say, something approaching authenticity (Barthel, 2001; Edensor, 2001; Olsen, 2002; Cary, 2004). It is only through fully merging the past and present that we can have cultural regeneration, especially for a culture that has been marginalized throughout the country's past and continues today to be marginalized through tourism.

Conclusion

Barthel notes that

> [P]eople visit historical sites in large measure to 'get in touch with history' . . . Like research scientists who demand to see experimental results . . . before they will believe them, visitors to historic sites want to see history with their own eyes.
>
> (Barthel, 1996: 2–3)

Increasingly visitors seek out heritage sites that are promoted in tourist literature(s) that have been produced by cultural entrepreneurs in an attempt to not only promote aspects of history for tourists but to regenerate culture. Although the commodification of heritage has been shown elsewhere to be problematic (Hewison, 1987; Graham et al., 2000; Smith, 2003), the very definition of a heritage site seems to be in constant flux.

Heritage sites are generally regarded as spaces where historic artefacts are preserved for education or recreation (Garrod and Fyall, 2000). Recently, however, it has been argued that heritage sites are not simply spaces where history is preserved, but spaces where emotive relationships are generated between the individual and the history being presented (Poira, 2001; Poira et al., 2004). Here heritage sites become spaces of representation (Bender, 1993). Such sites can be seen as attempts to re-present the past (Giddens, 1984; Urry, 2000) or as the past represented for the future (Crouch and Parker, 2003). They can be seen as hegemonic attempts to re-narrate history (Moscardo, 1996) or as a narrative tool used by traditionally marginal groups to contest the dominant image of their group (Parker and Wragg, 1999).

The inability of Black heritage spaces in New Jersey to promote cultural regeneration stems from their reliance on past and present categorizations (McIntosh and Prentice, 1999) (which ultimately stems from the disavowal of slavery as part of New Jerseyean culture). As Lowenthal notes, past and present must merge (1998), isolating one in favour of the other reifies both culture and identity. Much like Schwartz's (2004) examination of how interpretations of the Gettysburg Address change to reflect contemporary interests and Chronis' (2005) ethnographic analysis of how the narration of Gettysburg as a

tourist space incorporates current popular sentiments, successful cultural regeneration must go
beyond simply presenting history for tourists, it
must fuse the past and present. The failure to
materially commemorate or interpret the landscape in New Jersey, particularly Burlington
County, for Black heritage has blurred the distinction between place and culture and ultimately identity. Perhaps most importantly, the
inability to commemorate Black heritage sites
has not allowed present use of the past to critically examine culture. Thus many sites work
as spaces of tourism, but fail as instruments
of cultural regeneration. That is, where many
spaces can be consumed by tourists, the attempts
to re-imagineer New Jersey, especially Burlington
County, as a space of abolitionism and emancipation have not been successful.

Successful cultural regeneration has to go
beyond the dichotomization of tourist/local. Cultural regeneration has to merge not only heritage
and history, but the past. While Bruner asserts

that '[a]ny tourist attraction is subject to multiple
interpretations even if the producers attempt to
impose a monolithic meaning' (2004: 26), he
discounts the interpretative parameters that a
monological commemoration or interpretation
sets for the tourist and ultimately for the identity
of the residents.

New Jersey's Secretary of State Regina
Thomas was praised in the press for devoting
18 consecutive days to New Jersey history. On
the mission to bring history to life and to the
public she remarked, 'I don't look at history any
more as negative, as I did in the Civil Rights
movement, but as a positive' (Magyar and
Martinez, 2002). Thomas's comments are indic-
ative of the current relationship between history,
heritage and the past. We substitute heritage for
history and uncritical versions of history for the
past. The problem for heritage professionals
and cultural entrepreneurs is not only incorporating minority heritage into the tourist product,
but a minority past.

References

Apostolakis, A. (2003) The convergence process in heritage tourism. *Annals of Tourism Research* 30(4),
    795–812.
Ateljevic, I. (2000) Circuits of tourism: stepping beyond the 'production/consumption' dichotomy. *Tourism
    Geographies* 2(4), 369–388.
Ateljevic, I. and Doorne, S. (2003) Culture, economy and tourism commodities: social relations of production
    and consumption. *Tourist Studies* 3(2), 123–141.
Barthel, D. (1996) *Historic Preservation: Collective Memory and Historical Identity*. Rutgers University Press,
    Piscataway, New Jersey.
Barthel, D. (2001) Authenticity and identity: theme-parking the Amanas. *International Sociology* 16(2),
    221–239.
Bauman, J. (1995) Designer heritage: Israeli National Parks and the politics of historical representation. *Middle
    East Report* September–October, 20–23.
Bell, D. and Jayne, M. (2004) *City of Quarters: Urban Villages in the Contemporary City*. Ashgate, Burlington,
    Vermont.
Bender, B. (1993) *Landscape: Politics and Perspectives*. Berg Publishers, Providence, Rhode Island.
Birchall, D. (2004) *Burlington City, NJ*. Available at: http://08016.com/island.html (accessed 12 January 2005).
Blight. D. (2001) *Race and Reunion: the Civil War in American Memory*. Belknap Press of Harvard University
    Press, Cambridge, Massachusetts.
Bruner, E. (2004) *Culture on Tour: Ethnographies of Travel*. The University of Chicago Press, Chicago, Illinois.
Burlington County's More to Explore (1998) Available at: http://www.co.burlington.nj.us/tourism/history/
    looptour/african.htm (accessed 21 July 2005).
Cary, S. (2004) The tourist moment. *Annals of Tourism Research* 31(1), 61–77.
Chhabra, D., Healy, R. and Sills, E. (2003) Staged authenticity and heritage tourism. *Annals of Tourism
    Research* 30(3), 702–719.
Chronis, A. (2005) Coconstructing heritage at the Gettysburg storyscape. *Annals of Tourism Research* 32(2),
    386–406.
Cowie, J. and Heathcott, J. (2003) *Beyond the Ruins: the Meanings of Deindustrialization*. ILR Press, Ithaca,
    New York.

Cox, W. (2005) *Demographia*. Wendell Cox Consultancy Belleville, Illinois. Available at: http://www. Demographia.com/db-corecities1950htm (accessed 22 July 2005).

Crouch, D. and Parker, G. (2003) Digging-up Utopia? Space, practice, and land use heritage. *Geoforum* 34(3), 395–408.

Dann, G. (1998) The dark side of tourism. *Etudes et Rapports*, serie L, Vol. 14, x–y.

Dann, G. and Seaton, A. (2001) *Slavery, Contested Heritage and Thanatourism*. The Haworth Press, Inc, New York.

Edensor, T. (2001) Performing tourism, staging tourism: (re)producing tourist space and practice. *Tourist Studies* 1(1), 59–81.

Eichstedt, J. and Small, S. (2002) *Representations of Slavery: Race and Ideology in Southern Plantation Museums*. Smithsonian Institution Press, Washington, DC.

Eisinger, P. (2000) The politics of bread and circuses. *Urban Affairs Review* 35(1), 316–333.

Eisinger, P. (2003) Reimagining Detroit. *City and Community* 2(2), 85–99.

Garrod, B. and Fyall, A. (2000) Managing heritage tourism. *Annals of Tourism Research* 27(3), 682–708.

Giddens, A. (1984) *A Contemporary Critique of Historical Materialism*. Polity, Cambridge.

Graham, B., Ashworth, G. and Turnbridge, J. (2000) *A Geography of Heritage: Power, Culture and Economy*. Oxford University Press Inc., New York.

Hale, A. (2001) Representing the Cornish: contesting heritage interpretation in Cornwall. *Tourist Studies* 1(2), 185–196.

Harris, L. (2004) Slavery, emancipation, and class formation in colonial and early national New York City. *Journal of Urban History* 30(3), 339–359.

Harvey, D. (1989) *The Urban Experience*. Blackwell, Oxford.

Hewison, R. (1987) *The Heritage Industry: Britain in a Climate of Decline*. Methuen, London.

Judd, D. (2003) *The Infrastructure of Play: Building the Tourist City*. M.E. Sharpe Inc., Armonk, New York.

Judd, D. and Fainstein, S. (eds) (1999) *The Tourist City*. Yale University, New Haven, Connecticut.

Kammen, M. (1991) *Mystic Chords of Memory: the Transformation of Tradition in American Culture*. Knopf, New York.

Kirp, D., Dwyer, J. and Rosenthal, L. (1997) *Our Town: Race, Housing and the Soul of Suburbia*. Rutgers University Press, Piscataway, New Jersey.

Kirschenblatt-Gimblett, B. (1998) *Destination Culture: Tourism, Museums and Heritage*. University of California Press, Berkeley, California.

Law, C. (2002) *Urban Tourism: the Visitor Economy and the Growth of Large Cities*, 2nd edn. Continuum, NewYork.

Light, D. (2000) Gazing on communism: heritage tourism and post-Communist identities in Germany, Hungary and Romania. *Tourism Geographies* 2(2), 157–176.

Lowenthal, D. (1998) *The Heritage Crusade and the Spoils of History*. Cambridge University Press, New York.

Lutins, A. (2002) Dunkerhook: slave community? *Journal of Afro-American History and Genealogical Society* 21(1), 64–74.

Lyght, E. (1978) *Path of Freedom: the Black Presence in New Jersey's Burlington County 1659–1900*. E. & E. Publishers House, Cherry Hill, New Jersey.

Maygar, M. (2002) All-Black communities played key role in New Jersey's Underground Railroad. *New Jersey Heritage Magazine* 1(2), 44–46.

Magyar, M. and Martinez, P. (2002) Retracing the trail to freedom: New Jersey and the Underground Railroad. *New Jersey Heritage Magazine* 1(4), 14–21.

McIntosh, A. and Prentice, R. (1999) Affirming authenticity: consuming cultural heritage. *Annals of Tourism Research* 26(3), 589–612.

Melish, J. (2000) *Disowning Slavery: Gradual Emancipation and 'Race' in New England, 1780–1860*. Cornell University Press, Ithaca, New Yrok.

Miles, S. and Miles, M. (2004) *Consuming Cities*. Palgrave/Macmillan Press, New York.

Moscardo, G. (1996) Mindful visitors: heritage and tourism. *Annals of Tourism Research* 23(2), 376–397.

New Jersey Commerce, Economic Growth and Tourism Commission (2004) *New Jersey's African American Visitors Guide*. The Writing Company, Newark, New Jersey.

New Jersey Commerce, Economic Growth and Tourism Commission (2005) *New Jersey's African American Visitors Guide: the Family Reunion*. The Writing Company, Newark, New Jersey.

Olsen, K. (2002) Authenticity as a concept in tourism research: the social organization of the experience of authenticity. *Tourist Studies* 2(2), 159–182.

Parker, G. and Wragg, A. (1999) Networks, agency and (de)stabilization: the issue of navigation on the River Wye. *Journal of Environmental Planning and Management* 42(4), 471–487.

Parkinson, M., Foley, B. and Judd, D. (1988) *Regenerating the Cities: the UK Crisis and the US Experience.* Manchester University Press, Manchester, UK.

Perry, D. (2003) Urban tourism and the privatizing discourses of public infrastructure. In: Judd, D. (ed.) *The Infrastructure of Play: Building the Tourist City.* M.E. Sharpe Inc., Armonk, New York, pp. 19–49.

Pingeon, F. (1991) An abominable business: the New Jersey slave trade, 1818. *New Jersey History* 109(3–4), 15–36.

Poira, Y. (2001) Challenging the present approach to heritage tourism: is tourism to heritage places heritage tourism? *Tourism Review* 56, 51–53.

Poira, Y., Butler, R. and Airey, D. (2004) Links between tourists, heritage, and reasons for visiting heritage sites. *Journal of Travel Research* 43, 19–28.

Schouten, F. (1995) Heritage as historical reality. In: D. Herbert (ed.) *Heritage, Tourism and Society.* Mansell Publishing, London, pp. 21–31.

Schwartz, B. (2004) The new Gettysburg Address: fusing history and memory. *Poetics* 33, 63–79.

Schwartz, B. and Schuman, H. (2005) History, commemoration, and belief: Abraham Lincoln in American memory, 1945–2001. *American Sociological Review* 70(2), 183–203.

Shackel, P. (2003) *Memory in Black and White: Race, Commemoration, and the Post-Bellum Landscape.* AltaMira Press, New York.

Smith, M. (2003) *Issues in Cultural Tourism Studies.* Routledge, New York.

Taylor, J. (2001) Authenticity and sincerity in tourism. *Annals of Tourism Research* 28(1), 7–26.

Thorns, D. (2002) *The Transformation of Cities: Urban Theory and Urban Life.* Palgrave/Macmillian Press, New York.

Tunbridge, J. and Ashworth, G. (1996) *Dissonant Heritage: the Management of the Past as a Resource in Conflict.* John Wiley and Sons, London.

Urry, J. (1990) *The Tourist Gaze: Leisure and Travel in Contemporary Societies.* Sage, London.

Urry, J. (2000) *Sociology Beyond Societies.* Routledge, London.

Watson, J. (2002) Slavery in Middletown: what the 1798 Direct Tax reveals. *New Jersey History* 120(3–4), 3–45.

Wright, G. (1988) *Afro-Americans in New Jersey: a Short History.* New Jersey Historical Commission, Trenton, New Jersey.

Wright, G. (1998) *African-American Historic Sites.* Available at: http://www.co.burlington.nj.us/tourism/history/looptour/african.htm (accessed 19 December 2004).

Wright, G. (2002) *Steal Away, Steal Away . . . a Guide to the Underground Railroad in New Jersey.* New Jersey Historical Society, Trenton, New Jersey.

7 Sustainable Leisure and Tourism Space Development in Post-industrial Cities: the Case of Odaiba, Tokyo, Japan

Meiko Murayama and Gavin Parker

The car, the furniture, the wife, the children – everything has to be disposable. Because you see the main thing today is – shopping. Years ago a person, he was unhappy, didn't know what to do with himself – he'd go to church, start a revolution – something. Today, you're unhappy? Can't figure it out? What is the salvation? Go shopping.

(Miller, 1969)

Introduction

This chapter examines a particular type of mixed-use space – large-scale developments that are designed and built with the intention of generating tourism and leisure activity. It is argued that such developments owe a responsibility not just to (non-resident) visitors but also to the surrounding urban area and populations that live and work there, both now and into the future. Many authors have indicated that these spaces are one example of a mixed land use development or new urban fabric that is in danger of creating exclusive, unsustainable and segregated areas (Rowley, 1998; The Civic Trust, 2004). This critique implies the need for greater integration and engagement between a widening array of interests and beyond the generalized groupings of: 'developer', 'investor', 'planner', 'politician' and 'public'/'community'. This is deemed necessary to help provide a better quality of life for people who work and

live in or near the newly regenerated/redeveloped spaces, as well as to promote valued visitor experiences which support local economies. There appears to be a lack of balance and a lack of understanding between different interests in creating such playscapes and their ongoing regulation. This position leads towards the need to recognize better planning and integration of leisure/consumption-based development within mixed land use schemes with a view to creating more sustainable and durable amenity environments, as explained later.

The chapter also portrays how consumption and consumption spaces have become central features in late-Capitalist societies and have a major influence on how cities are redeveloped. A case study of the newly developed Waterfront City of Odaiba in Tokyo, Japan is used to argue that while a mixed land use approach has a critical role to play in bringing back vitality into the central part of the city, it must be well balanced and maintained. In the conclusion it is argued that the globalization of culture has significantly influenced this process of creating postmodern (read homogenized) urban landscapes of leisure and tourism and that in order to create more balanced and sustainable amenity environments, a more responsible and balanced approach to the design of these areas needs to be brokered in terms of the overall design and mix. This process needs the more active involvement of the leisure and tourism industry as stakeholders and a better understanding of the impacts of unbalanced leisure uses on the part of other local and national actors. In short we need to foster an engaged, educated and responsible leisure sector that is more fully included in urban regeneration deliberations.

Urban Regeneration, Consumption Spaces and Late-Capitalism

Consumption activity and leisure practice has become a more and more important part of people's lives and has been debated extensively over the past two decades (see Bourdieu, 1990; Miller, 1995; Miles, 1998; Lee, 2000; Hesmondhalgh, 2002). After the 1950s consumption levels steadily grew in the USA, Japan and Europe and by the 1980s, such advanced economies were transforming into post-industrial societies based around consumption activity and cultural industries and with urban development reflecting these trends.

Notably there has been a boom in the retail and leisure development sectors and more widely the role of tourism has grown phenomenally. In new urban developments, the tourism and leisure industry has tended to play a critical role; not only in terms of tourist spend but also in terms of influencing the physical and environmental, cultural and social aspects of these new spaces. These developments are knowingly created, as with theme parks, to elicit particular responses from visitors. This includes the design and orientation of physical structures, provision of quasi-public open spaces and the mix of uses and tenures as well as the use of particular construction and finishing materials.

It is not difficult to find postmodern architecture designed for consumers in the Central Business Districts of many North American and Japanese cities and this is also happening across the UK in cities such as Birmingham, Glasgow, Cardiff, Manchester and Leeds (as well as across London). This postmodernism has also been referred to as a 'standardization' or 'homogenization' delivered by market formulas and with little regard to local history, diverse needs or the preferences of local communities (Evans, 2001; Page and Hall, 2003; Savage et al., 2004).

At its worst this may lead to sterile 'non-place urban realms' (Auge, 1995; Page and Hall, 2003). This criticism has also been made regarding regeneration in non-Western cities, such as Singapore, Shanghai and Tokyo. These Asian cities have enthusiastically embraced 'Western' design in architecture and evidence of their own cultural heritage or 'authenticity' is hard to find in such places. Instead national or ethnic tradition is mixed where convenient (and profitable) as hyper-real elements of deemed acceptable cultural representation in these new urban spaces (see Wu, 2000; Savage et al., 2004; Sheller and Urry, 2004).

Cities evolve or transform continuously no matter how slow this process may appear, but the recent transformation of cities has been so dynamic and fast that people feel 'the sense of change' (Lifton, 1976; Knox, 1993) has intensified. The development and enhancement of cultural economies has become crucial for regeneration in city centres both in Europe and in North America as well as in Japan. Often, adjoining new leisure and tourism spaces pre-existing residents still reside, who typically live under national average income levels and who may not benefit from the jobs created or the consumption opportunities offered. These residents often do provide the low-skill workforce for expanding 'new consumption spaces' but the employment and incomes afforded by this kind of regeneration still leaves issues of equity and quality of life unanswered. Research in Birmingham and in East Manchester both confirm this (Ward, 2003; Murayama, 2004a). Often policymakers rationalize the redevelopment in their neighbourhood claiming to help local employment by creating new jobs and enhance their local environment. However, they do not necessarily benefit from it, as some older residents are relocated to give space for new buildings, or feel excluded from consuming in those spaces (Bianchini and Parkinson, 1993; Savage et al., 2004). Then several questions arise; some of which are longstanding and are only partly answered and some of which are not adequately addressed by the leisure and tourism sectors:

- Who are the true beneficiaries of such newly created spaces?
- What alternatives are considered?

- Are the wider impacts and possibilities of mixed-use amenity environments properly understood?
- Does an enhanced responsibility need to be brokered by and on behalf of the different stakeholders when such developments are being negotiated?

In the UK efforts are being made with partnership working, alterations to compulsory purchase powers, planning gain and engagement with communities in planning. However, there is little evidence of success on the above counts as yet, even in the more celebrated of development examples. City authorities often accept development schemes that are far from ideal, or that do not provide the kind of designs, mix of uses or mixed tenures which populations increasingly need.

Tourists inform and influence planners and developers indirectly. However, there is often little formal engagement between the 'locals', the tourist industry and planners or developers. Instead this relationship tends to be dominated by distant estimations, market research and the use of historic consumer data to plan new regeneration schemes with a view to leisure attractiveness – again part of the idea of the idealized 'amenity environment' (Murayama, 2004a). This relationship might be characterized as a market driven one where new regeneration spaces respond to the needs of capital and seek out consumers with disposable incomes. The resultant environments first and foremost must offer 'extraordinary' spaces for consumption and deliver premium income streams for investors. Other considerations tend to come a distant second, often despite the creation of public–private partnerships.

Mixed Land Use and 'Amenity Environments'

Jacobs (1961) argued for the need to return to and retain the diversity and juxtaposition of a mixture of land uses. However, despite Jacobs' persuasive points, for many traditional industrial cities the urban core was never conducive to a healthy happy existence for all. In others there was a decline of urban cores and city centres in the post-World War II period from a

position somewhere close to what we might now term sustainability – partly due to the existence of propinquitous communities and proximate uses. Indeed this is what Jacobs identified and argued to protect as planners and geographers began to recognize the economic process and social impacts of urban decline. Since then the mixed land use development approach has gradually gained recognition worldwide as a way of delivering sustainable places. Although it has been slow to gain popularity with large numbers of developers and investors – seen by them as more complex and risky undertakings. Innovative research on mixed land use development by the Urban Land Institute in 1976 (Witherspoon et al., 1976) spurred this on in the USA, however it was not until the mid-1990s that many British planners and developers seriously paid attention to the approach (Rowley, 1998, 2003) and evidence has begun to emerge that mixed-use schemes are viable economically as well as socially.

The idea of mixed-use development and the creation of more balanced and sustainable communities has been a feature of urban policy in the UK over the past 5 years – particularly since the publication of the Urban White Paper for England in 2000 (DETR, 2000a). However, the impacts of tourism and leisure on spaces can have a detrimental effect on efforts to create the balance between live, work and play that has been a byline for urban designers since the 1980s (Trancik, 1986; Locum Destination Review, 2003) and which has also informed the 'smart' growth concept in the USA (NAHB, 1999). The idea of Urban Villages (Aldous, 1992) and smart growth is based around integrated planning for more sustainable and 'liveable' communities.

In the UK there has been encouragement from government in recent years to promote mixed land use as part of the so-called 'urban renaissance' (DETR, 2000a, b). Though mixed-use development is officially promoted, the term is perceived to be ambiguous (see CABE/DETR, 2000; Murayama, 2004a). Mixed-use development can be organized in very different ways, for example: as a single building with different uses or an assemblage of various buildings each with different uses. In either of these formulations the degree or percentage floor space of mix can vary greatly, as can the range of the mix in terms of land uses. Often the objectives of different actors are traded-off and typically the needs of investors will predominate. It is worth noting that although a mixed land use approach can bring various benefits, the obstacles are often exaggerated (see DTLR, 2000; Rowley, 2003). Some developers are prepared to pay more for a development if they are confident of making better returns. In many cases these needs are based on conservative thinking based on minimizing risk, if not always on minimizing costs (see Guy and Henneberry, 2000; Gallimore and Gray, 2002).

One of the most important benefits of mixed land use is the potential to bring vitality back to the central parts of the city (Rowley, 2003). Well-designed mixes can give further synergetic effects; if pubs, cafés and restaurants are located on the ground floors of offices, then these places service workers and visitors during the day and potentially into the evening, thus extending the economic day and possibly creating safer spaces by dint of usage. Various activities and events can similarly attract further investment in city centres. Living within a walking distance from work, with easy access to cultural industries and other services can provide a better quality of life in inner cities. Such places can also prove attractive for urban living, such as *Brindleyplace* and the *Mail Box*

developments in Birmingham – but these are not always successful as we explain below.

A good mixed land use environment can contribute to the idealized 'amenity environment' as conceptualized in Fig. 7.1. The model is comprised of three elements: 'work', 'live' and 'play' dimensions, which are essential components for sustainable urban spaces and each is required for a better quality of life (Rowley, 2003; Murayama, 2004a). The x-axis represents 'work' (i.e. employment within the environment). The y-axis indicates residential space as expressed with the 'live' and the z-axis is the 'play' element for leisure and relaxation, and in which the tourism and leisure industry play key roles. However, the industry also impacts on the work and the live dimension – each are interconnected and affect each other. The simplicity of the model makes for versatile usage and application, but it also enables comparison of space compositions before and after regeneration and provides a template to assess how different spaces perform as amenity environments.

The model implies a careful mix with different activity opportunities for different user groups and which fulfils the needs of the market for economic viability. It can also be used to compare different mixed land use spaces. The smallest central triangle in the figure indicates there were few spaces for living, playing and working.

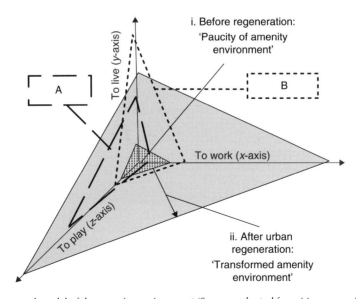

Fig. 7.1. Conceptual model of the amenity environment (Source: adapted from Murayama, 2004a).

After the regeneration living, working and play-ing spaces have been created and expanded as shown by the larger triangles. Space A has developed more play spaces with residential and less work spaces, on the other hand Space B is more residential in character with some play and work spaces. It should be emphasized that the ongoing monitoring and management of urban centres and amenity environments is crucial and this is an emerging key role for market-aware planners to undertake.

The idea is that the three elements of work, play and live, need to be combined in order to make a successful amenity environment, even though this may sound challenging. Leisure and tourism development is only one part of the urban fabric in this mixed use context, and plan-ners and developers need to be better empow-ered and have better economic information about leisure and tourism. Equally the leisure industry should be better informed about the need to aim for sustainable amenity environ-ments. Local politicians and policymakers also need to better understand the impacts of tour-ism. In the UK the well-documented story of the London Docklands provides an example of a deregulated planning approach that failed to provide adequate transport infrastructure or a sustainable mixed use (Brownill, 1990; Evans, 2001). Instead, retrofitting of the area has been required and this process has still left serious

questions over the process and structures in place to create anything approximating to a sus-tainable community. Although not primarily designed or envisaged as a leisure space, Lon-don Docklands exhibits some issues that parallel Odaiba, described below, as the case study 'amenity environment' that has attracted criti-cism in Japan – just as Docklands has in the UK.

The Odaiba Waterfront Sub-centre Development, Tokyo

The Tokyo Waterfront City, Odaiba, is located in Tokyo Bay on reclaimed lands, some of which date back to the 19th century when Japan was still closed to foreign countries (see Fig. 7.2). For-tress islands with defensive cannon, or 'Daiba', were built in the Bay to protect the capital from invasion. As a result the area has been known as 'Odaiba' to most of the Japanese population. Further islands were created in Tokyo Bay over decades as a result of waste dumping. Part of the reclaimed land became ironically known as Yumenoshima or 'dream island'.

In the 1980s the Tokyo Metropolitan Government (TMG) began planning for new development on these vast and virtually empty reclaimed land areas in the Bay. The original concept for the new area was to develop a 'teleport', as a main information hub and to

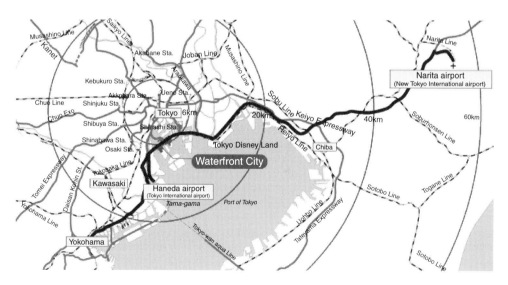

Fig. 7.2.   Location of Odaiba Waterfront City, Tokyo (Source: TMG, 2002).

build clusters of highly intelligent buildings in response to the development of the information age in the late 1980s (personal communication with H. Makino, planner at TMG, 2000). This was seen as particularly important as other world cities, such as New York and London had already been building similar hubs; for example London Docklands were researched and visited by Tokyo planners in the early stages of designing Odaiba (Hiramoto, 2000).

At the time of originally planning the area, the Japanese economy was booming and the price of land was rapidly increasing. Demand for office space was outstripping supply in central Tokyo. Therefore it was seen as urgent to build hi-tech offices in order to be competitive. TMG had promoted a policy, since the mid-1980s, of making sub-centres in central Tokyo, instead of having a single concentration of businesses. This was viewed as a method of helping to solve urban problems and dispersing urban functions and congestion around Tokyo (TMG, 2002). This plan for Odaiba was subsequently refined and developed, partly due to central government influence (see Hiramoto, 2000; Saito, 2003), to become a more mixed-use sub-centre (the seventh such node); known as the 'Odaiba: Tokyo Metropolitan Waterfront City' (see Fig. 7.2) and which was actually begun in the early 1990s. A public and private partnership company was established to build infrastructure including transportation (Hiramoto, 2000). TMG acts as landlord and leases lands to private companies who are responsible for their own building based on a master plan.

However, the economy and domestic politics severely affected the redevelopment of the area. The collapse of the so called 'bubble economy' in the early 1990s deterred investment and development. 'Tokyo Frontier', an international urban expo, was to open in March 1996 to celebrate and promote the new development. However, this was cancelled just 8 months before the opening due to the election of a new governor of Tokyo in April 1995. This caused much confusion as one of his prime election promises was to revise the development plan for Odaiba. Until then the development plan was made by a limited number of specialists and planners at TMG, and this had been widely criticized. Though new specialists were involved in the revised planning process, the final version of the plan was not significantly different from the old one and the final version of the scheme was published in late 1996. Due to the new political environment TMG introduced a new planning approach where particular areas of land were designated and planned and developed in close consultation with citizens. The idea was to create an innovative urban landscape where citizens felt a sense of ownership of the regeneration space (see TMG, 2005).

In 1999 yet another new governor was elected and he decided to reposition Odaiba as the strategic hub for leading industries for the 21st century, including IT and the creative industries. The revised plan also included high quality residential and leisure spaces (Saito, 2003). His aim was to revitalize Tokyo and make it more attractive to compete with other world cities (Saito and Thornley, 2003). Therefore Odaiba was to be developed as a showcase of what Tokyo could offer in terms of dynamic businesses, leisure space and residential environments (see Fig. 7.3).

The whole scheme is planned to be completed by 2016 and the people who work and live in the new urban sub-centre have been increasing steadily (see Figs 7.4 and 7.5) with a working population of around 70,000 and 42,000 residents anticipated by completion (TMG, 2005). By 2004 there was a workforce of 39,000 and a residential population 6,200 had been achieved and over 800 companies were operating from Odaiba by 2005 (TMG, 2005).

Odaiba is surrounded by the Port of Tokyo and is well connected to domestic and international airports by motorway. Expensive urban infrastructure has been developed including the 'Rainbow Bridge', which cost 128.1 billion yen (TMG, 1999, 2001) and opened in 1993. The crossing soon became one of the landmarks of Odaiba, and it serves as a main transportation route from the mainland to Odaiba stretching over 1.7 km (see Fig. 7.7). There are several transport methods to get to Odaiba. Some roads are still under construction and access by car can be frustrating. Bus services are available from three major terminal stations in central Tokyo and there are free shuttle bus services within Odaiba. Two train lines were constructed as part of the development; the subway line 'Rinkai-sen' and a new transit line 'Yurikamome', which is similar to the Docklands Light Railway.

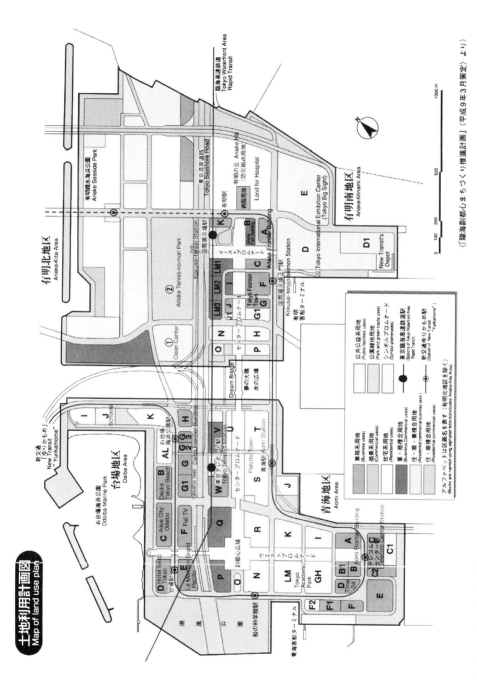

Fig. 7.3. Land use planning for Odaiba (Source: TMG, 2001).

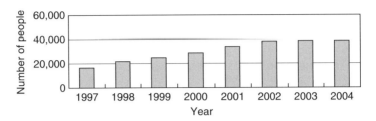

Fig. 7.4. Changes in working population in Odaiba (Source: TMG, 2005).

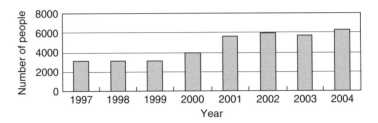

Fig. 7.5. Growth of resident population in Odaiba (Source: TMG, 2005).

Additionally a water bus plies between Odaiba and several piers and this method has become an attraction in its own right. Owing to the unique location of the regeneration zone the view from the window provides a panorama of Tokyo and of the modern architecture of Odaiba (see Fig. 7.7).

The construction costs of the area-wide transportation and on-site urban infrastructure provided by the public–private company were calculated as 2430 billion yen – approximately US$23Bn[1] (Bureau of Ports and Harbors, 2000; Saito, 2003). The rapid development of infrastructure resulted in a heavy financial burden for TMG and therefore commercial and office development became critical to Odaiba's economic viability (Hiramoto, 2000; Saito, 2003). Construction on Odaiba is still taking place and it is not easy to measure the impacts fully, however, the following figures were forecast (TMG, 1995: 1):

- Induced economic impacts for building and constructing infrastructure with an estimated multiplier effect of × 2.08 (i.e. about 6000 billion yen).
- The initial investment is estimated to bring in a further 12,000 billion yen (TMG, 1995).

- It is estimated 608 billion yen to be spent, bringing a further 1190 billion yen worth of production. This results in an anticipated multiplier effect of × 1.95 induced economic impact after the completion.

It appears that the optimistic early projections of economic impacts were far from the actual figures, especially after the Japanese bubble economy burst. TMG had to recalculate the figures again, and it was concluded that the area would only recoup its outlay by the year 2036 (Hiramoto, 2000: 250).

The initial idea of the regeneration was to build a teleport centre, and this has doggedly affected the outcome of the regeneration. Several major Japanese firms showed great interest in the area. It resulted in there being a concentration of multimedia industries, including: a telecommunication centre, broadcasting stations, as well as higher level education, research and development facilities, headquarters of several major Japanese companies, convention centre facilities, public sector offices of Tokyo Metropolitan Government and various cultural industries also continue to create employment. As it has been planned to be a vibrant new urban centre, it is also multifunctional; there are also: hotels, hospitals, schools, residential flats,

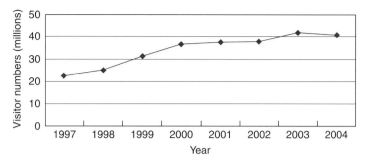

Fig. 7.6. Visitor numbers to Odaiba 1997–2004 (Source: TMG, 2005).

museums, beach areas, public open spaces, retail units, amusement parks, a multi-complex cinema, amusements such as a big wheel, world-class tennis courts and other sports and leisure related facilities.

In the 1980s when the development plan was made, depopulation was another serious problem in the central part of Tokyo, besides office demand issues and the need to revitalize inner cities with local communities. There are various reasons for this, but one historic reason is that people had been encouraged to live in the suburbs of Tokyo (Miyake *et al.*, 2004). This resulted in a significant gap between daytime and night-time populations[2] and this had become socially problematic. The other factor was the sharp rise in the housing market with house prices getting far too expensive in Tokyo. In response, local and national politicians promised to supply a large number of affordable public housing. As a result high density flats were planned for Odaiba with over 14,000 units allocated in the final plan, with 60% as public sector housing and the rest developed by the public sector for private ownership (TMG, 2005). These dwellings are designed to be of various sizes from single person households to bigger family accommodation. Additionally a kindergarten, primary school and junior high school were built among these new residential areas. As the scheme has progressed Tokyo politicians have wanted to increase the housing levels even more and as a result some public sector housing was built next to the major commercial zones, which has caused some friction between residents and visitors (Arisue Kenkyusitsu, 1996).

Odaiba is also located close to Tokyo Disneyland, which is hugely successful in drawing large numbers of visitors. It is located on a similar reclaimed land site in the neighbouring prefecture. Odaiba is seen by some as another type of theme park and it has quickly established itself as a major leisure and tourism space in Tokyo. Figure 7.6 shows a steady increase in visitor numbers since 1997 when over 22 million people visited Odaiba, only a few years after the completion of the Rainbow Bridge. These numbers rose to over 40 million visitors in 2004. This means it has become the most heavily visited area in greater Tokyo (TMG, 2005). The next section focuses on the newly developed cultural landscape and looks into what has attracted visitors to the area.

The cultural landscape and features of Odaiba

The 'Rainbow Bridge' is one of the main access routes to Odaiba and it has become one of the most photographed images in Tokyo. Visitors are attracted both during the daytime and in the evening when the bridge is illuminated. Passengers crossing the Rainbow Bridge will find many major large buildings on Odaiba which have distinctive designs, as if they are part of a huge showcase for postmodern architecture. There are virtually no small- or medium-size buildings of 'human scale', which are often seen in organically developed spaces, but very large-scale architecture predominates. The overall appearance looks futuristic, exotic and 'Western' to many Japanese eyes (see Fig. 7.7) but quite different from the older, organically developed areas of Tokyo which feature small shops, pubs,

Fig. 7.7. Replica of the Statue of Liberty, Odaiba with the Rainbow Bridge in the background.

restaurants and bathhouses closely cluttered together.

Odaiba provides diverse, if commodified, leisure activities including beach, wind surfing, boating, public parks with barbecues, an onsen complex (Japanese style hot spring spa with various attractions and bath pools), beauty treatments, sports facilities, shopping, eating and drinking, amusements, a cinema complex, indoor theme parks, pop-music and concert halls, convention and exhibition facilities, galleries and museums and the like. A generous proportion of the whole regeneration area (21% or 93 ha) is allocated to public parks and green spaces (TMG, 2005) and much of the waterfront spaces have been made into accessible public parks.

Creative industries (fashion, media and information industries) are given special emphasis in Odaiba (TMG, 2005). The Tokyo Fashion Town is built with the intention of making Odaiba a mecca for the creative and fashion industry. One of the key national broadcasting companies has located its headquarters on Odaiba. The building itself has become a popular attraction due to its architectural design, which includes an observatory and studio tours.

Trendy TV 'love dramas' using popular young actors and actresses dressed in top fashions, have been shot in Odaiba and such programmes have had a significant role in promoting Odaiba to potential visitors all over the country; sending out an image of Odaiba as a place for a 'fashionable urban lifestyle'.

Some of the most distinctive commercial developments in Odaiba are the shopping malls (Murayama, 2004b). Odaiba itself has been likened to an open-air theme park and the shopping malls have deliberately created themed shopping spaces. Developers have created the environments carefully, designing them specifically for different consumer niches. This approach encourages shoppers and diners to consume and spend money within these different environments (Hiramoto, 2000). Three of the shopping malls are discussed here. The first *Decks Tokyo Beach* is a shopping mall complex of nearly 80 outlets (18,700 m^2) with an indoor amusement park run by Sega, the Japanese software game firm (Sumisho Urban Kaihatsu, 2002). Within the mall, two levels of the building are branded as 'Little Hong Kong' and replicates typical Hong Kong streets with Chinese billboards and street signs (see Fig. 7.8). The space

Fig. 7.8.   The 'Hong Kong' themed area of one of the Odaiba shopping malls.

aims to provide shopping and dining experiences of Hong Kong. A nostalgic Japanese shopping space of the 1950–1960s occupies one floor, also created for the older and as well as the younger generations which replicates old streets and shops, restaurants and even public baths. Being surrounded by popular songs of the time and cheap sweets and toys displayed in old fashioned penny candy stores may bring back memories of childhood to older generations but at the same time something novel to the younger consumers.

The second shopping mall is labelled *Aqua City* (25,000 m²), which consists of over 100 cafés, restaurants, shops and a cinema complex. Well known names are seen in this complex, such as McDonald's, Starbucks, Cinnabon, Anna Miller's, Guess, Toys'R'us, Swatch, Agnes b., Coach, Godiva, HMV, Claire's, NEXT, The Body Shop and Eddie Bauer. More than 20% of the businesses operating in this shopping complex are funded via foreign capital (Aqua City Odaiba, 2002). A scale replica of the Statue of Liberty, which was brought from France to Japan (see Fig. 7.7), is placed outside of the mall and it has become a popular spot to take photos. Initially it was placed there temporarily for the celebration of 'French Year' in 1998, however it

has become so popular that it was decided to leave it there permanently.

The last shopping mall complex, and the biggest, is called Palette Town (72,800 m²), which houses *Venus Fort* and has 154 outlets. It is based around a recreated baroque European townscape, targeting female consumers in their 20s and 30s, and inspired by similar 'Forum shops' in Las Vegas (Mori Building, 2002). The developer aims for it to be a retail and leisure theme park with the concept being a 'fashion museum' (Kadota, 2001: 41). It aims to be a fashion leader with many products from abroad. The lighting of the ceiling changes regularly so that shoppers can experience sunrise, daylight, sunset and the night sky. There is an indoor fountain and piazza which can host small events and wedding ceremonies. This shopping mall also provides seasonal events, for instance during the Halloween season, costumed staff drive automatic carts in the mall and attempt to create a festive atmosphere for the season (see Fig. 7.9). A genuine replica of the Mouth of Truth (*Bocca della Verità*) from Rome, which became globally famous after the film *Roman Holiday*, is placed on the wall of the mall. This was presented when Japan was celebrating 'Italian year' in 2001 (see Fig. 7.10). This feature

Fig. 7.9. Halloween at the Venus Fort shopping centre, Odaiba.

Fig. 7.10. Replica of the Roman *Bocca della Verità* at the Venus Fort shopping centre, Odaiba.

attracts many shoppers and many take photos, just as they might in Rome.

Conclusion: Striking the Balance between 'Play, Work and Live'

Beyond Odaiba, residents of the wider Tokyo metropolis are surrounded by middle to high rise buildings in a densely built and cluttered urban neighbourhood; for them the sky of Tokyo is rather small, but in Odaiba it is spacious. Passengers on the Rainbow Bridge symbolically cross the water to wander into the 'foreign realm' that is Odaiba, and which offers them a different environment and a playscape akin to a theme park. Global capital and a range of exotic or culturally recognizable symbols have been carefully selected, organized and commodified for the Japanese market and for easy consumption for visitors ranging from school children to the elderly. In this new urban development, the tourism and leisure industry has played a critical role, not only as economic actor but also in the design and relative distribution of uses of the physical environment. The striking and incongruous architectural design and the presence of various leisure activities have made Odaiba one of the most popular destinations in Japan for visitors. Despite this success it is unpopular with some residents and workers who find the area difficult. While this reclaimed land was not initially planned to be a sub-centre of Tokyo, planners, developers, politicians and the market shifted their focus towards creating a mixed-use environment which included developing thousands of apartments.

The original Odaiba project was reworked and a 'dreamscape of consumption' has resulted but this area is a place of work for many thousands and a neighbourhood for many others. It is hugely successful as a combination of visitor attractions and the tourism and leisure industry, and a partial success as a sub-centre for businesses. Odaiba has, overall, been a qualified success but it is important to see Odaiba from a long-term perspective and in terms of its credentials as a sustainable environment; as a space with sustainable urban regeneration potential. In order to be competitive with other world cities TMG, developers and private investors are

making environments similar to many Western major city centres (see Saito and Thornley, 2003). Tokyo has sacrificed its sense of place, or even 'Japaneseness', in order to attract global businesses to create a novel 'work' and 'play' environment. Theme-park-like shopping malls are novel and they attract visitors, but only time will show their long-term durability and attractiveness and they demonstrably do not provide what residents need. Only bigger business chains or companies can afford to rent the larger commercial spaces, although some small- and medium-size businesses do rent spaces within these buildings. They are welcomed only if they fit the concept of the shopping mall. In this way many businesses are excluded from the new development.

In analysing Odaiba from the perspective of the three elements of the amenity environment model the 'play' dimension appears to work and appears to work for a cross-section of Japanese society, with a mix of activities and range of affordability on offer. Miyoshi (2000) has also analysed Odaiba's success with visitors, seeing it as a 'convenient resort' for urban dwellers. The environment is impressive and it has an atmosphere of the 'admirable West' that seems to appeal to the Japanese – indeed the 'exotic' is a recognized facet of leisure attractions around the world (Swarbrooke, 2002). Consumption in this new regeneration space is no longer only found in the activity of buying products, but also in consuming the environment itself, as Jackson and Thrift (1995) have noted. Odaiba has become an all-embracing consumer experience and the gap between a 'real' or 'authentic' place and a theme park has seemingly never been narrower than in Odaiba. This challenges us to reflect on even the possibility of such a distinction being viable in the post-industrial city (cf. Baudrillard, 1975). Without a conscious effort to provide for organic growth and the involvement of a wide range of interests Odaiba may struggle to be a fulfilling and vibrant community place.

Odaiba has become a major centre for business activities and the 'work' element has been expanding. As noted above, several major firms have moved their headquarters to Odaiba, further information, fashion, convention and exhibition industries are present and research-based offices are increasing, resulting in nearly 40,000

workers being employed in the area. Transportation, which was inconvenient for workers who
started to work there in the earlier stages of development, has been gradually extended and
improved. During holiday seasons, weekends
and when big events take place commuting still
becomes problematic. The situation was similar
in terms of food and drink retailers, the number
of restaurants were limited and this restricted
competition resulted in less choice and high
prices. It was not sustainable to eat lunch out on
a daily basis, though this situation too has improved in recent years (Kadota, 2001). It is also
important to question if Odaiba provides quality
spaces for workers to relax and to take breaks
during and after their working hours. Exploration
of the attitude of workers is one aspect of
Odaiba, and elsewhere, that is under researched
and requires further investigation.

The north-eastern part of Odaiba was initially planned to feature a major concentration
of residential areas. However, the political pressure which forced changes to the master plan
resulted in residential blocks being erected in a
space formerly designed to feature commercial
space and the original residential areas were not
developed by the time of writing. The residents
who now live next to the commercial areas and
the leisure facilities are disturbed by the passage
of many thousands of visitors and their needs
are subordinated to those of visitors and capital
(Arisue Kenkyusitsu, 1996). Although the political power of councillors at TMG succeeded in
increasing the number of residential flats in one
part of Odaiba, residents' quality of life was not
ensured at the same time. For example facilities such as supermarkets have been lacking
and decision makers should consider the integration of uses more carefully in future. As
already mentioned, the transportation system is
often over-congested, particularly during weekends, school holidays and when big events
take place. The large number of visitors over-
whelms those who live on Odaiba and the
location of the residential elements has also
been flawed, as noted above. Overall the 'live'
element needs improvement and a better
understanding of the needs required to deliver
a good quality of life for residents is required.
This can surely be derived from past experience and from engaging more thoroughly with
residents.

From the perspective of the amenity environment, the three elements are present but the
'live' and 'work' elements are overwhelmed by
the 'play' element. Tourists and leisure participants are the major beneficiary of the new
regeneration, however, the impacts of tourism
and leisure overwhelm the working and living
populations. Tourism and leisure space specialists appear to have a responsibility to voice the
range of benefits and problems that tourism and
leisure spaces may bring to 'work' and 'live'
communities and the industry must recognize
what is necessary to make more sustainable
environments for various users of the space.
Although a mixed land use approach has been
taken, it lacked detail, an understanding of different needs and the correct use of mix. The
economic and political environment severely
affected the process and development of
Odaiba. Some spaces must be allowed to be
developed organically over a longer period of
time with a mixture of small- and medium-size
buildings with open spaces – and given the public ownership of much of the area this must be
possible. Design guidelines are to be introduced
and some buildings may incorporate the more
traditional Japanese style. Indeed one building
used for onsen (hot spring) has already used
Japanese architectural design.

In closing this chapter it should be under-
scored that the making of the ideal amenity
environment offers a difficult challenge and
cannot be easily prescribed. There is still a need
for better and more carefully worked out design
and master planning with some spaces for
smaller organic development being part of the
solution. The selling of leases to a variety of
buyers and the active involvement of the leisure
and tourism industry in the design and
negotiation phases of these large mixed-use
developments may also help. Lessons should
have been learned from other developments
and applied in Odaiba. However, even the
most neatly planned and developed townscape
with architectural merit does not necessarily add
appropriate value to people's quality of life. The
challenge for the leisure and tourism industry is
to act more deliberatively and responsibly and
become a long-term partner in the governance
of towns and cities, helping to make the 'play',
'work' and 'live' elements of urban life work
better and be more sustainable. The foregoing

account also indicates an important area of research: to explore and better understand the impacts of playscapes within the wider sustainable communities agenda and to understand the needs of different interests (i.e. investors, tenants, residents, workers and visitors). For the tourism and leisure industries and those cities that are turning towards consumption activity and related land use to regenerate and sustain their economy, the need to work together responsibly is urgent.

Notes

[1] This was when the exchange rate between the US dollar and the Japanese yen was $1 = 113Y.
[2] It has been estimated that in 1999 the ratio of daytime to night-time population was 5 : 1 in Tokyo compared to New York with a 2 : 1 relationship (Hiramoto, 2000).

References

Aldous, T. (1992) *Urban Villages: a Concept for Creating Mixed-use Urban Developments on a Sustainable Scale*. Urban Villages Group, London.

Aqua City Odaiba (2002) *Aqua City Odaiba*. Available at: http://www.aquacity.co.jp (accessed 5 October 2002).

Arisue Kenkyusitsu (1996) *Tsukurareta-toshi: Rinkaifukutoshin wa risoukyou ka* (Artificial city: is the Waterfront City Utopia?). Unpublished report by University of Keio, Japan.

Auge, M. (1995) *Non-Places: Introduction to an Anthropology of Supermodernity*. Verso, London.

Baudrillard, J. (1975) *The Mirror of Production*. Telos Press, St Louis, Missouri.

Bianchini, F. and Parkinson, M. (eds) (1993) *Cultural Policy and Urban Regeneration: the West European Experience*. Manchester University Press, Manchester, UK.

Bourdieu, P. (1990) *Distinction. A Social Critique of the Judgement of Taste*. Sage, London.

Brownill, S. (1990) *Developing London's Docklands: Another Great Planning Disaster?* Paul Chapman, London.

Bureau of Ports and Harbors (2000) *The Results of Annual Visitor Numbers of New Waterfront City for 2000*. Tokyo Metropolitan Government, Tokyo.

CABE (Commission for Architecture and the Built Environment)/DETR (Department of the Environment, Transport and the Regions) (2000) *By Design. Urban Design in the Planning System: Towards Better Practice*. DETR, London.

DETR (Department of the Environment, Transport and the Regions) (2000a) *Our Towns and Cities: the Future – Delivering an Urban Renaissance*. DETR, London.

DETR (Department of the Environment, Transport and the Regions) (2000b) *Towards an Urban Renaissance – Mission Statement*. DETR, London.

DTLR (Department of Transport, Local Government and the Regions) (2002) *Mixed-use Development: Practice and Potential*. The Stationery Office, London.

Evans, G. (2001) *Cultural Planning: an Urban Renaissance?* Routledge, London.

Gallimore, P. and Gray, A. (2002) The role of investor sentiment in property investment decisions. *Journal of Property Research* 19(2), 111–120.

Guy, S. and Henneberry, J. (2000) *Cultures of Development: Property and Urban Regeneration*. Proceedings of the Cutting Edge Conference, Royal Institution of Chartered Surveyors Research Foundation.

Hesmondhalgh, D. (2002) *The Cultural Industries*. Sage, London.

Hiramoto, K. (2000) *The Tale of New Waterfront City: the Political and Economic Conflict of 'Odaiba'*. Chukoshinsho, Tokyo.

Jackson, P. and Thrift, N. (1995) Geographies of consumption. In: Miller, D. (ed.) *Acknowledging Consumption: a Review of New Studies*. Routledge, London, pp. 204–237.

Jacobs, J. (1961) *Death and Life of Great American Cities*. Random House, New York.

Kadota, K. (ed.) (2001) Tokyo favourite town, Odaiba. *Mapple Magazine* No. 137. Shobunsha, Tokyo.

Knox, P.L. (ed.) (1993) *The Restless Urban Landscape*. Prentice Hall, Englewood Cliffs, New Jersey.

Lee, M.J. (ed.) (2000) *The Consumer Society Reader*. Blackwell, Oxford.

Lifton, R. (1976) *The Life of the Self*. Simon and Schuster, New York.

Locum Destination Review (2003) The key to urban success. Live, work, play. *Locum Destination Review*, pp. 8–12.

Miles, S. (1998) *Consumerism: as a Way of Life.* Sage, London.

Miller, A. (1969) *The Price.* Secker & Warburg, London.

Miller, D. (ed.) (1995) *Acknowledging Consumption: a Review of New Studies.* Routledge, London.

Miyake, R., Siganos, A. and Sawai, Y. (eds) (2004) *Bunkashigen to Gavanansu* (Cultural Resources and Governance). Kajima Institute Publishing, Tokyo.

Miyoshi, R. (2000) *Odaibano-okite* (Rules of Odaiba). Diamond-sha, Tokyo.

Mori Building (2002) *Venus Fort.* Available at: http://www.mori.co.jp (accessed 7 October 2002).

Murayama, M. (2004a) *Understanding Urban Tourism: Urban Regeneration and Development in Birmingham.* Bunshindo, Tokyo.

Murayama, M. (2004b) Leisure and tourism and the development of new urban spaces in the global village. In: Conner, T. and Torimoto, I. (eds) *Globalization Redux: New Name, Same Game.* University Press of America, Lanham, Maryland, pp. 171–182.

NAHB (National Association of Home Builders) (1999) *Smart Growth. Building Better Places to Live, Work and Play.* NAHB, Washington, DC.

Page, S. and Hall, M.C. (2003) *Managing Urban Tourism.* Pearson Education, Harlow, UK.

Rowley, A. (1998) *Planning Mixed-use Development.* Royal Institution of Chartered Surveyors (RICS), London.

Rowley, A. (2003) Mixed-use development literature review. Report by Department of Real Estate and Planning, University of Reading, Reading, UK.

Saito, A. (2003) World city formation in capitalist developmental state: Tokyo and the waterfront sub-centre project. *Urban Studies* 40(2), 283–308.

Saito, A. and Thornley, A. (2003) Shifts in Tokyo's world status and the urban planning response. *Urban Studies* 40(4), 665–685.

Savage, V., Huang, S. and Chang, T.C. (2004) The Singapore River thematic zone: sustainable tourism in an urban context. *The Geographical Journal* 170(3), 212–225.

Sheller, M. and Urry, J. (eds) (2004) *Tourism Mobilities: Places to Play, Places in Play.* Routledge, London.

Sumisho Urban Kaihatsu (2002) *Decks Tokyo Beach.* Available at: http://www.odaiba-decks.com (accessed 5 October 2005).

Swarbrooke, J. (2002) *The Development and Management of Visitor Attractions,* 2nd edn. Elsevier Butterworth-Heinemann, Oxford.

The Civic Trust (2004) *Birmingham, Brindleyplace: Good Practice in the Management of the Evening Economy: a Case Study of Brindleyplace.* The Civic Trust, Birmingham, UK.

TMG (Tokyo Metropolitan Government) (1995) *Odaiba Waterfront City.* TMG, Tokyo.

TMG (Tokyo Metropolitan Government) (1999) *The Economic Impacts Studies of Development of New Waterfront City.* Tokyo Metropolitan Government, Tokyo.

TMG (Tokyo Metropolitan Government) (2001) *Tokyo Bay Area.* Tokyo Metropolitan Government, Tokyo.

TMG (Tokyo Metropolitan Government) (2002) *Tokyo Waterfront City.* Available at: http://www.kouwan.metro.tokyo.jp/rinkai/index.html (accessed 26 July 2005).

TMG (Tokyo Metropolitan Government) (2005) *Town Planning.* Available at: http://www.kouwan.metro.tokyo.jp/data/rinkai-plan/index.html (accessed 26 July 2005).

Trancik, R. (1986) *Finding Lost Space.* John Wiley, London.

Ward, K. (2003) Entrepreneurial urbanism, state restructuring and civilizing 'New' East Manchester. *Area* 35(2), 116–127.

Witherspoon, R.E., Abbett, J.P. and Gladstone, R.M. (1976) *Mixed-use Developments: New Ways of Land Use.* Urban Land Institute, Washington, DC.

Wu, F. (2000) The global and local dimensions of place-making: remaking Shanghai as a world city. *Urban Studies* 37, 1359–1377.

8 After the Circus Leaves Town: the Relationship between Sport Events, Tourism and Urban Regeneration

Andrew Smith

Introduction

It is increasingly common for cities to deploy mass or popular culture(s) to stimulate regeneration. Popular music (Aitchison and Evans, 2003), film (Schofield, 1996) and television (Tooke and Baker, 1996) have all been used in recent efforts. This represents a shift from established practice, where only 'high' culture was deemed capable of reversing urban decline. Sport initiatives are perhaps the most prevalent examples of these 'populist' regeneration schemes. The number of cities employing sport as a regeneration tool has increased in recent years, but so has the relative importance of sport initiatives within individual regeneration programmes. In some cities, sport is not merely allocated a minor role in helping to revive urban fortunes; but provides the 'centrepiece of regeneration efforts' (Austrian and Rosentraub, 2002: 550). Events and tourism are vital elements within this type of approach. Staging sport events is usually an intrinsic part of a sport-led strategy and tourism is often viewed as a key mechanism through which these events can assist regeneration. Yet the regeneration and tourism value of sport initiatives has been subject to much scepticism. As Long and Sanderson assert: 'just as the regenerative capacity of prestige cultural provision is limited . . . the efficacy of high profile sports development in aiding regeneration has been questioned' (1996: 28).

The tourism benefits have also been queried. Senior officials within the US travel industry have stated that sport 'has nothing to do with tourism or development', and have dismissed the contention that sport boosts tourism as akin to 'the emperor's new clothes' (Euchner, 1999: 222). The aim of this chapter is to assess such arguments by exploring the relationship between sport events, tourism and regeneration. Initial sections discuss the relationship between events and different types of regeneration. This is achieved via reference to a range of international examples. Subsequent sections focus more specifically on tourism, with a discussion of how tourism is affected by events strategies. In the final sections of the chapter, the case studies of Manchester 2002 and London 2012 are discussed to explore the way in which events have been used, and plan to be used, to encourage both urban tourism and urban regeneration. This focus on UK cities should provide a useful transatlantic comparison with the US perspective discussed by Heying *et al.* in Chapter 9.

Events and the Contemporary City

According to Connell and Page (2005) there are three main types of event; 'rolling events' that run from year to year; site specific 'one-off events'; and 'peripatetic events' where different cities compete to be the host. It is these latter 'footloose' events that provide the focus for this chapter. These events are typical of what have been termed 'hallmark' (Ritchie, 1984) or 'mega'-events (Hall, 1997) by academic commentators. Elite sport is the focus of many of these events. The mass audiences, celebrities, iconic structures and consumption associated with contemporary sport mean that sporting spectacles are perceived by cities as particularly valuable. Indeed, rather than merely comprising cultural celebrations, large sport events are now being used strategically by cities to achieve urban regeneration. According to Lipsitz (1984), this practice is underpinned by six key objectives: the creation of a 'big town' image; increased marketing power to attract new industry; additional employment and sales; new recreational opportunities for residents; renewed civic morale; and more interest in sport among the young. This broad range of envisaged outcomes emphasizes the potential links between events and multiple forms of regeneration: physical, social and economic. On a less explicit level, the importance of events to the contemporary city can be related to their compulsion to become centres of consumption through the 'organisation of spectacle and theatricality' (Harvey, 1989: 92). This desire to create spectacles is closely related to the contention that, rather than relying on the consumption of goods, it is valuable for cities to emphasize the consumption of experiences and pleasure, or what Harvey terms 'ephemeral services in consumption' (Harvey, 1989: 285). Staging large sport events is seen not only as a means of generating such consumption, but as an important way of symbolizing the transition of cities towards this envisaged role. However, there is nothing new or revolutionary about cities using sporting spectacles to achieve their objectives. As Tuan asserts, the city has always drawn attention to itself, and achieved power and status, through 'the scale and solemnity of its rites and festivals' (Tuan, 1977: 173).

Using sport events to achieve urban regeneration is both an illustration of, and an agent of, certain cultural shifts. Post-industrial cities are now deemed to be centres of play or entertainment which are 'saturated with signs and images to the extent that anything can become represented, thematised and made an object of interest' (Featherstone, 1991: 101). As Featherstone implies in his use of the term 'anything', the means by which cities pursue economic, cultural and symbolic capital have become increasingly diversified. The alleged collapse of 'the social' means that popular cultures have become regarded as 'more legitimate and the source of prestige and further up the symbolic hierarchy' (Featherstone 1991: 106). Therefore, post-industrial cities can become 'cultural' centres, not simply because of their association with the high arts, but also via associations with the mass or popular cultures, such as sport. Cities traditionally associated with industrial production are therefore able to compete with more established tourist cities by utilizing sport events to generate symbolic capital. This process is representative of a new role for cultural forms in cities. Whereas in previous eras, urban 'culture' was deemed to be one of the more desirable outcomes of economic growth, 'culture' is now deliberately exploited as a way of generating such growth in ailing industrial areas.

New urban developments aimed at encouraging tourist visitation are often aimed at the most lucrative consumers: the 'better off' (Bramwell and Rawding, 1996) or 'the right sort of people' (Harvey, 1989). Traditionally, sport in cities has been associated with the urban working classes, hardly the image that would be deemed to attract the 'right sort of people' to cities. But the increasing gentrification/sanitization of sport and the corresponding confusion of hierarchical consumer tastes means that sport is now regarded as an effective means of attracting affluent sectors of the tourist market. Whereas previously it may have been inherently contradictory to promote a city's sporting pedigree alongside more traditional forms of culture, the contention here is that not only is this now an appropriate partnership, but one that can be effectively sold to a new market of more eclectic, rounded tourists whose tastes aren't necessarily confined to the different ends of an orthodox cultural spectrum (Smith, 2005a).

There are also other possible explanations for the increasing deployment of sport events as regeneration 'tools'. Sport-led regeneration is an attractive compromise for cities that are seeking to attract external investment, but who are also keen to avoid accusations that they are deserting or suppressing local tradition and history. Sport has long been an important part of most cities. This means that an emphasis on sport events as a vehicle for urban regeneration may be less controversial than the use of more traditional cultural forms. For instance, it may avoid the sort of controversy generated by Glasgow's designation as the European City of Culture 1990 (Boyle and Hughes, 1991). This year-long event was criticized by some people who felt that the resulting representation of the city was 'not one sedimented down the years in Glaswegian consciousness, but one which encourages thinking about Glasgow in new terms, i.e. without having reference back to external reality' (Boyle and Hughes, 1991: 221). Although sport-led regeneration also presents a highly selective vision of the city, 'sanitising the real working class culture and cultural history' (Boyle and Hughes, 1991: 225), there is little doubt that sport has played a fundamental role in the development and daily life of these cities throughout the past 100 years. This may mean that sport is more readily accepted as a regeneration theme, not only placating sensitive residents, but also presenting a more credible image of the city to a critical external audience.

Before the relationship between tourism, events and regeneration can be understood, it is first necessary to explore the relationship between sport events and regeneration. As other chapters in this volume have identified, the term 'regeneration' has evolved from merely denoting environmental and infrastructural redevelopment in urban areas, to encompassing the revitalized provision of housing, employment, health, education and leisure services for those suffering disproportionately from the effects of industrial decline. Therefore opportunities for physical, social and economic regeneration are all discussed.

Events and Regeneration

Staging sport events often involves investment in new venues, thus providing opportunities for the physical regeneration of host cities. Nevertheless, it is perhaps worth noting a distinction between physical regeneration and mere urban development. Athens's Olympic initiatives designed for the 2004 Games were scattered around the city, with many built on greenfield sites in the urban outskirts. The location of these facilities and lack of spatial aggregation means this cannot really be considered to be an urban regeneration strategy (Beriatos and Gospodini, 2004). Instead the Athenian Olympic venues are examples of 'flagship development projects' (Carriere and Demaziere, 2002). This contrasts with Barcelona where new developments for the 1992 Olympic Games involved the concentrated recovery of brownfield sites. The reclamation of contaminated land is one reason why Barcelona's Olympic Village displays a 'high degree of adherence to sustainability principles' (Hemphill et al., 2004: 770). Yet even if dilapidated sites are redeveloped, sustainable regeneration is not guaranteed. To address this lofty ambition, an important consideration is to plan for the effective post-event use of such facilities. This helps to translate physical changes into wider regenerative benefits (Hemphill et al., 2004).

The most radical way of avoiding the under-use of venues is simply to dismantle them after the event. This was a strategy employed by Atlanta, USA, after the Olympic Games was staged there in 1996. The large number of temporary constructions and new venues that subsequently disappeared led some to label the 1996 event 'the disposable Games' (Rutheiser, 1996). This approach contrasts with that of Athens, where 95% of the projects planned for the Olympic Games in 2004 were permanent spatial structures (Beriatos and Gospodini, 2004). These cases highlight the dilemma faced by host cities: wanting to leave lasting physical legacy, whilst ensuring that money is not wasted developing and maintaining superfluous new facilities. Upgrading existing facilities is perhaps a more dependable way of avoiding expensive 'white elephants' and ensuring sustainable regeneration. This was the philosophy adopted during preparations for the 1984 Los Angeles Olympic Games (Andranovich et al., 2001). Such expediency matches the International Olympic Committee's (IOC's) latest, and rather negative, interpretation of event legacy which it sees as being ensured by cutting costs, reducing the size of the event and by avoiding unnecessary new sport arenas (Vigor et al., 2004). The IOC's approach is understandable in light of the innumerable instances of event venues that have subsequently been under-utlized (Chalkley and Essex, 1999). Malaysia spent a total of 561 m Malaysian Ringgits (£94 m) on stadia and infrastructure for the 1998 Commonwealth Games in Kuala Lumpur. The existing stadium and swimming complex were perfectly adequate for staging the Games, but new facilities were built to impress the watching international audience and to symbolize the achievements of the incumbent government (Silk, 2002). This example demonstrates the difficulties associated with using events to achieve regeneration, whilst simultaneously attempting to meet wider political objectives.

Events seem to leave a more positive physical legacy when they are used to accelerate or facilitate the accomplishment of existing plans. As Raco (2004) states, events should be embedded within other regeneration initiatives, and not act as a substitute for them. Accordingly, Carriere and Demaziere (2002) advocate an approach involving coherent urban development that includes an event, rather than using an event to encourage urban development. Barcelona provides the best example of such a strategy, as it had talked for over 25 years about many of the changes we now associate with the 1992 Olympic Games (Smith, 2005a). Principally, the event provided an important incentive and deadline to complete long held visions to develop road and transport infrastructure; housing, office and commercial developments; telecommunications; and hotel facilities. More money was spent on each of these types of development than new event facilities (Brunet, 1995). This ensured that the Olympic Games left a comprehensive physical legacy that provided the stimulus for subsequent economic regeneration.

The location of new facilities associated with events also influences the potential for regeneration. The recent trend to site event facilities at the edge of cities causes less disruption to residents and allows better access for spectators whilst events are being staged (Thornley, 2002). But it also means that facilities are often divorced from the communities they are supposed to be regenerating. For example, the Amsterdam Arena, developed as part of the Dutch capital's bid for the 1992 Olympics, was developed on a commercial site near to, but physically divorced from the Bijlmer district, one of the poorest neighbourhoods in the city (Thornley, 2002). This physical separation compromises the legacy of such facilities as evidence suggests that it is preferable to develop event facilities within disadvantaged communities, thus maximizing potential for local benefits. This is illustrated by the Stade de France, built as the centrepiece for the 1998 Football World Cup Finals, which has assisted the regeneration of the St Denis district of Paris in which it is situated (Dauncey, 1999). However, when siting event facilities within disadvantaged areas, organizers must ensure that they do not follow the established Olympic practice of simply 'bulldozing' existing communities to make space for new facilities and residents (Lenskyj, 2002).

Recent literature on events has suggested that it is insufficient to concentrate merely on the 'hard' physical legacy of events, as positive effects do not necessarily 'trickle-down' to the local people and businesses that need them most. Softer economic and social legacies also need to be addressed (Balsas, 2004). Accordingly, some events have involved deliberate attempts to encourage economic and social regeneration by providing new skills and support for local people. A common mechanism employed to achieve such effects is the use of volunteer programmes. Volunteers are needed to help facilitate events, and by training individuals and giving them direct experience of employment, new skills and confidence can be nurtured. In Lillehammer, Norway, host of the 1994 Winter Olympic Games, 79% of the volunteers surveyed felt that they had enhanced their skills by being one of the 9100 volunteers involved in the event (Kemp, 2002). The 2000 Sydney Olympic Games also involved an extensive volunteering scheme. The organizers spent $50 million on the recruitment, training, accreditation, acknowledgement, uniforms, feeding and transport of 62,000 volunteers. To reward their efforts, volunteers were given the chance to take up free tickets for the closing ceremony and the central business district (CBD) of Sydney was closed for half a day to provide volunteers with their own 'ticker-tape' parade.

The recruitment, training and management of voluntary staff is often very difficult (Webb, 2001). However, even if such efforts are successful, it is unclear whether this necessarily contributes to social regeneration. People who volunteer are often enthusiasts who have volunteered before, and tend not to be marginalized members of local communities. A more targeted approach focused on the most disadvantaged (and least skilled) helps to achieve genuine regenerative benefits for urban areas. Manchester's recent Commonwealth Games was the first to include an initiative where 'most participants came from groups with little sense of engagement with wider society' (Jones and Stokes, 2003: 204). A flexible training programme was formulated that offered participants the chance to volunteer for the Games and to obtain a nationally recognized vocational qualification. All participants were offered the chance to use new facilities in the period prior to the Games, including riding the Velodrome track at least once a month. Some groups, including people who were taught how to swim, were also given special access to the new aquatics centre (Jones and Stokes, 2003). Therefore, Manchester's volunteer programme was able to supplement skills development with wider social objectives. This is important, particularly as one of the UK's regeneration objectives is 'to enhance the quality of life of local people, including their health and cultural and sports opportunities' (Department of Environment, 1995: 2).

Alongside volunteering schemes, some cities have also adopted vocational training programmes in conjunction with events. As part of the $10 million construction industry training strategy implemented as part of the Sydney Olympic Games, 12,000 workers were trained, with special provision for workers from Aboriginal and non-English speaking communities (Webb, 2001). A pre-vocational programme for school leavers was also developed that enabled them to secure future employment in the industry. Large events are inextricably linked to construction employment, but major questions have to be asked about the actual number and quality of jobs which are supported by initiatives after the construction phase of an event (Loftman and Spirou, 1996). Therefore, it is important that wider employment and educational initiatives are pursued by event hosts. Greece adopted an Olympic Education programme in conjunction with the 2004 Games staged in Athens. This project was based on school initiatives adopted by previous Olympic hosts (Los Angeles, Calgary

and Lillehammer). Grammatikopoulos *et al.* note that these projects have tended to lack theoretical unity and subsequent evaluation, but assert that: 'they seemed to resonate with teachers as a source for integrated and imaginative pedagogical ideas and activities' (2004: 67). Lenskyj (2002) adds a note of warning that such schemes must not be led by commercial sponsorship. She cites evidence suggesting that the contents of Sydney's Olympic education packs left schoolchildren with the impression that McDonald's and the Games were indelibly linked.

Although new economic activity is often needed to stimulate economic regeneration, there is a danger that 'existing forms of employment . . . may be overlooked and undervalued' in event strategies (Raco, 2004: 35). Therefore, it is important to ensure that local companies and disadvantaged individuals are able to benefit from the lucrative contracts usually associated with large-scale events. The unsuccessful Cape Town bid for the 2004 Olympics involved a proposal whereby the Bid Company would offer 50% of its business transactions to commercial and professional enterprises from previously marginalized communities in the city. It also involved an Affirmable Procurement Policy (APP) which required that 30% of employees be local labour, which the Bid Company interpreted to mean the local neighbourhood. Such measures may be needed, particularly as evidence shows that events can actually harm local businesses, as well as assist them. Although Barcelona's Olympic regeneration is widely applauded, it involved the clearance of small manufacturing firms from Olympic sites. Hundreds of thriving small businesses were evicted from these areas which had traditionally offered low rents (Shapcott cited in Raco, 2004). Similarly, the Centennial Park constructed for the 1996 Olympic Games in Atlanta dislocated at least 70 businesses (Cherkis, 1996, cited in Whitelegg, 2000).

Just as there are events that can result in negative economic effects, there is the potential to engender negative social impacts, which planners should seek to minimize if regeneration goals are to be achieved. Some theorists have attempted to explain the effects that events have on host communities using social exchange theory. This framework implies that those who perceive that they have gained net benefits will think positively about an event and vice versa. After the Sydney Olympic Games in 2000, the main reason some residents were dissatisfied was because they perceived there to have been few personal rewards, with large personal costs (Waitt, 2003). Waitt also found that there was a worrying mismatch between public expenditure and perceived need and that the most disadvantaged were the least enthusiastic about the event (Waitt, 2003). Host cities need to be more aware that there are social consequences of events that affect host communities in the short and long term. With respect to the latter, cities must be careful not to remove access to community facilities to finance elite schemes. To allow the coherent development of Homebush Olympic Park for the Sydney Olympic Games, Auburn Local Government Area (LGA) was required to transfer rateable land to an adjacent council in exchange for land comprising part of the Olympic Park. The budget shortfall that this created meant that local community and youth services were suspended (Owen, 2002). Furthermore, due to the upgrading of various facilities to stage Olympic events, local people within both Waverley and Ryde LGAs experienced reduced access to, and control of, community facilities (Owen, 2002). Similar effects were felt in Sheffield, where local swimming pools were closed to fund high-spec facilities for the 1991 World Student Games. There is also a danger that events can have a negative effect on housing provision for local people. This is illustrated by several Australian examples. Despite the potential to develop new social accommodation, Lenskyj notes that the America's Cup (a prestigious sailing event) in Fremantle and Melbourne's bid for the Olympic Games were detrimental to housing (2002). She also reports that affordable rental accommodation in the eastern suburbs, inner city and inner west of Sydney became virtually non-existent by 2000, due to the Olympic Games staged that year. Events have also been associated with the sanitization of cities, with homeless people and travellers removed from prominent areas (Atkinson and Laurier, 1998). This provides a double whammy for evicted tenants who can no longer afford accommodation, but who also suffer from the withdrawal of support services for the homeless.

Managing and Planning Event Regeneration

Events will only achieve regeneration outcomes if they are properly planned and managed. The absence of rigorous planning approaches is an unfortunate, but seemingly established characteristic of event initiatives. As Chalkley and Essex point out, planning for major events often 'sits outside the existing categories of planning' (1999: 391). Similarly, Hall suggests that many event hosts have adopted a 'boosterist' approach, which he sees as 'a form of non-planning' (2000: 21). This is perhaps best exemplified by Sheffield's preparations for the 1991 World Student Games, which involved 'muddling through without a clear formal plan' (Bramwell, 1997: 174). Bramwell feels this lack of strategic planning resulted in missed opportunities for regeneration. Even when a more strategic approach has been undertaken by host cities, it has tended to be characterized by 'top-down' planning. There are few instances where communities have actively participated in the planning and implementation of event projects. Even in Barcelona, often lauded as an example of best practice, such involvement was conspicuously absent. As Calavita and Ferrer state: 'It would be tempting to ascribe, at least in part, the success of Barcelona's Olympics to a city-wide and neighbourhood participation process in its planning and implementation. But this is not the case' (2000: 804). Ironically, one exception to this prevalent deficiency was denied the opportunity to be fully realized. The (unsuccessful) bid for the 2004 Olympic Games prepared by Cape Town, South Africa, involved hundreds of visits to community groups by bid personnel. All aspects of the bid were independently assessed and submitted for community ratification (Hiller, 2000).

The frailties of event planning are perhaps explained, though not excused, by the apparent incompatibility of short-lived events with long-term planning. The deadlines and timetables associated with staging events often result in established planning procedures being compromised. Sydney's Olympic Games received plaudits such as 'The Best Games Ever' (Lenskyj, 2002) and 'The Collaborative Games' (Webb, 2001), but the Games President admitted that there were anti-democratic elements in the highly centralized system used to implement initiatives (Webb, 2001). Certain developments were 'fast-tracked' and certain procedures (e.g. environmental impact assessment (EIA) submissions) ignored. This made the Olympic organizers much less accountable to the community than under normal circumstances (Owen, 2002). The Games organizers were also accused of merely encouraging tokenistic input from LGAs and community groups. For example, the general manger of Auburn Council, the LGA in which the main Olympic Park is situated, complained that they were on a lot of 'paper-bag committees . . . yes, we're on a lot of committees, but I really question the substance or the impact or the effect that any of these have' (Owen, 2002: 301).

Event Regeneration and Tourism

The objectives of urban sport initiatives are diffuse and involve ambitions to achieve regeneration through a range of mechanisms. Newman (2002) suggests that urban authorities believe that staging sport events helps to resurrect the historical association between business, recreation, tourism and city centres. As this comment illustrates, tourism is often envisaged as both an impact of, and a mechanism for, event regeneration. Yet merely citing increased tourism activity as a key objective/justification does not necessarily mean that cities have developed rigorous plans to allow such effects to accrue. Again, Sheffield provides an illustrative example. Before, during and after the 1991 World Student Games, Sheffield City Council affirmed their desire to use the Games to generate and promote tourism. Despite this apparent commitment to tourism, Bramwell suggests that 'there was no clear view of how the World Student Games facilities could help the city's tourism industry' (1993: 17). As Bramwell recognizes, during the planning of the Games and in the immediate aftermath, there was no strategic plan that outlined 'specific objectives and precise mechanisms' that would ensure tourism benefits (1997: 170). This failure to develop rigorous tourism planning measures in association with events adds further weight to critics who have berated the regenerative power of tourism

more generally. This includes those who cite gentrification, urban polarization and community disenfranchisement as less desirable outcomes.

Although it is widely assumed that events will inevitably generate increased tourism receipts, this is not necessarily borne out by the evidence available. As Faulkner et al. (2001) identify, in many instances, cities staging large sport events such as the Olympic Games experience reduced visitor numbers during the event itself. This is due to a 'switching effect', where certain visitors deliberately avoid the extra expense and inconvenience associated with large events. In Sydney the large number of visitors attending the 2000 Olympic Games did not compensate for large number of 'switchers', who would have visited the city during that summer had the Games not taken place. As Euchner (1999) argues, the tourism benefits of event strategies are often exaggerated, because large sport events discourage tourist activity that would otherwise have occurred. This is further demonstrated by the research undertaken by Connell and Page (2005), who observed a 7.7% drop in local business caused by displacement of demand due to the World Medical and Health Games staged in Stirling, Scotland. The displacement of demand due to sport events should be of particular concern to the UK as the displaced tourism activity may actually have been more lucrative than that associated with event spectators. The small size of the UK means that, unlike in the USA, sport tourism does not result in a large proportion of lucrative overnight city visits. Therefore, the vast majority of sports fans are usually visitors or excursionists, rather than genuine tourists, and they tend to have little engagement with the cities they are visiting. This restricts economic impacts.

As well as directly displacing demand, it is also conceivable that sport-led regeneration initiatives could discourage tourism indirectly by detracting from, or diluting, other images that the city is attempting to develop. The potential for negative effects is highlighted by Higham's pessimistic assertion that cities staging major events 'stand to lose more than they can gain in terms of destination image' because of the possibility of detrimental media exposure (1999: 84). Chalip et al. (2003) view sport reimaging as an exercise in co-branding, where success depends upon the harmonization of the destination image and the event image. Their research revealed that images of the Gold Coast's natural environment were affected negatively by a motor race staged in the destination. This was because of the incompatibility of this type of event with this particular dimension of image (Chalip et al., 2003). Therefore, not all the imagery emanating from sport events is compatible with the images cities want to project. An illustrative example is provided by Rowe and McGurk (1999) in their evaluation of the relationship between sport and the image of Newcastle, Australia. This city enjoyed widespread media attention after its Rugby League team unexpectedly triumphed in a national final. Using a rather patronizing metaphor, the media were keen to draw parallels between the determination of the city's victorious team, and that of its blue-collar workforce. The resultant representation of Newcastle as a masculine, working class city, projected an image that was 'heavily reliant on the very properties that urban modernizers are attempting to de-emphasize' (Rowe and McGurk, 1999: 137). This dilemma perhaps helps to explain the conspicuous absence of regular sport events and established teams from official reimaging initiatives. Although Higham (1999: 89) contends that cities need to 'develop a greater understanding of the tourism development potential of existing/regular sport events and competitions', the need for a certain type of imagery, aimed at a certain target audience, suggests that this may be difficult to achieve. As Laurier states 'there is nothing more useless to a city-seller than a working class city that is still working class' (1993: 276).

Despite some of the cynicism noted above, many host cities have experienced large increases in visitor numbers in the years following an event. Although it is difficult to isolate the extent to which this was directly caused by an individual event, it is no coincidence that cities such as Seoul, Sydney and Barcelona have experienced larger tourism numbers for a sustained period after staging an Olympic Games. This effect is not merely due to increased international exposure and associated image enhancement. Infrastructural improvements, such as investment in airports, hotel space and new organizational capacity have assisted this trend. Positive effects are also sometimes a function of tourism marketing initiatives that are pursued in

parallel with events. Barcelona used its staging of the 1992 Olympic Games as a means of regenerating urban infrastructure and derelict land and to 'launch its tourism strategy for the next century' (Glyptis, 1991: 179). Similarly, Sydney used the 2000 Olympic Games to enhance its overall market position, to encourage repeat visits and to build new relationships amongst a fragmented tourism sector (Faulkner et al., 2001). Malaysia has also tied sport events to the development of its tourism industry (Van der Westhuizen, 2004: 1284). The successful 'Visit Malaysia Year', which increased tourism revenue by 190%, coincided with the staging of the 1998 Commonwealth Games (Van der Westhuizen, 2004). This example highlights that it is often unclear whether increases in tourism revenue are due to the effects of an event, or due to the effects of a wider tourism strategy employed in parallel with an event. Tourism development may also be explained by other external factors. The growth in short breaks and the rise of low-cost air carriers certainly assisted Barcelona's post-Olympic visitor numbers (Smith, 2004). As Hiller recognizes, a mega-event 'cannot be seen in isolation for other factors occurring simultaneously and independent of it' (Hiller, 1998: 53).

According to the rhetoric contained within the literature associated with event strategies, the main mechanism for positive tourism impacts is image enhancement. As Law identifies, cities use 'major sporting activities . . . to project a high status image of the city via media coverage which may help attract visitors' (Law, 1993: 94). There is certainly evidence that staging sport events can provide image benefits (Smith, 2005b). This is particularly important for cities aiming to address perpetual associations with heavy industry and industrial decline. Yet it is not entirely clear whether increased tourism revenues and regeneration inevitably follow from any resultant image enhancement. For Ritchie and Smith, even if destinations do experience image advancement 'it is not immediately obvious that this will translate into increased visitation levels, tourism receipts and/or other forms of economic development' (1991: 9). This is reaffirmed by Chalip et al.'s research where 'no direct effect of event media on intention to visit was found' (2003: 228). It is difficult to justify event regeneration via envisaged image and tourism effects if enhanced images don't deliver increased tourism receipts. This problem is further accentuated by evidence that a city's image is not necessarily an important factor in determining the consumption patterns of sport tourists. Evidence from both the consumers and the producers of sport reimaging appears to indicate that urban sport tourism is almost exclusively activated by the provision of attractive events, rather than via the images of cities (Smith, 2002). At present, developing an attractive image merely appears to assist urban sports tourism in an indirect manner, impressing event organizers and sport administrators, therefore allowing cities to secure events of sufficient quality to attract tourists. This is recognized by the Policy Officer-Sport of Birmingham City Council (UK) who states that the intended impact of sport initiatives in Birmingham was to 'demonstrate that we could adapt and provide a plethora of different settings which met sport's needs' (Personal communication, 1999). The target audience was the sport events industry, rather than sport tourists. Therefore, apart from attracting specific events, there is little evidence to suggest that urban sporting reputations directly influence tourists to visit particular cities.

Cities that have developed reputations as 'cities of sport' through events strategies need to capitalize more on such imagery if related strategies are to be justified. It is possible that a reorientation of urban sports tourism could allow sports imagery to have a more pronounced effect on tourism in cities. In the UK the concept of urban sport tourism is relatively undeveloped and is perceived as comprising the staging of regular and one-off elite sport events. The notion of a city that boasts a diverse range of sporting products including events, participatory activities, museums, tours, stadia, themed areas and halls of fame is something that has yet to be fully exploited by cities. This is something that is perhaps more developed in the USA, where cities are more likely boast to a coherent mix of sports attractions to complement the provision of elite events. Until more extensive provision is developed in UK cities, it is perhaps naïve to think that promoting a city as a 'city of sport' will attract sport tourists. This process may be assisted by exploring further the relationship between tourism and sport. In addition

to sports tourism, involving sport as a primary motivation for visitation, Hinch and Higham (2001) use the term 'tourism sports', which they consider to be 'sport as a secondary activity whilst travelling' (2001: 48). The challenge for cities may be to make more use of their sporting reputations, by providing a critical mass of tourism sport attractions which may generate 'tourism sports', as well as sports tourism.

Current provision of 'tourism sports' in cities is obstructed by various factors. Although urban sport is an attractive tourism product, the majority of tickets for regular events are pre-sold to season ticket holders, precluding 'opportunistic' or 'incidental' tourist engagement. As such, tourists are usually unable to watch the most popular sporting events staged in UK and US cities (Euchner, 1999). Furthermore, sport initiatives implemented recently in cities do not necessarily improve the provision of tourism sports because they were not initiated within a cohesive framework where tourism was an explicit objective. A vision of how to use initiatives to generate tourism was certainly lacking in the sport initiatives introduced in Birmingham, Manchester and Sheffield (UK) during the 1980s and 1990s (Smith, 2001). This is an important observation, particularly as Fretter (1993) suggests that an essential element of successful place marketing is 'a clear understanding of what you want to achieve' (1993: 165). Birmingham and Manchester inadvertently initiated sporting strategies as a result of opportunistic Olympic bids. Birmingham did not have a coherent and planned strategy at the onset of its recent sport initiatives, with an official that was involved throughout the process admitting that the 'policy followed the initiatives' (Personal communication, 1999). This situation was replicated some years later in Sheffield where urban sporting policy was prepared retrospectively once initiatives had already been implemented (Bramwell, 1997). In all three cities, it was never made clear how the development of sport initiatives could actually be used to pursue tourism objectives. The envisaged 'tourism sports' outcomes were particularly underdeveloped.

Although tourists benefit from the infrastructural legacy bequeathed by many sport events, the tourism potential of event sites is often neglected. Such areas have often been designed to accommodate hundreds of thousands of people and too many cities expect that they will automatically be attractive tourist zones even when events are not being staged. Although such spaces are usually well endowed with transport infrastructure, landscaping and public art, they are often in peripheral areas, exposed to the elements, and as they can be vast spaces, there are often inconveniently large distances between the different structures that might be of interest to tourists. Such spaces look spectacular when filled with large numbers of spectators, but rather pathetic when events are not being staged. This means they can be rather underwhelming tourist sites. Examples include the Greenwich peninsular in South East London, home of the infamous Millennium Dome, which is littered with enormous car parks, monumental green spaces and impressive transport facilities. This area dwarfs and disappoints the visitors who venture out of the city centre to take a closer look at the Dome. Certainly, those who have been to this and similar sites, will be wary of the claim that London's new Olympic park, the centrepiece of the 2012 Games; 'will appeal to visitors from around the UK and overseas as an important part of the capital's visitor experience' (London 2012, 2005: 28).

Before drawing conclusions about the relationship between sport events, tourism and urban regeneration, it is useful to consider examples of how UK cities have attempted to pursue regeneration through event-related tourism initiatives. Two such examples are reviewed below, including one city which has recently staged a large sport event, and another which has just earned the right to do so.

Manchester 2002

In 1995 Manchester was awarded the right to stage the 2002 Commonwealth Games. The city felt that the Games provided an unprecedented opportunity to secure lasting social and economic benefits and this was a key motivation for staging the event. A key mechanism for securing this legacy was the 2002 North West Economic and Social Programme (hereafter referred to as the Legacy Scheme). A successful bid was submitted to a national regeneration funding programme (the Single Regeneration

Budget Challenge Fund) for a programme running from 1999 to 2004. This award was supplemented with other private and public monies, providing an overall budget of £17.7 million, which funded a range of initiatives across the North West. The Legacy Scheme was noteworthy for several reasons. First, it aimed to deliver regional, rather than merely municipal, effects. Second, it was a programme which aimed to encourage neighbourhood level effects, rather than assuming that the benefits of large-scale projects would 'trickle-down' to the most needy. Third, it was essentially an 'event-themed' regeneration programme, rather than one which was 'event-led'. This involved delivering a range of social and economic projects that were only loosely linked to the Games. An event-themed approach had several benefits: it encouraged more dispersed effects, thus helping to meet the regional objectives cited above, and encouraged more diverse impacts, as tourism, educational, health, cultural and small- and medium-sized enterprise (SME) projects were pursued alongside those directly associated with sport.

The Legacy Scheme funded a total of seven individual projects. Although the objectives of the Scheme as a whole included '[to] support trade, inward investment and tourism strategies' (Manchester 2002 Ltd and the 2002 NW Partnership, Undated: 12), only one of the projects had tourism as its central focus. The 'Games XChange' was a project that aimed to capitalize on the opportunity offered by the Commonwealth Games to promote Manchester and the North West region as tourist destinations. This was achieved by providing information about the city/region to local people and visitors through a range of accessible, informative and innovative methods. The central aim was to provide an information-based legacy from the Games, and to promote Manchester and the North West as a tourist destination before, during and after the Commonwealth Games.

The fulcrum of the Games XChange project was the development of a central Visitor Centre. This Centre, located on Portland Street in central Manchester, was fundamental in delivering information to a range of stakeholders. It provided a medium though which local people, businesses and visitors to the region could gather

Commonwealth Games, city and regional tourist information. During the Games Manchester had to cope with additional tourist enquiries, hotel room requests and transport pressures. A lot of this additional workload was met by the Visitor Centre. The Centre offered an advanced and interactive experience for users and plasma TVs showing BBC coverage were introduced to focus attention on the event. An interactive website was also introduced to provide a further information point for people wishing to gather information about the Games. The success of these initiatives is demonstrated by their prevalent use. A total of 70,000 people used the Visitor Centre to gather information and the website had received around 1.5 million hits by the end of its initial funding in March 2005.

As the Games XChange project was concerned with providing an 'information-based' legacy, it also involved archiving the outcomes of Manchester 2002 programme for future generations. This included developing an image bank accessible to registered users. The organizers of London's 2012 Olympic Games bid and Melbourne's Commonwealth Games 2006 have already used these resources and asked directly for additional information, as have the Prime Minister's Office and two local authorities outside the North West (Birmingham and Newcastle). Archive materials will be stored at Manchester Central Library. In addition to the long-term tourism benefits generated, this should allow the project to leave a tangible legacy.

Perhaps the most innovative aspect of the Visitor Centre in Manchester was its regional perspective. The Centre was designed as one of the mechanisms for allowing the North West, rather than merely Manchester, to experience tourism benefits from the 2002 Games. This was achieved by allowing regional tourist boards the opportunity to contribute to the information stored and presented on site. Liverpool was particularly proactive in capitalizing on this opportunity and used the Games XChange project to increase the profile of its own (successful) bid to be European Capital of Culture 2008. Indeed, Liverpool paid for a permanent member of staff to work in the Visitor Centre, promoting the city. The opportunity was there for other local tourist boards to make more of the facility, though aside from Liverpool, Blackpool and Cumbria, few had the vision to do so.

A further innovative element of the Games XChange project was the promotion of attractions and venues to residents as well as visitors. Stands were set up within major supermarket chains in deprived areas of the city exhibiting information about forthcoming city and regional events. The stands promoted new tourist sites in the region such as the Imperial War Museum North and The Lowry Gallery. By marketing the city in this way to its residents 'on their doorstep', the project removed the requirement of disadvantaged groups to travel into central Manchester to gather information. Promotional work was also targeted at the large student population resident in Manchester, with around 40,000 leaflets distributed to city libraries and universities. With many students still unfamiliar with the city, this offered an ideal opportunity to disseminate information about Manchester and its wider region to a potentially lucrative residential and visiting friends and relatives (VFR) market.

As stipulated as part of its funding requirements, the project had an impact lasting beyond the end of the Commonwealth Games. The relationships built and lessons learnt meant that Manchester has been able to offer enhanced visitor services for subsequent events, including the Champions League Final. This took place at Old Trafford, home of Manchester United Football Club, in May 2003. Volunteers who had previously participated were offered the chance to assist once more, with the added incentive of the opportunity to learn some basic Italian. This assisted supporters of Milan and Juventus, the two Italian clubs who contested the Final. Games XChange also helped to stimulate other aspects of the region's tourism sector by pioneering the development of new materials. One initiative introduced in parallel with the Games was the 'Manchester Music Map' that highlighted places of specific musical interest in the city. This guide was produced in several different languages, including Japanese. Small-scale initiatives developed in association with events are critical if the momentum provided by a large event is to be properly capitalized upon. They also help to avoid a reliance on the benefits of flagship projects trickling down to tourism SMEs. Even though such initiatives may have tenuous direct links with the event itself, they can benefit from enhanced opportunities for funding, publicity and collaborative working that often accompany a major event. Indeed, diverse small initiatives that are not all sport orientated provide a more sustainable basis for tourism development, allowing a broad range of tourism enterprises to prosper. Accordingly, the 'Manchester Music Map' is regarded as a positive outcome of the Games XChange project.

As mentioned in earlier sections of this chapter, the time pressures associated with an event often compromise long-term objectives and there is evidence that this problem was applicable to the Games XChange project. The time period between the inception and actual operation of initiatives was very short and this presented certain challenges and limitations. The planning and fitting out of the Visitor Centre, and the training of its staff, were all completed in a 5 week period. Similarly, the website was also subject to a quick turnaround, with the entire project set up in approximately 12 weeks. The fixed deadline for both elements meant those involved working long hours to ensure successful delivery. These frame conditions also meant that new staff received little or no formal induction and were unable to obtain the full training required to meet the needs of their role. This meant the project did not entirely fulfil its obligation to meet the envisaged social and economic outcomes of the Legacy Scheme as a whole. These were heavily orientated towards skills development.

Although the Games XChange was the only Legacy Scheme project where tourism was the central focus, the other projects involved also assisted tourism. An innovative volunteering scheme (The 'Pre-Volunteer Programme') allowed disadvantaged individuals to gain qualifications in event management, whilst a highly successful business association initiative ('Prosperity') provided support for many small tourism businesses. The 'Lets Celebrate' project has also helped to support and manage cultural festivals in the North West, thus helping the region to secure valuable tourism attractions for many years to come. Tourism has also been taken into consideration at the main Commonwealth Games site at Eastlands, close to some of the most deprived parts of East Manchester. This site is now branded by Manchester as 'SportCity', illustrating the aim to provide a coherent set of sports attractions for residents and visitors. Although the site remains fairly bleak, visitors can hire bikes and receive cycling coaching at the Velodrome and take a tour of the new stadium, alongside attending scheduled events. Therefore, there is evidence that consideration of 'tourism sports' has been incorporated into the planning of this site. SportCity was also chosen as the location for the tallest piece of sculpture in the UK: 'The B of the Bang', and this has also increased visitor interest in this peripheral part of Manchester.

London 2012

It is hoped that some of the important lessons highlighted by Manchester's Commonwealth Games will be built into London's planning for the 2012 Olympic Games. The successful bid for the Games centred on the plan to use the event to regenerate a large part of East London, which has suffered disproportionately from the effects of industrial decline. The specific role of tourism in this regeneration is still unclear. However, in the months immediately prior to the city winning the Olympic candidature, a document was released that detailed the envisaged effects on tourism in London (London 2012, 2005). It asserts that London: 'does not intend to significantly increase tourism numbers through hosting the Olympic Games, but is seeking to enhance the visitor spend' (London 2012, 2005: 29). This reflects the high visitor numbers already enjoyed by the city, which means that spectacular increases such as those experienced by Barcelona and Sydney are unlikely, and perhaps even unwelcome. This realistic stance is somewhat contradicted in the same document which subsequently states that the Games 'will help to halt and reverse the recent decline in London's share of [world] tourism' (2005: 28). Greater market share is to be achieved by using the event to attract additional segments, particularly from the Far East, and to disperse existing visitors into different parts of London and into the rest of the UK. Such dispersal is a long-established objective of VisitBritain and VisitLondon, the relevant quangos responsible for national and local tourism marketing, respectively. It remains doubtful why the Olympics would succeed in delivering such impacts when decades of tourism public planning and intervention have patently failed to deliver a more equitable city and nationwide distribution of tourism. Most interestingly for the purposes of this chapter, the envisaged increases in tourist spending resulting from the Games are expected to 'act as a catalyst to regeneration' (2005: 31). This emphasizes that London does believe it can successfully use event-inspired tourism as a regeneration tool in East London and in adjoining areas. With respect to the latter, the bid document suggests that the concentration of new venues in East London will emphasize the 'sub-region' as a visitor destination. Therefore, more peripheral parts of East and South East London are deemed to be areas where new tourism development will be encouraged. There are also indications that the bid team feel that existing tourism attractions in East and South East London will be bolstered by the Games. The Millennium Dome, Woolwich Arsenal, Silvertown Aquarium and Maritime Greenwich are all highlighted as existing attractions that will benefit. However, it is not clear how this envisaged tourism-led regeneration will be achieved. The only explanation of the mechanism for these effects is given via reference to the South Bank in London. This part of London has recently been endowed with several new tourism attractions including the Tate Modern [Art Gallery], Shakespeare's Globe [Theatre] and Vinopolis [Wine Museum]; and is cited to demonstrate how tourism can assist the regeneration of an area. The validity of this analogy is questionable. Certainly, residents of the London borough of Southwark may not entirely concur that this new 'tourist bubble' (Judd, 1999) contained within a narrow riverside strip constitutes 'regeneration'.

With specific reference to developing tourism that extends merely beyond elite events, there is some evidence that London has attempted to consider such outcomes. The document states that London can expect to develop a new type of tourism: 'one based around sport and lifestyle, which is both high in value and a growing market' (London 2012, 2005: 32). London expects to offer an experience including 'cycle tours, a health and fitness element, as well as a variety of water sports' (London 2012, 2005: 32). This offers the faint hope that London may try to develop a coherent offer

including 'tourism sports' in addition to 'sports tourism' (Hinch and Higham, 2001).

Conclusion

The preceding discussion has highlighted that host cities tend to envisage the relationship between events, tourism and regeneration as being one represented by the process: EVENT → TOURISM → REGENERATION. Detailed consideration of the envisaged mechanisms through which this is to be achieved may lead to the conclusion that host cities see this relationship more specifically as: EVENT → IMAGE ENHANCEMENT → TOURISM → REGENERATION. This type of process typifies the approach adopted by Atlanta, USA, where the Olympic Games organizers emphasized that 'image, prestige and pride are the real residuals' which would provide a platform for subsequent urban revival (Rutheiser, 1996: 285). This approach relies on a very speculative process. Previous research certainly challenges the assumed 'tourism-regeneration' element, with some evidence also questioning whether cities can assume that increased tourism arrivals will always follow image enhancement (Ritchie and Smith, 1991; Chalip et al., 2003). The preceding discussion also highlights that cities cannot assume that all image effects will be positive, thus casting doubt on the initial part of the envisaged process ('event → image enhancement'). Unfortunately, early indications suggest that the organizers of the 2012 London Olympic Games also envisage the relationship between events, tourism and regeneration in the manner cited above. This may limit the positive outcomes of this mega-event.

The doubts expressed above do not render events, tourism and regeneration incompatible. Successful event regeneration may choose to ignore tourism as a mechanism, and even if it is incorporated, there are ways to combine events, tourism and regeneration more successfully. One way is to use regeneration in association with an event to deliver increased tourism receipts. This characterizes the approach taken by Barcelona, generally lauded as the most successful example of urban regeneration involving a large sport event (the 1992 Olympic Games).

This city has not been regenerated through tourism, instead tourism is one of the beneficial outcomes of developing a more attractive environment for city residents. The event was used as a means to generate funding, publicity and widespread support for more fundamental changes to the city. Manchester adopted a similar approach in its legacy planning for the Commonwealth Games. As Jones and Stokes (2003) suggest, the main regeneration benefit for East Manchester provided by the Commonwealth Games was the extra funding that was provided for wider regeneration projects. Alongside broader objectives, this has helped to fund initiatives that will assist tourism development. The focus on skills and social support means that social and economic regeneration should be assisted. However, unlike Barcelona, Manchester's regeneration programme was slightly dwarfed by the emphasis on the event itself, whereas ideally this relationship would be inverted. Events are most effective when they are used to assist, and to accelerate, the achievement of pre-existing plans and objectives. This means ensuring that events and associated initiatives are integrated into broader urban and regional regeneration programmes. As Raco (2004) states, events should be embedded within other regeneration initiatives, and not act as a substitute for them. Getting the right balance between regeneration and the event can also be assisted by developing regeneration initiatives in association with an event, but making sure that they exist independently of the event itself. This was a positive aspect of Manchester's strategy. It allows greater scope for sustained benefits at neighbourhood level, whilst using event associations to generate publicity for, and civic engagement with regeneration

initiatives. If programmes are too event driven, this will mean that initiatives will inevitably falter almost immediately once an event is over. Furthermore, there are fundamental limitations to what can be achieved if every initiative relies on direct event impacts. Uniting a series of ground-level initiatives under a coherent theme is a good way of achieving a compromise between top-down and bottom-up approaches to regeneration. This approach means that area-based initiatives can combine to give significant effects, rather than relying on the speculative effects of 'boosterist' schemes.

In terms of maximizing tourism benefits from events, it is essential that tourism impacts are properly planned. Too many cities simply assume that large sport events and associated international exposure will guarantee them subsequent tourism receipts. Urban authorities need to think about what tourism benefits developing an image as a 'city of sport' may bring, and how best to capitalize on those benefits. Cities should consider moving beyond mere event tourism by using event sites to house a coherent set of sport attractions that are accessible to tourists regardless of when they travel or whether they can get hold of elusive tickets. Manchester's development of SportCity in East Manchester is a good example. Furthermore, just as event regeneration should involve a diverse range of projects, some of which may only be tenuously linked to the event itself, cities should consider events as an ideal opportunity to launch a series of diverse tourism initiatives. If timed to coincide with major events, such initiatives will benefit from enhanced opportunities for funding, publicity and civic support; and should help to leave a durable legacy for cities long after an event's closing ceremony.

References

Aitchison, C. and Evans, T. (2003) The cultural industries and a model of sustainable regeneration: manufacturing 'pop' in the Rhondda Valleys of South Wales. *Managing Leisure* 8, 133–144.

Andranovich, G., Burbank, M. and Heying, C. (2001) Olympic cities: lessons learned from mega-event politics. *Journal of Urban Affairs* 23(2), 113–131.

Atkinson, D. and Laurier, E. (1998) Sanitised city? Social exclusion at Bristol's 1996 International Festival of the Sea. *Geoforum* 29(2), 199–206.

Austrian, Z. and Rosentraub, M. (2002) Cities, sports and economic change: a retrospective assessment. *Journal of Urban Affairs* 24(5), 549–563.

Balsas, C. (2004) City centre regeneration in the context of the 2001 European Capital of Culture in Porto, Portugal. *Local Economy* 19(4), 396–410.

Beriatos, E. and Gospodini, A. (2004) 'Glocalising' urban landscapes: Athens and the 2004 Olympics. *Cities* 21(3), 187–202.

Boyle, M. and Hughes, C. (1991) The politics of the representation of 'the real': discourses from the Left on Glasgow's role as European City Of Culture, 1990. *Area* 23(3), 217–228.

Bramwell, B. (1993) Planning for tourism in an industrial city. *Town and Country Planning* 62(1/2), 17–19.

Bramwell, B. (1997) Strategic planning before and after a mega-event. *Tourism Management* 18(3), 167–176.

Bramwell, B. and Rawding, L. (1996) Tourism marketing images of industrial cities. *Annals of Tourism Research* 23(1), 201–221.

Brunet, F. (1995) An economic analysis of the Barcelona 1992 Olympic Games: resources, financing and impact. In: Moragas, M. and Botella, M. (eds) *The Keys of Success: the Social, Sporting, Economic and Communications Impact of Barcelona'92*. Belleterra: Servei de Publicacions de le Universitata Autonoma de Barcelona, pp. 203–237.

Calavita, N. and Ferrer, A. (2000) Behind Barcelona's success story: citizen movements and planner's power. *Journal of Urban History* 26(6), 793–807.

Carriere, J. and Demaziere, C. (2002) Urban planning and flagship development projects: lessons from Expo 98, Lisbon. *Planning Practice and Research* 17(1), 69–79.

Chalip, L., Green, B.C. and Hill, B. (2003) Effects of sport event media on destination image and intention to visit. *Journal of Sport Management* 17, 214–234.

Chalkley, B. and Essex, S. (1999) Urban development through hosting international events: a history of the Olympic Games. *Planning Perspectives* 14, 369–394.

Connell, J. and Page, S. (2005) Evaluating the economic and spatial effects of an event: the case of the World Medical and Health Games. *Tourism Geographies* 7(1), 63–85.

Dauncey, H. (1999) Building the finals: facilities and infrastructure. In: Dauncey, H. and Hare, G. (eds) *France and the 1998 World Cup*. Frank Cass, London, pp. 98–120.

Department of Environment (1995) *Partners in Regeneration: the Challenge Fund Bidding Guidance*. Department of Environment, London.

Euchner, C. (1999) Tourism and sports: the serious competition for play. In: Judd, D. and Fainstein, S. (eds) *The Tourist City*. Yale University Press, New Haven, Connecticut, pp. 215–232.

Faulkner, B., Chalip, L., Brown, G., Jago, L., March, R. and Woodside, A. (2001) Monitoring the tourism impacts of the Sydney 2000 Olympics. *Event Management* 6, 231–246.

Featherstone, M. (1991) *Consumer Culture and Postmodernism*. Sage, London.

Fretter, A.D. (1993) Place marketing: a local authority perspective. In: Kearns, G. and Philo, C. (eds) *Selling Places: the City as Cultural Capital, Past and Present*. Pergamon, Oxford, pp. 163–175.

Glyptis, S.A. (1991) Sport and tourism. In: Cooper, C. (ed.) *Progress in Tourism, Recreation and Hospitality Management 3*. Belhaven, London, pp. 165–183.

Grammatikopoulos, V., Papacharisis, V., Koustelios, A., Tsigilis, N. and Theodorakis, Y. (2004) Evaluation of the training program for Greek Olympic education. *The International Journal of Educational Management* 18(1), 66–73.

Hall, C.M. (1997) Mega-events and their legacies. In: Murphy, P. (ed.) *Quality Management in Urban Tourism*. Wiley, Chichester, UK, pp. 75–87.

Hall, C.M. (2000) *Tourism Planning: Policies, Processes, and Relationships*. Pearson Education, Harlow, UK.

Harvey, D. (1989) *The Condition of Postmodernity*. Blackwell, Oxford.

Hemphill, L., McGreal, S. and Berry, J. (2004) An indicator-based approach to measuring sustainable urban regeneration performance, Part 2: empirical evaluation and case study analysis. *Urban Studies* 41(4), 725–755.

Higham, J. (1999) Sport as an avenue of tourism development. *Current Issues in Tourism* 2, 82–90.

Hiller, H. (1998) Assessing the impact of mega-events: a linkage model. *Current Issues in Tourism* 1(1), 47–57.

Hiller, H. (2000) Mega-events, urban boosterism and growth strategies: an analysis of the objectives and legitimations of the Cape Town 2004 Olympic bid. *International Journal of Urban and Regional Research* 24, 439–458.

Hinch, J. and Higham, J. (2001) Sport tourism: a framework for research. *International Journal of Tourism Research* 3, 45–58.

Jones, M. and Stokes, T. (2003) The Commonwealth Games and urban regeneration; an investigation into training initiatives and partnerships and their effects of disadvantaged groups in East Manchester. *Managing Leisure* 8, 198–211.

Judd, D. (1999) Constructing the tourist bubble. In: Judd, D. and Fainstein, S. (eds) *The Tourist City*. Yale University Press, New Haven, Connecticut, pp. 35–53.

Kemp, S. (2002) The hidden workforce: volunteers' learning in the Olympics. *Journal of European Industrial Training* 26(2/3/4), 109–116.

Laurier, E. (1993) Tackintosh: Glasgow's supplementary gloss. In: Kearns, G. and Philo, C. (eds) *Selling Places: the City as Cultural Capital, Past and Present*. Pergamon, Oxford, pp. 267–290.

Law, C.M. (1993) *Urban Tourism – Attracting Visitors to Large Cities*. Mansell, London.

Lenskyj, H. (2002) *Best Olympics Ever? The Social Impacts of Sydney 2000*. SUNY, New York.

Lipsitz, G. (1984) Sports stadia and urban development: a tale of three cities. *Journal of Sport and Social Issues* 8(2), 1–18.

Loftman, P. and Spirou, C. (1996) Sports stadiums and urban regeneration: the British and US experience. Paper presented at Tourism and Culture Conference University of Northumbria, Sept 1996.

London 2012 (2005) *Realising the Benefits of Hosting the 2012 Olympic and Paralympic Games*. London 2012, London.

Long, J. and Sanderson, I. (1996) Sport and social integration: the potential for community-based approaches to regeneration. In: Hall, C.M. *et al.* (eds) *The Role of Art and Sport in Local and Regional Economic Development*. Regional Studies Association, London, pp. 28–33.

Manchester 2002 Ltd and the 2002 NW Partnership (Undated) *The 2002 NW Economic and Social Programme 1999–2004: a Bid to the SRB Challenge Fund Round 5*. Manchester City Council, Manchester, UK.

Newman, H. (2002) Race and the tourist bubble in downtown Atlanta. *Urban Affairs Review* 37(3), 301–321.

Owen, K. (2002) The Sydney Olympics and urban entrepreneurialism. *Australian Geographical Studies* 40(3), 323–336.

Raco, M. (2004) Whose gold rush? The social legacy of a London Olympics. In: Vigor, A. *et al.* (eds) *After the Gold Rush: a Sustainable Olympics for London*. IPPR/DEMOS, London, pp. 36–49.

Ritchie, B. (1984) Assessing the impact of hallmark events: conceptual and research issues. *Journal of Travel Research* 23(1), 2–11.

Ritchie, B. and Smith, B. (1991) The impact of a mega event on host region awareness: a longitudinal study. *Journal of Travel Research* 30(1), 3–9.

Rowe, D. and McGurk, P. (1999) Drunk for three weeks: sporting success and city image. *International Review for the Sociology of Sport* 34(2), 125–141.

Rutheiser, C. (1996) *Imagineering Atlanta*. Verso, New York.

Schofield, P. (1996) Cinematographic images of a city: alternative heritage tourism in Manchester. *Tourism Management* 17(5), 333–340.

Silk, M. (2002) 'Bangsa Malaysia': global sport, the city and the mediated refurbishment of local identities. *Media, Culture and Society* 24, 775–794.

Smith, A. (2001) Sport-based regeneration strategies. In: Henry, I. and Gratton, C. (eds) *Sport in the City: the Role of Sport in Economic and Social Regeneration*. Routledge, London, pp. 127–148.

Smith, A. (2002) Reimaging the city: the impact of sport initiatives on tourists' images of urban destinations. PhD thesis. Sheffield Hallam University/University of Sheffield, UK.

Smith, A. (2004) Barcelona. In: Foster, N., Pomfret, G., Smith, A. and Whalley, P. (eds) *Barcelona and Catalonia: a Fieldwork Guide*. Sheffield Hallam University, Sheffield, UK, pp. 29–66.

Smith, A. (2005a) Conceptualizing image change: the reimaging of Barcelona. *Tourism Geographies* 7(4), 398–423.

Smith, A. (2005b) Reimaging the city: the value of sport initiatives. *Annals of Tourism Research* 32(1), 229–248.

Thornley, A. (2002) Urban regeneration and sport stadia. *European Planning Studies* 10(7), 813–818.

Tooke, N. and Baker, M. (1996) Seeing is believing: the effect of film on visitor numbers to screened locations. *Tourism Management* 17(2), 87–94.

Tuan, Y. (1977) *Space and Place: the Perspective of Experience*. Edward Arnold, London.

Van der Westhuizen, J. (2004) Marketing Malaysia as a model Muslim state: the significance of the 16th Commonwealth Games. *Third World Quarterly* 25(7), 1277–1291.

Vigor, A., Mean, M. and Tims, C. (2004) Introduction. In: Vigor, A., Mean, M. and Tims, C. (eds) *After the Gold Rush: a Sustainable Olympics for London*. IPPR/DEMOS, London, pp. 1–35.

Waitt, G. (2003) Social impacts of the Sydney Olympics. *Annals of Tourism Research* 30(1), 194–215.

Webb, T. (2001) *The Collaborative Games*. Pluto, Sydney.

Whitelegg, D. (2000) Going for gold: Atlanta's bid for fame. *International Journal of Urban and Regional Research* (24), 801–817.

9 World Class: Using the Olympics to Shape and Brand the American Metropolis

Charles H. Heying, Matthew J. Burbank and Greg Andranovich

Bidding for and hosting the Olympics has become a popular strategy for urban regeneration in American cities. The competition to become an Olympic city is intense. For instance, eight cities vied to become the US contender for the 2012 Games, with New York City the eventual winner. Cities may also bid over an extended period of time. Salt Lake City's winning bid for the 2002 Winter Olympics was its fifth attempt over a span of 30 years (Burbank *et al.*, 2001:125). For city leaders there are substantial rewards for the difficult task of winning the Games: the promise of increased tourism, the ability to be counted among the 'world class' cities and the opportunity to use the revenues generated by the Olympics to leverage large-scale urban regeneration (Heying *et al.*, 2005).

In this chapter, we examine the reasons for and consequences of using the Olympics to shape and brand the American metropolis. To introduce our case, we briefly describe how cities are adapting to the changing contours of a global economy and how this leads cities to seek out high-profile events like the Olympics. We then discuss why the Olympic strategy is so compelling that cities will spend years seeking the opportunity to host the Games. Finally, we explore the role of the Olympics in shaping the city and the conflicts this generates between those who benefit from these new landscapes of consumption and those whose places and meanings are appropriated in the process.

We view these issues through the lens of two case studies, the 1996 Atlanta Olympics and New York City's unsuccessful bid to host the 2012 Games.

Urban America is engaged in a transformation with consequences as great as those that followed the industrial revolution. The global restructuring of the economy, aided by the intensity of technological applications, is creating a landscape of uneven development. Industries in the manufacturing sector and the jobs they generate are migrating to locations with lower costs and fewer regulations. At the same time, America has become a suburban nation where the separation of living and working spaces is more pronounced and inequalities more evident. These changes have prompted a search for ways of making cities more attractive places to live and work. Recognizing that the new economy of cities cannot be based on luring back manufacturing jobs, city leaders have begun to address what some have characterized as the 'economy of flows' in order to try to capture a share of the flow of words, images, ideas, money and people in an increasingly mobile world (Appadurai, 1990; Clarke and Gaile, 1998; Clark *et al.*, 2002; Florida, 2005). As part of this effort, urban regeneration strategies often focus on attracting the creative class, among others, back to the downtown core by providing amenities and creating distinct neighbourhoods. And as leisure and tourism have become more important components of consumer spending, consumption has become a focus of urban regeneration. Efforts to regenerate US cities in symbolic and instrumental ways reflect the emergence of the global economy and its influences, but also highlight the conflicts and controversies in changing the use patterns of cities (Gottdiener, 1997; Judd and Fainstein, 1999). The strategies available to city leaders seeking to revitalize parts of their city or to alter its image, however, are typically constrained by a lack of resources as well as the challenges of policymaking in a federal system. Thus, for US city leaders, playing host to a large scale, global event such as the Olympic Games can be seen as a rare and attractive opportunity.

The Logic of the Games

Why is the Olympic strategy so compelling for US city leaders? In three words: tourism, image and regeneration. Tourism is one of the largest and fastest growing sectors of the global economy. For the USA in 2003, domestic and international expenditures on travel and tourism equalled $546 billion, generated 7.2 million jobs and contributed $95 million in tax revenues (TIAA, 2005). Cities compete vigorously to increase their attractiveness within the well-defined circuit of tourist destinations. They continually reshape their urban landscape to create a distinct place identity that is diversionary yet seems authentic (Judd and Fainstein, 1999). The Olympics provide an irresistible opportunity to take tourism and place promotion to a new level. In the short term, millions of dollars are projected for direct and indirect tourist expenditures. Over the long term, the city expects to benefit from new venues such as sports stadia, from media exposure and from its association with a dramatic and heroic event (Heying *et al.*, 2005). However, recent studies suggest that the reality may fall short of the claims. Critics argue that pre-Olympic estimates gloss over short-term factors such as the displacement of events or travellers seeking to avoid the disruption of the Games. And careful studies of the long-term impacts question whether the Olympics have lasting effects on tourist arrivals (Preuss, 2000; Kasimati, 2003).

Generally, modelling tourist impacts is extremely difficult because other variables such as city location and changes in exchange rates tend to overwhelm any Olympic effect (Spurr, 1999).

The possibility for cities to improve their image and alter their status within the hierarchy of world cities is also compelling. The Olympic Games are the world's premier sporting event and the Olympic rings the world's most recognizable brand image (Morgan and Pritchard, 1998). For 17 days, the city is host to an event that attracts a global viewing audience. During that time, the city becomes something more than a backdrop for a sports event; it becomes sponsor, namesake and partner in the production of a highly symbolic drama. Cities that host the Games can claim 'world class' status and co-mingle their place identity with the heroic imagery and internationalism associated with the Olympic brand.

But the close identification of the city with the Games creates both opportunity and risk. The host city must demonstrate its local distinctiveness by showcasing its culture and heritage. Simultaneously, it must stage a global event under the watchful eyes of the International Olympic Committee (IOC) that jealously guards its brand from being hijacked or oversold (Heying *et al.*, 2005). As the premier international sports event, the Olympic Games also become a focal point for concerns that can stigmatize the host city: Munich elicits memories of terrorist acts, Mexico City and Moscow political protest, Montreal fiscal irresponsibility and Salt Lake City corruption (Guttman, 2002).

The 1996 Centennial Olympics in Atlanta provides an example of the difficulty of enacting the Olympics as a place branding event. To win the bid, Atlanta promoted its human rights reputation exemplified by the work of Martin Luther King. But this vision of social moderation was shattered by a politically motivated bombing in Centennial Olympic Park, later linked to an anti-abortion protester. Atlanta also promoted itself as an international destination city; the cultural, economic and transportation hub of the new South. But the international press and the IOC experienced a different reality including communication and transportation problems and lacklustre venues (Burbank *et al.*, 2001). The overall impression of a shoddy over-commercialized event prevented the President of the IOC, Juan Antonio Samaranch, from bestowing the customary salutation of 'best Olympics ever' on Atlanta (*Atlanta Journal Constitution*, 1996). For Atlanta, using the Olympics to achieve 'world class' status was more problematic than expected.

New York City's bid for the 2012 Olympics provides a different prospective on Olympic branding. Although New York already has 'world class' stature, its rank is not assured in the global inter-city competition for tourists and mobile capital (Shovall, 2002). Bidding for the Olympics provided New York with an opportunity to put the city's image out in the global media and reinforce its brand as a tough competitor, an international city, a place of opportunity where people from all over the world come to follow their dreams (Andranovich and Burbank, 2004). These identities resonated with Olympic values and were authentic representations of the city, linking back to iconic images like the Statue of Liberty and reinforcing the message of a city bouncing back from a tragic event. Even though New York was not successful in winning the bid, it was successful in asserting its brand identity.

For city leaders the real prize of the Olympics is the opportunity to reshape the urban landscape in a way that makes the city appealing to the 'economy of flows', that is, the investments, travellers, creative workers, entrepreneurial firms and global corporations that are seeking high amenity, high opportunity locations. On several levels the Olympics are ideally suited to help a city achieve this goal. Financially, there is the potential to use future Olympic revenues as seed money to leverage public and private investment for regeneration projects. For the 1996 Atlanta Olympics, the $432 million spent on facilities and infrastructure by the independent organizing committee leveraged an additional $395 million in private funds and $2.08 billion in government funds (Burbank *et al.*, 2001:117).

Structurally, the Olympics encompass nearly all types of regeneration strategies: festival, sports, public space, heritage and infrastructure. More importantly, the Olympics provide a focusing event that helps city leaders weave together a regeneration coalition. Creating a sustainable coalition is especially problematic in the US context where: (i) corporate power is hegemonic but

increasingly less interested in local issues as it extends its global reach; (ii) the legal powers of local government are limited and planning domains are Balkanized; and (iii) central cities are facing a declining tax base caused by the hollowing out of their industrial base, voter resistance and state limitations on taxing power. The Olympics help to mobilize fragmented urban coalitions, force adherence to a development timetable and attract scarce external resources to regeneration initiatives.

The Olympics are an attractive strategy for regeneration. The promise of increased tourism, the attainment or reassertion of 'world class' status, the ability to attract resources and focus the interests of coalition partners, are all enticements for city leaders to pursue this difficult strategy. But with the Olympics so firmly driven by the impulse of creating new spaces of consumption, it is likely that benefits of regeneration will flow primarily to elites and not to those who occupy the spaces targeted for development. In the next sections, we examine how this plays out in two US case studies, the 1996 Atlanta Olympics and New York City's bid for the 2012 summer Games.

Atlanta and the 1996 Olympic Games

Atlanta was selected to host the 1996 Olympics by the IOC in 1990. In the euphoric moments after Atlanta's victory, Maynard Jackson, the city's mayor, stated his intention to use the Games to help regenerate Atlanta. Jackson spoke of the need to scale 'the twin peaks of Atlanta's Mount Olympus': the first peak being to stage the best Games ever and the second to 'uplift the people of Atlanta and fight poverty in the process' (Roughton, 1991: F3). The mayor's pronouncement was consistent with the proposed locations for Olympic venues. Atlanta's 'Olympic Ring' encompassed 15 of the city's poorest and most neglected neighbourhoods. While urban regeneration was not an explicit goal of the bid committee, expectations that urban regeneration would benefit the residents were heightened. In large part this was because Atlanta, unlike Los Angeles, did not have existing 'world class' facilities and had to build them. To fulfil his pledge to make regeneration work for the poorest residents, Mayor Jackson established the Corporation for Olympic Development (CODA), a quasi-public organization with a mission to revitalize the Olympic Ring neighbourhoods (Andranovich *et al.*, 2001). Unfortunately, as the history of the Atlanta Olympics shows, neither the hopes of Mayor Jackson nor the expectations of poor residents were realized. Why and how this took place is described in the stories of Atlanta's Olympic Stadium, Techwood/ Clark Howell housing complex, Centennial Olympic Park and CODA.

Atlanta's Olympic Stadium was the vehicle for accommodating the joint need of the city and a professional sports team for a high-value sports attraction. Among US cities, competition is intense to attract or retain footloose professional teams. For cities, professional sports teams are major tourist attractions and iconic indicators of major league status. Team owners create bidding wars between locations to get them to build or renovate stadiums (Eisinger, 2000). Atlanta's promise to construct a new stadium for the Olympics led to some joint planning for post-Olympic use. Both the city and Ted Turner, the CEO of Turner Broadcasting and owner of the Atlanta Braves baseball team, were eager to replace the ageing and poorly designed Fulton County Stadium. The availability of Olympic revenues to finance a new stadium combined with a strategic threat by Turner to move his team to the suburbs produced a sweetheart deal for Turner and solved a problem for the city (Rutheiser, 1996). Turner got naming rights, revenue control and a 25-year lease on a state-of-art stadium that doubled the value of his baseball franchise. The city retained a major tourist attraction and got a new stadium for the cost of infrastructure upgrades (Unger, 1996).

While the stadium deal seemed to be a win-win situation, not everyone benefited. The African-American residents of the Summerhill neighbourhood who would bear the brunt of construction and displacement saw the stadium deal as part of a long history of community disruption. Between 1965 and 1990, Summerhill had been decimated by the construction of two freeways and the Fulton County Stadium, thereby forcing out 13,000 of its 16,000 residents (Foskett, 1993). When Summerhill activists voiced their concern over the stadium, the

Atlanta Committee for the Olympic Games (ACOG) successfully framed their actions as selfish and obstructionist (*Atlanta Journal Constitution*, 1990). In the end, their protests produced few tangible concessions and the stadium project was completed largely as envisioned by corporate and city leaders.

The imperative of Olympic development affected other low-income communities. Techwood/Clark Howell was a 1200 unit public housing project that provided homes for low-income Blacks in central city Atlanta. It was a historic structure, the first public housing built in a US city. It was well designed and remained functionally sound despite poor management and neglect. Security in and around the facility was poor and the area became known for its high crime rate. The land it occupied had long been coveted by its neighbours, Coca Cola and Georgia Tech. In the early 1970s, Central Atlanta Progress, the city's premier business association, developed a plan to tear down the structure and replace it with higher income housing. But this was rejected by Maynard Jackson, Atlanta's first Black mayor, when he took office in 1974 (Allen, 1996).

The Olympic bid refocused attention on the public housing community. A proposal by Georgia Tech to construct the Olympic Village in close proximity to Techwood evoked long-standing concerns of race and class. Georgia Tech President, John Crecine, bluntly stated what many in the business community were thinking:

> Number one, there is one of the finest international corporations [Coca-Cola]. Two, here is one of the world's finest technological institutions [Georgia Tech]. And here is one of the world's best cesspools [Techwood]. It doesn't play well.
>
> (Dickerson, 1991: A14)

As planning for the Olympics progressed, several more proposals emerged to replace Techwood/Clark Howell. The business community pushed for full-scale removal, but Mayor Jackson supported renovation. Events in 1994 tipped the balance in favour of removal. Bill Campbell, a new business friendly mayor, took office and replaced the director of the Atlanta Housing Authority (AHA) with a corporate lawyer who made clear her belief that housing the neediest was not the responsibility of the AHA. At the national level, changes in HOPE VI, a programme that provided funds for public housing renovation, lowered its standards requiring one-for-one replacement housing for existing residents and also allowed for the complete demolition of struggling housing projects. While these plans formally required approval by tenants, the need for approval was effectively circumvented by a strategy of forced removals for violation of rules or unpaid rents resulting in the depopulation of all but 10% of the units (Keating and Flores, 2000).

The final proposal, approved by the US Department of Housing and Urban Development, provided $42 million of federal funds for the $100 million project. The 1200 units of public housing were levelled and replaced by Centennial Place, 900 units of low-rise, mixed-income condominiums. An 'architecturally significant' building that formerly housed Techwood's library was renovated, and a marker, with a sanitized history of the public housing project, was placed nearby. Fewer than 8% of the original Techwood/Clark Howell residents took occupancy in Centennial Place. In the post-Olympic period, the model developed for Centennial Place was repeated for other public housing projects throughout Atlanta resulting in the loss of an additional 4170 low-income housing units. A corner of the Techwood property closest to Georgia Tech became the site for the Olympic Village towers. ACOG contributed $47 million to help finance the construction of the Olympic Village that, after the Games, became housing for Georgia Tech students (Burbank et al., 2001:109–112).

Securing the area that was occupied by Techwood/Clark Howell prepared the way for a grander scheme of urban regeneration. Centennial Olympic Park, at 22 acres, is one of the largest public open spaces built in a modern city. The plan for the park did not appear in Atlanta's Olympic bid, nor did it come from a groundswell of public interest, rather it emerged from the collusion of elite interests and the opportunity of the Olympic moment. The area had long been targeted for redevelopment by downtown business groups because it was close to Atlanta's shopping, hotel and convention complexes. From the perspective of elite leaders, what stood in the way of its redevelopment was its proximity to the Techwood/Clark Howell projects (Rutheiser, 1996). The Olympics provided a justification for the removal of this housing complex and its replacement with the Olympic Village towers and the mixed-income Centennial Place condominiums.

There were many corporate beneficiaries of the new park. The Georgia World Congress Center, a convention and entertainment complex managed by a state authority, got a palatial lawn for its front yard. The Atlanta Journal Constitution and the Chamber of Commerce, whose headquarters now overlook a park rather than an industrial district, also benefited from a value-enhancing amenity. Coca Cola Corporation expanded its headquarters on a large parcel it assembled along the park's northern boundary. Similarly, Turner Broadcasting invested $27 million to renovate its CNN Center and Omni Hotel (Burbank et al., 2001:106–109). Turner also replaced Omni Coliseum with a new $217 million complex, Philips Arena, home to his professional hockey and basketball teams. Turner credited the creation of Centennial Olympic Park with his decision to make these investments and keep his teams downtown (Turner, 1999). Local governments were also beneficiaries. While the creation of the park removed land from the tax rolls, the increased value of the new facilities more than compensated for the loss.

One of the cruel ironies of the development of Centennial Olympic Park was that it directly contradicted ACOG's policy of only funding venue construction. ACOG had used this policy to resist claims that Olympic funds should help ease the social or economic problems of poor neighbourhoods (Hill, 1993). According to ACOG, helping residents was the responsibility of CODA, the quasi-public organization created by Mayor Jackson. Unfortunately, CODA was not up to the challenge. From the beginning it was hampered by conflicting agendas and poor management. Major Jackson envisioned CODA as a way to attract private funds for projects like bridges, sewers and streets (Hill and Roughton, 1992). Neighbourhood residents expected it to focus on immediate needs like housing and jobs. ACOG and downtown business interests saw it as a way to make poor neighbourhoods presentable for the Games (Roughton, 1992). Not unexpectedly, it was the business agenda that prevailed. Of the

$76 million raised by CODA, nearly all of it went towards urban landscaping projects such as parks and street improvements in the downtown business area or pedestrian corridors leading to Olympic venues. Less than a tenth of the funds went to projects that directly affected poor neighbourhoods (Burbank *et al.*, 2001:92–93).

The Atlanta Olympics mobilized the business community and transformed the downtown to focus on consumption, and in the process rebuilt the city's downtown in ways that adhered to the larger institutions' visions of the city. Olympic organizers were able to take advantage of the IOC's requirements for world-class facilities as well as the city government's structural weaknesses regarding the use and transformation of downtown space to ensure that Olympic and corporate needs were met even if public needs were not. In American Olympic bids since, the politics of regeneration have remained the focal point for local bid committees, as the US candidate city in the 2012 competition illustrates.

New York City's 2012 Bid

New York's bid was as outsized as the city. Total capital investment for the Olympic Village, sports venues and infrastructure was estimated at $7.6 billion, the most ambitious of all international competitors. The bid emphasized compact and accessible venues concentrated in four sports clusters (New York Committee for the Olympic Games (NYCOG), 2004). Our discussion will focus on two projects: the Olympic Stadium and the Brooklyn Arena. These proposals shared some common attributes: (i) professional sports teams looking for new stadiums; (ii) complex partnerships that included large but hidden public subsidies; and (iii) organized and outspoken opposition.

In describing the financial commitment to the proposed Olympic Stadium, New York's bid was effusive and confident:

> The city and state governments have committed to provide funding for the essential infrastructure to redevelop the Hudson Yards area on Manhattan's Far West Side, including platforms over the rail yards upon which the Olympic Stadium and Olympic Square Park will be built, the expansion of the Javits Convention Center, a network of new parks

> and boulevards, and the extension of the subway system. The New York Jets American football team has committed $800 million to build the Olympic Stadium.
>
> (NYCOG, 2004: Vol. 1, p. 105)

The statement was accurate but incomplete. Indeed, the Jets football franchise was very interested in moving from a stadium they shared in New Jersey to their own stadium in New York. Their interest dovetailed with the need to construct the Olympic Stadium and the city's desire to expand the adjacent Javits Convention Center (Bagli, 2002). It is also correct that the Jets made a financial promise of between $600 and $800 million towards what was projected to be a $3.4 billion Olympic Square project. Also there was government commitment as both Mayor Michael Bloomberg and Governor George Pataki were both strong supporters of the stadium proposal. For its part, the city had agreed to spend an estimated $150 million to construct the platform over the rail yards and was committed to a $500 million Javits Center expansion (NYCOG, 2004). In addition the Metropolitan Transit Agency had agreed to work exclusively with the Jets on a leasing arrangement for the development rights over the Hudson Yards. The mayor also promoted an extension for the No. 7 subway as part of the necessary transportation infrastructure. The key to financing the subway extension was a redevelopment proposal along the Midtown Manhattan avenues that led to Olympic Square. In a complicated scheme, increased tax revenues generated by the new development would be dedicated to paying back the subway bonds (deMause, 2004a).

But the apparent clarity and certainty of agreements described in the bid document glossed over intense neighbourhood opposition, labyrinthine financing schemes and political rivalries. One of the neighbourhood organizers of the Clinton Special District Coalition that opposed the stadium put their position succinctly, 'It's not about sports, it's about real estate' (Crumpacker, 2002). The coalition outlined their concerns in the *2012 Contra-Bid Book* (Clinton Special District Coalition, 2002) that was sent to all members of the IOC. They argued that the massive new commercial space proposed for Midtown (equivalent in scale to ten Empire State Buildings) would drive out residents and small business owners, decrease diversity and overwhelm the natural evolution of the neighbourhood. Citing a study by the New York City Independent Budget Office, they also questioned the optimistic tax revenue projections for funding the No. 7 subway extension. They were especially concerned that the funding scheme would divert revenues from the more critically needed Second Avenue Subway. Academic critics argued that the state-funded Javits Center expansion was ill advised, coming at a time when convention centre space in the USA was overbuilt, attendances were declining and rents heavily discounted (deMause, 2004a).

Support at the state level was also more tenuous than the bid book implied. State Assembly President Sheldon Silver was not a supporter of the stadium. He accused Mayor Bloomberg of trying to side step city council and state legislative oversight (deMause, 2004b). Silver noted that more than half of the money the Jets had committed to the stadium came from the sale of tax-free bonds by a semi-public development corporation. While the Jets would make payments to the corporation to retire the bonds, these payments would be made in lieu of paying real estate taxes. According to Silver, these lost revenues constituted a public subsidy of over $1 billion. Silver also had political reasons to oppose the stadium. The lower Manhattan district he represented was slow to recover from the impact of the 9/11 attacks that destroyed the World Trade Center. He feared that the Olympic Stadium and Midtown plans would overshadow the redevelopment of lower Manhattan (Pressman, 2005). His resistance was decisive. As chair of the Public Authorities Control Board, an obscure three-person state panel that oversees statewide public debt, he stopped the stadium proposal. The veto took place only weeks before the final IOC decision and undermined any chance New York had to win the bid (Bagli et al., 2005).

The Brooklyn Olympic Arena received much less citywide attention than the West Side stadium, but it also provoked intense local opposition. The proposed arena was the third most expensive Olympic site after the Olympic Stadium and Olympic Village (NYCOG, 2004). Like the Olympic Stadium the plan called for the arena to be constructed on a platform over rail yards owned by the Metropolitan Transit Authority.

But this was only part of a $3.5 billion dollar project that would redevelop 24 acres of prime real estate in Brooklyn, adding the 18,000-seat arena and 17 high-rise buildings. The plan was pushed by developer Bruce Ratner who had purchased the New Jersey Nets professional basketball team and wanted to move them to Brooklyn (Cardwell, 2005).

The project received the support of the mayor, governor and the borough president but was opposed by Develop Don't Destroy Brooklyn, a coalition of 18 neighbourhood groups, and the Downtown Brooklyn Leadership Coalition, a group of clergy representing eight churches (Develop Don't Destroy Brooklyn, 2005a). Opponents argued that the arena was a Trojan horse for the 17 skyscrapers, and the entire project was a boondoggle (Carreira, 2005). They showed that the proposed arena would occupy only 10% of the project area, that 15% would come from public streets sold to the developer, and that 45% would be purchased from private parties under threat of condemnation. Opponents were incensed that the deal was being structured to bypass the city's land use review process and that it would include over $1.5 billion in tax subsidies in the form of direct infrastructure investment, tax exempt bonds for construction, exemption of construction materials from sales tax, and a 30 year property tax exemption (Develop Don't Destroy Brooklyn, 2005a). They also argued that the proposed affordable housing strongly favoured the wealthy with 83% of units being targeted at those above the median income, and 64% to those with double the median income (Develop Don't Destroy Brooklyn, 2005b). Ratner, the developer, was also accused of strong-arm tactics, forcing those who accepted his purchase offers to sign agreements to withdraw from any group that opposed the project, remove signs, testify in favour of the project, and work to get non-sellers to agree to his price (Gallahue, 2004).

It is hard to know what effect the opposition had on New York's bid. Six months before the IOC chose London for the 2012 Olympics, the Brooklyn Rail, a borough newspaper, declared that the seemingly unstoppable Olympic Arena project was no longer inevitable (Carreira, 2005). When the IOC site visit team came in February 2005, activists opposing the Brooklyn Arena and the West Side stadium met with them to express their opposition (Wisloski, 2005). The site visit team later noted the uncertainty of the Olympic Stadium as a weakness in New York's bid. Their concerns about public support were reinforced when an IOC sponsored poll revealed that only 59% of New Yorkers favoured having the Olympics in New York City, the lowest of all competitors (Topousis and Singer, 2005). While it is uncertain whether the bid failed because of political infighting or citizen opposition, what is certain is that winning the Olympics would have changed the debate. Flagging projects would have got a huge push and the imperative of the Games would have weakened the voices of the opposition.

Conclusion

For city leaders who are able to organize the resources for large-scale change, the Olympics are an ideal strategy to focus urban regeneration and intensify land use in the city's core. The number and scale of opportunities presented by a mega-event such as the Olympics brings powerful actors to the table who can make things happen. Promised benefits, such as increased tourism or jobs from large-scale construction projects, build public enthusiasm and suppress resistance. But these massive interventions produce opposition and displacement. Those who are truly marginalized in the new economy, such as those who lived in Techwood/Clark Howell public housing in Atlanta, often lack the resources to resist and are summarily displaced. In other locations, such as Brooklyn, where some regeneration is already taking place, the controversy is over the speed and scale of change, who will control it and who will pay for it. Those who resist often prefer gradual transformation where benefits flow to the small businesses, entrepreneurs and residents who are already in place. Yet resistance is difficult because of the financial and political power promoting Olympic development. These conflicts also extend to the meanings of place. Cities are the embodiment of place-associated meanings and people take pleasure when these meanings are authentically projected on to a global stage. Becoming an Olympic city is attractive because it encourages individuals and their places to be enrolled in a project of heroic effort, celebration and internationalism. But the scale of the projects and the machinations of the powerful that displace the weak and exclude ordinary citizens dim the flame of Olympic enthusiasm and appropriate meanings of places for the sole purpose of instrumental commercialism. As a lever for regeneration, the Olympics have perhaps passed a point at which they can work for the ordinary citizen, but for elites, in a seemingly ungovernable city, the Olympics may be one of the few strategies of sufficient stature to withstand the thousand blows of oppositional interests.

References

Allen, F. (1996) *Atlanta Rising: the Invention of an International City 1946–1996.* Longstreet Press, Marietta, Georgia.

Andranovich, G. and Burbank, M.J. (2004) Regime politics and the 2012 Olympic Games: New York and San Francisco bids. *California Politics and Policy* 8, 1–18.

Andranovich, G., Burbank, M.J. and Heying, C.H. (2001) Olympic cities: lessons learned from mega-event politics. *Journal of Urban Affairs* 23, 113–131.

Appadurai, A. (1990) Disjuncture and difference in the global cultural economy. *Theory, Culture and Society* 7, 295–310.

Atlanta Journal Constitution (1990) ANUF [Atlanta Neighborhoods United for Fairness] is too much [Editorial]. *Atlanta Journal Constitution*, 30 November, A18.

Atlanta Journal Constitution (1996) IOC: the royal pains of the Games [Editorial]. *Atlanta Journal Constitution*, 11 October, A16.

Bagli, C.V. (2002) West Side plan envisions Jets and Olympics. *New York Times*, 1 May, B1.

Bagli, C.V., Rutenberg, J., Cooper, M. and Steinhauer, J. (2005) Requiem for New York stadium: overtures were made too late. *New York Times*, 8 June, A1.

Burbank, M.J., Andranovich, G.D. and Heying, C.H. (2001) *Olympic Dreams: the Impact of Mega-Events on Local Politics*. Lynne Rienner Publishers, Boulder, Colorado.

Cardwell, D. (2005) Instant skyline added to Brooklyn Arena plan. *New York Times*, 5 July, A1.

Carreira, B.J. (2005) The AtlanticYards project: no longer 'inevitable'? *The Brooklyn Rail*, 3 February, p. 1.

Clark, T.N., Lloyd, R., Wong, K.K. and Jain, P. (2002) Amenities drive urban growth. *Journal of Urban Affairs* 24, 493–515.

Clarke, S.E. and Gaile, G.L. (1998) *The Work of Cities*. University of Minnesota Press, Minneapolis, Minnesota.

Clinton Special District Coalition (2002) *2012 Contra-Bid Book*. Clinton Special District Coalition. Available at: http://hellskitchen.net/develop/olympics/contra-bid-book.pdf (accessed 6 August 2005).

Crumpacker, J. (2002) N. Y. neighbors unite to fight Olympic bid. *San Francisco Chronicle*, 21 October, A1.

deMause, N. (2004a) Blank check for Hudson Yards. *Village Voice*, 10 August, 18.

deMause, N. (2004b) The Jets' end run. *Village Voice*, 23 November, 20.

Develop Don't Destroy Brooklyn (2005a) *Atlantic Yards News*. Develop Don't Destroy Brooklyn. Available at: http://www.developdontdestroy.org/AYards_News.pdf (accessed 6 August 2005).

Develop Don't Destroy Brooklyn (2005b) *Anatomy of a Sweetheart Deal*. Develop Don't Destroy Brooklyn. Available at: http://www.dddb.net/dummies/sweetheartanatomy.pdf (accessed 6 August 2005).

Dickerson, J. (1991) If Techwood's a cesspool, why haven't we helped? *Atlanta Journal Constitution*, 22 March, A14.

Eisinger, P. (2000) The politics of bread and circuses: building the city for the visitor class. *Urban Affairs Review* 35, 316–333.

Florida, R.L. (2005) *Cities and the Creative Class*. Routledge, New York.

Foskett, K. (1993) Olympic stadium reaps suspicion planted 30 years ago. *Atlanta Journal Constitution*, 7 March, A14.

Gallahue, P. (2004) Tout of bounds: Ratner forces apt. sellers to hype Nets arena. *New York Post*, 16 June, 4.

Gottdiener, M. (1997) *The Theming of America: Dreams, Visions, and Commercial Spaces*. Westview, Boulder, Colorado.

Guttman, A. (2002) *The Olympics: a History of the Modern Games*. University of Illinois Press, Champaign, Illinois.

Heying, C.H., Burbank, M.J. and Andranovich, G. (2005) Taking the measure of the Games: lessons from the field. *Plan Canada* 45, 20–22.

Hill, A.E. (1993) Neighborhood leaders' first reaction: wrong priority. *Atlanta Journal Constitution*, 19 November, A7.

Hill, A.E. and Roughton, B.J. (1992) New city board will plan, guide '96 renovations. *Atlanta Journal Constitution*, 10 October, A1.

Judd, D.R. and Fainstein, S.S. (eds) (1999) *The Tourist City*. Yale University Press, New Haven, Connecticut.

Kasimati, E. (2003) Economic aspects and the summer Olympics: a review of related research. *International Journal of Tourism Research* 5, 433–444.

Keating, L. and Flores, C.A. (2000) Sixty and out: Techwood Homes transformed by enemies and friends. *Journal of Urban History* 26, 275–311.

Morgan, N. and Pritchard, A. (1998) *Tourism Promotion and Power: Creating Images, Creating Identities*. John Wiley, New York.

New York Committee for the Olympic Games (NYCOG). (2004) *NYC2012 Bid Book*. Available at: http://www.nyc2012.com/en/bid_book.html (accessed 6 August 2005).

Pressman, G. (Host) (2005) Interview: Sheldon Silver discusses the proposed construction of a New York Jets stadium, New York education and his family. WNBC.com. Available at: http://www.wnbc.com/news/4516898/detail.html (accessed 6 August 2005).

Preuss, H. (2000) *Economics of the Olympic Games: hosting the Games 1972–2000*. Walla Walla Press, Sydney.

Roughton, B.J. (1991) The challenge. *Atlanta Journal Constitution*, 21 July, F3.

Roughton, B.J. (1992) Atlanta Olympics update '92. *Atlanta Journal Constitution*, 20 September, H6.

Rutheiser, C. (1996) *Imagineering Atlanta: the Politics of Place in the City of Dreams*. Verso, London.

Shovall, N. (2002) A new phase in the competition for the Olympic gold: the London and New York bids for the 2012 Games. *Journal of Urban Affairs* 24, 583–599.

Spurr, R. (1999) Tourism. In: Cashman, R. and Hughes, A. (eds) *Staging the Olympics: the Event and its Impact*. University of New South Wales Press, Sydney, pp. 148–156.

TIAA (Travel Industry Association of America) (2005) *Economic Impact Fast Facts*. Available at: http://tia.
    usdm.net/pressmedia/economic_2003.html (accessed 6 August 2005).
Topousis, T. and Singer, H. (2005) NYers cool to Games: IOC. *New York Post*, 3 March, 2.
Turner, M. (1999) Philips Arena: a new downtown: 'defining moment'. *Atlanta Journal Constitution*,
    12 September, p.15.
Unger, H. (1996) Braves' new stadium swells franchise value. *Atlanta Journal Constitution*, 22 February, C2.
Wisloski, J. (2005) Arena foes stuck in Olympic spin cycle. *The Brooklyn Paper*, 5 March, 15.

10 Touring Templates: Cultural Workers and Regeneration in Small New England Cities

Myrna M. Breitbart and Cathy Stanton

Introduction

The growth of culture-led regeneration raises questions about how the social and economic benefits are balanced and distributed. How, for example, does cultural tourism serve the differing needs of cultural producers, property owners, real estate developers and marginalized groups in a given area? How sustainable or marketable are such projects once many towns and cities within a region have embraced them? Within the burgeoning literature on the subject, many have noted that the widespread adoption of these strategies may be leading to a kind of cultural homogenization masquerading as local variety – what one critic has called 'eclectic conformity' (Holcomb, 1993: 142; see also Short, 1989; Dicks, 2003). At the same time, some have charged that the types of places and cultural economies being created through culture-based redevelopment tend to reinforce rather than challenge the growing exclusions and inequalities of the global capitalist economy (see, for example, Zukin, 1995; Deutsche, 1996; Edensor, 2005). Others maintain that local autonomy, variation and resistance to globalized flows of capital and culture can be found within officially-sanctioned cultural projects, and that it is a mistake to tar all such efforts with the same brush (for defence of this view see Castells, 1994; McNeill, 1999). These are crucial questions for those concerned with social

and economic justice and who want critical and counter-hegemonic views to exist within the new public spaces of heritage areas, cultural quarters, tourist attractions, arts districts and similar ventures.

In this chapter we propose an angle of approach that has thus far been underutilized in the literature. Focusing on small New England cities and the former textile city of Lowell in particular, we investigate 'culture industry' workers whose labour is an integral part of cultural tourism and culture-led regeneration projects. Evans and Foord term these people 'cultural intermediaries':

> professionals and semi-professionals working in the interface between cultural activity (creative production and arts organizations) and the regeneration system (local/regional authorities, regeneration companies, development agencies, housing providers).
>
> (Evans and Foord, 2003: 171)

These workers are part of what John Urry, following Pierre Bourdieu, refers to as the 'new petty bourgeoisie' and what Richard Florida has famously termed the 'creative classes' – the educated, white-collar, mobile, professional workers who produce the ideas, experiences and services fuelling much of the activity at the leading edge of contemporary capitalist development (Urry, 1990; Florida, 2002). Their structural status varies widely from positions of considerable power to very tenuous short-term contracts. Overall, they occupy an ambivalent middle ground between local and outsider, for-profit and non-profit enterprises, dominant and marginalized groups, and the demands of mobile capital and local needs. These interstitial roles make cultural intermediaries a useful group to study in relation to questions about balancing different interests within cultural tourism and regeneration projects. Their work also presents an opportunity to explore the effects of professionalization, communication and mobility within such projects, and to ask how these factors contribute to standardization, adaptability, participation and innovation.[1]

Post-industrial New England

Industrial capitalism found its first home in the USA in New England. In the early days of American industrialization, utopians sought the ideal formula for melding agriculture with industry, efficiency with fair-mindedness. Paternalistic manufacturers in New England sought to address the problems posed by industrial capitalism through the design and construction of new manufacturing cities like Lowell, Massachusetts, in the hopes of attracting a reliable workforce and providing the power for large mills. For more than a century prior to World War II, New England's economy was dominated by industries producing consumer goods such as textiles, apparel, shoes and paper. By the 1970s, this mill-based employment dropped to only one tenth of all jobs in the region, producing serious unemployment and factory abandonment in every state in the region (Harrison, 1982). The image of New England factories, once a metaphor for social and technological progress, came to be linked instead with lowered self-esteem among residents and dark images of vacant mills with padlocked gates and boarded up storefronts on once-thriving Main streets. In the face of ongoing difficulties in generating new employment opportunities, these images have often proved persistent, although this has begun to change with the growing viability of the region's post-industrial economy. More positive mill images have been revived in many 'reinvented' cities, which once again proudly point to their industrial histories and landscapes.

Recent studies that document the growing role of cultural production in New England's economy have contributed to the publicizing and proliferation of this revitalized image. The Creative Economy Initiative started in the late 1990s with a partnership between the New England Council (a business organization), government, cultural leaders and six state art agencies scattered throughout the region. In June 2000, the New England Council released a study, *The Creative Economy: the Role of Arts and Culture in New England's Economic Competitiveness*, which produced compelling evidence of the 'creative sector' as an important economic force in the regional economy. This sector was made up of 'creative clusters' of non-profit and commercial enterprises, a 'creative workforce' and 'creative communities' with high concentrations of both. Statistics (e.g. that the creative economy comprises 3.5% of New England's total job base) are widely shared among arts advocates and cultural workers, and gain the attention of business and politicians. A second report, *Blueprint for Investment in New England's Creative Economy* (New England Council, 2001) examines how creativity contributes to the region's cultural economy and makes recommendations about how to grow and invest in this sector. Drawing on models from all over the world, the blueprint suggests a range of targets and initiatives to reach them.

Cultural Workers: the Johnny Appleseeds of the New Creative Economy

Urban cultural development strategies are diffusing rapidly across the New England landscape. This often involves the transformation of abandoned mills into new cultural, retailing and living spaces. It also involves the re-framing of narratives about these spaces and the re-formation of the public's image of key parts of a city, mixing imagery and symbolism with the physical transformation of space. Where early regeneration efforts of the 1970s and 1980s emphasized a trajectory of innovation, decline and rebirth, more recent narratives speak of a long arc of continuous challenge and innovation in New England. Cultural intermediaries in small cities have provided a key voice to both narratives, as they help transform once-abandoned spaces and generate cultural performances and new marketing and image-making strategies. For many, this has involved a shift from first seeing investment in culture as amenity alone, to seeing it as a replacement for industry and eventually as an important component of large-scale makeovers.

The idea of using the arts and culture to jump-start the economy did not originate in one particular New England city. Artists and creative entrepreneurs, local and state-level cultural policymakers, researchers, arts advocates, public historians and even real estate developers have long been involved in local and grass-roots redevelopment efforts based on cultural strategies, and were thus poised to become full fledged advocates of cultural economic development once the environment was ripe. It is sometimes difficult to identify the source of cultural workers' optimism or their ability to convince mayors and planners of the potentials of cultural production in the face of high unemployment, empty mills and lingering negative images. Many of their visions for change include ridding cities of the symbols of decline before replacing them with new prideful reconstructions. The question of where culture-driven revitalization fits within this vision for change in small- to medium-sized post-industrial cities is not well explored. How do places that have lived with notoriously negative images, anachronistic economies and numerous sites of industrial decay, come to believe that at least a part of their economic recovery depends upon something as elusive (or material) as the arts?[2]

All the New England cities under study here have experienced deindustrialization and a range of failed attempts to lure industry back.[3] For mayors, economic developers, realtors and cultural intermediaries, the failure of past revitalization approaches (especially the demise of their downtowns and removal of historic buildings through 'urban renewal' and outlying shopping mall construction) is a key motivator for taking the city in a dramatically new direction. Mayor Barrett of North Adams, Massachusetts, admits that he was not initially enthralled with the idea of a Museum of Contemporary Art (MoCA) as a vehicle for economic recovery. But faced in the 1980s with a 14% unemployment rate, approximately 75,000 m^2 of empty mills, 28 vacant buildings downtown, and the closing of the town's large employer, Sprague Electric, he realized that 'art was the only game in town'.

Models for new creative economies often come from places outside New England. For example, when Worcester, Massachusetts, decided to create a 'cultural corridor' downtown, a coalition began immediately to research similar strategies around the USA. This outward gaze was common, and often driven by personal travel. According to one developer from Lowell,

> The original arts development that we did when I was on the Preservation Commission, which is at Market Mills Artists Working Space, came about because when I was living in Alexandria I saw the Torpedo factory down there and we were trying to create something similar here. And certainly we've gone to a lot of other places. The Preservation Commission used to make field trips. We went to Savannah and San Antonio . . . Portsmouth, New Hampshire, places have had their successes and that's stimulated ideas and different ways to do things . . . No one should be that proud that they can't try and take other formulas for success.

Cultural intermediaries also identify New York's Soho and Greenwich Village or the Bay Area around San Francisco as examples. While mostly seen in a positive light, these examples are sometimes referred to as illustrations of what *not* to emulate due to resulting gentrification and displacement. Charlie Hunter, a painter and music promoter in Bellows Falls, Vermont, draws on his observations of Tribeca in New York City, and smaller 'artsy towns' such as Hudson, New York and New Hope, Pennsylvania, to describe what he would like to avoid. For many artists, the experience of once living in a gritty warehouse district of a large city and then unwittingly being displaced through gentrification, is motivation for seeking a different route. For example, Jerry Beck, Director of the Revolving Museum, which moved from the Boston waterfront to Lowell, experienced displacement in Boston, and now harbours a vision of artists owning their own spaces.

> I mean these are the lessons that go across the country. Look what happened to every arts community . . . I had friends in San Francisco.

> I used to look up to their alternative program
> there . . . and I was like blown away . . . when
> I found that that whole community was
> devastated and what was happening in Boston
> and New York and is continually happening.
> It's very clear. If you didn't own the building
> you're gone . . . artists move in to these
> forgotten spaces and gentrification just follows.

This desire to distinguish between big city scenarios and what may be possible or desirable in
smaller cities may explain why Richard Florida's
optimistic ideas about cultivating creative environments to attract new business have such
appeal in smaller industrial communities. The
arts- and tourist-based gentrification observed
by cultural workers and social critics such as
Zukin (1991) are seen as 'big city' phenomena
in part because they require massive infusions
of capital. In contrast, people often see Florida's
ideas about attracting creative people as requiring smaller investment. A beautiful setting and
proximity to nature, smartly transformed historic
structures that reference a gritty past, or even a
liberal political climate that supports alternative
lifestyles, may be deemed sufficient to attract
this creative class. Many small New England
cities fit this bill.

Cultural intermediaries also generally love
the older industrial urban aesthetic and the possibilities it presents for creative transformation.
Urry notes how such individuals attempt to 'subvert the bourgeois order through minimal luxury,
functionalism, and an ascetic aesthetics' (1990:
95). Robert McBride, an artist and cultural advocate in Bellows Falls, Vermont, grew up in the
Bay Area, lived among artists in Manhattan, and
was then introduced to Bellows Falls by friends.
What attracted him to this small post-industrial
town was the 'urban grittiness' and aesthetics of
train bridges and historic architecture. Once living there full time, he began to talk with locals
and read about many failed renewal strategies.
Now he says he feels no compulsion to develop
an overall 'game plan', only to 'dust Bellows
Falls off'. His contribution, given his background,
is to do cultural planning. Gregarious and enthusiastic, he is continually on the lookout for creative risk takers to generate ideas for events and
activities that both engage residents and draw
outsiders. Charlie Hunter, mentioned above, is
one of those creative risk takers McBride proudly
lured to Bellows Falls.

Cultural intermediaries in many New
England cities present their ideas for building
on creative resources at a time when policymakers are increasingly open to using all identifiable resources to craft economic opportunities.
The two studies by the New England Council
mentioned above opened avenues of communication between these individuals as a class
and local policymakers. Both reports entice private business people, politicians and planners
to think seriously about the creative side of the
economy and provide dramatic and convincing
quantitative evidence to support the wide
impact of culture on the region's economy.
Some have criticized the reports, arguing that
the economic cluster analysis on which they are
based reduces the rationale for art and culture
to purely economic terms. Nevertheless, the
studies serve the important purpose of giving
arts advocates and cultural workers a platform
from which to approach mayors and local planners. They lend support to what were previously
perceived as unconvincing artist-driven pas-
sions. Once a strong case for cultural production
is made through economic-impact pie charts
and bar graphs, the channels of communication
with policymakers open.

But how have these studies and others
migrated across New England and into the
planning lexicon at such an astonishing rate of
speed? Key venues for dissemination are statewide and regional gatherings sponsored by such
cultural organizations as the Massachusetts Cultural Council (MCC) and the Vermont Council
on Culture and Innovation. These groups hold
meetings all over New England with such titles
as 'Linking Arts, Culture and Economic Development' and 'Creativity Sparks Economy: Cultural Tourism in Western Massachusetts'. They
attract planners, mayors, cultural workers and
economic developers who listen to countless,
inspiring stories from small cities similar to their
own. These stories illustrate how arts and heritage initiatives, cultural marketing campaigns
and building regeneration are contributing real
economic dollars to local economies. Some
panelists present the theories of cultural economy gurus, such as Richard Florida and Charles
Landry. Robert McBride points to a talk by
Florida on how the so-called 'creative class'
could use their talents to help struggling cities
attract new investment, as a real 'turning point',

inspiring him to take his ideas to a broader audience, seek state support, and eventually to host his own Creative Forum in Bellows Falls.

Consultants responsible for many of the cultural economy impact studies have also organized numerous conferences in New England. Beate Becker, founder and executive committee member of the New England Economy Council and author of the *Blueprint for Investment in New England's Creative Economy* (New England Council, 2001), consults with cities across the nation that want to examine their own potential for development. With Becker's help, Worcester, Massachusetts developed a master plan for cultural development that includes the formation of an arts/industry district, gallery and incubator space, a 'cultural corridor' and public–private partnerships. Advised (and initially funded) by the MCC, Worcester also created the new position of Cultural Development Officer to guide these efforts.

Grants officers, responding to the economic impact reports with programmes that directly encourage cultural economy initiatives and provide technical support, are also present at these conferences. Those who administer programmes for state cultural organizations are important conduits for tales of cultural redevelopment across New England. For example, at a recent forum on the creative economy held in Springfield, Massachusetts, one such officer from the MCC recounted how, 25 years earlier, she and others had renovated a five-story warehouse in South East London near the River Thames into art studios and a theatre. Describing herself as 'naïve, energetic and political', she told how they borrowed tools, passed out flyers about arts events, and eventually turned the space into a local gathering place. Fast forwarding to the present, she discussed how that same 'irrepressible' level of commitment to the arts and community building is necessary but must now be augmented by 'entrepreneurship'.

Such cultural intermediaries have been instrumental in transporting the concept and specific implementation strategies for cultural-based economic development from one small city in New England to another. Whether leading field trips to New Bedford to see cultural economy projects such as AHA! (Art-History-Architecture) or speaking about such initiatives in cities contemplating cultural economy initiatives, these intermediaries combine their own enthusiasm for the arts with skilful and compelling presentations of data about positive economic outcomes. They share specific details from other cities and provide advice on preparing and improving funding applications. It becomes possible to trace the direct influence of these intermediaries in the replication of ideas from one city to another throughout the region.

Individual artists and cultural advocates also play a key role in spreading the concepts and practices of the creative economy around New England. Extensive social networks connect these people to one another around the region. Whether these connections are made through visiting each other's events and exhibits, or established through common experiences of displacement from places such as the Fort Point warehouse district of Boston, it is remarkable how many artists scattered around New England know one another and use their personal connections to disseminate ideas about the creative economy. McBride is not alone in saying that he derives much inspiration for organizing as a cultural worker from these social connections and that he thrives on meeting new people and sharing ideas. In Bellows Falls, he utilized his status as a newcomer to promote what once seemed like outrageous ideas to anyone who would take the time to stop and chat. Though the concept of a museum or affordable residences for artists downtown seemed foreign to locals, he gained their trust by volunteering his time, investing some of his own money in downtown real-estate conversion, and generally acting like a persistent 'spark plug'.

As former Mayor Cianci of Providence and Mayor Barrett from North Adams became minor celebrities for the cultural economy initiatives in their cities, and the print and TV media picked up on these examples, other New England cities have become more open to envisioning a future that is quite distinct from their industrial past. They are beginning to strategize with cultural workers about how to sell cultural economy ideas and historic preservation to city councils, local Chambers of Commerce and private investors. In the process, cultural workers learn ever more effective and convincing strategies for approaching public policymakers. And, as intermediaries in the process, they play multiple roles, similar to those outlined by Fleming in the European context – information resource, collaborative project initiator and broker between the arts world, private developers and public policymakers (Fleming, 2004).

With all of the ideas for cultural economic initiatives circulating around New England, it is not surprising that policymakers openly admit to importing ideas from their neighbours. In explaining why he rejects the idea of 'high-priced consultants' Mayor Barrett of North Adams, Massachusetts says, 'Why should I, when I can "steal" ideas from other Massachusetts cities?' (most notably, the strategy of providing live/work spaces downtown for artists). Several cultural workers and developers in Lowell acknowledge Providence, Rhode Island as the inspiration for their Arts Overlay District and live/work downtown-zoning ordinance, even as they proclaim their city to be the first in the state to develop a true cultural plan. Holyoke's former Director of Planning travelled to New Bedford, Worcester and Providence before promoting an arts/industry district in his downtown, while New Bedford's Mayor admits that the idea of AHA! (Art-History-Architecture) came directly from Providence, Rhode Island's gallery night. Not to be upstaged by their neighbours, Worcester, Massachusetts also claims to originate ideas that Lowell and Providence have never even conceived of – for example, arts-based development that looks beyond the downtown to neighbourhoods, and the position of Cultural Development Officer. Meanwhile Providence claims that its Performing Arts Center was the inspiration for Worcester's proposed Center for the Performing Arts (Breitbart, 2004). And on it goes.

Many of these initiatives are new and it is not yet clear whether this migration of ideas is leading to standardization or providing a myriad of rich and different creative economic opportunities. Also far from clear is whether these developments are merely replicating familiar patterns of competing cities offering incentives to lure new residents, businesses and attractions, or whether newer models of cultural production and collaboration are emerging in the wake of the older industrial economy. One place where we can begin to trace these processes over three decades is Lowell, Massachusetts.

Case Study: Public Historians in Lowell, Massachusetts

Lowell, Massachusetts offers an exceptionally high-profile example of industrialization, deindustrialization and post-industrial culture-led regeneration in the region and beyond. Deindustrialized in the 1920s and considered one of New England's most down-and-out mill cities, Lowell was one of the first places to adopt culture-based regeneration strategies. A broad local coalition of educators, ethnic and historical groups, city planners, artists, neighbourhood activists and politicians successfully mobilized state and federal support for cultural projects beginning in the 1960s. From the beginning, supporters of these plans envisioned culture as a way of enhancing the city's overall quality of life and attracting tourism, reinvestment and new residents – a way, in the words of one of the project's first visionaries, of 'becoming a good address again'.

These efforts culminated in 1978 with the creation of Lowell National Historical Park, an innovative urban labour history site that has served as a flagship development. The city's cultural landscape now includes many museums, festivals, educational and performing arts centres, examples of landscape and architectural restoration, sports facilities and public art.

Lowell's reputation has changed strikingly in recent years, and it is now regarded as an exemplar of the revitalized ex-mill town – what *Historic Preservation* magazine called 'the relevant precedent emulated by gritty cities worldwide' (Freeman, 1990: 32). Although much of its success can be attributed to its proximity to Greater Boston, Lowell's culture-led redevelopment also shines on its own merits. Regrettable measures of its success include rapidly rising downtown rents and real estate values, coupled with persistently high poverty rates, particularly among recent immigrants. Many familiar signs of gentrification have appeared. For example, in 2002 the city energetically wooed the Revolving Museum, which had ironically been displaced from Boston's redeveloping waterfront. Within a month of the museum's re-opening in Lowell, a neighbouring art store and gallery, whose owner had been among the city's most longstanding champions of local artists and community art shows, lost its lease, only to be replaced by an upscale housewares boutique. 'Frankly', the local paper editorialized, 'that's part and parcel of what happens when a real estate market perks up' (*Lowell Sun*, 2002).

Within Lowell's new cultural economy, historians – particularly those in the field now known as 'public history' – have long played a prominent role. The field of public history *per se* emerged in the USA during the 1970s out of a shortage of jobs in academic history departments, an influx of public funding for cultural projects, and the leftist sensibilities of many academically trained historians wishing to connect their work to broader audiences. Training programmes began in the late 1970s and early 1980s, embracing the work of archivists and curators but professionalizing additional roles such as museum educators, interpretive and exhibit planners, and consultants on preservation law and policy (Conard, 2002; Liddington, 2002). Early graduates of these programmes often stepped into jobs linked with the American bicentennial and the concurrent 'heritage boom' of the 1970s, and with publicly funded reinvestment in depressed places like Lowell. Both kinds of projects – the celebratory and the ameliorative – were woven into the knowledge and service sectors which were becoming increasingly important segments of the US economy. Linked with economic redevelopment projects and commercial or quasi-commercial ventures, the work of public historians is suspended somewhere between the categories of 'public' and 'private'. It also bridges the categories of amateur and professional, local and outsider, making public historians true 'cultural intermediaries' in Evans and Foord's sense.

Just as Lowell was an early adopter of culture-led revitalization, Lowell National Historical Park (NHP) was among the first projects substantially shaped by the newly professionalizing field of public history. One of Lowell NHP's first historians recalled his colleagues realizing one day, 'Oh, my God, there's no road map here. We're doing something that people will look back on some day.' Lowell's culture-led regeneration has been widely studied and emulated. Another early planner at the national park reported, 'We entertained more delegations from all over the place in [the park's early] years . . . areas that have wound up . . . becoming heritage areas. The western Pennsylvania crowd, . . .

delegations from England . . ..' Players in Lowell's redevelopment have subsequently moved into positions in similar projects throughout the region and beyond, and Lowell NHP retains its iconic status for many in the public history field; in the words of one younger public historian, 'In my universe . . . Lowell looms very large on the horizon . . . Everybody I studied in graduate school or studied *with*, had a hand in this place.'

The first public historians at Lowell NHP embraced the concept of using the present-day city itself as an interpretive text, 'an artifact of the industrialization process' (Weible, 1991: xi). They welcomed the 'public-private' model: 'We were activists . . . and we felt that the purpose of public interpretation is to give people a sense that you make your own history, and if making your own history means using your history to make money, then that's a good thing.' The left-leaning sensibilities of many public historians emerged in exhibits that not only emphasized working people's history, as the local coalition had insisted, but took a distinctly critical view of industrial capitalism and its social consequences. 'Most of us young people on the staff,' one early park planner noted, 'thought of ourselves as a little subversive.'

This phrase – 'a *little* subversive' – is telling. While they were acting out of politically progressive values, these cultural intermediaries were not interested in storming the barricades of late industrial capitalism. They accepted the underlying logic of the economic restructuring project their work was asked to contribute to, and welcomed the employment that such projects were beginning to offer for academically trained, publicly-inclined historians. In the decades since the creation of Lowell NHP, the abundant public funding of the 1970s has dwindled and the political climate in the USA has favoured an increasingly market-driven vision of social and economic development. In this changed setting, jobs have become scarcer and leftists in the field of public history even less willing or able to challenge that vision in direct or consequential ways.

An examination of public historians' socio-economic backgrounds suggests one reason for this reluctance. The families of many of these white-collar knowledge workers often only recently entered the middle classes. The attainment of the level of material comfort that comes with that status was quite fresh in their family or personal memories, creating a particular set of responses that have helped shape their work lives. For many, this recent socio-economic mobility also created a sense of discontinuity and disconnection – a disconnection that they seemed to address, in part, through their choice of jobs in the field of history. In the words of one Lowell NHP employee:

> To me, thinking back, [coming to work in Lowell] was connecting with the farm-to-factory story, what my family had gone through . . . and how so little of that seems to have gotten passed down . . . from generation to generation . . . But . . . the point of education is *not* to work in a factory, *not* to work on a farm, and to work behind a desk . . . I guess, the white-collar professional middle class existence was the goal . . .. And I lived that dream! [laughs] The National Park Service – perfect middle-class bureaucrat existence!

Another suggested that her choice to pursue a public history career was linked to the material production that had once taken place in the buildings where she worked: 'I reside more or less in the world of ideas, but I think why I like public history, and museum work, is because I like the tangible aspect.' For these workers, then, their work lives help them to fill perceived gaps in their own lives. These are the same gaps experienced by many visitors to Lowell NHP, who often come to bridge the disconnections in their own histories, which include immigrants and factory workers.[4] The work of public historians in Lowell thus helps create a linear narrative about industrialism, a new cultural product whose producers and consumers use it to locate themselves in relation to their own post-industrial lives.

Moreover, they pursue this act of location within an economy that is putting new kinds of pressures on both their leftist values and their middle class status. Although Lowell's public historians, like most cultural workers, are not primarily driven by financial ambitions, they are reluctant to give up creature comforts. In the words of one park employee, 'I have a schizophrenic relationship with capitalism . . . I have a strong collective sense of democracy and justice that really is not necessarily compatible with something I might want to buy at the Gap, you know.' Working in the cultural sector – in this case, in the relative security of the US National Park Service – appears to be a way to balance the conflicting demands of their critical values and their desires for comfort. However, public history and similar fields are now so thoroughly embedded in cities' economic survival that this choice does not insulate workers from the vicissitudes of post-industrial capitalism. These stresses make public historians more reluctant to pose critical challenges to the larger projects within which they work, reducing the likelihood that they will use their work in oppositional or counter-hegemonic ways. One strategy available to cultural workers facing such demands is to place new emphasis on reports and their own credentialing professional organizations, to shore up their status, maintain some degree of control over the demands placed on their work, and justify its social importance. These strategies often contribute to standardization and a narrowing of the range of voices in cultural projects.

This narrowing of perspectives can be seen within Lowell's redevelopment efforts. Like many such projects, Lowell's began as a local effort, primarily by educators. Once the city began to attract outside funding, non-local professionals (known in Lowell as 'blow-ins') came to play a more prominent role in planning, celebrating its cultures and interpreting its past. Urban planners, public historians, folklorists and others who have come to Lowell since the 1970s have often posed a challenge to existing networks and practices. The city has also seen enormous immigration from South East Asia, Latin and South America, Africa and elsewhere. At times, this blending of disparate voices – local people with a long-established stake in the city's culture-led revitalization project, 'blow-ins' with their own visions for the city and their own professional affiliations, and recent immigrants – has resulted in a productive tension that has broadened the expression of ideas and possibilities within the overall redevelopment effort. Such was the case with the national park's unusually critical interpretation of industrial and labour history, which built on local insistence that the park focus on working people but also drew on the sensibilities of a generation of 'new social historians' inspired by the work of leftist scholars like E.P. Thompson, Herbert Gutman and others.

In more recent years, however, this productive tension appears to have dissipated, perhaps because the range of local voices has narrowed. 'Public' meetings and programmes at Lowell NHP between 2000 and 2002 attracted audiences from an extremely limited pool of people, many of whom had long-standing connections with the cultural institutions active in the redevelopment project. These people are not widely representative of the city's population, particularly its working class population. They come from Lowell's professional and management classes, and have few ties (other than symbolic ones) to the industrial history that is being mobilized to create the 'new Lowell'. People from this group have developed enduring relationships with the 'outsider' public historians and other cultural workers whose contributions are essential to the overall project. While the locals still cast themselves in a some-what oppositional role – 'We still never let [the Park Service] totally off the hook,' in the words of one local cultural activist – deference now clearly goes both ways, with the established local voices often ceding ground to the park without a struggle. Contention over specific issues is often like a family dispute in which everyone is ultimately on the same side. Those already within the pale are circumspect about who is admitted to this inner circle of localness. Recent immigrants, with their particularist agendas and widely dispersed loyalties, pose a particular challenge, as their presence validates the city's celebration of ethnicity and culture but also threatens to disrupt it.

Loyalty to the city over time is of paramount concern for the local people who have seen their community climb so painstakingly from deep depression to relative post-industrial success. Both new immigrants and professional outsiders are placed in some sense on probation until their loyalty has been proven. Martha Norkunas, a folklorist active in the development phase of the national park and related ventures, has written that, 'Lowell is a place where one is known, and one's family is known . . . People here earn their authority to advocate ideas through loyalty to the city, longevity, and ethnic associations' (2002: 30). While this undoubt-edly contributes to the unusually high level of cohesiveness and continuity that have been hallmarks of Lowell's cultural realm over the decades, it also works to slow or block internal challenges or the inclusion of new perspectives about the city's possible futures, and to define 'localness' in quite a narrow way.

Conclusion

What can this investigation of cultural workers in Lowell and other small New England cities tell us about the issues of standardization and inclusion within culture-led tourist and regeneration efforts? Our case of Lowell illustrates how the professionalization of jobs within the cultural sector and the continued volatility of the new cultural economy may combine over time to exert a centripetal force which limits participation and narrows the scope of what is defined as 'local' within redevelopment projects based on cultural strategies. Lowell's example also shows that as heritage-related ventures have become more entrenched and institutionalized, they have lost much of their early critical edge and the kinds of community-oriented energies that were evident in the first stages. Further, public history, heritage tourism and related fields have lost 'market share' throughout New England in recent decades as competition among cities and towns has increased and as newer cultural ventures – notably the cultivation of projects based on visual and performing arts, cultural festivals and related retailing – have come more to the forefront of planning and marketing efforts.

It seems possible that sheer newness is in fact the real cultural product being marketed through these efforts, and that longevity and institutionalization within cultural projects may undermine the flexibility cities need in order to maintain a vital and adaptable cultural presence in the region. We have also documented the growth of a close-knit regional network of cultural workers who disseminate very similar patterns of development throughout the region. This may further work against the emergence of alternative models that critically question or radically reinvent those patterns. Like manufacturing before it, the cultural sector is also on a trajectory to create ever-larger entities in the pursuit of new economies of scale. This shift from local to regional planning and decision making may limit local control and further reduce local participation.

At the same time, our research suggests certain areas of possibility for reinvigoration of the kinds of critical and community-oriented energies that were evident in the early stages of Lowell's redevelopment and that have surfaced more recently elsewhere. Unlike larger metropolises, many smaller New England cities are moving towards regional cooperation, encouraged in part through the social connections among cultural workers and their involvement with advocacy organizations. Two examples are the newly formed Vermont Council on Culture and Innovation and the Western Massachusetts Arts Alliance. Both sponsor 'Creative Economy' forums to share ideas for extending the cultural economy sector and for promoting their regions as unique tourist destinations. They also act as clearinghouses of information about local talent, arts and cultural organizations, and events. Whether regional cooperation enables more diverse constituencies to be recognized and stems the competitive ethos of development, however, remains to be seen.

The recent turn towards more diverse forms of cultural production and away from earlier investment in 'heritage' projects may also rejuvenate critical and community-oriented energies. Dynamic arts-led projects may be a way to inject new vigour into historical projects themselves, via such productions as the recent collaboration between the Massachusetts Museum of Contemporary Art (MoCA) in North Adams and Historic New England, entitled 'Yankee Remix: Artists Take on New England' (see Stanton, 2005). It also seems possible that as an overarching concept, 'art' may in fact have greater potential for ongoing renewal, participation and invention, as compared with 'history', which appears to many people as something finished and static.

Artists currently enjoy increased visibility and public and private support in New England's small cities. This provides cultural and financial capital that they may also use to challenge purely economic rationales for their work and advocate for more inclusive and critical approaches to cultural production. There are signs that this is happening in Lowell. For example, Jerry Beck plans to use his Revolving Museum to tap into the creativity of residents by working with more community-oriented artists and educators, and by dispersing tourist-attracting public art installations to neighbourhoods outside of downtown. He and other cultural workers

believe that the use of the arts for community building can coexist with cultural economy initiatives. They express concern about the emerging gentrification that their work may be helping to spawn, and speak sincerely of a desire for cultural projects that are inclusive of a wide range of voices. Whether this concern generates a deeper civic commitment to social justice projects or is neutralized over time also remains to be seen.

A hopeful view is that these undercurrents of awareness and discontent provide a potential opening that can capitalize on the current energy within many artistic communities in the region for reinventing culture-led developments along more participatory and egalitarian lines. Indeed, the mobilization of cultural planning on a regional level may itself open space for this kind of reinvention, offering, as it does, a way for cultural intermediaries in many small cities to work collaboratively rather than in competition with one another. Further study of culture-led regeneration projects in New England's small cities will reveal whether these potentials are realized over time.

Notes

[1] As yet there has been little extended critical or ethnographic investigation of the cultural sector as a workplace occupied by specific kinds of people acting out of a set of historical and socio-economic contexts that motivates and shapes their work. Florida's writing about the creative class describes and analyses but does not probe critically into context and motivation. A few writers (for example, Snow, 1993; Handler and Gable, 1997) have produced fine ethnographies of cultural workers at work, but have similarly drawn lines between their subjects' work and non-work lives. Zukin (1995) has asked the kinds of questions we are proposing here in relation to restaurant workers – that is, how do their cultural and socio-economic backgrounds shape their choice of work and how are the products of their labour shaped by these in turn? However, she has not extended her exploration to cultural workers in a broader sense or more specifically to those professionals whose labour helps to shape culture-led redevelopment projects in significant ways.

[2] This is the question that Nancy Kelly poses in her documentary 'Downside Up' (from New Day Films in 2002) about the impact of the new

Massachusetts Museum of Contemporary Art (MoCA) on the city of North Adams.

[3] Myrna Breitbart conducted research involving interviews on the dissemination of ideas about culture-based revitalization in small New England cities as well as cities in the North Midlands of England from 2003 to 2005 and is continuing to expand this work on the comparative cultural economy of small post-industrial cities into a book. She has also been involved in long-term ongoing participatory action research and ethnographic fieldwork on the role of culture-driven revitalization in the city of Holyoke, Massachusetts. Ethnographic fieldwork in Lowell, Massachusetts was conducted between 2000 and 2002 by Cathy Stanton as the basis of her doctoral dissertation (see Stanton, 2006). This project involved interviews with 54 people at Lowell National Historical Park and elsewhere in the city's cultural institutions, as well as considerable participant-observation at tours, festivals and other cultural performances, and surveys of national park visitors.

[4] This finding parallels Dicks's research at a Welsh coal mining heritage site, which revealed that 'virtually all the visitors I approached had some close or distant family connection, either to the place or to coal-mining in general' (2003: 128).

References

Breitbart, M. (2004) Blueprinting SoHo: the geographic life of the idea to transform space and economy through artists and the arts. Paper presented at the Association of American Geographers Annual Meeting, 14–19 March. Philadelphia, Pennsylvania.

Castells, M. (1994) European cities, the informational society and the global economy. *New Left Review* 204, 18–32.

Conard, R. (2002) *Benjamin Shambaugh and the Intellectual Foundations of Public History*. University of Iowa Press, Iowa City, Iowa.

Deutsche, R. (1996) *Evictions: Art and Spatial Politics*. MIT Press, Cambridge, Massachusetts.

Dicks, B. (2003) *Culture on Display: the Production of Contemporary Visitability*. Open University Press, Maidenhead, UK.

Edensor, T. (2005) *Industrial Ruins: Space, Aesthetics and Materiality*. Berg, London.

Evans, G. and Foord, J. (2003) Shaping the cultural landscape: local regeneration effects. In: Miles, M. and Hall, T. (eds) *Urban Futures: Critical Commentaries on Shaping the City*. Routledge, London, pp. 167–181.

Fleming, T. (2004) Supporting the cultural quarter? The role of the creative intermediary. In: Bell, D. and Jayne, M. (eds) *City of Quarters: Urban Villages in the Contemporary City*. Ashgate, London, pp. 93–108.

Florida, R. (2002) *The Rise of the Creative Class: and How it's Transforming Work, Leisure, Community and Everyday Life*. Basic Books, New York.

Freeman, A. (1990) Lessons from Lowell. *Historic Preservation* November/December, 32–39.

Handler, R. and Gable, E. (1997) *The New History in an Old Museum: Creating the Past at Colonial Williamsburg*. Duke University Press, Durham, North Carolina.

Harrison, B. (1982) Rationalization, restructuring and industrial re-organization in older regions: the economic transformation of New England. Working Paper #72, February, Joint Center for Urban Studies of MIT and Harvard University.

Holcomb, B. (1993) Revisioning place: de- and re-constructing the image of the industrial city. In: Kearns, G. and Philo, C. (eds) *Selling Places*. Pergamon Press, Oxford.

Liddington, J. (2002) What is public history? Publics and their pasts, meanings and practices. *Oral History* 30(1), 83–93.

Lowell Sun (2002) Lost energy [Editorial]. *Lowell Sun*, 5 August, p.13.

McNeill, D. (1999) Globalisation and the European city. *Cities* 16(3), 143–148.

New England Council (2000) *The Creative Economy: the Role of Arts and Culture in New England's Economic Competitiveness*. New England Council, Boston, Massachusetts.

New England Council (2001) *Blueprint for Investment in New England's Creative Economy*. New England Council, Boston, Massachusetts.

Norkunas, M. (2002) *Monuments and Memory: History and Representation in Lowell, Massachusetts*. Smithsonian Institution Press, Washington, DC.

Short, J.R. (1989) *The Humane City: Cities as if People Matter*. Blackwell, Oxford.

Snow, S.E. (1993) *Performing the Pilgrims: a Study in Ethnohistorical Role-Playing at Plimoth Plantation*. University Press of Mississippi, Jackson, Mississippi.

Stanton, C. (2005) Outside the frame: assessing partnerships between arts and historical organizations. *The Public Historian* 27(1), 19–37.

Stanton, C. (2006) *The Lowell Experiment: Public History in a Postindustrial City*. University of Massachusetts Press, Amherst, Massachusetts.

Urry, J. (1990) *The Tourist Gaze: Leisure and Travel in Contemporary Society*. Sage, London.

Weible, R. (ed.) (1991) *The Continuing Revolution: a History of Lowell, Massachusetts*. Lowell Historical Society, Lowell, Massachusetts.

Zukin, S. (1991) *Landscapes of Power: from Detroit to Disney World*. University of California Press, Berkeley, California.

Zukin, S. (1995) *The Cultures of Cities*. Blackwell, Cambridge, Massachusetts.

11 Cultural Policy and Urban Restructuring in Chicago

Costas Spirou

In response to the global restructuring of industry in the 1970s and 1980s and the increasing inter-urban competition for investment and jobs, cities affected by manufacturing decline have adopted pro-growth local economic development policies as a means of securing their economic futures. This chapter examines how Chicago, a city that previously was dependent on manufacturing industry, has sought to improve its economic position and raise its national and international profile via locally driven strategies focused on facilitating the physical, economic and cultural restructuring of its downtown area. The chapter proceeds to highlight potential distributional consequences of such investment for disadvantaged groups.

The increased internationalization of economic activity has provided the primary driving force for the formulation and implementation by cities of pro-growth local economic development policies. Indeed, it is argued that declining cities unwilling to adopt entrepreneurial policies focused on encouraging economic growth, are contributing to their own economic demise (Kotler *et al.*, 1993; Fainstein, 1994). Given these trends, many city leaders and locally based coalitions have felt compelled to undertake or facilitate massive restructuring of the physical fabric of their respective cities (and particularly the downtown areas), in order to maintain or improve the position of their city in the global economic hierarchy. Thus, it is argued

that adoption of pro-growth local economic development policies represent the only practical course of action as local governments endeavour to achieve financial prosperity within their jurisdictions (Fainstein, 1994).

As cities search for innovative ways to reshape their core areas, culture industries and amenities have become an integral part of urban redevelopment (Lash and Urry, 1994; Zukin, 1995; Clark, 2003). In recent years, entertainment and gaming districts in US cities such as those in Baltimore, New Orleans and San Diego have been spruced up with the aim of capturing the discretionary spending of local residents and tourists. Waterfront areas and their associated recreational facilities have received great attention in the revitalization efforts of Baltimore, New Orleans, New York City and Philadelphia. In Atlanta, Chicago, Milwaukee, Minneapolis, Pasadena and Philadelphia enclosed shopping malls have anchored downtown redevelopment plans. Finally, new or expanded convention centres in Chicago, New York, Kansas City and Orlando seek to tap the wellspring of large-scale trade shows and conventions. These projects, in turn, count on spin-off hotel, restaurant and entertainment expenditures to stimulate their cities' economies (Frieden and Sagalyn, 1989; Judd and Fainstein, 1999; Law, 2002; Judd, 2003).

Under the leadership of Mayor Richard M. Daley (1987–present) Chicago has engaged in a series of projects aimed at redefining its public spaces along cultural tracks. Downtown redevelopment projects, along a 4-mile area of Chicago's lakefront, have been central to the planning agenda of city government. These projects are intended to position Chicago as a major beneficiary of the national/international travel and tourism sector. The restructuring of Navy Pier as a recreational/exposition facility, the recent transformation of Northerly Island into a recreation/education park, the creation of the Museum Campus and the expansion of McCormick (convention centre), the recent transformation of Soldier Field [Chicago Bears of the National Football League (NFL)] and the construction of the Millennium Park reveal the culturally based, pro-growth ideology of this city. City assessments indicate that near 30 million visitors come to Chicago each year. During the record breaking year 2000, over 120,000 jobs were attributed to domestic tourism, with over $180 million in local taxes deriving from the same source. The direct impact of domestic travel to Chicago that year was $8.5 billion (Spirou, 2006). However, some argue that one of the outcomes of this direction has been a misguided prioritization of public investment, resulting in diminishing support for social and economically disadvantaged groups.

Chicago's New Direction: Lakefront and the Economy of Culture

The 2000 census identified the Chicago metropolitan population nearing 8.3 million residents, with about 2.9 million living in the City of Chicago (Bureau of the Census, 2000). Chicago's economy has been historically identified with manufacturing for many decades going back to the 19th century. Yet, like many other American cities, due to extensive economic restructuring occurring in the 1970s and 1980s, the city experienced considerable manufacturing decline and population loss. Following the 1950 census depopulation persisted until 2000, when for the first time Chicago observed a 115,000 population increase.

In 1999, *Industry Week*, a leading trade publication, ranked Chicago as the number one metropolitan area for manufacturing in the country.

According to the publication, manufacturing jobs in the nine-county area increased from 651,147 in the fourth quarter of 1994 to 769,598 in the third quarter of 1998. Yet the city itself experienced a manufacturing employment decline from 265,150 to 214,348 (Miller, 1999). Similarly, according to the *Manufacturers' News Inc.*, during that same period, the number of manufacturing plants in the city declined from 4328 to 4172 (Gaines, 2000). The booming of the overall economy in the USA left many people working in this sector of Chicago's economy unemployed as the loss of 156 plants translated to 3297 lost jobs. When compared to other areas around the country, the organization identified excessive county tax burdens on commercial and industrial properties, additional local sales and gasoline taxes, and high city payroll taxes as the primary reasons for these alarming trends (Gaines, 2000). According to *World Business Chicago*, a public–private economic development corporation, 17.99% of the city's labour force worked in manufacturing in 1990. That percentage dropped to 12% in 2001.

While the above assessments on these recent Chicago trends can be argued as part of larger structural shifts, the city's performance on manufacturing job creation has been disappointing. Efforts to create environments for such growth have been largely unsuccessful. An example of such an effort would be the empowerment zones initiative. This $100 million federally supported programme was expected to bring jobs and private investment to some of the most disadvantaged neighbourhoods of the city in the west and south side. Mayor Daley viewed the programme as the source of many area employment opportunities, and he predicted that 5000 jobs and $2 billion were attainable programme outcomes. Yet, this 1994 initiative did not fully meet these expectations and in 1997, Daley conceded that after an investment of $43 million, 'roughly 400 new private sector jobs [were created]' (Simpson, 1997).

The one area that received the attention of the Mayor and where the city administration is proud of its public policy initiatives and accomplishments is Chicago's lakefront. Though Daley often references Chicago's most famous city planner Daniel Burnham and his declaration: 'The lakefront by right belongs to the people',

Daley has also viewed the lakefront as the foundation of Chicago's new economic engine – culture. From 1989 until 2003 over $11 billion have been expended by the City of Chicago in public infrastructure investments that according to Tiffany Hamel, Director of Business Development for *World Business Chicago*, will 'lay the foundations [for the city] to remain a thriving, global, economically diverse city that is always thinking toward its future, no matter what' (Hamel, 2003).

Extensive renovations as in the case of Navy Pier (an entertainment destination spot), realignment of major transportation routes as in the case of Lake Shore Drive for the creation of the Museum Campus, introduction of new lakefront cultural projects such as the Millennium Park, and 'mayoral battles' over Meigs Field and Soldier Field, have come to define recent city administrations, and in the process shape Daley's legacy. This attention to the most visible cultural side of the city, the intense showcasing of its world-class museums and entertainment venues at its central core, has further shifted Chicago's identity from that of a 'manufacturing centre' to a centre of tourism, a centre of social experience, recreation, leisure, urban tourism, fun and play.

After a decade of physical restructuring the Mayor proudly commented in his 2000 State of the City address:

> And with tourism numbers at an all-time high, the rest of the world is finally discovering what we have known for a long time: Chicago is a beautiful, diverse, welcoming and culturally rich city – on a par with the greatest cities in the world.
>
> (Daley, 2000a)

Navy Pier and the Millennium Park

Navy Pier, located on Chicago's lakefront has a long history of being connected to the city. The pier opened for the first time to the public in 1916 and at a cost of $4.5 million it primarily served as a centre of business and recreation. The public increasingly visited the area, especially after its accessibility expanded owing to the addition of its own streetcar. Theatres and restaurants made the place a popular destination spot and in the 1920s it is estimated that attendance reached 3.2 million visitors annually. The attendance to the pier declined during the Great Depression, though even during that period, it continued to be a Chicago favourite. During World War II, the city leased the pier to the Navy and its public use was restricted as it was utilized as a training centre for pilots and other military personnel. After the war, the University of Illinois used the pier as one of its branch campuses, while its function as a public space of choice persisted. In the 1970s and 1980s, the pier fell into disrepair as its use by the University of Illinois ceased. Efforts to revitalize the pier were unsuccessful and the area became a symbol of urban decay (Wright, 1996).

The revitalization of the 1006 m pier began in 1989 by the Metropolitan Pier and Exposition Authority. At a cost of $200 million, Navy Pier was completely redesigned and opened to the public in 1995. The facility includes the Chicago Children's Museum, a 2973 m^2 indoor botanical garden, a 15-storey Ferris wheel, street entertainment areas with outdoor stages, an IMAX theatre, retail concessions, restaurants, food courts, a skyline stage, a festival hall, a huge ballroom and 50 acres of parks and promenades, among other attractions. The initial boom of the project was so impressive that public officials viewed Navy Pier as having a positive effect on the revitalization of nearby housing in the Streeterville community (Kaiser, 1997; McCarron, 1997; Bernstein, 2004). The latest addition to the Navy Pier complex is the $27 million, 900-seat Chicago Shakespeare Theatre, which opened in the autumn of 1999 (Jones, 1998). Owing to the extensive renovations however, many of the original structures were torn down and the pier is no longer on the National Register of Historic Places (Reardon, 1992).

The Navy Pier complex is the most popular attraction in the City of Chicago. According to the Chicago Office of Tourism, Chicago Convention and Tourism Bureau, the attendance exceeded 7 million in 1997 and in 1999 that number surpassed 7.75 million (Bergen *et al.*, 2005). In 2002 the number of visitors to Navy Pier neared the 8.4 million mark and in 2003, 8.7 million visited the pier generating $45.8 million for the year. To that end, multiple corporate sponsors have utilized the access to a large number of visitors for marketing and promotional purposes. What is certain about Navy Pier in Chicago is that today it is viewed by Chicagoans and visitors alike as a centre of entertainment and recreation and a generator of substantial tax revenue for the city.

The Lakefront Millennium Project is the most recent, culturally based development effort of the Daley administration. In 1998, Mayor Daley announced his plan for a major expansion of the park system along the lakefront. This proposed expansion was initially projected at a cost of about $150 million. Over $120 million was to be generated from the issuing of revenue bonds. Corporate sponsors and private donations were expected to provide the remaining $30 million. The project, on 16.5 acres would feature an outdoor performance stage, an indoor theatre, a skating rink, gardens and concession stands. The city would schedule performances by the Grant Park Symphony Orchestra and would utilize the amenities for other musical festivals. A parking garage would be constructed directly beneath the park, on land currently home to a rail yard. Proceeds from the two-level, 2500-space parking garage, would be used to pay off the bonds. The completion of the project was scheduled for the summer of 2000 (Shields, 1998).

A year later, the Chicago Department of Transportation announced an expansion of the previous plan. New additions to this plan included a warming house and a restaurant for an ice skating rink, an increase in seating from 500 to 1500 in the planned indoor theatre, a commuter bicycle centre, a glass greenhouse pavilion and an improved design of the music pavilion with good sight lines. The size of the park also increased to 24.6 acres. According to Ed Uhlir, Millennium Park Project Director: 'Grant Park is Chicago's front yard. Sadly this 16-acre corner of the park has been a blight for too long. Millennium Park will remedy that with a plan that brings Chicagoans together on a year-round basis' (City of Chicago, 1999).

One of Millennium Park's central projects has been the Frank Gehry band shell design of the music pavilion. Heralded architect Gehry had an enormous impact on the city of Bilbao, Spain, where, in 1997, he built the highly acclaimed Guggenheim Bilbao Museum. His signature massive steel trellis, unveiled in 1999, would be built over a seating area for 11,000

spectators, the new home of the Grant Park Symphony Orchestra. Employing similar architectural principles, Gehry contributed the design of a nearby bridge connecting the pavilion with the Daley Bicentennial Park to the east and across Columbus Drive.

The Millennium Park Project has been hampered by cost overruns and delays. For example, initially scheduled to be completed in 2000, Frank Gehry's band shell opened in the summer of 2004. While early cost estimates required $17.8 million for the structure, the actual cost ballooned to $50 million. Initial projections for the flowing stainless steel bridge were around $8 million but surpassed the $13 million mark (Kamin, 2003). The cost of the entire park development ballooned to $450 million when it finally opened in 2004. While earlier, Mayor Daley (1998) in a letter to the people of Chicago, described the Millennium Park as 'an exciting new cultural destination for families and children, and an economic magnet for visitors and conventioneers' the Mayor, recently, placed the project in a historical context by indicating that this is a 'civic project [that] marks the new Millennium as no other project ever before undertaken in the history of Chicago' (City of Chicago, 2003).

Museum Campus

The Museum Campus can be viewed as one of the most aggressive plans of Mayor Daley's culturally driven redevelopment agenda during the last decade. The vision to join the grounds of the Field Museum of Natural History, the Shedd Aquarium and the Adler Planetarium and thus create a museum campus, required the re-routing of the northbound, five-lane Lake Shore Drive, which cut through and separated these cultural institutions. With the approval of a bond in 1994 for the expansion of nearby McCormick Place (Chicago's major convention centre) funds were allocated for the South Lake Shore Drive project. At a cost of more than $120 million, the Metropolitan Pier and Exposition Authority carried out the project with city and state financial resources (*Planning*, 1995).

After the completion of the relocation of Lake Shore Drive to the west, additional work was conducted to add 57 more acres, including expansive greenways, massive landscaping, raised terraces, pathways and land bridges designed to cover the old multilane thoroughfare. To put into perspective the size of this project, consider that more than 91,446 m³ of dirt were displaced and the ground was lowered by as much as 6.7 m to create a tiered lawn (Kamin, 1998).

Devoted to recreation and culture this new complex, south of Grant Park, opened in 1998 and on the whole has received the approval of civic leaders, local government and other groups. The new grounds of the Museum Campus became a favourite location for Daley to promote his extensive planting programme. According to Blair Kamin (1999), one of the most respected architectural critics in Chicago, 'Mayor Richard M. Daley has been Chicago's Johnny Appleseed, carrying out a simple (and politically popular) idea: the more trees the better.' In the spring of 1999, 114 linden trees along with bushes and ground cover were planted at a cost of $1 million.

The purpose of the Museum Campus was to create a destination place and increase the attendance at the three museums for both Chicagoans and tourists. According to the Chicago Office of Tourism, the museums attracted 3.7 million attendees in 1997 and in 2002 that number increased as it neared 4 million visitors. With recent museum expansions, such as the completion of a $40 million upgrade at the Planetarium, a new construction exhibit at the Aquarium and a $10 million addition to the Field Museum, that number is expected to increase. On its own, this project along the lakefront shows the Mayor's commitment and desire to engage in fundamental physical restructuring of the area to advance his vision of Chicago as a city of culture (Mendieta, 1999).

Meigs Field and Soldier Field

Though the Mayor of Chicago successfully managed to advance the above culturally based projects without political opposition, this proved not to be the case with Meigs Field and Soldier Field. The proposed transformation of Meigs Field, a small airport in operation on Northerly Island near the Museum Campus, into a public park, received intense resistance by then Governor Edgar of Illinois and the corporate community of Chicago. The facility was primarily used to provide business leaders easy access to the downtown area. Scheduled to commence in 1996, the 50-year airport lease with the Chicago Park District, would not be renewed. Instead, according to the mayoral proposal, the space would be altered to create a 91-acre park at a projected cost of $27.2 million. The plan would link the park to the Museum Campus and would include botanical gardens, playgrounds, wetlands, a nature centre and a sensory garden for the visually or hearing impaired. The island would be accessible by a ferry and a rubber-wheeled trolley. According to city projections the 'superpark' would generate over $30 million a year in revenue from parking, concessions, souvenirs and other fees and it would draw more than 350,000 visitors annually. This environmental park would be fully accessible to the disabled, as ramps would extend to the lake, fully accommodating those using pushchairs and wheelchairs (Hill and Borsky, 1996).

The plan faced political opposition from Governor Edgar. He challenged the Mayor who had earlier shown limited support for the Governor's third commercial airport proposal. The Edgar proposal would add an additional commercial airport in north-eastern Illinois, and located outside the city limits, the plan would pose competition to both city airports, O'Hare and Midway. Daley had also resisted the Governor's plans for expansion of Chicago's convention centre to create McDome, an indoor stadium for the Bears of the NFL. Arguing that closing Meigs would negatively effect the transportation of the region, the State filed a lawsuit to take control of the property. Given the extensive legal battle ahead over control of Chicago lakefront property and rights between the City and the State, the two reached a compromise early in 1997. The agreement would allow for the reopening of the airfield, which had shut down in the autumn of 1996 after the lease had expired. Then following a 5-year period of operation, the city would proceed with its plans to create a park on Northerly Island. According to a press release by the Office of the Mayor, Daley indicated that:

> The compromise is good for the long-term future of Chicago. The original Meigs Field lease on Northerly Island ran for 50 years. We have to wait another five years to create a

family and tourist's Park on Northerly Island –
but it will be worth the wait. From the very
beginning, I have supported negotiation on this
issue – but with one condition. In the end, the
best use of Northerly Island is for it to become
a part of our lakefront museum campus.

(City of Chicago, 1997)

In the summer of 2005 the Charter One
Pavilion opened on Northerly Island, a 7500-
seat venue offering outdoor concerts and live
entertainment to music fans (Kot, 2005).

In recent years nearby Soldier Field, home
of the Chicago Bears of the NFL, has also
become part of this culturally based image
advanced by Mayor Daley. Stadium development has proved capable of reshaping urban
space even at the neighbourhood/community
level (Spirou and Bennett, 2002). Located adjacent to the Museum Campus to the south,
Soldier Field opened in 1924 and since then it
has been identified as an integral part of the
city. The facility is owned and operated by the
Chicago Park District and its major tenants,
the Bears, have been leasing the stadium. The
relationship between the city and the ownership
of the team has been contentious, especially
after 1986 when the team won the Super Bowl
and began to argue against the antiquated
Soldier Field, advancing pressure for a brand
new facility with a large number of luxury
skyboxes.

As the team explored multiple options both
in the city, the suburbs and even in neighbouring Indiana, Mayor Daley continued to support
the Soldier Field choice, because of its lakefront
location and its proximity to the Museum
Campus. Sport as a form of culture surely fits
the vision of the lakefront and its presence
would complement the city of culture theme.

In the summer of 2000, following many
years of 'battles' over locations and financing,
Bears' officials and Mayor Daley settled old differences and jointly began to promote an
ambitious proposal for a new stadium that
included substantial redevelopment of the surrounding areas. This most recent proposal to
renovate Soldier Field promised to deliver to
the franchise a state of the art sport facility
wrapped in the existing historic stadium shell.
At the same time the Mayor would take another
step in his campaign 'to restore the Lakefront',
a central piece of his administration's ongoing

effort to improve Chicago's downtown and
near downtown public spaces (Osnos and
Pearson, 2000).

The cost of the Soldier Field renovation
surpassed the $680 million mark with the Bears
contributing $200 million and the remainder
being financed by Chicago's 2% hotel-motel
tax. The Illinois Sports Facilities Authority
(ISFA), an agency created to oversee construction of another Chicago stadium, the New
Comiskey Park in the late 1980s, issued bonds
to cover the city's share of stadium construction
costs. The physical plan specified a new football
stadium set within, though also rising substantially above, the classical colonnades crowning
Soldier Field's east and west facades. Extensive
underground parking has been added and surface parking areas to the south of the stadium
were landscaped, adding more than 15 acres of
green space to the lakefront. Overall, 1300 trees
of 45 different species were planted, a sledding
hill was configured and a children's garden has
been created (Ford, 2004). The new facility
opened in 2003, and is in concert with the city's
larger vision of keeping Soldier Field as part
of the lakefront, positioning it as an additional
piece to the available entertainment venues
along Chicago's front yard (Spirou and Bennett,
2003).

Chicago's Downtown Strategy: Social
Implications and Impact

Though the City of Chicago over the last
few years invested a tremendous amount of
resources and attention to reshaping both the
physical and the cultural standing of its lakefront,
its neighbourhoods have been faced with a series
of economic and social challenges. In that regard
health care, social inequality, problems in education and poverty rates continue to plague the
city. City leaders have turned to tax increment
financing (TIF) districts and the federal empowerment zones as a way to assist various socially
and economically ailing communities. Questions
though do remain about the long-term effect and
positive contributions of these programmes.

Real challenges for the city administration
exist in the neighbourhoods as the number of
Chicago communities in which the population

in poverty exceeded 40% increased from 48 (population 156,270) in 1970 to 184 (population 396,200) in 1990. In addition, Chicago in 1997 accounted for 55.3% of Illinois' welfare caseload, though it possessed 23% of the state's population (Miller, 1999). Furthermore, according to the US Bureau of Labor Statistics, while unemployment decreased in Chicago through the 1990s the unemployment rate for African Americans (13.8% in 1997) remained at least double the rate of Whites (5.4% in 1997). Most troubling has been the unemployment rate among Blacks between 16 and 19 years of age (43.3% in 1997) in comparison to that of Whites between 16 and 19 years of age (17% in 1997) (Chicago Reporter, 1999).

The 2000 census has also shown that Chicago is facing some serious difficulties as it attempts to reduce poverty. While the poverty rate in Illinois was 11.6%, the poverty rate in Chicago was 19.6% (2000 US poverty rate was 11.3%). Similarly, the 2000 median family income in Illinois was $55,545 per annum while in Chicago that figure was $42,724. Regarding poverty, the highest rates continue to be in the predominantly minority communities in the south and west sides of the city. Many of these have rates of poverty exceeding 40% with a few surpassing the 50th percentile (Illinois Poverty Summit, 2003).

The city is also struggling to deal with health care, especially in African American neighbourhoods. Sixteen community areas average fewer than two doctors per 10,000 population. Together these areas are 69.5% Black and 8.1% White. On the other hand, 15 community areas average more than 16.8 doctors per 10,000 population. Together these areas are 55.4% White and 29.2% Black (Medical Marketing Services, 1997). Similarly, both the life expectancy and the mortality rates vary across the city by race. The communities with the highest rates of mortality between 1995 and 1997 are found in the predominantly African American communities of the west and south sides. Ten of the 11 areas with the highest death rates are at least 90% African American. The average life expectancy in 1992 was also the longest for the mostly White north-west side (75–79.7 years) and the shortest for mostly African American west and south sides (58–64.9 years) (Pardo, 1999).

Issues of housing have also emerged. The emphasis on developing the cultural amenities of the lakefront has encouraged an upsurge in the cost of residential housing in the downtown area. In the Near South Side (just south of the Loop) the number of loans increased from 760 with a value of $145 million (2000) to 1443 with a value of $310 million (2001) to 1497 loans with a value of $461 million (2002). The number of loans in the Loop also increased from 1149 with a value of $227 million (2000) to 1889 with a value of 351 million (2001) to 1937 with a value of $466 million (2002). Finally, according to Crain's Chicago Business (2004), Chicago's South Loop ranked as having the second most affluent residents by mailing zip code across the entire metropolitan area with a median annual household income of $193,939. This reality has placed enormous pressure on middle income residents who are now priced out of the area and local community organizations are attempting to promote the importance of diversity and the need for affordable housing in the area (Gibson, 2004).

Education has also proved challenging. In the early 1990s the Chicago Public School system was identified as one of the worst public school systems in the USA. Since then, Mayor Daley has attempted to revert the negative publicity associated with that distinction by focusing on strict accountability measures, mandatory summer school and extended days. Yet, high school dropout rates continue to plague the public school system. Overall dropout rates in 1993, 1994 and 1995 have been around 43% and in 1995, 25 high schools recorded rates greater than 50%. The highest dropout rate in 1995 was at Phillips Academy (71.8%) on the south side of the city. These figures amplify the formidable task facing the city when one considers that the nationwide dropout average in 1992 was 10.8% (Kaneya, 1998).

The city is also falling behind in educating its adults. In 2000, the average percentage of adults without a high school diploma in Illinois was 18.6%. In Chicago that number was 28.2%. Specifically, 47 out of 77 Chicago community areas had at least 25% of adults lacking a high school education. Fifteen areas have non-completion rates in excess of 40% (Illinois Poverty Summit, 2003).

Conclusion

Over the last 15 years, the City of Chicago, under the leadership of Mayor Daley has engaged in extensive physical restructuring of the lakefront in an effort to redefine the city as one of culture, entertainment and recreation. The Mayor successfully managed to choreograph the cooperation of various local agencies and, where necessary, asserted his authority to give the lakefront an immense facelift. The transformation of the lakefront will continue as millions of public dollars are earmarked to be spent in the next few years.

Along with these trends, a new vision for the city has emerged, one which will come to define its future. Conventions and tourism are of primary importance and a source of considerable revenue. The total number of visitors travelling to Chicago in 1992 was 23.74 million. By 1997, that number had increased to 27 million and it reached an all time high of 32.39 million in 2000 (*Chicago Convention and Visitors Bureau*). While the volume experienced a decline owing to September 11th, the city expects a healthy rebounding in the years to come.

In his 2000 speech at the annual meeting of the Chicago Conventions and Tourism Bureau, Daley reminded those in attendance that:

> Anyone who thinks Chicago is falling behind in the convention and tourism business had better go back and check the numbers . . . [I want] a city on the cutting edge of technology and on the leading edge of tourism and travel.
>
> (Daley, 2000b)

At the same time, the attention to the lakefront and the building of Chicago's new economy of culture has not solved the problems in the neighbourhoods of the city. Many of the social and economic challenges remain and attention to solving these problems persists. The utilization of the empowerment zones and the TIF districts has not produced the projected outcomes. In the end, well-paid jobs are what is mostly needed, something that the convention and tourism industries have not been shown to be capable of providing. Furthermore, crime is on the rise and the city ranked first in the number of homicides among large urban centres both in 2002 and in 2003.

Finally, the intense residential housing changes, caused by the explosion in the construction of new and converted housing in the downtown area, have proved to have a wider impact. Current minority residents find it increasingly difficult to maintain their housing units due to increased property taxes. Public housing developments are pushed aside to make room for upscale, luxury units. This has resulted in gentrification and displacement, and has altered the socio-economic character of various area neighbourhoods. The case of Chicago reveals that the advancement of cultural policy in search of economic opportunities derived from tourism and leisure has the potential to generate substantial strain and as a result produce forces capable of considerable urban restructuring at the physical, social and economic realms.

References

Bergen, K., McCormick, J. and Yates, J. (2005) Navy Pier, ten years later. *Chicago Tribune*, 28 August, pp. 1 and 22–24.

Bernstein, D. (2004) Just a quiet night at home. *Crain's Chicago Business*, 3 May, p. 13.

Bureau of the Census (2000) *2000 Census of Population*. Bureau of the Census, US Department of Commerce, Washington, DC.

Chicago Convention and Visitors Bureau (n.d.) Home page. Available at: www.choosechicago.com (accessed 14 March 2006).

Chicago Reporter (1999) Chicago's unemployed [Editorial]. *Chicago Reporter*, May, pp. 12.

City of Chicago (1997) Mayor Daley announces compromise plan on Northerly Island. Meigs to reopen for five years, then become park. Press release from the Office of the Mayor, Richard M. Daley, Mayor, 6 January.

City of Chicago (1999) New millennium plans unveiled to Chicago Plan Commission on March 11, 1999. Department of Transportation, Richard M. Daley, Mayor, March.

City of Chicago (2003) Chicago's Millennium Park. Office of Tourism, Richard M. Daley, Mayor, May.

Clark, T.N. (2003) The city as an entertainment machine. In: Clark, T.N. (ed.) *Research in Urban Policy*. Elsevier/JAI, Boston, Massachusetts, p. 338.

Crain's Chicago Business (2004) Most affluent communities. *Crain's Chicago Business*, 29 November, p. 32.

Daley, R.M. (1998) A letter to the people of Chicago. 20 August, p. 1. Available at: http://egov.cityof chicago.org/ (accessed 24 September 2005).

Daley, R.M. (2000a) State of the City address. 19 January. Available at: http://egov.cityofchicago.org/ (accessed 24 September 2005).

Daley, R.M. (2000b) Speech at the annual of the Chicago Conventions and Tourism Bureau. 24 March. Available at: http://egov.cityof chicago.org/ (accessed 24 September 2005).

Fainstein, S. (1994) *The City Builders: Property and Planning in London and New York*. Blackwell, Oxford.

Ford. L. (2004) Soldier Field landscaping takes shape. *Chicago Tribune*, 26 April, section 2, p. 1.

Frieden, B.J. and Sagalyn, L.B. (1989) *Downtown, Inc.: How America Rebuilds Cities*. The MIT Press, Cambridge, Massachusetts.

Gaines, S.L. (2000) Manufacturing jobs vanish amid strong sector. *Chicago Tribune*, 13 January, section 3, p. 5.

Gibson, L. (2004) Affordability among the South Loop's Affluence. *Chicago Journal*, 22 April, p. 1.

Hamel, T. (2003) Chicago blue skies? *Economic Focus* 3(5), 1–2.

Hill, J. and Borsky, D. (1996) City lifts veil on hopes for Meigs wetlands, botanical gardens are included. *Chicago Tribune*, 2 July, section 5, p. 6.

Illinois Poverty Summit (2003) *Atlas of Illinois Poverty*. Spring. Heartland Alliance for Human Needs and Human Rights, Chicago, Illinois.

Jones, C. (1998) The location is the thing: Chicago's Shakespeare Rep poised for move to Navy Pier, and perhaps for wider recognition. *Chicago Tribune*, 1 February, p. 16.

Judd, D.R. (2003) *The Infrastructure of Play: Building the Tourist City*. M.E. Sharpe, Armonk, New York.

Judd, D.R. and Fainstein, S.S. (1999) *The Tourist City*. Yale University Press, New Haven, Connecticut.

Kaiser, R.L. (1997) Blazing a trail through lost Chicago. *Chicago Tribune*, 5 August, p. 1.

Kamin, B. (1998) Reinventing the lakefront: to shape the shoreline. *Chicago Tribune*, 26 October, section 5, p. 1.

Kamin, B. (1999) City has a field day planting trees – with mixed results for the museum. *Chicago Tribune*, 8 July, section 5, p. 1.

Kamin, B. (2003) Steel appeal. *Chicago Tribune*, 6 July, section 7, p. 5.

Kaneya, R. (1998) Dropout rates still plague public schools. *Chicago Reporter*, May, p. 3.

Kot, G. (2005) Stunning skyline. *Chicago Tribune*, 27 June, section 5, p. 1.

Kotler, P., Haider, D.H. and Rein, I. (1993) *Marketing Places*. Free Press, New York.

Lash, S. and Urry, J. (1994) *Economies of Signs and Space*. Sage, London.

Law, C.M. (2002) *Urban Tourism: the Visitor Economy and the Growth of Large Cities*. Continuum, London.

McCarron, J. (1997) Downtown unchained? The building boom is back. *Chicago Tribune*, 11 August, p. 1D.

Medical Marketing Services (1997) *Census Estimates*. Claritas Inc., San Diego, California.

Mendieta, A. (1999) Planetarium shines new. *Chicago Sun-Times*, 30 September, p. 16.

Miller, W.H. (1999) Sick cities – healthy regions. *Industry Week* 248(7), 96–101.

Osnos, E. and Pearson, R. (2000) Bears, city say this may be real deal for Soldier Field. *Chicago Tribune*, 15 August, p. 1.

Pardo, N. (1999) Life cut short for city's minorities. *Chicago Reporter*, April, p. 1.

Planning (1995) Lake Shore Drive [Editorial]. *Planning* 61(2), 42.

Reardon, P. (1992) Navy Pier off US historic list. *Chicago Tribune*, 18 February, p. 2C.

Shields, Y. (1998) Chicago plans issue for park expansion. *Bond Buyer*, 2 April, 324(30364), p. 3.

Simpson, B. (1997) $43 million later, Chicago has fewer new jobs in the empowerment zone. *Chicago Reporter*, June, p. 1.

Spirou, C. (2006) Urban beautification and the construction of a new municipal identity in Chicago. In: Koval, J., Bennett, L., Demissie, F. and Bennett, M. (eds) *The New Chicago: a Social and Cultural Analysis*. Temple University Press, Philadelphia, Pennsylvania (in press).

Spirou, C. and Bennett, L. (2002) Revamped stadium . . . new neighborhood? *Urban Affairs Review* 37(5), 675–702.

Spirou, C. and Bennett, L. (2003) *It's Hardly Sportin': Stadiums, Neighborhoods and the New Chicago*. Northern Illinois University Press, DeKalb, Illinois.

World Business Chicago (n.d.) Home page. Available at: http://www.worldbusinesschicago.com (accessed 14 March 2006).

Wright, G. (1996) Decaying pier gets a life preserver. *Building Design & Construction* 37(2), 36.

Zukin, S. (1995) *The Cultures of Cities*. Blackwell, Cambridge, Massachusetts.

12 Philadelphia's Avenue of the Arts: the Challenges of a Cultural District Initiative

Anna Maria Bounds

Introduction

Over the last 20 years, cultural, economic and political elites in Philadelphia (Pennsylvania, USA) have been developing a cultural district, the Avenue of the Arts, a 1 mile block of performing arts venues, hotels, restaurants and office buildings. This chapter describes how diverse leaders from the government, arts and business sectors worked together to implement this cultural district in the hope of using cultural amenities as tools for generating tourism and reviving a declining downtown area. It examines the challenges of implementing cultural district initiatives in the American context where cultural planning decisions are often driven by key project stakeholders and real estate and economic developers rather than in conjunction with cultural policies or cultural planning administrators.

Cities have always been the centre of cultural and economic activity (Hall, 1998); however, there is now an increasing overlap between these two realms (Scott, 2000). Cultural resources are now viewed less as expressions of locality or urbanity than tools to revitalize urban economies (Bianchini, 1993). Cultural initiatives are valued as urban regeneration projects because they improve images of cities, attract affluent tourists and residents (as well as their corporations) and diversify the local economic base. The Avenue of the Arts case illustrates this intersection of the arts and economic development

as city officials and elites supported the cultural district initiative as a means to bolster both the image and the economy of Philadelphia.

While the Avenue of the Arts initiative was designed to cover two different areas, in the south of the city centre and one to the north, this study focuses on the nine projects to the south, that is on South Broad Street, the core performing arts district. The first section of the chapter discusses the rationale behind cultural district initiatives and presents the Avenue of the Arts case. The second section analyses the roles of the local government, the private sector and arts organizations in implementing Philadelphia's cultural district.

The Avenue of the Arts initiative is a vital case for examining the development of cultural district initiatives for three reasons. First, the development of cultural attractions such as cultural districts and regional performing arts centres is on the rise (See Strom, 2002). Second, within cultural district literature, the Avenue of the Arts initiative is considered a model case for local government participation in cultural district development and management (Frost-Kumpf, 1998; Brooks and Kushner, 2001). The initiative's complexity and expansive nature – the proposed development of nine core projects involving the participation of diverse actors ranging from the state government to small local performing arts companies – also allows for the investigation of cultural district implementation

© CAB International 2007. *Tourism, Culture and Regeneration* (ed. M.K. Smith)

in multiple contexts and levels of organizations. Third, the initiative represents an effort to restore the economic and social importance of the declining South Broad Street as well as the declining city of Philadelphia by relying on the city's cultural assets to increase revenue from its tourism and hospitality sector (Hodos, 2002).

The Rise of Cultural Districts

Cultural district initiatives are part of the shift in urban development from representing cities as places of production to cities as places of consumption (see Zukin, 1995; Hannigan, 1998; Fainstein and Judd, 1999). Rather than being prized for their productive capacities, cities are now valued for their cultural and entertainment attractions. Quality of life standards are now measured by a city's range of lifestyle amenities such as its cultural institutions, nightlife and sports venues (Clark *et al.*, 2002). Recognizing that cultural amenities appeal to the service sector and its affluent workers, entrepreneurial local governments have sought to attract these workers as both residents and tourists through an extensive array of cultural and entertainment urban development projects (Evans, 2001). Such entertainment projects are numerous. They include the early example of Baltimore's Inner Harbour, a waterfront festival marketplace (Levine, 1987); the redevelopment of New York's Times Square, an entertainment district (Reichl, 1999); and the construction of Newark's New Jersey Performing Arts Center (NJPAC), a regional performing arts centre (Strom, 1999).

Examples of cultural districts include London's South Bank (Newman and Smith, 2000) and Dublin's Temple Bar (McGuirck, 2000). In the USA, interest in cultural districts has been increasing, with more than 90 cities having developed or planning cultural districts as a means for revitalizing their downtown areas (Frost-Kumpf, 1998). Drawing from early examples such as New York's Lincoln Centre, cultural districts exist in American cities of all sizes from Pittsburgh's Cultural District to Houston's Museum District to Rock Island, Illinois's Arts District.

As a type of arts-based development project, cultural districts are thought to have a multiplier

effect, attracting interest and revenue to the city (Frost-Kumpf, 1998; Brooks and Kushner, 2001). By improving the quality of life of downtown, arts-based projects attract tourists and professionals to the area. Increased downtown activity promotes other types of economic development such as retail shops, restaurants and hotels. As a result, the local government benefits from revenue generated from tourism as visitors to a district spend money on food, lodging and retail purchases.

South Broad Street: Center City's Cultural Destination

The Avenue of the Arts initiative promised the possibility of restoring both Philadelphia and South Broad Street, which had become a 'symbolic boulevard of broken dreams' (Lemann, 2000: 42), to their former glory. With roughly 1.5 million people, Philadelphia is the sixth largest city in the USA (US Census Bureau, 2002). Its population is almost evenly divided between Whites (45%) and Blacks (43%). Once a prominent manufacturing city that specialized in textiles, its top employment sectors are now services, management and retail. Like other large north-eastern cities, Philadelphia is experiencing decline.

Mayor Edward G. Rendell (1992–2000) saw the cultural district initiative as a tourism-based economic development strategy that would increase tax revenue for a city that had been drained of its population and employment. The combination of structural changes in Philadelphia's economic base, a change in demographics reflecting an increase in the low-skilled and poor population and the exit of the middle-income population, as well as reduced federal support of cities, pushed Philadelphia into severe fiscal crisis (Inman, 1995). Given this economic climate, Rendell began to look for projects that offered the possibility of generating revenue and employment for Philadelphia's failing economy. His hope was that the Avenue of the Arts initiative was such an opportunity.

The Avenue of the Arts is located along a mile-long section of South Broad Street in Philadelphia's Center City (see Fig. 12.1). Since its completion in 2001, the district now contains

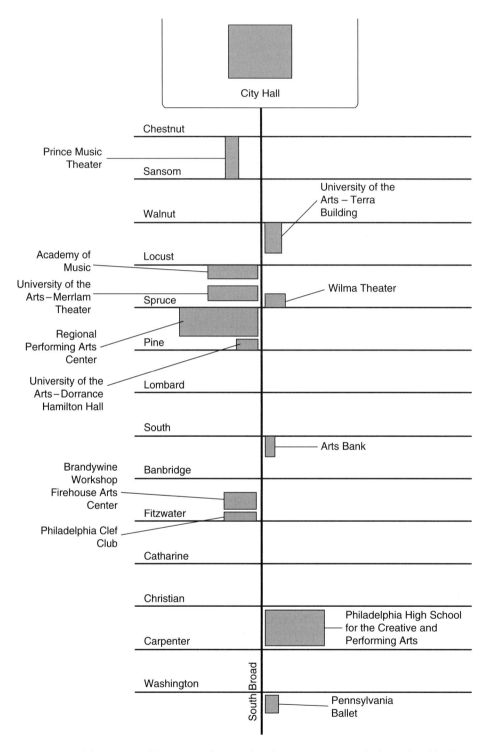

Fig. 12.1. Map of the Avenue of the Arts: implemented performance venues and other cultural facilities.

11 cultural and educational institutions and seven venues, providing over 10,000 performances seats. Total investment for the initiative was $378.4 million, with over $75 million from the state and over $30 million from the local government (Avenue of the Arts, Incorporated, 1999). In 1999, the district generated over $157 million in revenue annually, providing 2800 full-time and over 1000 part-time jobs (Pennsylvania Economy League, 1999).

South Broad Street's history as a cultural destination begins in the late 19th century (see Strom, 2000). This main boulevard blossomed with the development of several theatres, meeting halls, office buildings and luxury hotels (Skaler, 2003). Facilities ranged from Kiralfy's Alhambra Palace, a Moroccan-inspired performance venue for large musical productions, to the historic Union League, a club for members of a patriotic social society that supported Abraham Lincoln. At this time, the Academy of Music, Philadelphia's premiere grand opera house, was also constructed. Built in 1857, the Academy is the oldest operating grand opera house in the USA. One of Philadelphia's cultural treasures, it features an opulent interior that still captivates audiences. From 1901 until the construction of the Kimmel Regional Performing Arts Centre in 2001, the Philadelphia Orchestra performed at the Academy of Music. The Academy of Music continues to be the home of the Pennsylvania Ballet and the Opera Company of Philadelphia. Beyond its critical mass of cultural institutions, South Broad Street was also the location for important citywide celebrations, such as Philadelphia's annual Mummer's Day parade, and the destination for annual conventions.

In addition to becoming the city's cultural destination, South Broad Street also became the city's commercial centre. Commerce shifted from Society Hill to Broad Street with the construction of Philadelphia's City Hall at Center Square (the intersection of Broad and Market Streets) in 1871. As a result, important banking and office buildings were also built on South Broad Street. By 1910, South Broad Street had become known as 'Hotel Row', with the opening of five prominent hotels. Sparked by South Broad Street's vitality, 'Hotel Row' was soon followed by 'Millionaire's Row', which consisted of several blocks of grand brownstones.

With the development of new office space in the western section of Philadelphia, South Broad Street began to decline in the 1980s. By the end of 1990, three office towers in the western section of the city added roughly 280,000 m^2 of office-suite space (Warner, 1990). This construction boom shifted the city's financial centre from Center City to the west of City Hall (Beauregard, 1989). The new office buildings provided important amenities and technological improvements that the older buildings on South Broad Street could not provide without extensive renovations. As a result, office buildings on South Broad Street experienced high vacancy rates as their tenants, prestigious law firms, began to move from older buildings in Center City to modern new office towers (Warner, 1990).

Despite its decline, South Broad Street had several important cultural attractions that could support a cultural district initiative. The Academy of Music was still in use. The Academy of Music and its major resident companies, the Philadelphia Orchestra, the Pennsylvania Ballet and the Opera Company of Philadelphia were considered to be important anchors of attraction for the district's development. The University of the Arts was now located on South Broad Street. The Pennsylvania Ballet had purchased a building for teaching and rehearsal space further south at Broad and Washington Streets. Based on these factors, momentum began to grow for developing South Broad Street into the Avenue of the Arts, a performing arts cultural district.

Implementation of the Avenue of the Arts

The development of the Avenue of the Arts can be divided into three phases: (i) the creation of the first performing arts centre plan, The Academy Center Plan, in 1981; (ii) the development of the William Penn Foundation's 'Cultural Corridor' initiative, its own cultural district plan, in 1989; and (iii) the implementation of a comprehensive plan during the Rendell Administration. In each of these stages, a different key stakeholder assumed leadership of the initiative.

The Academy Center Plan and the William Penn Foundation's cultural district initiative

In 1978, South Broad Street business and cultural leaders created the Avenue of the Arts Council (AAC) to redevelop South Broad Street as a cultural destination. The AAC was comprised of about 30 cultural, business and educational institutions, including the renowned Academy of Music and Philadelphia Orchestra (Avenue of the Arts Council, 1981).

By 1980, the AAC had created annual festivals and produced The Academy Center Plan, a proposal for a performing arts complex. The complex would include the Academy of Music and a new concert hall for the Philadelphia Orchestra. The Philadelphia Orchestra had been performing in the undersized and overbooked Academy of Music, which was also used by the Pennsylvania Ballet and Opera Company of Philadelphia.

Council leaders argued that if the Orchestra had a new, larger hall it could sell more seats and record performances in its own venue (Avenue of the Arts Council, 1980). They proposed construction of a 3000-seat hall plus a 500-seat hall across the street from the Academy. The complex would be managed by the Academy of Music. The leaders envisioned the three venues comprising a new 'Academy Center' analogous to Lincoln Center in New York.

The AAC leaders sought to purchase a parcel of city-owned land for the new performance venue. However, the AAC learned that Mayor Rizzo's administration had agreed to sell part of the tract to hotel developers for a parking garage (Hine, 1981). The AAC was forced to consider other locations.

In 1986, the Orchestra Association voted to build a new hall at Broad and Spruce Streets (Hine, 1986). The Philadelphia architectural firm of Venturi, Rauch and Scott Brown and Russell was hired to design the project (Hine, 1987). The Orchestra still failed to raise substantial revenue and, in 1989, tried a new strategy to generate contributions. The Orchestra released the preliminary design plans for the concert hall to the general public. The strategy 'backfired' however, as the public perceived the plan as too contemporary and stark. While the estimated project cost was $95 million, the Orchestra had raised only $18 million (Fleeson, 1989).

At the end of 1989, the William Penn Foundation launched the 'South Broad Street Cultural Corridor' plan, a separate cultural district initiative. The plan contained several smaller projects that would be located about a mile south of City Hall. The Foundation funded or managed the development of four projects: the relocation of the Brandywine Graphics Workshop, an African-American printmaking facility and exhibition space; the Arts Bank, a 250-seat venue for local performance companies; the Clef Club for the Performing Arts, a jazz venue and archives centre for jazz as an American art form; and the High School for the Creative and Performing Arts (CAPA), which would be relocated to the historic Ridgway Library, after it was renovated (William Penn Foundation, 1990).

Project implementation during the Rendell Administration

After 5 years of trying, the Orchestra had raised only $24 million of the estimated $112 million cost for its new venue. The situation called for different leadership. The answer was to be found in 1992 with the new mayor, Edward G. Rendell. After searching for a project to boost the city's economy, unify its tourist offerings and enhance its image, Mayor Rendell discovered it in the evolving Avenue of the Arts initiative (personal interview, 29 May 2002). At this point, the initiative consisted of developing or renovating nine venues (see Table 12.1).

To advance the projects, Rendell established the Avenue of the Arts, Inc. (AAI), a nonprofit management entity (Salisbury, 1993). The AAI would be responsible for overseeing development and promoting the initiative as an economic development project. Rendell relied on the Philadelphia Industrial Development Corporation (PIDC), the city's economic development agency, to provide technical assistance and resources to projects. The AAI's Board of Directors was also comprised of local elites, charged with making development and fundraising decisions.

Mayor Rendell obtained state funding with assistance from the PIDC that spurred additional private contributions. For example,

Table 12.1. Avenue of the Arts core projects (1992–2001) (Modified from: Central Philadelphia Development Corporation, 1992).

Project	Description	Projected total cost in 1992 (millions US$)
Academy of Music renovation	Renovations to historic opera house, to be used by Opera Company of Philadelphia and Pennsylvania Ballet	18.3
Wilma Theater (300 seats)	Construction of new venue for Wilma Theater Company	6.1
Concert hall and public garage (2800 seats, 500 spaces)	Construction of concert hall for use by Philadelphia Orchestra	139.1
Drama Guild/AMTF theatres (750 and 400 seats)	Construction of joint theatre space by Drama Guild and American Music Theater Festival (AMTF)	17.5
Recital hall (800 seats)	Construction of smaller hall as part of concert hall project	16.5
Arts Bank (248 seats)	Renovation of bank building as theatre for community performing arts groups	3.7
Brandywine Workshop	Renovation of vacant firehouse and the construction of new building for use by Brandywine Workshop (a visual arts organization dedicated to printmaking)	3.1
Clef Club (100 seats)	Renovation of a building into a jazz venue and archive	2.4
Ridgway Library (CAPA classrooms)	Renovation of a city-owned building into a high school for the creative and performing arts	24.0

Walter H. Annenberg, an influential philanthropist, agreed to contribute $20 million and ten corporations pledged at least $1 million in contributions (Salisbury, 1992). Through both the AAI and the PIDC, the Rendell administration provided funding, planning and technical assistance for the smaller projects such as the Brandywine Workshop and CAPA.

Within a 4-year span, the smaller projects were implemented. In 1993, the first smaller cultural facility opened, the Brandywine Workshop (Sozanski, 1993). In 1994, a ribbon-cutting ceremony kicked-off the Arts Bank's week-long opening festival – a noteworthy event that marked the first new theatre opening on Broad Street in over 60 years (Salisbury, 1994a). The Clef Club opened in 1995. In 1996, the Wilma Theater was able to open due to the support of the mayor's wife, Judge Marjorie O. Rendell, who used her skills as a bankruptcy lawyer and negotiator to help secure funding (Saline, 1997). CAPA opened in the refurbished

Ridgway Library in 1997. According to CAPA's principal, Ellen Savitz, both the Mayor and his wife helped to raise the $31 million required for the new school from city and state agencies as well as foundations, corporations and private contributors (personal interview, 23 October 2001).

The ongoing struggle of the Philadelphia Orchestra

Despite the progress of the small projects, the Philadelphia Orchestra's plan for a new performance venue was still floundering. Rendell and other powerful actors supported the plan, but Walter Annenberg and R. Anderson Pew, chairman of the Pew Charitable Trusts, wanted the Orchestra to continue its tradition of performing at the Academy of Music. They spearheaded a drive to renovate the Academy's interior to better accommodate the Orchestra; however, the plan was abandoned because its changes were too radical (Dorbin and Sokolove, 1994).

To accomplish its goal of creating a district that represented a new period in Philadelphia's cultural legacy, the local government tried to save the Orchestra's project by revising the performing arts company's concert hall plan. First, the local government broadened the number and type of actors participating in the project. Chaired by Marjorie O. Rendell, a working group comprised of key actors from Philadelphia's cultural and business sectors was formed to engage in problem solving and build consensus for a revised strategy. The group concluded that constructing a larger performing arts centre offered the best solution and the widest appeal. Rather than serving just one arts organization, the larger project would provide the Orchestra with a new concert hall and offer smaller performance spaces for other resident companies. In 1997, a new architect and a prominent real estate developer were hired to bring much-needed credibility to the completely restructured project (Patel, 2001; Ellen Solms, personal interview, 4 April 2002).

The new architect hired was Rafael Vinoly who had recently received critical acclaim for his design of the Tokyo International Forum, a $1.5 billion performing arts complex and convention centre (Ferrick, 1997). Willard Rouse, III, a powerful Philadelphia real estate developer, was charged with overseeing the project. In 1998, the Vinoly design was released including a 2500-seat concert hall, a multipurpose theatre, and a 130-car underground parking garage, at an estimated cost of at least $200 million (Dorbin, 1998). To fund the new project, revenues from both the Orchestra's concert hall project ($100 million) and the previously proposed performing arts centre ($25 million) were pooled, along with an additional $20 million from the state (Dorbin, 1999).

In 2000, the new Regional Performing Arts Center was permanently renamed the Kimmel Center – in honour of its single largest private donor, Sidney Kimmel (founder of the women's apparel group, Jones New York), who contributed $15 million to the project. In December 2001, after Mayor Rendell's term expired, the Kimmel Center opened with a sold-out $5000-per-ticket gala for an exclusive audience of patrons and supporters (Tommasini, 2001).

Failed projects

Although the initiative had many successes, it also had failures. Despite operating at almost full capacity, the Arts Bank closed in 1997. It could not meet costs owing to the end of subsidies by the William Penn Foundation. While the Arts Bank was operated by the University of the Arts, its rental rates were subsidized by the William Penn Foundation. After the subsidies ended, community groups could not afford the rental rates (Dorbin, 1997). To compound matters, the Arts Bank was located in an area generally perceived as unsafe and offered neither onsite parking nor nearby dining facilities. As a result, the Arts Bank was subsumed by the University of the Arts for its own use.

The Clef Club also ceased operations in 1997. Prior to joining the initiative, Clef Club members differed about the club's planned relocation. Some older members were reluctant to move from a building where the group had been since 1972. They were concerned about the group's ability to retain its autonomy and African-American identity if it were to join the Avenue of the Arts (Carter, 1993). The younger members favoured participation but the older members feared losing control to the Sassafras Corporation, the non-profit management entity established by the William Penn Foundation to oversee the project. Clef Club President Bill Carney attributed the club's collapse to lack of interest by Avenue of the Arts officials and its location five blocks south of the regional performing arts centre (personal interview, 30 May 2002). Carney also cited a lack of sufficient funding and the building's poor design as problems (personal interview, 30 May 2002). Today, the building is open only for certain events but mainly sits dark. Unlike the Arts Bank, however, the function of the Clef Club cannot be redirected. According to the former President of the PIDC, William Hankowsky, the William Penn Foundation deeded the building without a reverter clause, which would have required ownership of a failed venue to revert back to either the AAI or William Penn (personal interview, 30 May 2002).

Another failed project was the Joint Theater, first conceived in 1992, when the Philadelphia Drama Guild and American Music Theater Festival (AMTF) announced plans to build a performing arts centre (Keating, 1992). The plan was abandoned in 1993, however, due to the Drama Guild's financial problems and challenges of designing a theatre to satisfy the needs of both organizations at reasonable cost (Keating, 1993).

One year later, the AAI announced a revised plan for the Joint Theater project, as a larger complex to house the AMTF, the Drama Guild, Philadanco, the Chamber Music Society and Concerto Soloists (Salisbury, 1994b). The AMTF withdrew from the project when Marjorie Samoff, its founder and director, decided to build an independent theatre (Salisbury, 1995). The Philadelphia Drama Guild became defunct. Although the plan for this arts centre stagnated, the AMTF did open its new venue, the Prince Music Theater (Keating, 1999).

Lesson Drawing

The Avenue of the Arts case raises three critical issues for cultural district implementation. The first issue centres on understanding the strategies used by the Rendell administration to guide the initiative. Second, the level of philanthropic influence on specific projects should also be assessed. Lastly, the impact of the managerial and financial strength of participating arts organizations on a district's implementation should also be determined.

With the Rendell administration, the Philadelphia local government transformed from a disinterested party to a key proponent of the initiative. When Mayor Rendell took office, little progress had been made in making the cultural district a reality. However, during his two terms, Rendell used his power as a government leader to create a network of philanthropic, business, cultural and governmental elites dedicated to implementing the Avenue of the Arts. The Rendell administration drove the initiative forward through five means: (i) its development of a tourism-based policy agenda; (ii) its establishment of a non-profit management entity and use of the PIDC to direct control of the project; (iii) its success in winning public and private funding; (iv) its push to complete smaller projects to buttress the initiative; and (v) its re-conceptualization of the concert hall project

as a regional performing arts centre to create broad appeal for the initiative.

The first step in Rendell's decision to salvage the project was the recognition that the initiative matched Rendell's policy agenda of strengthening the city's tax base by increasing its tourism and convention sector. After determining that the project provided a good image and had economic potential, Rendell worked to bring needed actors and resources to the project. Because the plan lacked adequate funding, Rendell engaged in intense fundraising. Rendell's ability to gain funding was his most important contribution to the project. As a result, the Avenue of the Arts network expanded both vertically (into the state government) and horizontally (across philanthropists, corporations and arts organizations) (see Agranoff and McGuire, 2003).

Rendell sought to consolidate policy efforts and increase revenue streams by relying on two quasi-public agencies to direct the initiative's implementation, the AAI and the PIDC. By promoting the initiative as an economic development project, the AAI generated political and financial support. The PIDC also became crucial to guiding the initiative. In addition to arranging financing, the PIDC provided direct leadership to specific projects when needed. Through the AAI and the PIDC, Rendell was able to direct the initiative and to provide mechanisms for removing obstacles to implementation.

Mayor Rendell first focused on implementing the smaller Avenue of the Arts core projects. Unlike the larger concert hall project that still required substantial funding and suffered from a lack of support, the smaller projects had funding. The scale of these projects suggested short timelines for completion so they offered the advantage of increasing momentum for the completion of the concert hall. Marjorie O. Rendell was instrumental in implementing many of these projects. As Allan Edmunds, the Executive Director of Brandywine Workshop explained, 'Mayor Rendell and his wife were a powerful combination for moving the Avenue of the Arts initiative forward. Mayor Rendell was able to put his "weight" behind the project while Judge Rendell was the driving force, providing direct leadership and bringing quality people to the project' (personal interview, 29 July 2002).

The re-conceptualization of the concert hall project as a regional performing arts centre was spearheaded by Marjorie O. Rendell. As the leader of the performing arts centre group, she facilitated communication among a group of diverse elites and motivated the group to commit their resources (time and money) to overcoming challenges to constructing the project. Through a broad base of support, the project was completed, offering the Orchestra a graceful resolution to its dilemma and providing other performing arts companies the chance to become part of the district. The performing arts centre opened in 2001, over 20 years after the Philadelphia Orchestra started the project, but only 5 years after the Rendell administration took control of the project.

The opening of the Kimmel Center was crucial to the Avenue of Arts initiative because it was the district's anchor of attraction. Its completion, along with other projects, boosted tourism and sparked the renewal of South Broad Street. However, the project represents the Avenue of the Arts network's limited success in implementing the cultural district. In the effort to ensure that the performing arts centre was completed, the network focused most of its resources on the reinvention and management of this project. By the time that the performing arts centre plan was launched in 1997, two Avenue of the Arts projects, the Arts Bank and the Clef Clubs had already failed. Due to the loss of William Penn subsidies and the lack of a long-term funding strategy, the Arts Bank could not meet its costs despite operating at almost full capacity. Based on the contractual agreement between the University of the Arts and the William Penn Foundation, which the PIDC helped arrange, the venue was subsumed by the university for its own use. The Clef Club's bad location (farther down South Broad Street), poor interior design and organizational mismanagement caused its closure.

The failure of these projects raises questions about the participation of philanthropic organizations in cultural district initiatives. Funding from the William Penn Foundation was crucial to the success of the district (providing funding for studies and specific projects). Its efforts also increased the diversity of the initiative. However, the Foundation's failure to provide stipulations in its agreements with cultural organizations undermined the strength of the district. The Foundation's inability to lead projects indicates that difficulties may arise when a foundation seeks to expand beyond its traditional expertise in grant making to new types of support such as project management.

The managerial and financial strength of arts organizations is also a key factor in cultural district implementation. By 'going it alone', the Philadelphia Orchestra did not bring key actors into the project and secure their commitment to building the concert hall. Instead, the Philadelphia Orchestra alienated key funders and other performing arts companies. Key funders wanted to support a project that benefited more than one arts organization, while others resisted the Orchestra's move from the Academy of Music. Alienating other performing arts companies meant that the concert hall project shrunk its base of support. In trying to develop a concert hall, the Orchestra moved beyond its expertise in classical music into trying to manage a real estate project. It achieved its objectives only after Rendell revised the project into a broader goal that supported multiple arts organizations.

The Avenue of the Arts case demonstrates the evolution of a cultural district initiative as it has been influenced by key public and private stakeholders. Key actors shared the roles of defining, funding and managing the district. The Avenue of the Arts initiative suggests three key recommendations for the implementation of cultural districts. First, city officials and prospective funders should be aware that arts organizations often lack the technical knowledge to undertake large projects such as the development of a new performance space. Traditional fundraising and administrative expertise that prove valuable in typical arts capital campaigns may not be an applicable skill set for other processes related to cultural projects such as real estate development. Second, for cultural projects to be successful, they need to benefit multiple cultural organizations to bolster political and financial support. Lastly, the local government's ability to manage projects should not be overlooked. The local government's unique resources, such as its access to funding and expertise in negotiation, can be used as strategies to revive struggling projects.

References

Agranoff, R. and McGuire, M. (2003) *Collaborative Public Government: New Strategies for Local Government.* Georgetown University Press, Washington, DC.

Avenue of the Arts Council (1980) *Academy Center Draft Proposal.* Avenue of the Arts Council, Philadelphia, Pennsylvania.

Avenue of the Arts Council (1981) *Interim Report: Academy Center for the Performing Arts.* Avenue of the Arts Council, Philadelphia, Pennsylvania.

Avenue of the Arts, Incorporated (1999) *Extending the Vision for South Broad Street.* Avenue of the Arts, Incorporated, Philadelphia, Pennsylvania.

Beauregard, R.A. (1989) City profile: Philadelphia. *Cities* 6(4), 300–308.

Bianchini, F. (1993) Remaking European cities: the role of cultural policies. In: Bianchini, F. and Parkinson, M. (eds) *Cultural Policy and Urban Regeneration: the West European Experience.* Manchester University Press, Manchester, UK, pp. 1–19.

Brooks, A.C. and Kushner, R.J. (2001) Cultural districts and urban development. *International Journal of Arts and Management* 3, 4–15.

Carter, K. (1993) Clef club split over move to Ave. of the Arts. *Philadelphia Inquirer,* 14 July, p. E1.

Central Philadelphia Development Corporation (1992) *The South Broad Street Economic and Cultural Development Plan.* Philadelphia, Pennsylvania.

Clark, T.N., Lloyd, R., Wong, K. and Jain, P. (2002) Amenities drive urban growth. *Journal of Urban Affairs* 24(5), 493–515.

Dorbin, P. (1997) Avenue not finale for arts, survival not always a given on Broad Street. *Philadelphia Inquirer,* 6 July, p. B1.

Dorbin, P. (1998) Performing arts centre moves to centre stage. *Philadelphia Inquirer,* 17 April, p. A1.

Dorbin, P. (1999) PA comes through for arts centre. *Philadelphia Inquirer,* 8 July, p. A1.

Dorbin, P. and Sokolove, M. (1994) Orchestra revokes plan for the academy. *Philadelphia Inquirer,* 22 July, p. A1.

Evans, G. (2001) *Cultural Planning: an Urban Renaissance?* Routledge, London.

Fainstein, S. and Judd, D.R. (1999) Global forces, local strategies, and urban tourism. In: Judd, D.R. and Fainstein, S. (eds) *The Tourist City.* Yale University Press, New Haven, Connecticut, pp. 1–17.

Ferrick, T. (1997) Architect chosen for arts centre. *Philadelphia Inquirer,* 18 April, p. B1.

Fleeson, L. (1989) Orchestra is granted $3 million. *Philadelphia Inquirer,* 28 December, p. F3.

Frost-Kumpf, H.A. (1998) *Cultural District Handbook: the Arts as a Strategy for Revitalizing Cities.* Americans for the Arts, New York.

Hall, P. (1998) *Cities in Civilization.* Pantheon, New York.

Hannigan, J. (1998) *Fantasy City: Pleasure and Profit in the Postmodern Metropolis.* Routledge, London.

Hine, T. (1981) Broad and Locust: where business could meet posterity. *Philadelphia Inquirer,* 4 June, p. B1.

Hine, T. (1986) New concert hall: decisions have only just begun. *Philadelphia Inquirer,* 30 June, p. I1.

Hine, T. (1987) Orchestra chooses Venturi. *Philadelphia Inquirer,* 21 July, p. A1.

Hodos, J.I. (2002) Globalisation, regionalism, and urban restructuring: the case of Philadelphia. *Urban Affairs Review,* 37(3), 358–379.

Inman, R. (1995) How to have a fiscal crisis: lessons from Philadelphia. *The American Economic Review* 85(2), 378–383.

Keating, D.J. (1992) Philadelphia Drama Guild gets some company in its search for new theater site. *Philadelphia Inquirer,* 25 May, p. E3.

Keating, D.J. (1993) Two theater companies drop plan of joint site. *Philadelphia Inquirer,* 29 April, p. E1.

Keating, D.J. (1999) Princely debut, the city's latest theatrical venue. *Philadelphia Inquirer,* 16 March, p. E1.

Lemann, N. (2000) Letter from Philadelphia: No Man's Town. *The New Yorker,* 5 June, p. 42.

Levine, M.V. (1987) Downtown redevelopment as an urban growth strategy: a critical appraisal of the Baltimore renaissance. *Journal of Urban Affairs* 9(2), 103–123.

McGuirck, P.M. (2000) Power and policy networks in urban governance: local government and property-led regeneration in Dublin. *Urban Studies* 37(4), 651–672.

Newman, P. and Smith, I. (2000) Cultural production, place, politics on the South Bank of the Thames. *International Journal of Urban and Regional Research* 24(1), 9–24.

Patel, R. (2001) The house that Rouse built. *Philadelphia,* December, pp. 126–163.

Pennsylvania Economy League (1999) *Moving in Harmony: the Union of Arts, Business and Lifestyle on the Avenue of the Arts.* Pennsylvania Economy League, Philadelphia, Pennsylvania.

Reichl, A. (1999) *Reconstructing Times Square: Politics and Culture in Urban Development*. University of Kansas Press, Lawrence, Kansas.

Saline, C. (1997) Portrait of a (first) lady. *Philadelphia*, March, pp. 54–128.

Salisbury, S. (1992) Annenberg donates to arts avenue. *Philadelphia Inquirer*, 12 December, p. A1.

Salisbury, S. (1993) Avenue of the Arts gets an executive director. *Philadelphia Inquirer*, 13 May, p. B1.

Salisbury, S. (1994a) Millions given to city arts corridor. *Philadelphia Inquirer*, 19 January, p. B1.

Salisbury, S. (1994b) City buys Broad Street site for retooled arts complex. *Philadelphia Inquirer*, 26 March, p. A1.

Salisbury, S. (1995) A bump in the road for the Avenue of the Arts. *Philadelphia Inquirer*, 29 January, p. G1.

Scott, J.A. (2000) *The Cultural Economy of Cities*. Sage, London.

Skaler, R.M. (2003) *Images of America: Philadelphia's Broad Street South and North*. Arcadia, Charleston, South Carolina.

Sozanski, E.J. (1993) A double milestone for the Avenue of the Arts. *Philadelphia Inquirer*, 8 December, p. E1.

Strom, E. (1999) Let's put on a show: performing arts and urban revitalization. *Journal of Urban Affairs* 21(4), 423–436.

Strom, E. (2000) Cultural coalitions past and present. Paper presented at the Urban Affairs Association Conference, May.

Strom, E. (2002) Converting pork into porcelain: cultural institutions and downtown development. *Urban Affairs Review* 38(1), 3–21.

Tommasini, A. (2001) In Philadelphia, new hall's sound is in the ear of the beholder. *New York Times*, 17 December, p. E1.

US Census Bureau (2002) *City and County Data Book 2000*. US Department of Commerce, Washington, DC.

Warner, S. (1990) Grand old dames bow to Center City's skyscrapers. *Philadelphia Inquirer*, 22 October, p. D1.

William Penn Foundation (1990) *Annual Report*. William Penn Foundation, Philadelphia, Pennsylvania.

Zukin, S. (1995) *The Culture of Cities*. Blackwell, Cambridge, Massachusetts.

13 On the Water's Edge: Developing Cultural Regeneration Paradigms for Urban Waterfronts

Andrew L. Jones

Introduction

A major phenomenon of the 1980s and 1990s was the interest expressed in the redevelopment and regeneration of derelict or decaying waterfront sites, especially in inner city areas. Indeed, the regeneration of many derelict docksides was very much a mark of the 1980s and 1990s urban planning and regeneration strategies. This was highlighted at the time by remarks from observers such as Torre and Warman who highlighted in quite apt terms the relationship and juxtaposition between waterfront sites, regeneration and inner city areas.

> The waterfront is now a magic ingredient quenching the desire of many companies for an environmentally pleasing workplace.
> (Warman, 1990)

> It is at the edge that man is at his best that life is most vibrant. It is the lure of water, its spells, its reflection, its endless movement and change, that best captures man's imagination and provides a variety of applications from business to recreation, from calm to passive activities, the water's edge is where life is most diverse and unique.
> (Torre, 1989)

Today it is well documented that waterfront projects have become commonplace in the process of urban regeneration worldwide. Indeed the revitalization of docklands and associated waterfront development areas has been discussed at length by a number of authors such as Breen and Rigby (1985), Hoyle et al. (1988), Falk (1989), Meyer (2000) and more recently by Burayidi (2001), Marshal (2001), Falk (2003) and the Urban Land Institute (2004). All have extensively documented the changing relationship between port and city interfaces, the changing socio-economic character of port-cities and highlighted the regeneration opportunities that have resulted.

The changes in spatial and socio-economic order have indeed presented considerable new opportunities for the reassessment of substantial areas of city docklands and waterfront areas. These regeneration ideas and concepts were initially developed in the USA during the 1970s. This new approach largely reflected a regeneration strategy that promoted and increased residential, recreational, tourism, commercial and associated public land uses which, in many cases, often became dominant features. During this period, these newly created urban waterfront environments were often referred to as the new 'Central Waterfront'. In many instances these ideas provided the basic ingredient or 'model' for the regeneration of urban waterfronts globally. As a consequence many North American cities embarked upon major dockland and waterfront regeneration initiatives which have not only spanned the east and west coasts, with notable examples in San Francisco, Oakland, Seattle, New York, Boston and Baltimore, but have also seen notable inland initiatives in, for example, Toronto and Chicago.

Elsewhere, particularly in Europe and the UK, the pace was slower in engaging with this new waterfront phenomenon. However, despite the slow start the early 1980s did see a number of major global, European and UK cities, including Sydney, Yokahama, London, Barcelona Copenhagen, Hamburg, Rotterdam, Liverpool, Birmingham and Glasgow, embarking on ambitious dockland and waterfront regeneration which largely demonstrated remarkable transformations of decaying docklands, dilapidated warehouses, derelict wharfs and substandard housing areas.

By the mid-1980s the vocabulary of waterfront regeneration was clearly established in the mindset of developers, local authorities and national government departments as the benefits of waterfront locations became more apparent. In this respect the revitalization of waterfronts is now perceived as a key element in the wider processes of national, regional and local government urban policy and urban renewal strategies. In many instances the focus on waterfronts through government urban policies has become synonymous with the socio-economic objectives of government urban policy programmes across the Western world.

During the late 1980s and early 1990s waterfront regeneration projects thus became uniquely placed to create new social facilities, expand employment and provide a real foundation for the environmental, economic and social regeneration of many urban areas. Nevertheless, as projects grew in scale and complexity, growing concerns were often raised questioning the approach to many projects. Indeed, as several exponents revealed at the time, many proved controversial in economic, social and political terms. The USA increasingly provided lessons in what to avoid when regenerating waterfronts and in the more sobering economic climate of the mid- to late-1990s many regeneration projects had to take a much more pragmatic approach (Gordon, 1997).

The American Festival Market Approach

The American regeneration experience, supported by federal government reconstruction initiatives, did indeed provide valuable pointers for government regeneration agencies around the world. Strong executive powers of the US local authority system and a favourable tax environment encouraged many entrepreneurs to invest in American city dockland areas (Hambleton, 1991; Breen and Rigby, 1996). These ideas were very much transposed to 'globalized' urban policy initiatives which encouraged a 'prototype model' based upon public urban regeneration agencies, a variety of publicly funded regeneration finance and moreover a political focus based on priorities to support economic development (Thornley, 1992). Several additional factors prompted a general revitalization of US port-cities which included changing demography, availability of cheap residential property, growing heritage awareness, growing quality of life awareness, the desire to live closer to work, and the growing importance of urban tourism. Indeed, it seemed that in absolute terms the USA led the world in the extent of its waterfront revitalization programme. As a result American waterfront regeneration focused primarily upon rehabilitation and redevelopment consisting of a wide development mix including residential, recreational, commercial, retail, service and tourist facilities. This largely became the typical development model or paradigm within the USA and shaped the 'export model' that was to characterize many waterfront development projects in other parts of the world including Asia, Australasia, Europe and the UK. Essentially residential, recreational and tourist related uses were often the predominant development mix in this model. They included private residences, retail leisure, chiefly of the 'festival market' type, marinas and other boat related uses. Secondary to this, museums, commercial facilities, sport and light industrial uses were often integrated. The total theme, however, was very much orientated to residential-leisure which was often enhanced by periodic festivals and special events (Breen and Rigby, 1996; Marshal, 2001; Falk, 2003).

These factors led to the many important urban waterfront regeneration schemes that characterized the successful reclamation of derelict waterfronts in many parts of the USA. Although it is beyond the scope of this chapter to discuss these in detail, some of the more influential projects included the Inner Harbour

Baltimore, Quincy Market Boston, the Pierhead Building New York, San Diego's waterfront village, Giradelli Square and Fisherman's Wharf San Francisco (Hoyle et al., 1988). All provided catalysts and influential development criteria for projects worldwide.

The downturn of the US and world economy during the late 1980s and early 1990s slowed the process of regeneration. In fact several US waterfront regeneration projects during the 1990s experienced economic as well as social difficulties. This has notably been primarily in the commercial and retail sectors of developments. As early as 1991 Dutton documented a downturn but suggested that in many instances this would not be a particularly serious problem if developments adhered to certain development criteria. These, he surmised, were largely related to three key areas, notably: (i) the extent to which commercial uses were diversified; (ii) the extent to which tourism development was catered for; and (iii) the extent to which high environmental excellence was achieved (Dutton, 1991). Similar problems at the time were reported by Winterbottom (1989), Suttles (1991) and Breen and Rigby (1990) and have been repeated more recently by concerns expressed on waterfront projects in Cleveland, Chicago, New York and Toronto by Cleveland Urban Development Commission (CUDC) (2001) and Levick (2004).

Global Waterfront Development

Waterfront and dockland renewal projects outside the USA and particularly in Europe and the UK have been generally far more pragmatic. Nevertheless the US experience was a major influence in orchestrating global, European and British urban regeneration policy developments over the last two decades and as such, American experience did provide the framework for dockland revival across much of the world (Department of Environment (DoE), 1990; English Tourist Board (ETB), 1988, 1989). Outside Europe projects such as Darling Harbour in Sydney, Yokohama Bay in Japan and Lambton Harbour in New Zealand became disciples of the American model. At the forefront of European waterfront regeneration were examples such as

Barcelona's Ramblar del Mar, Bilbao and the Guggenheim, and Rotterdam's dockland waterfront. Within the UK the London Docklands was one of the first British examples. However, since the inception of this project in 1981 there have been several other comprehensive waterfront regeneration schemes, some completed and some now in the process of completion. Well established and successful UK examples now include: Liverpool's Albert Dock, Cardiff Bay, Gloucester Docks, Bristol Docks, Birmingham's Broad Street, the Dockyards of Portsmouth, Glasgow's Clydeside, Salford Quays, London's South Bank, Manchester's Castlefields, Newcastle's Quayside and Sheffield's Canal Basin. In Europe other notable waterfront schemes have been initiated in, for example, Genoa, Copenhagen, Helsinki, Oslo and Hamburg. Indeed a recent study by Falk (2003) has identified a considerable number of projects still underway.

Post-2000 – the Waterfront Global Phenomenon: Success and Failure

The extent, pace and scale of waterfront development projects and associated activities has thus been far-reaching and still continues to grow. At the start of 2005 the concept of 'Waterfront Renaissance' still clearly remains an atavistic desire of many developers, planners, architects and visitors alike around the globe. The growth associated with tourism development has also been exponential and a phenomenon without parallel with many waterfront locations creating new leisure and tourism quarters as a basis for new urban tourism and regeneration initiatives. San Francisco's Fisherman's Wharf and Bristol's floating harbour and the Arnolfini development, one of the first US and UK examples, respectively, very much reflected this approach. Baltimore's and Cardiff Bay's festival type market/leisure quarters have also reflected this approach, New York and Salford Quays provide other examples. The list is extensive and too long to consider in this chapter. However, these examples have not only changed the face of run-down city quarters but in more strategic terms have changed the character of both cities and regions. This, in turn, has provided unprecedented opportunities for new economic development, inward investment and of course new tourism and leisure related initiatives.

As a consequence there is now much evidence to support the arguments for waterfront regeneration and much of this suggests that there are real returns to be had from investing in water-related projects. These have included: high real estate and property investment returns; socio-economic regeneration for inner city communities; the development of new visitor markets; job creation; environmental enhancement; historic conservation; city and regional promotion; and improved infrastructure.

It would, however, be naïve to suggest that there are only positive features to waterfront regeneration. Indeed, as far back as 1985 there were growing concerns being expressed in the USA about the direction and focus of waterfront renewal projects. As a result, several key issues have emerged that concern some of the more detailed aspects of waterfront regeneration. These have included: problems associated with waterfront 'fashions' and commercial exploitation at the expense of community need; problems associated with land use mix and the 'standardization' of waterfront development schemes; problems of funding, commercial failure, the securing of community or social benefit; problems of 'political dogma' with an overemphasis on private sector-led initiatives; and problems associated with social conflict especially between indigenous community groups and new development (Fisher, 1997; Gordon, 1997; Dovey, 2004).

Learning Past Lessons: Developing Future Successful Paradigms

Evidence to evaluate waterfront regeneration projects is both extensive and disparate. Research has tended to centre around visitor numbers, investment levels and visitor expenditure levels generated by the new attractions. In some, the impact developments have had upon the social and physical environments in which they are placed has also been assessed, for example research by Brookes (1988), Gordon (1997), Levick (2004) and Dovey (2004). Despite a rather *ad hoc* approach to evaluation, the scale of, and number of waterfront projects is

nevertheless impressive. Many existing data imply or suggest that there are real returns to be had from investing in water-related projects. There are several sources of literature that outline the advantages that such waterfront regeneration projects can bring to an area in decline, for example MSI (1990), Meyer (2000), Marshal (2001), Falk (2003) and Urban Land Institute (2004). With this track record, it is clear that there are many tangible, although usually fiscal, benefits that waterfront regeneration projects have made. Some of the more pronounced advantages include:

- high real estate values, which can be especially advantageous to the property investment market;
- new economic regeneration opportunities for declining inner city areas;
- new visitor expenditure through the multiplier often creating new investment and employment opportunities;
- the upgrade of poor inner city environments, clearance of derelict land, utilization of urban land, improved infrastructure and increased accessibility;
- more effective and sustainable use of urban resources;
- conservation and reuse of historic buildings and local heritage;
- improvement of the water ecology, encouraging the rehabilitation of local water and aquatic life;
- improved urban marketing strategies for the promotion of an area or a city to encourage inward investment and tourism;
- growth in housing markets and the associated rise of confidence in the property investment markets;
- improved social and community provision.

Together with these benefits there are also concerns that pressure from private and public developers has often led to short-term exploitation and overdevelopment, with little or no provision for environmental and social safeguards. In research carried out by the US Department of the Interior, several emerging conflicts were highlighted (DoE, 1990). They included:

- problems associated with federal reductions in waterfront project funding and public funding cut-backs;

- loss of waterfront character by replicating waterfront development 'models' and applying them to sites which may differ considerably from one another;
- difficulties associated with private sector interests competing with public access needs and other public interests;
- removal of traditional working and living waterfront practices – 'the working waterfront';
- several commercial failures;
- over reliance on the public provision of infrastructure to make a scheme successful.

Other authors have also raised concerns on these lines which often highlight emerging conflicts between profit orientated development and interrelated concerns for social equity, heritage and conservation (Falk, 2003).

Hambleton's earlier interpretations of this problem (1990, 1991) indicated that existing evidence pointed to the domination of the private sector with deprived or community groups gaining little or nothing from the regeneration process. His review of Levine's work showed that many downtown developments, taking Baltimore as an example, have helped to create a dual city of 'haves' and 'have nots'. As a consequence he suggested that city neighbourhoods had continued to deteriorate and, for local communities, public interest had been unable to secure quality employment and city public space. He surmised that regeneration interests had largely been restructured to meet the various interests of developers, tourists and upper income consumers (Hambleton, 1991). Falk (2003) has also expressed more contemporary analysis in similar terms.

Indeed, findings such as these are paralleled with concerns now being voiced within general debates and agendas on regeneration. In this respect there has certainly been growing concern related to large dockland regeneration schemes, especially issues that have raised concern regarding the misdirection of public funding and policy. Developments in places such as London, Barcelona, New York and Chicago have taken the brunt of most criticism which often relates to fundamental problems of design quality, public accessibility, gentrification, public utility provision and social policy decisions. These are now well documented and have led

to broader national and international debates on waterfronts that increasingly question regeneration policy guidelines. Again it is beyond the scope of this chapter to provide a detailed critique of these growing issues but clearly there are fundamental issues at stake. In this context criticisms over the last decade have been aimed largely at the lack of democratic accountability, *ad hoc* public funding, problems with social equity, under-representation of local community interests and major environmental concerns. Questions have also been raised regarding the effectiveness of the development agencies in bringing about meaningful urban regeneration. Several key issues now present themselves, including problems:

- associated with waterfront 'fashions' and commercial exploitation at the expense of community needs;
- associated with land use mix and the 'standardization' of waterfront development schemes and the appropriateness of these;
- of funding, commercial failure and the securing of community or social benefit, including public accessibility and public facilities;
- of 'political dogma' with an overemphasis on private sector led initiatives;
- of social conflict especially with indigenous community groups.

Moving Forward: from Waterfront Regeneration to Cultural Regeneration?

The issues of waterfront regeneration including questions concerning the problems associated with regeneration panaceas, design paradigms, public facility provision, public–private sector partnerships and broader concerns between economic and social objectives are now widely known. It is clear that development strategies should rely increasingly on a balanced economic and social provision of facilities and ensure that future strategies concentrate upon public–private sector partnerships that secure the integration of appropriate waterfront related uses. In this context the regeneration 'model' adopted or applied and the extent to which public–private sector partnerships are encouraged is critical. Lessons also suggest that there is a need to establish clear public sector and private sector objectives prior to implementing projects. Without such objectives waterfront regeneration projects will, in many instances, be in danger of becoming short-term answers to economic development requirements rather than longer-term initiatives that aim to rehabilitate often run-down urban areas and docklands for all interested parties. As a result it has become increasingly necessary to make sure that all current and future developments be considered as part of a more comprehensive regeneration strategy that should embrace both economic and social objectives and aim to achieve well balanced and integrated social and economic policy objectives for the future prosperity of these areas.

Several examples of successful schemes have evolved over the last decade. Often they tend to be smaller scale schemes than the more prestigious developments and in contrast are frequently the result of public–private sector partnerships. In the USA they include examples such as the Minneapolis Riverfront District, Oakland Waterfront Trail, Beerline Neighbourhood Milwauki and Hudson River Park New York. UK examples include London's South Bank, Gloucester Docks and Swansea's Maritime District. Indeed it is now interesting to see that in the USA innovative waterfront regeneration is highlighted by the award of annual prizes for 'excellence on the waterfront', using criteria such as best environmental protection and enhancement, best historic preservation and adaptive use, best parks and recreation and best neighbourhood (Waterfront Centre, 2004).

European states have usually reflected this more publicly spirited approach to regeneration. As an example, Spain has been a major lead player in this respect. The rehabilitation of Barcelona in Catalunya has been much praised for its ambitious and innovative plans. The reclamation of substantial waterfront areas for public open space and other leisure orientated activities has played a large part in this regeneration process. The Olympic Games, held in the city in 1992, were obviously the catalyst for this regeneration. Nevertheless, this dynamic process has continued. In 1995 the city hosted a major planning exhibition titled 'La Ciutat De la Gent' (City of the People). At the forefront of this was the construction of La Rambla Del Mar

(Street of the Sea) a major new waterfront walkway and leisure area for the city. In broader European terms, the objectives and aims of the Barcelona experience fit well with the policy for future regeneration strategies. It is perhaps such examples that are small scale and largely publicly orientated, as well as innovative that will provide the new waterfront regeneration paradigm.

It is encouraging to see that more publicly spirited approaches or models are being increasingly adopted as the template for the more recent and future regeneration projects. It is a model that embraces both the benefits of the more commercially orientated American examples together with the more publicly spirited approach of regeneration that is seen within Continental Europe and elsewhere. These are sentiments expressed by Falk's assessment on the future of waterfronts that highlighted the criteria for successful regeneration, which included for example such criteria as creating a spirit of place, providing a cared-for public realm, respecting the past, integration with surrounding areas, community attractions, being resourceful and utilizing waterfront resources to the full (Falk, 2003).

Midway through 2005 it is optimistic to see that the urban regeneration debates of the 1980s and 1990s and the political controversies that were apparent at that time have now largely been offset by more positive and inclusive approaches that embrace this all-encompassing model. With respect to this there now appears to be a more general acceptance towards innovative, more focused and specialized policy alternatives for regenerating waterfront and inner city areas. Significantly, government and academics alike are now increasingly recognizing the importance and contribution that urban tourism and cultural regeneration can contribute to the growth of cities and their associated inner areas and waterfronts. In this respect, contemporary urban initiatives have more recently started to focus on culture and cultural regeneration and have been increasingly funded through less traditional government sources and include more private sector involvement.

Such initiatives have involved the development of locally based cultural strategies in partnership with local authorities who are increasingly turning to 'cultural resources' to both stimulate new economic activity and to aid physical regeneration of urban environments, waterfronts and communities. For example, Wales in the UK has encouraged this approach and cities like Swansea with its new waterfront and maritime cultural strategy is a case in point. In general, however, the future success of waterfront regeneration strategies will be increasingly tied to a development paradigm that reflects more prescribed development criteria and one which encourages inclusivity, mixed and innovative projects that promote good planning, the creation of innovative urban design and vision, cultural sensitivity, vitality and momentum, equitable financing and appropriate development scale. All these attributes provide the basis from which urban waterfront initiatives can successfully be used as prime micro-market methods for the wider regeneration that will befit a city's future economic, social and cultural growth.

Acknowledgements

Thanks go to the local authorities in the UK, the USA and Europe who supplied data, documents and plans.

References

Breen, A. and Rigby, D. (1985) Urban waterfront: positive directions, urban problems. In: *Proceedings from Myrtle Beach Recreational Conference*. February. Dept of Interior, Myrtle Beach, South Carolina, pp. 60–80.

Breen, A. and Rigby, D. (1990) Who's waterfront is it anyway? *American Planning Journal*, February, 10–12.

Breen, A. and Rigby, D. (1996) *The New Waterfront: a Worldwide Urban Success Story*. Higher Education, London.

Brookes, J. (1988) Cardiff Bay renewal strategy: another hole in the democratic system. *Planner*, January, 16–23.

Burayidi, M.A. (2001) *Downtowns: Revitalising the Center of Small Urban Communities*. Routledge, New York.

Cleveland Urban Development Commission (CUDC) (2001) Symposium puts Cleveland's waterfront in global perspective. *CUDC Quarterly* 1(4), Summer.

Department of Environment (DoE) (1990) *US Experience in Evaluating Urban Regeneration*. Her Majesty's Stationery Office (HMSO), London.

Dovey, K. (2004) *Fluid City: Transforming Melbourne's Urban Waterfront*. Routledge, London.

Dutton, C. (1991) Sustaining regeneration on the Eastern Seaboard. *Planning*, 28 June, 15–16.

English Tourist Board (ETB) (1988) *Waterfront Renaissance. Tourism in Action*. ETB, London, pp. 1–5.

English Tourist Board (ETB) (1989) *Growth of Waterside Magnets. Tourism in Action*. ETB, London, pp. 2–3.

Falk, N. (1989) On the waterfront. *Planner*, 6 October, 11–15.

Falk, N. (2003) *Turning the Tide*. Urbed, London.

Fisher, B. (1997) *Elements of the Urban Waterfront*. Van Nostrand Reinhold, New York.

Gordon, D.L.A. (1997) *Battery Park City: Politics and Planning on the New York Waterfront*. Routledge, New York.

Hambleton, R. (1990) *Urban Government in the 1990s: Lessons from the USA*. SAUS, Bristol.

Hambleton, R. (1991) American dreams urban realisation. *Planner*, 28 June, 6–10.

Hoyle, B., Pinder, D. and Hussain, M. (eds) (1988) *Revitalising the Waterfront: International Dimensions of Dockland Redevelopment*. Belhaven Press, London.

Levick, E. (2004) *Seaport: New York's Vanished Waterfront*. Smithsonian Books, New York.

Marshal, R. (2001) *Waterfronts in Post Industrial Cities*. Spoon Press, London.

Meyer, H. (2000) *City and Port: Transformation of Port Cities: London, Barcelona, New York and Rotterdam*. Routledge, London.

MSI (Marketing Research for Industry) (1990) *MSI Data Report Back. Waterside Development UK*. MSI, London, pp. 1–6.

Suttles, G.D. (1991) *Forever Open and Free: the Struggle for Chicago's Lakefront*. University of Chicago Press, Chicago, Illinois.

Thornley, A. (1992) *Urban Planning under Thatcherism*. Routledge, London.

Torre, L.A. (1989) *Waterfront Development*. Van Nostrand Reinhold, New York.

Urban Land Institute (2004) *Remaking the Urban Waterfront*. Urban Land Institute, Washington, DC.

Warman, C. (1990) Business taken to working on water. *The Times*, 25 July, p. 4.

Waterfront Centre (2004) Home page. Available at: http://www.waterfrontcentre.org/awards2004.html (accessed 15 August 2005).

Winterbottom, S. (1989) Baltimore Power Plant: assessment of failure. *Urban Land*, January, 2.

14 Born Again: from Dock Cities to Cities of Culture

Patricia Avery

Introduction

Urban environments have become increasingly important foci for the implementation of government-led policies and initiatives designed to improve the social, economic and physical fabric of our towns and cities. The economic aspects of using culture for regeneration are widespread and indeed, many of the achievements of the last decade are impressive, ranging from the natural process of regeneration to arts and culture-led initiatives.

This chapter examines the changing role of dockland cities and urban regeneration strategies that have transformed the image and fortunes of previously derelict ports. It provides examples of how dock cities have been an integral part of an urban renaissance story (Cardiff Bay and Albert Docks, Liverpool), compares the different approaches to culture-led regeneration and considers the experience of two cities that have made use of the benefits (and potential benefits) arising from the EU designation of 'European City of Culture 2008' awarded to Liverpool and Cardiff's unsuccessful bid for the title. It is significant that these two cities have in common the designation of European City of Culture. The aim is to assess the contribution that former docks are making to urban renaissance though culture, the arts and heritage. Comparisons will be made between the two cities, in particular through their policies and

success in attracting tourism and community development, and to allow conclusions to be reached as to the effectiveness of the approaches adopted, with implications for 'good practice' in other contexts.

British cities have experienced a profound restructuring of their economic and social fabric since 1945. Some change has obviously been economic – the decline in traditional manufacturing, for example. But apparently social changes, like the drift of populations from centre to suburb, have had an impact on the local community and economy alike.

> This erosion of individual commitment to the city has been accelerated recently by the trend towards private provision in all areas of daily life, from transport to leisure. Urban renewal initiatives have in the past tended to overlook the importance of the social factors in their pursuit of economic growth.
> (Landry *et al.*, 1996)

Increasingly there is seen to be a role for artists in regeneration as the value of the arts in urban developments is being promoted by government, local authorities and other development agencies (Park, 2004). The main roles assigned to the arts in this process include beautification and/or contribution to an identifiable icon or iconic building to encourage tourism and investment in an area. The creative industries are also proving to be effective in providing employment and diversification for local economies. Indeed, the contribution of the arts and culture in regeneration is increasingly quantified and cultural expression offers the city an opportunity to forge its own world of unique meanings in the face of the dominant corporate priorities and styles of the consumer age. As a result there is a growing interest in the role of the arts and wider cultural factors in restoring something of the quality of urban life.

The Attraction of Ports and Waterfronts

Port cities have a special cosmopolitan charm that makes them particularly attractive to artists, tourists and developers, although the special contribution of the arts to urban development is usually analysed as a matter of heritage (Lorente, 2000). At most, certain publications have paid tribute to the role of new cultural venues as 'flagships' of image management and urban regeneration. Where the arts and cultural quarters have capitalized on such areas, indeed the cultural element has often been the catalyst for regeneration, Lorente points out that the birth of art districts is not merely the consequence of a renewal process but also a catalyst for the further reuse of other nearby derelict buildings for art purposes and, in general, for the boosting of standards of living.

The urban waterfront is part of our national heritage and docks, ports and rivers all have an important role to play in urban regeneration, capitalizing on the 'magic' that waterfronts can create, particularly as far as residential and leisure uses are concerned. They also offer some of the best opportunities for promoting an urban renaissance and in attracting people back to live, play and work in urban areas. Port cities have demonstrated that it is possible to create places that have a distinctive flavour while making the most of their heritage. Baltimore and San Francisco were the inspiration for many early waterfront developments, and both London Docklands and Cardiff took their inspiration from the USA. The redevelopment of Liverpool docks, which included the 'Tate of the North', a maritime museum and television studio, was a high-profile cultural regeneration initiative which set the tone for the 1980s.

According to Falk (2004) the 'winning schemes' that attract most praise and are most frequently visited are successful in both economic and social as well as physical terms. The overall message is that urban waterfronts that capitalize on culture and heritage can provide the catalyst for urban renaissance. Waterfront areas present a special challenge because their catchment areas are intrinsically limited by the barrier water presents. The waterfront and ports are the roots of many of our towns and cities, and contain a large amount of derelict and under-utilized urban land, and therefore have an important role to play in urban regeneration. It is, however, and quite naturally, the largest cities that have received the most publicity, and they face quite special challenges (Falk, 2004). However, if waterside developments are in fact contributing to the 'urban renaissance' they must be judged in wider terms than their direct economic impact alone.

Culture has been the driving force for breathing life into both Cardiff and Liverpool docks as both cities suffered from considerable dereliction and decline in their economies. Cultural activity is seen as the catalyst and engine of regeneration (Evans and Shaw, 2004) through design and construction (or reuse) of a building or buildings for public or business use, the reclamation of open space or the introduction of an activity which is then used to re-brand a place. The search for the Capital of Culture 2008 created an extraordinary momentum and the competition to become European Capital of Culture in 2008 demonstrated how entire cities could be revived by a substantial programme of regeneration, boosting tourism numbers and greatly enhancing the quality of life.

Successful schemes using the arts share a capacity to identify potential in seemingly intractable and difficult areas. Often it is a run-down building or location whose structures seem inappropriate for our time. The ugly and depressing nature of industrial legacies are often seen as wasted space and of little value for conventional commercial developers, but today they have turned out to be an asset for the mass of small traders and artists who came to populate these spaces. However, artists and indeed communities have now been pushed out, as the lack of affordable housing tends to drive them into substandard accommodation or even homelessness. As a consequence the social structure of most town centres does not reflect the social structures of society as a whole. Landry *et al.* (1996) affirms that the presence of artists and other cultural producers in declining urban areas can help break cycles of decline. What these tales demonstrate is that a weakness can become a strength when looked at from another angle; location may have a bad image in the eyes of some, but it may be exactly what others are looking for. The connection between urban regeneration and culture is so easily made because of the low perception of the quality of life in the modern city, and the arts are seen as a resource through which that quality of life might be improved.

Liverpool and Cardiff have shown that museums and art galleries are also a successful investment, for they can become catalysts of further urban regeneration when an 'arts district' emerges close by (Lorente, 2000). Obviously this is not a medicine suitable for every city with problems of urban decay, because not every place has the artistic background and the cultural glamour of Liverpool and, to a lesser extent, Cardiff. But there are plenty of declining ports in Europe whose pedigree as artistic metropolises qualifies them for a similar cure expecting the same results. It is surely no coincidence if some of the most successful examples of the 'Cultural Capital of Europe' festival, like Glasgow (1990), Antwerp (1993) and Lisbon (1994), have produced arts-led rehabilitation of decayed waterfronts.

> Museums in general and art galleries in particular are not a panacea able to heal ailing ports everywhere, but they can work as catalysts of urban regeneration of port-cities in decline. In this respect cultural policies in Liverpool and possibly Cardiff are succeeding where more celebrated cases like London and Dublin have failed.
>
> (Lorente, 2000)

Over the last decade, Liverpool and Cardiff have undergone a transformation. In the case of Liverpool docks and Cardiff Bay this has been startling, even more so as both cities were suffering from a problem of self-image. Yet, despite this, they have increased their popularity as tourist destinations and, increasingly, as retailing centres. There is a cultural dimension to this, as Cardiff and Liverpool have a special charm: they are vastly proletarian, cosmopolitan and multicultural cities. Their people are renowned in their respective countries for their vivacity, humour and strong community loyalties. Economic decline, unemployment, crime, depopulation, urban dereliction and social violence have been endemic in Liverpool and Cardiff since the world economic crisis of 1974, with particular virulence in the early 1980s (Cousins *et al.*, 1980). Liverpool has now re-invented itself and re-imagined its future, largely due to its investment in culture at the heart of regeneration.

The Case of Liverpool: Port of Call for Culture

The transformation of Liverpool from urban 'basket case' to textbook case for design-led regeneration has been one of the most remarkable turnarounds in recent city history. However, we should not be too surprised. Since Liverpool's first rise to greatness in the 18th century, the city has always displayed an innovative and sophisticated approach to public space, civic architecture and urban culture. It was the Atlantic economy and then the Industrial Revolution that created modern Liverpool. Sadly, the 20th century was not so kind to Liverpool. The end of empire, the development of deep docks in Europe and the collapse of Britain's industrial base left the Liverpool economy marooned. Some criminal post-war planning finished off those parts the Luftwaffe bombing had missed. By 1982 the *Daily Mirror* described Liverpool as 'a showcase of everything that has gone wrong in Britain's major cities'. But over the last decade, Liverpool has undergone a startling renaissance. The changes began originally with the regeneration of the docklands in the wake of the 1981 riots. And from the first days of the 1984 Liverpool Garden Festival, art and culture have proved central to the changes. New architectures, public spaces and galleries have helped transform the city's 'no-go' image.

Today, Liverpool is engulfed in a period of dramatic change. Private investment is pouring into the city, a new light rail system has just been announced, and Liverpool Vision, the UK's first urban regeneration company, is promoting a number of landmark developments, including the fourth Grace building. Liverpool Vision, a new private regeneration company was established in 1999, whose main aim was to regenerate the city centre. However, it was clear to critics of previous regeneration policies that the trickle-down theories that had dominated the city for nearly 20 years would continue. But there is also the possibility of unknowingly losing the very things that make Liverpool so special. Most people are familiar with a number of its iconic structures: the buildings of the Pier Head, the Albert Docks, St Georges's Hall or the two cathedrals, but these provide merely a taste of the city's historical and architectural wealth. For while many provincial cities embarked upon radical clearance and redevelopment programmes in the second half of the 20th century, Liverpool's economic misfortunes prevented many of its plans from being implemented. Consequently, the city retains a significant proportion of the built fabric constructed during its heyday.

The rich historical legacy bequeathed to contemporary Liverpool raises a number of significant issues. Within the city centre there is considerable development, bringing with it not only the potential loss of individual buildings but also the prospect of substantial alterations to the character of some of the country's most outstanding areas of 20th century townscape. While developer interest has increased dramatically, the scale of Liverpool's decline is such that it will take a considerable period of recovery to completely transform the city's fortunes. Many problems remain: in outlying areas and pockets of the city centre the economic imperative remains low and the historic environment is showing the results of decades of under-investment. In recent years several prominent buildings have passed the point of no return and have been demolished as dangerous structures. HELP (Historic Environment of Liverpool Project) was developed by English Heritage in 2002 as a response to local needs. Liverpudlians have deep associations with the historical environment and want to see something done about the features that give the city its distinctive identity. While the public call for action is clear, a considerable degree of uncertainty remains over the extent and value of Liverpool's historic resource.

A second jointly funded post was established to take forward Liverpool's bid for World Heritage Site status as 'the supreme example of a commercial port at the time of Britain's global influence'. The choice of Liverpool as Capital of Culture 2008 underlines the historic importance and sheer quality of waterfront, warehouse district and commercial centre. The World Heritage Site status has proved a useful means of focusing attention upon the historic environment – a tangible goal for galvanizing support from partners. First and foremost, World Heritage status for Liverpool provides the international acknowledgements by independent experts that Liverpool is a city of global significance. Together with Liverpool's success as Capital of Culture for 2008, World Heritage Site status will be a convincing factor in creating a new image for Liverpool as a vibrant cultural and historic city. With the official United Nations Educational, Scientific and Cultural Organization (UNESCO) heritage designation, Liverpool is now better placed to attract an informed sector of the cultural tourist market, as visitors will be keen to see the tangible evidence of what justifies the honour of World Heritage status. 'What is now clear is that, in many cases, far form obstructing change, the remains of the past can act as a powerful catalyst for renewal and stimulus to high-quality new design and development' (Department for Culture, Media and Sport (DCMS), 2001).

The rise and rise of Albert Dock

Liverpool's Albert Dock was designed by Jesse Hartley as the first enclosed dock warehouse in the world made entirely out of non-combustible materials: cast-iron, brick and granite. It opened in 1846 and closed in 1972, but it was defunct long before that time (Ritchie-Noakes, 1984). With its five blocks, each of five storeys, it is Britain's largest Grade 1 listed building. Its restoration, which cost £30 million, was conducted by the Merseyside Development Corporation (MDC), one of the Urban Development Corporations created by the government of Margaret Thatcher in 1980 in opposition to some Labour-led local councils (Parkinson and Evans, 1988). The riots of 1981 prompted the MDC to seek quickly a highly visible area for physical regeneration in part of the 865 depopulated acres under their control in Liverpool, Sefton and the Wirral. But Albert Dock was almost wiped off the face of modern Liverpool, as in the 1970s suggestions were made that the complex was to be demolished to make way for a massive concrete car park. However, after largely unsuccessful attempts to redevelop the south docks for industrial and commercial purposes, they turned towards a tourism and leisure-led strategy. In 1984, an area of 50 ha of derelict oil installations, naphtha tanks and a domestic rubbish tip was developed into a greenhouse and theme gardens at a cost of £30 million, to hold an 'International Garden Festival' attracting two million visitors.

In the intervening decades the once-derelict quayside warehouses have been gradually converted into a thriving mixed-use development. When the dock scheme was first proposed, Liverpool was at rock bottom. When the first part – the Edward Pavilion – opened in 1984, coinciding with the influx of Garden Festival visitors, local cynics said it would never prosper. It was too small, too far from town, too little on offer, too crowed and too cramped. Yet, leaflets at the time showed a glamorous, futuristic 'village'. Lights shone over the water; yachts were moored near massively expensive apartments; there were restaurants and wine bars, leisure facilities and shops. It was Liverpool of the future!

Why Liverpool won

Rotterdam hosted the Royal Institute of British Architects (RIBA) annual conference, which focused on the regeneration of Liverpool. A discussion was held on what was going to drive regeneration in Liverpool, capital of culture, the region, the city or the private sector? Opinions were mixed (both the public and the private sector were felt to have failed the city in the past), the vital issue of what was going on with the fourth Grace building prompted a comment: 'if we can't decide, it won't happen'. Emblematic building came in for a lot of criticism, as did the idea that culture, broadly speaking, was used to revive declining cities. Liverpool's win as European Capital of Culture for 2008 promised to bring with it significant regeneration to tackle a falling population, rising unemployment and community decline (Social Exclusion Unit, 2005). In beating strong opposition

from Birmingham, Bristol, Cardiff, Newcastle-Gateshead and Oxford, the title will see Liverpool try to repeat the success of Glasgow. The judges singled out regeneration as a significant factor in Liverpool's bid. They found that Liverpool's bid:

> targets support to disadvantaged communities and includes a large number of events designed to appeal to a wide cross section of people. The long-term benefits are envisaged as making the city a better place to visit, live and work.
>
> (BBC News, 2003)

Liverpool's European Capital of Culture title will be an opportunity for Liverpool to show that culture is central to the life of the city, and demonstrate the contribution culture can make to regeneration and social inclusion. Liverpool's capital of culture team claim the win will bring at least £2 billion in investment plus an additional £200 million in tourism revenue in the run-up to 2008 with an extra 1.7 million visitors expected to visit the city.

The real impact of Liverpool's successful bid to become the European Capital of Culture is indeed a success story, but there are criticisms that the benefits of Liverpool's culture crown might be overestimated (Weaver, 2003). The real economic benefits could be just a fraction of that estimated by the organizers, it has emerged. When Liverpool was chosen ahead of five other bids the news was greeted as a major financial boost to the city, and predicted to create 14,000 jobs and generate £571 million for the local economy. But a report commissioned by Liverpool City Council into the economic impact of becoming Capital of Culture estimates that it would only directly create 1390 jobs and £53 million of revenue – just 10% of the headline prediction. Interim findings of the report were used to suggest that a successful bid would create considerably more employment. The leader of Liverpool Council, Mike Storey, claimed that if the city were selected 'there would be thousands of new jobs and a huge growth in new industries'. However, the full report by consultants ERM Economics (2003), the team behind Liverpool's bid, reveals that most of that growth would happen anyway! It predicts that by 2012, around 12,200 jobs would be created in Liverpool's cultural sector – defined as tourism, sports, heritage and the creative industries. This prediction is based on 'trend growth, cultural investments and a successful capital of culture bid'. But only 1390 of the jobs, and an additional £53 million of revenue could be directly attributed to a successful culture bid (ERM Economics, 2003).

Setting out Liverpool's strengths, Sir Jeremy Isaacs, chairman of the judges' panel stated that what swung it for Liverpool was a

> greater sense . . . that the whole city is involved in the bid and behind the bid. The pack of cards that Liverpool holds in the visual arts is enormously strong . . . the splendours of the waterside in Liverpool and the city centre are at least as architecturally imposing and magnificent as any of the cities.
>
> (BBC News, 2003)

The judges also pointed to a city that 'looked good, sounded good and feels good to be in'. In Thomas O'Brien's (Chief Executive of the Merseyside Partnership) view, the success of Liverpool came down to three factors:

> Our international status – Liverpool is a city that is well known in North America and across Europe. The second factor was the strength of our cultural offering. Our reputation for music is second to none while our museums have a national status. And thirdly there is our architecture – we have more listed buildings than anywhere else in England except for London.
>
> (BBC News, 2003)

Some critics claim that developments associated with the Capital of Culture, such as art galleries and museums are representative of only one type of culture and that working-class culture or minority ethnic cultures are ignored. Liverpool has had its fair share of promises since the Scarman Report of 1981 and Michael Heseltine's infamous visit to the charcoaled remains of the Toxteth riots. They got the International Garden Festival and Albert Dock projects in the belief that tourism would provide much needed employment for the local area. But the Garden Festival closed down, and the site was left derelict for a number of years until recently it was sold on again to a private developer, despite strong opposition. Research has recently revealed that workers were brought in from outside to rebuild large sections of Albert Dock. The campaigning group, People Not Profit

believe the regeneration bodies are deliberately excluding local people from decisions about regeneration and that 'city of culture and regeneration is used cynically by professionals and those in power to line their own pockets' (Guy, 2004). Richard Kemp, the city's former regeneration committee chairman, said the success of the bid was based on the existing economic growth in the city: 'The Capital of Culture does not come down from Mars, it is about building on what we are already doing' (Weaver, 2003).

When Liverpool won the European Capital of Culture, there was again talk of a bright future for everyone on Merseyside. There was a new-found confidence particularly in relation to the regeneration bodies. They began to intensify not only their regeneration plans, but also their cultural plans. Critics of the present regeneration policy began to argue that the 'whole notion of culture and regeneration was now being defined by those who stood to make huge profits out of it' (Guy, 2004). Local campaigning group People Not Profit argued that 'culture and regeneration, to those controlling the money means expensive cafés, wine bars and restaurants, luxury flats, and expensive retail outlets' (Guy, 2004). Others have talked about a city centre that is becoming 'sterile', 'cultureless', of feeling like ghosts in their own city. And with a huge emphasis on regeneration publicity focusing on attracting visitors and tourists from more wealthy regions, and with the building of numerous luxury apartments, many question the relevance that regeneration has for local people.

Cardiff Bay: All Things to All Developers

Cardiff Docks and the associated land once formed part of the biggest port in the world at the end of the 19th century. Following the decline of the export of coal in the early 20th century, the docklands relied on the expanding steel industry and associated engineering works to provide employment for one of the most multiracial and cultural cities of its time. But since the decline of the steel industry, the industrial areas of the bay degenerated and became an area languishing in its former glory. The history of Cardiff Bay goes back 20 years when Nicholas Edwards, then Welsh Secretary, visited the docks and its 3000 acres of industrial dereliction and announced out of the blue that a barrage would be built leaving the mudflats beneath a 400 acre lake to provide a neat, attractive centrepiece of regeneration and development.

Cardiff had no choice. If it wanted regeneration, it had to be the barrage. The area was to be tidied up, to become a freshwater Baltimore, a post-industrial Venice – all things to all developers! The Cardiff Bay barrage, which turned 400 acres of what was then called Tiger Bay, into a lake, cost £200 million to build and now costs almost £20 million a year to run. It is one of the most expensive and destructive civil engineering schemes undertaken on the British coastline, yet it was conceived as a purely political project, with no substantial economic or ecological justification (*Society Guardian*, 2000). The government encouraged development, largely by removing constraints, but the main effect was the creation of numerous bijoux homes for middle class executives. Businesses which relocated into the dockland area needed skilled staff and these had to be recruited from outside. Meanwhile, local people, who could not afford to occupy the smarter waterfront properties, were displaced on to less desirable estates. A primary task set before the Cardiff Bay Development Corporation was to construct a link between the city centre and its waterfront. The Cardiff Bay area covers an area equal to one-fifth the size of Cardiff, and is a natural extension of the city centre. The new Bay, according to Duncan Syme, would:

> enhance the environment, making it visually appealing to companies considering relocation to the city and region as a whole, bringing in visitors and tourists to the leisure and cultural attractions that could be established, with an 'arc of entertainment' around the Bay's Inner Harbour.
>
> (Cardiff Bay Development Corporation, 1990a)

Regeneration strategy

In 1988, after public consultation with local authorities, business interests and local communities, the Cardiff Bay Development Corporation adopted what Duncan Syme describes as an 'innovative, visionary and flexible' strategy that was also achievable (*Locum Destination Review*, 2000). The *Cardiff Bay Regeneration Strategy* (Cardiff Bay Development Corporation, 1988) set out to achieve:

> a dynamic new waterfront city to transform utterly an area of dereliction, wasteland and low order uses. The site is of great scale and quality, and offers the city the potential of generating new forms and levels of development in economic, housing, cultural, leisure and tourism terms. The strategy involves harnessing this potential to the benefit of the city and in particular to create a magnet for investment in Wales as a whole.

The strategy points out that 'regeneration involves a process, not a plan'. The tourism proposals envisaged a series of major visitor attractions combined in a major urban tourism focus on the waterfront, cultural and heritage attractions combined with residential and other leisure uses including pubs, restaurants and cafés. The policy was to 'conserve the heritage of buildings, structures and engineering artefacts, and to ensure its integration harmoniously into the new developments and draw inspiration from the history' (Cardiff Bay Development Corporation, 1988).

Ben Thompson and associates of Boston, a leading urban designer for waterfront developments, prepared the brief for the heartbeat of the regeneration area, the Bay's Inner Harbour, which is now the focal point of what the Corporation has named the Millennium Waterfront. The Cardiff Bay Development Corporation was officially wound up on 31 March 2000. By this time, it had received a total of £500 million in grant aid, which was used to secure private investment of around £1.8 billion. The revitalized Cardiff Bay is already recognized as a thriving destination for business, leisure and living. Over 16,000 permanent new jobs have been created, admittedly, in Syme's words, 'just over half of the target set out in the official regeneration strategy document at the project's birth, but an admirable achievement nonetheless in the light of the national economic recession of the early 1990s' (*Locum Destination Review*, 2000). Not all those employees working in Cardiff Bay companies are Cardiff residents; nearly a third of all employees in the Bay travel to work from the Valleys and the Vale of Glamorgan. A total of 4500 new homes have been built or are under development. Complementing the commercial appeal of the destination are the leisure and culture facilities for visitors and residents alike. In addition to the restaurants and hotels on offer, a national ice-rink has been developed, along with an international arena, a centre for visual arts and a constellation of attractions on the waterfront. The new Millennium Centre has been recently constructed, providing a home for Welsh National Opera and many other companies.

A particular kind of contradiction, between development and ecology, is found in the policy for art in the redevelopment of the dock area of Cardiff. Like the London Docklands, this scheme is geographically adjacent but separated in ambience and land use from the city, substituting 'bay' for 'docks'. Public art has played a role in the regeneration of Cardiff Bay and the *Strategy for Public Art in Cardiff Bay* (Cardiff Bay Development Corporation, 1990b) proposed an arts' plan costing £30 million, £16 million to be provided through a percent for art scheme enforced by the Development Corporation. It makes the usual business case for art on the grounds of its perceived role in urban economic regeneration; a possible source of the strategy's assertions is the claim that the arts are effective in attracting visitors to a town, enhancing the visual quality of the environment and providing a focal point for community pride. The strategy translates arguments from the cultural industries and the arts in general to public art, claiming that the visual arts 'have usually spearheaded the process of urban regeneration' (Cardiff Bay Development Corporation, 1990a: 15), for which no evidence is given (Miles *et al.*, 2000). Cardiff Bay Arts Trust (CBAT), the arts and regeneration agency, have transformed much of the Bay through their innovative approaches to opening up social and public spaces through temporary and permanent public art pieces and explain:

> The transformation of post-industrial cities is a multidisciplinary practice. The importance of imaginative and innovative approaches, as well as participation of and ownership by citizens are high on the agenda of municipal authorities and regeneration companies.
>
> (CBAT, 2004)

But there are criticisms that the most contentious recommendation, which exposes the value-free ethos of the report, is that the 'entire barrage' (seen by ecologists as devastating for the bay's wildlife) should be a 'work of art' (Cardiff Bay Development Corporation, 1990a: 22).

Cardiff's waterfront is an exemplar of the ways in which a city can make visible its rich physical and cultural heritage, weaving it into the essence of its material quality. Indeed, it is home to a diversity of international cuisine and the bars, restaurants and clubs of Mermaid Quay provide an attractive destination for visitors, underpinned by the cultural activity located in the Bay, including festivals, watersports and outdoor performances. Cardiff Bay has achieved some of its aims and has indeed undergone enormous transformation from a declining area to a popular destination for local people and visitors and Cardiff is currently celebrating its centenary as well as its status of capital of Wales for over 50 years. Its bid to become Capital of Culture 2008, although unsuccessful, has given Cardiff the impetus to build on its cultural and artistic assets and celebrate its achievements over the past decades. Cardiff already had a cultural infrastructure that has grown from very distinctive stories. The Executive Summary put forward in its bid points out that:

> Cardiff 2008 will reflect the cultural values of inclusivity, respect for diversity, learning and growth. The themes for Cardiff 2008 place culture at the centre of the relationships of individuals to their city and the city to the country.
>
> (Cardiff City Council, 2002)

Cardiff celebrated its role and the impetus that being short listed for the title has given the city in the run up to its centenary celebration in 2005. Speaking on behalf of Cardiff 2008, Lynne Williams who was leading the city's bid, said that the competition has 'galvanized our communities and focused attention worldwide on the artistic and sporting excellence of Cardiff and Wales' (Cardiff City Council, 2004). She continued: 'Whilst Cardiff has not gained the ultimate prize, it is still on a cultural roll. The city is still accelerating its drive and ambition to become a truly European capital.' As a European Centre of Culture, Cardiff becomes an integral part of a European network of cultural cities, and will benefit from future international collaborations. As well as an increased profile throughout the UK and internationally, the accolade also means that Cardiff will benefit from being part of a £6 million, 3-year marketing campaign in Europe. Cardiff is now demonstrating its cultural ambitions with a year-long national celebration in 2005 as it celebrates its centenary and 50th anniversary as capital of Wales. Secretary of State for Wales, the Rt. Hon. Peter Hain, said:

> Initial disappointment at Cardiff not achieving the European Capital of Culture Bid 2008 must not mask the very real success our capital city has achieved in making the shortlist. Cardiff has been given a tremendous impetus to artistic and cultural activity in the city and we must now build on that. Just by making the shortlist, Cardiff has raised its profile in the UK and VisitBritain [British Tourist Authority] will be promoting the city as a 'centre of culture' for the next three years.
>
> (Cardiff City Council, 2004)

Russell Goodway, the Leader of Cardiff Council and chair of Cardiff 2008, said:

> The Liverpool team deserves to be congratulated. We felt that Cardiff had put together an exceptional bid – so Liverpool's must have been of an incredibly high standard. The short-listed cities are all required to work closely with the Capital of Culture during 2008, and I want to ensure that Cardiff plays a leading role in this respect. We recognize the potential benefits of collaborating with Liverpool to put in place an outstanding cultural festival that demonstrates all that is good about the UK in a European context. The 2008 process has had real benefits for Cardiff. It has demonstrated the talent and creativity that exists in local communities. Without exception, organizations throughout Wales have supported Cardiff to the hilt, and such cooperation will continue in the future. We must not lose the momentum. The transformation of Cardiff will continue. The 2005 celebrations will confirm the City's ability to punch above its weight on the European stage. Cardiff will continue to develop as an ambitious and creative city with strong international connections. Culture is Cardiff's core business and it will remain Cardiff's core business.
>
> (Goodway, 2005)

Despite the recognition of the accolades and recognition of being a Capital of Culture, it is not without its critics. Cities are becoming more competitive anyway. Bianchini (1993) estimates that policies only make sense if the prospects are realistic.

> The direct impact of 1980s cultural policies on the regeneration of employment and wealth was relatively modest, in comparison with the role of culture in constructing positive urban images, developing the tourist industry, attracting inward investment, and strengthening the competitive position of cities.
>
> (cited in Smiers, 1997: 112)

Andreas Wiesand (Director of the Institute of Cultural Research, Bonn) points to the 'hubbab approach' coming forth from those policy intentions, and notes that they will eventually simmer down. As an example he points to Glasgow:

> Marketing does not suddenly make Glasgow the cultural capital of Europe. In itself it is an interesting city, but it would be better if it would refrain from promoting itself with all that rubbish you are obliged to put out when you are selected to be 'European Cultural Capital' for a year. It costs money and it helps nobody.
>
> (Norwood, 2001)

Renato Nicolini, member of the Italian parliament goes further and suggests that 'it is time we dispense with the outdated project of a yearly European cultural capital. It does not correspond at all with the real cultural and artistic movements throughout Europe' (Norwood, 2001). It could be said that cities that have such a number of cultural offerings can become over-visited. Eduardo E. Loxano, head of a study centre for municipal cultural policies, sounds an alarm bell for his city Barcelona and other cities that are presently much praised for their cultural climate: 'a fashionable city is an endangered one' (cited in Norwood, 2001).

Analysis

A comparison may now be made between the experience of culture-led regeneration in Cardiff Bay and Albert Docks, Liverpool. This will be done by considering the achievements of the two cases in terms of broad regeneration outcomes and mixed uses, criteria that are derived from the conceptual frameworks that underpin 'culture-led' approaches to regeneration. In the case of Cardiff Bay, the regeneration strategy has achieved some of its objectives in terms of broad regeneration outcomes. But whilst it attracted a considerable amount of investment in uses such as leisure/entertainment and lifestyle, many businesses in the area were displaced as were the local communities, and they were forced to relocate to the outer fringes of the bay. Many people lack access to the relatively exclusive benefits that have been created, following the process of gentrification, feeling left out and disconnected to the bay. While new housing has been created, this would seem to have been occupied largely by relatively affluent residents. It may be suggested that this process has arisen in large part as a result of the concentration on image enhancement at the expense of 'holistic' regeneration objectives (McCarthy, 2002).

Similarly, in the case of Liverpool, the aim of generating employment seems to have been largely unfulfilled, and tourism numbers have not been sustained since the designation of the city as European Capital of Culture 2008. However, there are signs that by 2008, the large efforts being put into events and programmes should ensure that tourist numbers will increase significantly. But again, the concentration on an image and marketing-led approach to the development of cultural facilities and initiatives would seem to have contributed to a lack of sustainable outcomes in this case. There are also criticisms that creeping homogenization is sweeping the waterfronts of Britain. Sales brochures for developments from Cardiff to London, Poole to Manchester, bear an eerie resemblance to one another. 'Why do all new dock and riverside developments have to look the same?' asks Graham Norwood (2001). Indeed, this is worrying, despite the fact that dockside regeneration and the redevelopment of inner-city waterfront properties is usually to be applauded. Hall (1998) observes:

> It is evident that new and upstart cities do not immediately develop as strong centres of culture, however dynamic their economies. The likelihood is that places with a unique buzz, a unique fizz, a special kind of energy, will prove more magnetic than ever for the production of products and, above all, the performance and quality of its services. It is for that same reason

that cities, to be successful, have concentrations of historic buildings, significant museums and galleries, and charming residential quarters, then they will be equally attractive to well-heeled cosmopolitan residents and to that special kind of short-term resident, called a tourist.

(Hall, 1998: 963)

Cardiff Bay has invested heavily in consultants' studies and infrastructure, which have paid particular attention to quality. Indeed, the landscaping details around the waterside could have come from one of the many excellent case studies published by the Waterfront Centre in Washington. But in the drive to emulate Baltimore and Sydney, they may have missed out on the potential to make the most of Cardiff's heritage, including the ever-changing coastal landscape and a rich stock of existing buildings. Mount Stuart Square is an area with the character and potential of Birmingham's Jewellery Quarter and Bradford's Little Germany and buildings such as the Coal Exchange could have been used as a basis for growing cultural industries organically. The strategy seems to have been based largely on the idea that creating a fixed stretch of water, rather than a tidal bay, would generate the values from new housing and prestige offices that would justify the public investment. Such a strategy assumes that amenity can be used to shift activities to where they are most needed. Perhaps, if the strategy had focused on creating a new park to link the city centre with the Bay, and development had been planned over a 20-year time span, more could have been achieved for less public expense. A series of sustainable urban neighbourhoods, while not as dramatic, could generate the confidence needed for private investment. This is not to criticize the efforts of the Development Corporation or the work of urban design and planning consultants, but to suggest a fundamental change is needed in the way we evaluate waterside and dockside regeneration projects.

Tentative Conclusions

A number of tentative conclusions may be reached by this comparison of different approaches to 'culture-led' regeneration. The case of Albert Dock illustrates the achievement of a number of focused aims in conjunction with a closely targeted policy and implementation process. By comparison, the use of cultural development to further regeneration aims in Cardiff seems to be more broadly based, bringing together economic, social and environmental aspects of regeneration. Both Cardiff Bay and Albert Dock have overcome problems of dereliction and negative images. Historic preservation of port waterfronts can, and should go beyond merely keeping old buildings, saving not only the buildings, but also their utility and local morale. The legacy of winning Capital of Culture for Liverpool and Cardiff's enhanced profile is impressive, but forging a new identity for the city nationally and internationally is not just about creating an 'image' to attract the tourists – it is about the city once again rising to its natural level of world importance. But what the two cases demonstrate is that levels of success of urban regeneration policies cannot be adequately measured in solely physical terms.

A conclusion to be drawn from Cardiff and Liverpool is the existence of a pattern of arts-led urban renewal processes. Such has been the process in both cities to some extent, but this is not to say that every commercial venture has been a success story in the recovery of derelict buildings in the area. In Liverpool especially, spaces for the production of art, such as artist studios and community centres, were not the prime movers for the revitalization of derelict areas of the city centre. It would be helpful if those involved adopt a more realistic and compromising approach regarding the funding of arts and urban regeneration. If waterfront developments are in fact contributing to the 'urban renaissance' they must be judged in wider terms than their direct economic impact alone. A different framework is needed to design and manage successful projects, and also to judge how much to invest in them. In addition, research by the Urban and Economic Development Group (URBED) (Falk, 2004) drew attention to the point that Britain was following the example of American cities, whereas it should be trying to emulate continental cities. Most continental cities have always treated their waterfront as part of the city's heart and soul, thus making them successful economically, as well as desirable places to live (Falk, 2004). As CBAT (2004) puts it:

> The transformation of post-industrial cities is a multidisciplinary practice. The importance of imaginative and innovative approaches, as well as participation of and ownership by citizens are high on the agenda of municipal and regeneration companies.

So the precise causal relationship between culture and regeneration remains elusive (Hall, 1998: 15). The central question now is precisely how and why a city renews itself, exactly what is the nature of the creative spark that kindles the urban fires. Culture plays a variety of different roles in regeneration, from approaches where culture is the starting point to ones where culture is part of a broader regeneration strategy. However, there are gaps in the evidence base that need to be addressed to ensure that culture's impact is more clearly understood and consistently measured. A number of perennial questions remain about the effectiveness of cultural regeneration schemes. One area for research is the question of the extent to which artists are involved in the decision-making process as a precondition for sustainable regeneration. Future research could also address the impact of the arts on social regeneration and whether they have more to offer in complex areas of social deprivation, on which regeneration depends.

References

BBC News [UK edition] (2003) Why Liverpool won. 4 June, pp. 1–2. Available at: http://www.news.bbc.co.uk (accessed 15 November 2005).

Bianchini, F. (1993) *Urban Cultural Policy in Britain and Europe: Towards Cultural Planning.* Griffith University, Nathan, Queensland, Australia.

Cardiff Bay Development Corporation (1988) *Cardiff Bay Regeneration Strategy: the Summary*. Cardiff Bay Development Corporation, Cardiff.

Cardiff Bay Development Corporation (1990a) *Wales Millennium Waterfront*. Cardiff Bay Development Corporation, Cardiff.

Cardiff Bay Development Corporation (1990b) *Strategy for Public Art in Cardiff Bay*. Cardiff Bay Development Corporation, Cardiff.

Cardiff City Council (2002) Cardiff European Capital of Culture 2008: Take me somewhere good. Bid document, Executive summary. Cardiff City Council, Cardiff, p. 7.

Cardiff City Council (2004) Congratulations Liverpool. Press release, June 2004, Four Communications. Available at: www.cardiff.gov.uk/capitaltimes/get.asp? cat (accessed 12 May 2005).

CBAT (2004) Ain't no love in the heart of the city. Press release. Cardiff Bay Arts Trust (CBAT), Cardiff.

Cousins, L. *et al*. (1980) *Merseyside in Crisis*. Merseyside Socialist Research Group, Birkenhead, UK.

Department for Culture, Media and Sport (DCMS) (2001) *The Historic Environment: a Force for Our Future*. DCMS, London.

ERM Economics (2003) *A Socio-economic Impact Assessment of Liverpool's Capital of Culture Bid*. March. Liverpool City Council, Liverpool.

Evans, G. and Shaw, P. (2004) *The Contribution of Culture to Regeneration in the UK*. A report to the Department for Culture, Media and Sport (DCMS), London.

Falk, N. (2004) Turning the tide. Available at: http://www.urbed.com/cgi-bin/get binary doc object (accessed 15 November 2005).

Goodway, R. (2005) Cardiff 2008 Ltd announces wind-up of company. Available at: www.cardiff.gov.uk/capitaltimes/get.asp (accessed 20 November 2005).

Guy, D. (2004) *Liverpool, a City being Regenerated, But Who is Benefiting?* NERVA, Liverpool.

Hall, P. (1998) *Cities in Civilization*. The Orion Publishing Group, London.

Landry, C., Green, L., Matarasso, F. and Bianchini, F. (1996) *The Art of Regeneration: Urban Renewal through Cultural Activity*. Comedia, Stroud.

Locum Destination Review (2000) Born again: the resurrection of Cardiff Bay. *Locum Destination Review* 2, 6–8. Available at: http://www.locum-destination.com/pdf/LDR2born-again.pdf (accessed 18 March 2006).

Lorente, J.P. (2000) Art neighbourhoods, ports of vitality. In: Bennett, S. and Butler, J. (eds) *Locality, Regeneration and Divers{c}ities*. Intellect, Bristol, UK.

McCarthy, J. (2002) Encouraging culture-led regeneration. Paper presented at the European Urban Research Association (EURA) Conference *Urban and Spatial European Policies: Levels of Territorial Government*, 18–20 April. Turin, Italy.

Miles, M., Hall, T. and Borden, I. (eds) (2000) *The City Cultures Reader*. Routledge, London.

Norwood, G. (2001) Britain's identikit waterfronts. *Sunday Times*, 22 April, p. 12.

Park, A. (2004) Current perspectives on the role of art in urban development. Do artistic interventions benefit a community? Art in Community Settings, Birkbeck College, University of London. Available at: www.msdm.org.uk/sos-ok/perspectives.html (accessed 15 November 2005).

Parkinson, M. and Evans, R. (1988) *Urban Regeneration and Development Corporations: Liverpool Style*. European Institute for Urban Affairs, working paper no 2, Liverpool.

Ritchie-Noakes, N. (1984) *Liverpool's Historic Waterfront: the World's First Mercantile Dock System*. Her Majesty's Stationery Office (HMSO), London.

Smiers, J. (1997) European cities – first sow, then reap. In: Miles, M., Hall, T. and Borden, I. (eds) *The City Cultures Reader*. London, Routledge, pp. 112–115.

Social Exclusion Unit (2005) Liverpool culture win sparks regeneration. Office of the Deputy Prime Minister. Available at: http://www.socialexclusion.gov.uk/news.asp?id (accessed 20 November 2005).

Society Guardian (2000) The regeneration game. *Society Guardian*, 16 October. Available at: http://society.guardian.co.uk/regeneration/story (accessed 15 November 2005).

Weaver, M. (2003) Benefits of Liverpool's culture crown 'overestimated'. Available at: www.society.guardian.co.uk/regeneration/story/ pp.1–3 (accessed 21 November 2005).

15 Interpretative Planning as a Means of Urban Regeneration: Recife, Brazil

Brian Bath and Paula Goncalves

Introduction

In April 2003, an interpretative plan for the historic port island of the city of Recife in the north-east of Brazil was finalized by a team of British consultants and local planners. The aim of the plan was twofold. First and foremost, to place interpretation at the heart of the planning process and explore it as a tool for urban regeneration. Second, to organize internal and external visitor demand on a citywide scale, via projects that revealed the city's history. This chapter discusses the contents and implications of the plan. It will do so by looking initially at concepts of regeneration and interpretation, the context in which the plan emerged and the area it targeted. Then it will discuss the techniques used to match target audience needs to the plan. Finally, it will consider the challenges posed to traditional approaches to planning in general and urban regeneration in particular.

Regeneration and Interpretation

Regeneration policy is currently one of the cornerstones of local urban development in the West (Robertson, 1995, 1999; Crouch et al., 2003). As a result, the sight of renewed, traditional urban areas in cities as diverse as Berlin, London and Barcelona; New York, Baltimore and Montreal; Montevideo, Rio de Janeiro and Quito, comes hardly as a surprise to visitors and inhabitants alike.

Revitalization, rehabilitation, re-qualification, renaissance and renewal are but a few of a range of terms used to describe a welter of state-led strategies aimed at re-orientating existing urban occupations and conditions in the West (Harvey, 1989). The use of the prefix 're', from Latin meaning 'again', is not without consequence as it inextricably invokes connotations of a new life for the areas targeted. However, the kind of new life, who benefits and who does not, can be as diverse in nature and number as the terms available to define such strategies. In Brazil, for instance, regeneration (or the preferred term of revitalization) is more often than not used to denote strategies pursued and developed under the umbrella of conservation of historic sites (Zancheti et al., 1995; Brito, 2002). In Britain, regeneration has seemingly moved away from a set of conservation-based, 'special, targeted, time-limited activities funded by centrally-designed grant regimes to . . . [a] rationale for the management of whole areas' (Russell, 2000: 5).

Distinctions of approach aside, an inescapable feature of the history of regeneration strategies in the West is the way in which they entail the attraction of new capital to areas from which they have been previously withdrawn (Berman, 1988; Harvey, 1990). Moreover, in the present, as in the past, regeneration remains a key, controversial competitive tool for contemporary cities looking for an opportunity to redevelop and reclaim low land-rent areas (Davis, 1990; Jessop, 1997; Smith, 2002).

As one of the key driving forces of contemporary economies, tourism has become an important source of income to cities and, hence, an inescapable means of achieving such a goal (Bianchini, 1999; Jokilehto, 1999; Urry, 2002; Smith, 2003). Notwithstanding, cities seeking to reposition themselves in the international, national and regional economy have more often than not resorted to a means of regeneration that is based, among other things, in strategic place marketing. That is, the ability of a city or a segment of the city to promote its distinct advantages (intrinsic features, goods, products and services) to visitors (business and pleasure), residents and workers, business and industry and export markets in order to improve its relative competitive position (Kotler et al., 1993; Ward, 1998). In this context, one could argue that 'interpretation' emerges as one of the tools available for those seeking to identify and communicate their distinct advantages.

Interpretation is an activity that emerged in the late 1950s from attempts by park rangers in the USA to engage and sustain more effectively the interest of visitors. It is defined by the American National Association for Interpretation (NAI) as 'a communication process that forges emotional and intellectual connections between the interests of the audience and the meanings inherent in the resource' (NAI, 2005: 1). The resource in question can be a place, event and/or artefact.

If planning is the collaborative act of defining a course of action, a method for getting from one setting or set of circumstances to another, then interpretative planning can be defined as 'official guideline for the resource management body which sets forth the policies concerning development, philosophy and operation of a . . . programme' that aims to communicate the meaning of a particular resource or set of resources (as quoted in Goodey, 1994: 303).

Goodey (1994) suggests that processes of interpretative planning are, in principle, influenced by the resource-focus of the local authority department initiating the process, by the type of research informing the definition of themes and stories, and awareness of market conditions and orientation (visitor preferences and taste).

Moreover, he argues that for an interpretative plan to be viable, to become reality, it must involve broad consultation (public, private and voluntary organizations), management of interdisciplinary skills (research, analysis, design) and financial support. Three types of plans are identified: novel (where no previous professionally developed interpretation is provided), remedial (where a review of an existing interpretation is required) and generative (where interpretation is used to create a sense of place). The case study in this chapter falls into the novel plan category.

Recife is a city of three million inhabitants located in the north-east coast of Brazil. In 2003, it became the first city in the country to engage in the production of an interpretative plan for the port island where the city originally started 466 years ago. Target of a programme of regeneration that started in 1987, the area is widely perceived to be one of the city's key competitive advantages in relation to other tourist destinations in the country's north-east such as Fortaleza and Salvador. However, one could argue that its potential as an area crucial for the organization of tourist demand on a city-wide scale in 2003 was, and in many ways still remains, underdeveloped.

This chapter looks in more detail at the antecedents of the plan and the area it targeted. More significantly it looks at how interpretation can help match the interests and aspirations of audiences to a regeneration plan.

Setting the Scene

In October 1999 a conference organized by the Recife branch of the British Council (BC), the Pernambuco State Government and the Recife municipality (British Council, 1999) offered professionals involved in heritage conservation a first glimpse of interpretation and its techniques. A well-established practice in countries such as the UK, USA and Australia, interpretation was hardly known in Brazil.

As a result of this conference the Recife branch of BC, local conservation planners and three British interpretation designers forged a partnership aimed at exploring the potential of interpretation as a planning tool. A series of missions and meetings in Recife and various locations in the UK followed, culminating with a week long interpretative workshop involving around 50 planners, students and experts (Goncalves, 2000). Of the three project areas chosen two were large, traditional historic sites targeted by regeneration initiatives. Curiously, the third area was a half-century-old occupation called Brasilia Teimosa, one of Recife's oldest and most interesting low-income communities. This choice initially raised questions about the notion of 'historic' and interpretation as a practice associated with things 'historic'. In the years that followed, however, it was the work in this area that presented the most interesting outcomes. Local people, with the help of local artists, explored their fishing community tradition in panels that helped to improve two of the areas' few open spaces: the beach square and the local water fountain.

However, it was not until 2003 that an opportunity to explore the potential of interpretation as a comprehensive regeneration tool emerged. This opportunity was granted by the Monumenta Programme, Brazil's first conservation-specific line of finance. The Programme resulted from a partnership between Brazil's Ministry of Culture (MinC), the Interamerican Development Bank (IDB), United Nations Educational, Scientific and Cultural Organization (UNESCO) and four Brazilian municipalities participating in the Programme's experimental round (UNESCO, 2000). Recife was one of these cities. The area targeted by the Programme in the city was the southern corner of the port island of Bairro do Recife. The central core of the island had been itself the object of a slow, but gradual process of regeneration since the late 1980s. Respectable bars and restaurants were brought in to replace the low-income brothels and cheap whisky bars that benefited from sailors, workers and untaxed goods flowing in and out of the port. The southern corner of the island was the next stage in the city's regeneration strategy.

This time, the 17th-, 18th- and 19th-century buildings empty or in disrepair and the hostels and small industrial supply shops they housed were targeted. In Recife, funding from Monumenta fostered, among other things, the restoration of monuments, street refurbishment, parking facilities, building refurbishment, training for the tourism sector, institutional support and heritage educational programmes (Monumenta, 2005). The idea behind the Monumenta investments was to promote the economic sustainability of its investment by requiring, among other things, that interpretative techniques be used to make historic environments profitable and self-sustained. Tourism and the organization of visitor demand were important dimensions of such a strategy, particularly in a city lacking focal points, places, centres where visitors (notably external visitors) could find out what products are on offer in and around the city. It was within this context that the interpretative plan came about.

General Methodology and Project Structure

Work on the interpretative plan started in November 2002 and was to last for 4 months. The plan involved three broad phases of development, with a final presentation phase. Each phase involved one or more of the British team visiting Recife and working with the Recife planners for a week or more, followed by the Recife team carrying on with that phase of work throughout the month. Table 15.1 summarizes the tasks undertaken during each phase and the expected results.

The general methodology was followed throughout the project, but there were inevitably some variations due to practical considerations. For example, thematic development and clarification continued during all phases. The iterative nature of the development process is again highlighted in the next section on aims and objectives. It is also important to point out that too much time was spent on the product and presentation development phases. As a result, the 'Funding and implementation' tasks were rushed through and not completed effectively. While consultation had been reasonably comprehensive during the research and development phases, there was no time to establish project 'owners' or to get agreement to funding commitments from interested organizations and parties. In fact, this was a lengthy process beyond the scope of a 4-month project. However, it is an essential step if the plan is to become a reality.

Table 15.1. Summary of the tasks undertaken and expected results during each phase of the interpretative plan (Source: URB-Recife/Monumenta, 2003).

Content	Tasks	Results
Phase 1: Research		
Aims and objectives	• Discuss the final results required from the interpretative planning process in general and detailed form • Agree area and scope of the interpretative planning process	• Written aims and objectives
Audience	• Review/summarize existing tourism data • Consult with local government agencies, organizations and businesses • Carry out interviews with the audience directly in order to define audience profile and level of interest and awareness of the site	• Summary of tourism in the area • Visitor profile • Analysis of interests and awareness
Existing plans and strategies	• Review existing documents • Consult with relevant agencies and individuals to establish their existing and future strategies, plans and projects	• Map of existing and planned interpretative projects in area • Summary of relevant strategies and policies
What to say to the target audience(s)	• Review existing historical sources • Consult with local historians, people, businesses and relevant societies • Summarize most important stories as general themes	• Create 'story box' of all relevant stories linked to people of the area • Summary of history of area • Relevant themes
Where stories need to be told	• List most important locations in the area (interpretative resources) relevant to selected themes • Carry out subjective site condition survey and map the area • Compare locations of resources and target audiences in relation to site conditions	• Establish best locations for interpretation of themes • Match with existing interpretative projects • Identify potential new interpretative projects in relation to themes, resources and audience interests
Phase 2: Community consultation and project identification		
Involve the community directly	• Consult with community leaders • 'Planning for Real' workshops with community members • Hold discussion groups to evaluate proposals	• Obtain community opinions on existing and proposed plans • Generate community input into new interpretation
Identify interpretative projects for development	• Identify any existing or planned interpretative projects for further development (from existing plans and strategies in Phase 1) • Identify any potential new interpretative projects (from those identified as needed in Phase 1) • Use SWOT analysis to select • Consult with interested parties as required/appropriate	• Final list of projects for detailed planning

Continued

Table 15.1. *Continued*

Phase 3: Detailed plan and projects

Content planning of selected projects	• Develop detailed objectives (learning, behavioural and emotional) • Detail relevant themes and stories • Select appropriate media and techniques • Outline storylines/storyboards	• Initial project definition plan
Operational planning of selected projects	• Identify any associated works • Identify appropriate management and staffing • Prepare detailed cost plan and outline business plan • Prepare implementation schedule	• Detailed project proposal document
Funding and implementation	• Establish potential sources of funding • Identify potential project 'owners' and management • Prepare design briefs for development team	• Negotiated funding and management plans • Final design briefs

Phase 4: Presentation and recommendations

Final report and presentation	• Collate all reports on findings • Prepare final report on proposals	• Presentation of final report to all relevant authorities • Recommendations for further actions

As can be seen from the range of tasks to be undertaken by the Social, Planning and Tourism groups (identified in Phases 1 and 2 of Table 15.1), all involved personal interviews, consultations with interested parties, audience surveys and in some cases participation. The main slant of the methodology was thus to increase contact between the interpretative planners and the different target audiences they were planning for. The aim of this process is to gain a clear understanding of the attitudes, interests, needs and expectations of all the target audiences (and in an interpretative plan this includes the political audience as much as the person on the street). Once this has been established it is possible to begin forming links between known interests, the stories that need to be told, and the most appropriate way of telling them. In a sense it is akin to marketing, matching product development to expressed consumer needs and interests. Even more so when the consumer is not yet aware that he or she has a need for or interest in the product or products.

Aims and Objectives: Evolution and Iteration

This phase was initially undertaken between the lead consultant, Brian Bath of Interpretive Design Limited, and the client, Monumenta. It was agreed that aims and objectives were likely to evolve during the project and this proved to be so. Initially there were two aims: to propose a strategic interpretative plan for Bairro do Recife; and to develop specific interpretative projects for Bairro do Recife as part of a phased implementation plan.

However, by the end of the research phase it had become evident that there was a major requirement to inform the inhabitants and workers in the Bairro of the importance of their cultural heritage. A third aim was added: to increase the awareness of all inhabitants, workers and visitors in Bairro do Recife of the significance of its cultural heritage for Pernambuco and Brazil.

Finally, by the end of the community involvement and project development phase (Phase 2 in Table 15.1) the four aims were replaced by a single general objective with a more specific chronological dimension:

> To develop a strategic interpretative plan for Bairro do Recife, including specific interpretative projects that can be implemented in stages and that will increase the awareness of inhabitants, visitors and workers of the significance of the locality in the past, the present and the future.

This last change came out of the continued development of themes to be pursed in product development, and the team's growing familiarity with the historical and regeneration context in which the plan would be implemented. The main theme, as finally formulated, stated:

> Bairro do Recife was, and continues to be, a gateway between Brazil and the rest of the world, a gateway for merchandise, people and cultural influences.

Given the large amounts of data generated by the various aspects of research undertaken it was necessary to be continually open to the need to review overall aims and objectives and the bases on which the interpretative products were developed.

The specific objectives of the project also changed as the project progressed. In the list below, objective 7 was added at the end of the community research phase (Phase 2) in response to expressed needs from the community.

1. To develop an interpretative planning process that can be applied to specific projects in Bairro do Recife and throughout the city of Recife.
2. To enable community participation in the interpretative planning process through, for example, consultation and workshops.
3. To take account of existing studies and strategies for Bairro do Recife in the interpretative planning process.
4. To develop detailed interpretative plans and proposals for a range of exemplar projects in Bairro do Recife.
5. To provide materials for a publication to disseminate the interpretative planning process developed during the project.
6. To identify relevant research that will contribute towards the development of an argument for attracting World Heritage Site status for Bairro do Recife.

7. To develop sustainable projects that will, where possible, provide new job opportunities for the local population.

Consultation and Community Involvement

Phases 1 and 2 both involved extensive consultation and community participation. There were several levels of involvement depending on the person or persons involved and the most effective way of obtaining their input. The first three of the following methods were used mainly, but not exclusively, by the Tourism Group, led by the lead consultant Brian Bath.

Personal interviews

Businessmen and politicians were generally interviewed individually and at their offices or premises. Over 50 individual interviews were held with various members of the community including managers of government organizations with a strong presence or influence in the area, shopkeepers, bar and restaurant owners, hotel owners, street traders and taxi drivers.

Panel discussions

These were held where more than one important individual could be brought together to discuss the issues faced by the project. Tourism organizations, hotel associations and trade associations were more comfortable in this context, as were representatives of the local low-income Pilar community.

Street surveys

In order to find out first hand who was in the Bairro at certain times of day, and essentially to establish their origins and interests, street surveys formed an important part of the data gathering. Sample sizes were not excessively large (at about 300 per survey) but large enough to give a useful picture and for some of the participants in the project to gain first-hand knowledge of the people who lived and worked in the Bairro.

'Planning for Real' days

The 'Planning for Real' techniques were originally developed in Scotland for community-based interpretation and were conducted by consultant Rona Gibb, leader of the Social Group. These days involved sessions on the street for the general public, and sessions with schools and special groups. From the groups each person was asked a series of specific questions about likes and dislikes in relation to the environment and asked to put a flag (with their reaction written on it) on a map to indicate its whereabouts. The placing of flags generates discussion. Other dimensions of their relationship with the environment and the community were also explored. All participants could see the previous responses.

Qualitative surveys

These were included on a partnership basis with consultants working for a local government office in Pilar.

Because of the political, social and economic sensitivities involved in the project team working with the low-income Pilar community on the Bairro, special emphasis was given to professional involvement. Many social workers and community development officers were already working with the community and the project was fortunate that many of them were able to give time to the project. What could have been a long process of gaining community trust was shortened by working with the existing authorities and thus gaining access to community

leaders in a relatively short time. Equally, as some consultation work had begun, it was possible to work in partnership with relevant bodies. Essentially, our Social Group comprised these workers, some of the other participants, and one specialist in community interpretation from Britain.

Apart from within the Pilar area, there was no attempt to use public community discussion groups. This would have been an alternative source of input, but many of the participating local planners felt that only those interested in pursuing their own agendas would participate, and that the voices that were never usually heard would be better accessed through the street interviews and 'Planning for Real' sessions.

When one talks of working with the community it is useful to elaborate somewhat on what that community comprises. There were two resident communities in the Bairro: one lived in the hostels placed within the historic buildings of the southern segment of the island and the other on a squatter settlement placed in the middle section of the island. As Table 15.2 shows, the population of the Bairro as a whole had been diminishing considerably since the beginning of the 20th century. This trend emerged as a result of successive rounds of urban renewal intervention that led the area's residents to gradually move to other areas of the city, particularly the suburbs. In the 1990s, however, as the hostel population continued to decrease, the squatter settlement population, formed initially in the 1970s, increased considerably, becoming the largest concentration of residents in the Bairro.

Finally, in the detailed project development phase, specialists and interested parties

Table 15.2. Changes in population in Bairro do Recife and the Pilar community.

Residents in	Date of survey	No. of inhabitants
Bairro do Recife	1910	13,204
	1913	5,146
	1923	3,206
	1970	1,670
	1991	566
The Pilar community	1987	87
	1998	370
	2001	403

related to each project were interviewed and brought into discussions. Consultation remained a priority throughout project development.

While the Social Group worked mainly with the local communities and residents, the Tourism and Planning groups worked to establish the broader context in which regeneration initiatives were to be developed. Not least was the concern that most of the broader 'community' in the Bairro were people who only worked there by day, and those who visited the cultural attractions at one time or another. Desk research, personal interviews and street surveys revealed an interesting picture.

General Tourism Context

While the number of tourists visiting Pernambuco and Recife has been growing dramatically over the last few years, there has been very little apparent growth in the number of visitors to the Bairro (URB-Recife/Monumenta, 2003). In fact, shop and restaurant owners in the fashionable Rua Bom Jesus were concerned that numbers were falling, and previous regeneration initiatives were proving unsustainable in the present setting.

Most visitors (80%) cite 'natural attractions' as their main reason for visiting. Many will be staying at beach resorts outside Recife and can remain relatively isolated from their surroundings. However, there are also many tourists in the city's hotels who are also attracted by the beaches. Tour buses from these hotels and the surrounding beach resorts bring groups to see the urban features of Recife, including the Bairro. Increasingly, tourists from cruise ships docking in Bairro do Recife will focus their tours on Recife and Bairro do Recife rather than the beaches. However, historic and cultural heritage is only the main motivation for visiting Recife for 6% of visitors. The great majority of all visitors to Recife are Brazilian (92%). Only 8% of visitors are from abroad. Most are Portuguese or Argentinean.

Interviews with tour group leaders showed that most visits to Bairro do Recife by organized groups are in the early morning or evening. In the mornings they are taken to Marco Zero Square, and then into Rua Bom Jesus. Some may briefly visit the Synagogue, a recently regenerated site. These groups stay only about 30 minutes. They are most often en route to another destination. As they visit in the early morning most shops, bars and temporary exhibitions are closed. During the day the Bairro is mainly peopled with those who work or are on business there. However, some school groups arrive in coaches to visit temporary exhibitions in cultural centres. There are very few tourists around during the daytime. In the evenings, the majority of visitors are Recife residents visiting the bars and restaurants of Rua Bom Jesus, many attracted by the numerous special events held in the nearby Praca Arsenal. Some tour groups may come in the evenings to spend time in one of the bars or restaurants of Rua Bom Jesus or to buy souvenirs in the Sunday Handicrafts Fair.

Street interviews revealed that two-thirds of respondents had little or no knowledge of the significance of their surroundings, despite some having worked there for 40 years. It was also found that all groups – tourists, workers and inhabitants – were slightly more interested to know about the regeneration work that was going on about them than the historical significance of their surroundings. This was an important key connection between all target audiences and the stories we were defining and led to the inclusion of further aims for the project.

General Political and Strategic Context

This was explored mainly by the Planning Group who established maps to show all existing initiatives and plans, including those completed, in hand and intended. Our aim was to work within the existing planning structures, using the interpretative plan as a means to link the visions and strategies of different departments into an integrated regenerative plan.

Environmental Context

The Planning Group also used a new environmental quality evaluation technique devised by Professor Brian Goodey, the leader of the group. This involved 20 observers working in pairs making extensive visual surveys of the locality, the surveyors making scored qualitative judgements on a number of previously agreed criteria, for example condition of pavements, street lighting, aesthetic appeal, historic importance. These scores were then transferred to colour-coded maps and could have been put on GIS and updated.

The process defined the qualitative reaction to views out from the Bairro (important in an area that is an island) as well as establishing the environmental quality on streetscapes. These data were used as the basis for the product development process, using existing areas of quality, identifying their connections (or lack of them) and using new products to integrate them.

The group also identified the initial interpretative resources and the themes connected with them. This was done through a process of brainstorming with professionals and academics as well as desk research. All groups were involved in identifying potential thematic material during personal interviews. These were to have been compiled in a 'story box', but in practice few stories emerged this way. Instead a catalogue of resources was begun which included buildings, street furniture, characters, stories and musical associations.

Developing the Themes for Product Development

While the Planning Group were responsible for the initial list of resources it took some time to move from lists of objects and places to actual themes. This was necessarily so in such a rich cultural environment. Indeed, as Professor Goodey observed, it was the richness of the immaterial culture that almost overwhelmed the importance of the material. Certainly from the start it had been evident that the place existed and had evolved and subsequently declined because of its port and associated services. At first, the emphasis was put on the sugar trade as a linking theme, as this generated the wealth that had led to the different building phases. However, as more was revealed about the political importance of the port as a landing place for members of political movements from France, bringing new ideas of freedom and equality, and as a meeting place for dissidents in later years, it became clear that its importance was

far wider. Many waves of people had arrived here and moved to other areas of Brazil. The main theme gradually evolved to focus on Bairro do Recife as a gateway between Brazil and the rest of the world.

Combining the results of different surveys of interests with the interests of local historians, government departments and the project groups' evaluation of what would interest the identified audiences, the following further topics were identified as being important to an understanding of the main theme. These were:

- the locality – islands, rivers and sea;
- the port – its growth and decline;
- cultural development;
- Dutch, Portuguese and 'Paris Tropical' periods;
- the Bohemian way of life; and
- conservation and regeneration.

Interpretative Product Development

The process of product development involved deduction and creativity. It was known who the visitors were, where they went and when they went there. Additionally, there was a broad understanding of their interests and expectations. The overall theme had been formulated and the richness of each of the stories and their links to the overall theme were understood. Also it was widely accepted that the existing interpretative offer was slim, contributing to the short stay times of tourists. The list of planned interpretation was impressive, including a Museum of Carnival and Frevo (a local carnival dance), a major visitor orientation centre (Casa do Acucar) and a heritage route through the Bairro (to be included in the city's tourism master plan), and three projects planned by Porto Digital (an information and communication technology-driven regeneration initiative in the Bairro). Other projects included historic trails, access to heritage spaces in selected buildings, and a large 'Sea World' experience in the port area.

Existing and proposed projects were then analysed in terms of how well they could tell the stories implied by the gateway theme, and bring it to the fore. The gaps in the overall offer were then explored and new projects brainstormed.

Over 30 new project ideas were generated by the team. These ranged from grand projects like the 'City of Water' spectacular aimed at attracting tourists using the city's hotels to smaller projects like interpretation panels at the bus stops aimed at gaining attention from local workers and inhabitants.

All of these new projects were then put through analysis of their strengths, weaknesses, opportunities and threats (SWOT analysis), which included relevance to themes, attractiveness to the target audience, appropriateness in the locality, and relevance to existing plans and strategies. These were subsequently mapped taking particular account of environmental quality and existing or imminent developments.

Above all, however, there was great awareness among project coordinators and participants of the need for a central focus for a visit to the Bairro. One could argue that this centre already existed in the form of Marco Zero Square. However, while the Square had been renovated, it was more often than not an empty space except when special events were taking place in the evenings. Interestingly enough, one of two buildings placed on each side of the Square had been renovated as a leisure and cruise ship terminus. However, due to difficulties associated with the depth of water being insufficient for docking of large cruise ships, the building had been left virtually empty.

Given that the Square was the major point of arrival in the Bairro, it became a natural option for developing visitor orientation and as the starting point for any visitor interested in exploring the Bairro. Four projects emerged as the most relevant in organizing visitor demand in and around the island.

The first project was Casa do Acucar (Portuguese for 'House of Sugar') since it could give all the conceptual orientation not only for the Bairro and the city, but also for Pernambuco state as a whole. As mentioned earlier, the story of sugar is inextricably linked to the story of the city and the region and it also allowed cultural practices such as gastronomy and dance to be brought in. The underused warehouse sitting opposite the terminus on the other side of Marco Zero Square was identified as the most suitable for this use.

The second project involved the recently redeveloped, yet largely empty terminus building itself that could quickly become a focus for boat trips around the island and up the rivers of Recife.

The third project involved Marco Zero Square itself as the starting point for heritage trails around the Bairro during the day, as well as an ongoing venue for special events in the evenings. The trail would link historic landmarks, view points and the redeveloped 17th-century customs house (Casa da Alfandega, a shopping centre on the other side of the island) with Marco Zero Square. A novel idea for an animated trail through the artistic quarters linking these elements was also developed. Visitor safety is always an important factor in Brazil, and the existing tourist areas are often heavily policed at night. Beyond this lay darkness. The rationale of the animated trail was to create a safe, bright route from the shopping centre and the attractions nearby, with the restaurants and bars of Bom Jesus Street. Local artists would interpret aspects of the Bairro with projections, graffiti, music and dance.

The fourth project involved one of the buildings owned and restored by the Porto Digital initiative: the entrance to the headquarters of the State Science and Technology Secretariat (SECTMA) building. This had already been developed as an exhibition space and the director of SECTMA was positive about the relevance of interpretative planning.

For each of the selected projects a detailed storyline was written, elaborating the chosen theme. Layouts and media plans were developed and a 10-year business plan created to demonstrate the sustainability of the project and the economic benefits it could bring in terms of jobs and income.

At this stage, the project ran out of time and money and the team had to focus on producing presentations of the overall project, the interpretative plan and the detailed projects they had been working on. The presentations were to a public audience as well as senior figures in the government and community. While the results were well received by government and planning agencies, notably in the tourism sector, to date, none of the projects have been taken forward. This is at least partly the result of the funding and implementation stage not having been taken far enough, and also of major administrative shifts in the Brazilian coordination of the Monumenta Programme and the priorities of local government as a whole since that time.

Conclusion

Regeneration is one of the cornerstones of Western cities' attempts to change existing urban conditions. However, interpretation is rarely fully integrated into the urban planning process. During the initial consultation phase of this project it was noted that different municipal departments were developing their own plans rather than an integrated regeneration plan. As this chapter has suggested, an interpretation-based approach to regeneration planning can help not only to assess user expectations, but ultimately to match interpretative product development with the different needs and interests of the identified target audiences.

The process of consultation relied on three different techniques, tourism and marketing, environmental analysis, and community consultation, reflecting the diversity of the plan's audience on the one hand, and the economic, historic, social and political dimensions of regeneration planning on the other. Tourism and market analysis provided most of the material for developing new interpretative products, but this was given context and support by the environmental analysis and community consultations. In so doing, the process endorsed well-known audience expectations and revealed others not yet identified by local planners. In the case of the latter, the most interesting findings are the unexpected numbers of local residents and workers who had little or no knowledge of the significance of their surroundings and the great interest tourists, workers and inhabitants had in learning more about the two-decade process of regeneration of the area.

As the project was being developed, it became increasingly clear that an integrated approach to the visions and strategies of the different agencies and departments involved in the regeneration of the Bairro do Recife was needed. The interpretative plan is a useful starting point in the pursuit of such an approach. Moreover, the plan puts forward the means to organize visitor demand on a citywide scale. This is something the city of Recife as a whole and the Bairro do Recife area in particular are still lacking.

The project identified numerous potentially sustainable interpretative products that could fulfil the expressed needs of the local community for employment opportunities, as well as extending the leisure and tourism value of the area for visitors, workers and residents alike. The process of developing the interpretative plan for Bairro do Recife demonstrated the potential of bringing together different disciplines in an integrated planning process. Interpretative planning offers the opportunity for cities to pursue regeneration as part of an integrated response to the pressing social, cultural and economic needs of Western cities in the 21st century. Moreover, it can help cities to reveal what makes them distinct from others, their unique identity, not only to outside visitors, but ultimately to residents, workers and commercial enterprises.

References

Berman, M. (1988) *All that is Solid Melts into Air – the Experience of Modernity*. Penguin, New York.

Bianchini, F. (1999) Cultural planning for urban sustainability. In: Nystorm, L. (ed.) *City, Culture: Cultural Processes and Urban Sustainability*. The Swedish Urban Environment Council, Kalmar, Sweden, pp. 34–51.

British Council – Recife branch (1999) *Conferencia Brasil-Reino Unido de Patrimonio e Desenvolvimento*. Conference Proceedings, British Council, Recife, Brazil.

Brito, M. (2002) Pressupostos da reabilitação urbana de sítios históricos no contexto brasileiro in IPHAN. Available at: http://www.iphan.gov.br/proprog/seminarioreabi.htm (accessed 10 August 2005).

Crouch, C., Fraser, C. and Percy, S. (2003) *Urban Regeneration in Europe*. Blackwell, Oxford.

Davis, M. (1990) *City of Quartz : Excavating the Future in Los Angeles*. Verso, London.

Goncalves, P. (2000) *Workshop de Planejamento Interpretativo*. British Council (Recife branch)/Fidem/PCR, Recife, Brazil.

Goodey, B. (1994) Interpretative planning. In: Harrison, R. (ed.) *Manual of Heritage Management*. Butterworth Heinneman, Oxford, pp. 303–311.

Harvey, D.W. (1989) *The Condition of Postmodernity: an Enquiry into the Origins of Cultural Change*. Blackwell, Oxford.

Jessop, B. (1997) The entrepreneurial city: re-imagining localities, redesigning economic governance, or restructuring capital? In: Jewson, N. and MacGregor, S. (eds) *Transforming Cities*. Routledge, London, pp. 28–42.

Jokilehto, J. (1999) *A History of Architectural Conservation*. Butterworth-Heinemann, Oxford.

Kotler, P., Haider, D.H. and Rein, I. (1993) *Marketing Places Attracting Investment, Industry and Tourism to Cities, States and Nations*. The Free Press, New York.

Monumenta (2005) Acompanhamento online: Recife' in Monumenta. Available at: http://www.monumenta. gov.br/acompanhamento.php?cid=18 (accessed 5 September 2005).

NAI (National Association for Interpretation) (2005) What is interpretation? Available at: http://www. interpnet.com (accessed 15 August 2005).

Robertson, K.A. (1995) Downtown redevelopment strategies in the United States: an end-of-the-century assessment. *Journal of the American Planning Association* 61, 429–437.

Robertson, K.A. (1999) Can small-city downtowns remain viable? *Journal of the American Planning Association* 65, 270–283.

Russell, H. (2000) *New Commitment to Regeneration – Progress and Policy Lessons*. Local Government Association Research Report 15. Local Government Association, London.

Smith, M.K. (2003) *Issues in Cultural Tourism Studies*. Routledge, London.

Smith, N. (2002) New globalism, new urbanism: gentrification as global urban strategy. *Antipode* 34, 427–450.

UNESCO (2000) Recife e a primeira beneficiada. Available at: http://www.unesco.org.br/noticias/revista_ant/ noticias2000/nu400/nu400c/mostra_documento (accessed 5 September 2005).

URB-Recife/Monumenta (2003) *Plano Interpretativo do Bairro do Recife – Relatorios 1,2,3 and 4*. URB-Recife, Recife, Brazil.

Urry, J. (2002) *The Tourist Gaze: Leisure and Travel in Contemporary Societies*, 2nd edn. Sage, London.

Ward, S. (1998) *Selling Places: the Marketing and Promotion of Towns and Cities 1850–2000*. Routledge, London.

Zancheti, S., Marinho, G. and Milet, V. (1995) *Estratégias de Intervenção em Áreas Históricas*. Mestrado em Desenvolvimento Urbano, Recife, Brazil.

Conclusion

Melanie K. Smith

This volume has attempted to illustrate many of the complexities and contradictions inherent in the process of regeneration, as well as offering case studies and examples of good practice. Whilst the phenomenon of *cultural* regeneration is still in its relative infancy, many decades of urban redevelopment have demonstrated clearly that certain approaches are more successful than others. Most of the authors in this volume indicate, for example, the importance of local resident involvement in, and perceptions of, regeneration schemes. Of course, it is always easy to bandy around 'buzzwords' based on intangible and symbolic outcomes, yet increasingly there seems to be a commitment in cities to local issues with political support and funding to match. Government demands for hard evidence of the success of culture-led regeneration schemes has resulted in agencies and practitioners attempting to collect more qualitative data (e.g. relating to quality of life, community perceptions). This has arguably given a new impetus to the approaches taken to regeneration and helped to close the gap between rhetoric and reality. Regeneration projects are often so extensive and ambitious, that aspirations are not always met, but clearly there has been a step in the right direction in many of the case studies given.

Culture and tourism were once seen to be the icing on the cake in regeneration schemes after economic and social issues had been addressed (clearly an ongoing process), but evidence suggests that this situation is changing, and that more integrated approaches are being adopted. Indeed, cultural and tourism developments can become the catalysts for regeneration, sometimes providing a new level of hope for cities which have declined seemingly beyond all other hope. Flagship projects, events and festivals, innovative and iconic architecture, the development of cultural and creative quarters, and the promotion of ethnoscapes can all help to raise the profile of cities and create unique branding opportunities. More importantly, they can help to strengthen economies and enhance social cohesion.

Nevertheless, care must be taken to recognize the limitations of cultural and tourism developments, as governments and the public cannot live on symbolic benefits alone! The most recent research by Florida (2002) and others suggests that there is an inextricable link between culture, creativity, economics, business and technology. Whilst the creation of new public museums, galleries, events and festivals can serve a useful social and educational function, they will only succeed if they can become profitable businesses too. If they are constructed in idealistic isolation and fail to connect with local residents or tourists, they can become disastrous 'white elephants'. Instead, they must demonstrate enough potential to be attractive to businesses, and encourage investment and long-term funding and sponsorship opportunities (no mean feat in the field of arts and culture). Cultural purists may reject the notion of a cultural–commercial partnership, but it is surely an inevitable feature of the postmodern urban landscape.

Fears about standardization, homogenization and gentrification are, however, not unfounded. The dominance of serial reproduction as a result of copy-cat schemes and a lack of imagination and innovation can lead to sterile and alienating landscapes. On the other hand, consumers (including tourists) have a contradictory thirst for the familiar, the comfortable and the safe, at the same time as craving novelty and excitement. Smith (2005) refers to the concept of the 'new leisure tourist', who has a very short attention span, little time to spend, but often a substantial income. He or she therefore seeks a series of expensive thrills within a short space of time. Rojek (1993) and Sheller and Urry (2004) have noted the importance of playfulness in tourism destination development, and Pine and Gilmore (1999) highlight the growing importance of the 'experience economy'. It seems, therefore, that destinations increasingly have to provide a predictable and comfortable infrastructure (e.g. hotels, transport, services), whilst dreaming up ever new and fantastical attractions. The most successful 'new' destinations are clearly those that can manage this demanding balance (e.g. Dubai). It is more difficult for historic or former industrial cities that have an ageing infrastructure and limited space and investment for new developments.

The success of new developments is, however, seemingly unpredictable. A scheme can work exceptionally well in one destination (e.g. a modern art museum), whilst failing miserably in another. This can be the result of a number of complex factors. For example, the Millennium Dome in Greenwich, London (2000) is often cited as being a 'failure' despite being the most popular visitor attraction in Europe during the year that it remained open. It also contributed significantly to the local economy in terms of job creation and acted as a catalyst for a number of environmental and social developments (see Smith and Smith, 2000). Nevertheless, the notoriously negative press was mainly due to excessive political intervention, as well as its dramatic cost (£800 million or so). It has also remained empty for the past 5 years and may

remain so until the 2012 London Olympics (assuming the architectural fabric lasts that long!). This is not the only example of an expensive 'white elephant' (numerous Olympic Games and Expos suffered the same fate), though lessons are at least being learnt from previous mistakes. For example, the importance of long-term legacy has been recognized and is now being built into the bidding process for large-scale projects.

Many of the case studies in this volume indicate how expensive mistakes can be avoided, and most authors make some suggestions as to how the critical success factors of regeneration can be maximized. Increasingly creative approaches to development and design are being taken (e.g. see Richards and Wilson, Chapter 2); charismatic and dynamic leadership is emerging (e.g. see Bounds, Chapter 12); public spirited initiatives are complementing commercial ones (e.g. see Jones, Chapter 13); long-term outcomes are being planned for, especially in the context of sporting mega-events (see Smith, Chapter 8 and Heying et al., Chapter 9); local issues are being prioritized alongside international development and tourism projects (e.g. see Murayama and Parker, Chapter 7); and integrated approaches to cultural and community planning are being implemented (e.g. see Smith, Chapter 1 and Bath and Goncalves, Chapter 15).

However, it is suggested in some of the chapters that cities can sometimes be *over* planned for, and that some 'organic' development should be allowed to flourish. This is particularly important in alternative or fringe areas of cities (e.g. as highlighted by Maitland, Chapter 3, and Aiesha and Evans, Chapter 4). Creativity tends to develop more readily in areas that have a high 'Bohemian Index' according to Florida (2002) and it is well documented that many of the most interesting regeneration processes have been led by artists in a somewhat ad hoc fashion.

The development of ethnoscapes and the interpretation of ethnic cultures may, however, require some political support (as indicated by Shaw, Chapter 5 and Harvey, Chapter 6). Although culture and tourism can help to bolster political and financial assistance, they should not become substitutes for true social and welfare support. Indeed, Breitbart and Stanton (Chapter 10) suggest that however important the arts and creativity may be to the regeneration of an area, they are often very elusive and intangible, and cannot therefore replace or entirely compensate for industrial development. Bounds (Chapter 12) also notes that arts organizations frequently lack the ability to manage large-scale projects and extensive budgets. Harvey (Chapter 6) shows that the development of tourism spaces of consumption based on ethnic cultures and heritage can be successful, but that this is not the same as regeneration in a true sense (i.e. maximizing economic and social advantages and helping to resolve political conflicts). Similarly, Spirou (Chapter 11) demonstrates that one can be rather too idealistic about the benefits of culture and tourism-led regeneration, which cannot necessarily alleviate problems of poverty, crime and unemployment. Finally, Avery (Chapter 14) highlights the need for more research on the contribution of the arts to social regeneration, which she notes have been traditionally overlooked in favour of economic advantages.

However, it would be misrepresentative to end this Conclusion on a pessimistic note. Many of the chapters have indicated the richness, creativity, innovation and ambition of regeneration projects in a wide range of contexts. No form of development, whether it be based on culture, tourism or regeneration can be expected to compensate for economic decline, environmental decay or social unrest. They can only alleviate some of the problems and tensions, and give new hope to cities.

It would be misguided to suggest that there could be a 'checklist' for all cities hoping to embark on a 'successful' regeneration scheme, especially given that similar schemes can easily fail in different contexts. However, several factors seem to emerge as being rather critical to the future of regeneration. A summary is therefore provided in Box C.2.

One of the most interesting aspects of this international project has been to realize that whatever the context (be it Europe, the USA, Asia, Australasia), the issues and dilemmas surrounding cultural regeneration are broadly similar. Most practitioners and planners face political and financial difficulties at some stage, which often hinder their ability to be truly aspirational. Many large projects succeed on one level (e.g. they become popular tourist attractions), but can fail on another (i.e. they fail

---

Box C.2. A summary of critical success factors for cultural regeneration.

- Accept that regeneration cannot 'save' cities that are in the throes of decline. It can only ameliorate them.
- Recognize that culture and tourism cannot always compensate for, or replace industrial development.
- Try not to overestimate the importance of intangible and symbolic aspects of regeneration.
- Be aware that copy-cat schemes cannot necessarily work in different contexts. Research on local social and cultural environments is therefore essential.
- Aim for innovation and uniqueness in design, attractions development, and branding. Some (calculated) risks will be necessary.
- Acknowledge that new and unusual developments may not be instantly popular with the public.
- Understand the importance of the relationship between culture, creativity, commerce, business and technology.
- Encourage charismatic and dynamic leadership coupled with financial realism and adequate budgets and funding opportunities.
- Accept that joined-up thinking and stakeholder collaboration are time-consuming and expensive to undertake.
- Appreciate that community consultation is important, but that true representation is rare and consensus is seldom reached.
- Provide political and social support for ethnic minorities and other marginalized or under-privileged groups whenever possible.
- Apply a flexible approach to planning allowing organic development to flourish where appropriate.
- Undertake adequate and realistic research on both the quantitative and the qualitative benefits of culture-led regeneration.

---

to attract or interest local residents). Even as tourist attractions, their appeal can be short lived resulting in inadequate legacies for a destination. Conversely, projects can be developed with considerable local community involvement (e.g. small-scale arts programmes, festivals) only to lack the commercial support to be viable in the long term.

The changing fortunes of both tourist desti-nations and culturally regenerated areas lead to a certain degree of insecurity, due to the unpre-dictability of economic, environmental and social conditions. The postmodern world can be a relatively unstable one. Yet, at the same time, there have never been so many opportunities for new and innovative developments, which build not only on global business opportunities and technological change, but also embrace social and cultural diversity. Pessimists might conclude that regeneration is just another 'flash-in-the-pan' phenomenon that has helped to plug the gaps in economic and social decline. However, the editor and authors have attempted to dem-onstrate that within the academic/practitioner community, there is excitement, dynamism and great hope for the future.

References

Florida, R. (2002) *The Rise of the Creative Class*. Basic Books, New York.

Pine, J.B. and Gilmore, J.H. (1999) *The Experience Economy*. Harvard Business School Press, Boston, Massachusetts.

Rojek, C. (1993) *Ways of Escape: Modern Transformations in Leisure and Travel*. Palgrave Macmillan, London.

Sheller, M. and Urry, J. (eds) (2004) *Tourism Mobilities: Places to Play, Places in Play*. Routledge, London.

Smith, M.K. (2005) New leisure tourism: fantasy futures. In: Buhalis, D. and Costa, C. (eds) *New Tourism Consumers, Products and Industry: Present and Future Issues*. Butterworth-Heinemann, Oxford, pp. 220–227.

Smith, M.K. and Smith, K.A. (2000) Surviving the millennium experience: the future of urban regeneration in Greenwich. In: Robinson, M. (ed.) *Developments in Urban and Rural Tourism*. Business Education Publishers, Sunderland, UK, pp. 251–267.

Index

Note: page numbers in *italics* refer to figures and tables; those with suffix 'n' refer to notes.